More advance praise for *Limited Wants, Unlimited Means:*

"I know of no literature of social inquiry more fascinating for an economist than that regarding hunter-gatherer societies, where we have a chance to see human nature in the raw. Of course, there is no such thing as 'human nature' nor any condition that can be called 'raw.' But the men and women who hunt, gather, fight, and laze in this book are nonetheless the closest we can get to seeing the utility-maximizing monads of our texts stripped of the trappings of 'civilization.' I must warn my colleagues, however, that they are likely to be in for a shock. These pages are as dangerous as they are fascinating—dangerous, that is, to the premises on which rests so much of our economic thought. All the more reason to read this collection, which will not only save its readers an expensive trip, but perhaps give them the intellectual adventure of a lifetime."

—Robert Heilbroner,
Norman Thomas Professor Emeritus,
New School for Social Research, and
author of *Economic Transformation of America*

"Modern hunter-gatherers—like all pre-agricultural humans and indeed all species in the 3.5 billion year history of life—live as populations within the context of local ecosystems. Agriculture changed the human status, making us the first species to live outside local ecosystems. Now, as a globally interconnected economic force, we six billion humans have re-emerged as a part of the natural system, this time of the global system 'Gaia.' Gowdy's presentation of these essays invites us to ask: What can we learn from hunter-gatherers about how to handle this unfamiliar experience of living inside a natural economic system?"

—Niles Eldredge,
Department of Invertebrates,
The American Museum of Natural History

♦ ABOUT ISLAND PRESS ♦

Island Press is the only nonprofit organization in the United States whose principal purpose is the publication of books on environmental issues and natural resource management. We provide solutions-oriented information to professionals, public officials, business and community leaders, and concerned citizens who are shaping responses to environmental problems.

In 1994 Island Press celebrated its tenth anniversary as the leading provider of timely and practical books that take a multidisciplinary approach to critical environmental concerns. Our growing list of titles reflects our commitment to bringing the best of an expanding body of literature to the environmental community throughout North America and the world.

Support for Island Press is provided by Apple Computer, Inc., The Bullitt Foundation, The Geraldine R. Dodge Foundation, The Energy Foundation, The Ford Foundation, The W. Alton Jones Foundation, The Lyndhurst Foundation, The John D. and Catherine T. MacArthur Foundation, The Andrew W. Mellon Foundation, The Joyce Mertz-Gilmore Foundation, The National Fish and Wildlife Foundation, The Pew Charitable Trusts, The Pew Global Stewardship Initiative, The Philanthropic Collaborative, Inc., and individual donors.

LIMITED WANTS, UNLIMITED MEANS

LIMITED WANTS, UNLIMITED MEANS

A READER ON HUNTER-GATHERER ECONOMICS AND THE ENVIRONMENT

Edited by John M. Gowdy

Island Press WASHINGTON, D.C. / COVELO, CALIFORNIA

Library of Congress Cataloging-in-Publication Data

Limited wants, unlimited means : a reader on hunter-gather economics and the environment / edited by John M. Gowdy.
    p.   cm.
    Includes bibliographical references (p.   ) and index.
    ISBN 1-55963-555-X (paper)
    1. Hunting and gathering societies. 2. Human ecology. 3. Sustainable development.   I. Gowdy, John M.
    GN388.L55   1997
    304.2—dc21   97-32425
                                                 CIP

Printed on recycled, acid-free paper ∞ ✪

Manufactured in the United States of America
10   9   8   7   6   5   4   3   2   1

Contents

Foreword

The world's hunting and gathering peoples—the Eskimo, Australian aborigines, African Bushmen, and similar groups—represent the oldest and perhaps most successful human adaptation. Until 12,000 years ago, virtually all of humanity lived this way. In recent centuries, hunters have retreated precipitously in the face of the steamroller of modernity. Fascination, however, with hunting peoples and their ways of life remains strong. Hunters and gatherers stand at the opposite pole from the dense urban life experienced by most people; yet those same hunters may have the key answers to some of the central questions about the human condition: Can people live without the state or the market? Can people live without accumulated wealth or "advanced" technology? Can people live in nature without destroying it?

Working in highly diverse cultures, anthropologists have long been familiar with such questions. Yet what is daily fare for anthropologists may provide serious challenges to the orthodoxy of other disciplines. For most economists, the supremacy of the market, the sanctity of property, and the centrality of the doctrine of economic man are the sacred tenets of their craft. Orthodoxies of any kind deserve careful scrutiny, and for economic orthodoxy, with its grip on the lives of billions, this is especially true. Are there alternatives to the economic arrangements that are deemed natural and inevitable in the contemporary world? John Gowdy answers with a resounding yes. This intriguing collection of essays is a welcome sign that within the temple of economic thought the monolith may be breaking up. Gowdy, a respected economist with training in anthropology, has assembled a lively and irreverent collection to address two questions: Are there alternate ways of managing human economic affairs, and do the world's hunting and gathering peoples have something to teach us?

Now a wider readership can be exposed to what anthropologists have known for some time: there are peoples who lived, until quite recently, without the overarching discipline of the state: they lived in small groups without centralized authority, standing armies, or bureaucratic systems, and exchanged goods and services without recourse to markets. Yet the evidence indicates that they lived together surprisingly well, solving problems among themselves largely without courts or prisons and without a particular propensity for violence. It was not the situation that Thomas Hobbes, described as "the war of all against all." By all accounts, life was not "nasty, brutish, and short." With relatively simple technology—wood, bone, stone, fibres—they were able to meet their material needs with a modest expenditure of energy, leading American anthropologist and social critic Marshall Sahlins to call them, in an essay reproduced here, "the original affluent society." Most striking, the hunter-gatherers demonstrated a remarkable ability to survive and thrive for long periods, in some cases thousands of years, without destroying their environment.

The contemporary industrial world exists in highly structured societies at immensely high densities and enjoys luxuries of technology that foragers could hardly imagine. Yet that world is sharply divided into the haves and the have-nots, and after only a few millennia of stewardship by agricultural and industrial civilizations the environments of large portions of the planet lie in ruins. Therefore the hunter-gatherers may well be able to teach us something, not only about past ways of life but about long-term human futures as well. If technological society is to survive it may have to learn the keys to longevity from fellow humans whose way of life has lasted at least one hundred times longer than industrial commercial "civilization."

Led off by in chapter 1 by Sahlins' classic "The Original Affluent Society" (1972), the essays collected here represent a cross section of thirty years of anthropological writing. To the economists' view of *homo economicus,* stategizing to maximize and minimize, Sahlins proposes that hunter-gatherers are best seen as in business for their health. Their means may be limited but so are their ends, offering a Zen alternative to the unlimited wants of a consumer economy. Other essays found in this book critically develop this theme by offering empirical evidence from such peoples as the Innu, !Kung, Hadza, and Nayaka.

In defining and understanding foraging peoples, their hunting and gathering subsistence is only one part of a three-part definition. A distinctive social and economic organization and a characteristic cosmology and worldview sets foragers apart from farmers and herders. All three sets of criteria have to be taken into account in understanding hunting and gathering peoples today.

The basic unit of social organization of most, but not all, hunting and gathering peoples is the band, a small-scale nomadic group of 15 to 50 people related by kinship. Band societies are found throughout the Old and New Worlds and have a number of features in common.

First, they are relatively egalitarian. Leadership here is less formal and more subject to constraints of popular opinion than in village societies governed by headmen and chiefs. Leadership in band societies tends to be by example, not by fiat. The leader can persuade but not command. This important aspect of their way of life allowed for a degree of freedom unheard of in more hierarchical societies, but put them at a distinct disavantage in their encounters with centrally organized colonial authorities.

Mobility is another characteristic of band societies. People tend to move their settlements frequently, several times a year or more, in search of food, and this mobility is an important element of their politics. People in band societies tend to "vote with their feet," by moving away rather than submitting to the will of an unpopular leader. Mobility is also a means of resolving conflicts that would be more difficult for settled peoples.

A third characteristic is the remarkable fact that all band-organized peoples exhibit a pattern of concentration and dispersion. Rather than live in uniformly sized groupings throughout the year, band societies tend to spend part of the year dispersed into small foraging units and another part of the year aggregated into much larger units. The Innu (Naskapi) discussed by Leacock would spend the winter dispersed in small foraging groups of 10 to 30 people, while in the summer they would aggregate in groups of 200 to 300 at fishing sites on lakes or rivers. It seems clear that the concentration dispersion patterns of hunter-gatherers represents a dialectical interplay of social and ecological factors.

A fourth characteristic common to almost all band societies (and hundreds of village-based societies as well) is a land tenure system based on common property regimes. These regimes were, until recently, far more common worldwide than regimes based on private property. In traditional common property regimes, while movable property is held by individuals, land is held by a kinship-based collective. Rules of reciprocal access make it possible for each individual to draw on the resources of several territories. Rarer is the scenario where the whole society has unrestricted access to all the land controlled by the group.

Sharing is the central rule of social interaction among hunters and gatherers. There are strong injunctions on the importance of reciprocity. Generalized reciprocity, the giving of something without an immediate expectation of return is the dominant form within face-to-face groups. Its presence in hunting and gathering societies is almost universal. This, combined with an absence of private ownership of land, has led many observers from Lewis Henry Morgan on to attribute to hunter-gatherers a way of life based on "primitive communism."

Nurit Bird-David in an essay reproduced here notes, that many, but not all, hunter-gatherers have a notion of the giving environment, the idea that the land around them is their spiritual home and the source of all good things. This view is the direct antithesis of the Judeo-Christian perspective of the natural environment as a "wilderness," a hostile space to be subdued and brought to heel by the sheer force of human will. This latter outlook is seen by many ecological humanists as the source of both the environmental crisis and the spiritual malaise afflicting contemporary scoiety.

Hunter-gatherers in recent history have been surprisingly persistent. As recently as 1500 AD, hunters occupied fully one-third of the globe, including all of Australia and most of North America, as well as large tracts of South

America, Africa, and northeast Asia. The twentieth century has seen particularly dramatic changes in their life circumstances. The century began with dozens of hunting and gathering peoples still pursuing ancient, though not isolated, ways of life in small communities, as foragers with systems of local meaning centred on kin, plants, animals, and the spirit world. As the century proceeded, a wave of self-appointed civilizers washed over the world's foragers, bringing schools, clinics, administrative structures, and, not incidentally, taking their land and resources in the process.

The year 2000 will have seen the vast majority of former foragers settled and encapsulated in the administrative structures of one state or another. And given the tragic history of the forced acculturation of hunter-gatherers, one can imagine that the millennium might bring to a close a long chapter in human history. But will it? I believe not. Hunter-gatherers live on, not only in the pages of anthropological and historical texts, but in an estimated forty countries worldwide. Their hundreds of thousands of descendants, only a generation or two removed from a foraging way of life, have created a strong international voice for indigenous peoples and their human rights.

What makes the contemporary hunters and gatherers so intriguing is that, far from simply being victims of history, in many parts of the world they have become political actors in their own right, mounting land claims cases, participating in the environmental movement, lobbying for their rights with governments and the United Nations, addressing wider audiences through the media, and finally being increasingly sought out by spiritual pilgrims from urban industrial societies.

As we approach the millennium, there is an increasing preoccupation with where we have come from and where we are going. The accelerating pace of change and the ceaseless transformations brought about by market forces have had the effect of obfuscating history and creating a deepening spiritual malaise. For centuries philosophers have sought the answers to humanity's multiple problems in the search for the holy grail of "natural man." At the same time, other more powerful forces have been appropriating in the name of "progress" the lands and resources of the world's hunting and gathering societies. These same forces have branded the search for economic alternatives a futile excercise driven by myth and romanticism. Thus we are doubly indebted to John Gowdy, first for rekindling economic imagination in an age of sharply reduced expectations and second for bringing to a broader readership the evidence from ethnographic research that, out there, beyond the baleful light shed by capitalism, other ways of life are possible.

Richard B. Lee

A Note from the Editor

This collection of essays is only a brief introduction to the rich anthropological and sociological literature on nonagricultural societies. For the most part, the articles included here deal only with the most frequently studied cultures, the !Kung Bushmen of southern Africa, the Hadza of Tanzania, and the Australian Aborigines. No attempt is made to provide a representative sample of the great variety of hunter-gatherer lifestyles. Nevertheless, I believe not only that these provocative and well-written papers are interesting in their own right but also that bringing them together in one source will serve to enliven the debate about ecological sustainability and social equality. In particular, these essays drive home the point, in a way that studies of industrial societies cannot, the indissoluble connection between social and environmental harmony. Hunter-gatherer societies were environmentally sustainable because they were egalitarian, and they were egalitarian because they were environmentally sustainable.

The ideas presented in this volume, like all ideas, are not new. It is hoped, however, that presenting them from a novel perspective might have an effect that has been elusive until this point. It would be particularly rewarding if my own profession, economics, would be a little more inclusive after reading about the many successful ways in which human society can be organized other than through competitive markets. I truly believe that the economics profession is poised to shed its skin of centuries-old dogma and once again play a constructive role in meeting the environmental and social challenges the human race faces as many of the old paradigms prove inadequate to meet today's ecological and social problems.

Of the hundreds of students, teachers, colleagues, and friends with whom I have shared these ideas, I owe the greatest debt to the following. First and foremost, I owe a debt of gratitude to my teacher, Nicholas Georgescu-Roegen, who always had it right, and to William Miernyk, without whose encouragement I might never have started down a path that has made my own intellectual life so rewarding. My gratitude also goes to John Davis, editor of the *Review of Social Economy,* for encouraging my interest in the bioethics of hunter-gatherer societies. I would like to thank two (of many) colleagues at Rensselaer Polytechnic Institute, Carl McDaniel and Sabine O'Hara, for discussing these and many other ideas with me for hours on end. Most of all, I would like to thank the graduate students in Rensselaer's ecological economics program for their enthusiasm, their dedication, and their infectious optimism that the world can be made a better place.

Finally, I would like to thank my wife, Linda, and my daughter, Anna, without whose love, patience, and understanding my world would be empty.

Back to the Future and Forward to the Past

Economics is defined in most textbooks as "the study of the allocation of scarce resources among alternative ends." Humans, it is said, have unlimited wants and limited means to satisfy these wants, so the inevitable result is scarcity. We cannot have everything we want, so we must choose what we would have. Every act of consumption is thus also an act of denial, resulting ultimately in deprivation. In this dismal state of affairs, our job as economic beings is to allocate our limited incomes so as to get the greatest enjoyment possible from the relatively few things we are able to buy.

The central irony of this volume is that hunter-gatherers, people who lived with almost no material possessions for hundreds of thousands of years, enjoyed lives in many ways richer and more rewarding than ours. A far cry from their portrayal as primitive savages struggling to survive during every waking moment, these people had structured their lives so that they needed little, wanted little, and, for the most part, had all the means of fulfilling their needs at their immediate disposal. The !Kung of southern Africa, for example, spent only twelve to nineteen hours per week getting food. Young people were not expected to work until they were well into their twenties; nor were people expected to work after age forty or so. They spent their abundant leisure time eating, drinking, playing, and socializing—in short, doing the very things we associate with affluence.

In addition to (or perhaps in concert with) their abundant leisure time, hunter-gatherers also enjoyed an amazing amount of personal freedom. Among the !Kung and the Hadza of Tanzania, there were either no leaders at all or temporary leaders whose authority was severely constrained. These societies had no social classes and no discrimination based on gender. They were also environmentally sustainable. The Aborigines of Australia, the Hadza, and the !Kung had technologies and social systems that allowed them to live for tens of thousands of years in equilibrium with their environments, without destroying the resources on which their economies were based.

We are taught that only after the "discovery" of agriculture did humans have enough leisure time to build culture and civilization; only then did we become truly human. But the more we learn about hunter-gatherer cultures, the more we realize that the value system of modern market capitalism does not reflect "human nature." Assumptions about human behavior that members of market societies believe to be universal truths—that humans are naturally competitive and acquisitive and that social stratification is natural—do not apply to many hunting and gathering peoples. Yet in a very real sense, in the sense of having abundant leisure and unlimited access to all they needed, these hunter-gatherer societies were more affluent than our own.

The Culture of the Market

All cultures have a set of beliefs or organizing principles that serve not only to guide behavior but also to explain and justify the existing state of the world. Western cultural beliefs, in particular, serve to justify the peculiar material relationship that has evolved among the members of our society and between humans and the rest of the world. Our culture sees class divisions as inevitable, even desirable, and views nature as a collection of "natural resources" to be used to fuel the engine of economic growth and technological progress.

My own particular tribe, that of academic economists, has its own belief system to explain and justify the world of commerce we have created, typified by the notion of "economic man." This "man" is naturally acquisitive, competitive, rational, and calculating and is forever looking for ways to improve his material well-being. He rations his time from an early age on to get the training needed to earn an income, and he carefully allocates this income among the dizzying array of goods and services available in the marketplace.

Today, we in the West hardly recognize the idea of economic man as a cultural belief, as opposed to a universal fact, because it accurately describes most of us. We may joke about the irrationality of our species, but as individuals we all believe deep down that we are fairly rational and consistent in the choices we make. We believe that to want more and more things is a natural human attribute. We value the individual above society. Competition and expansion, not cooperation and stability, describe the rules by which our world operates. We are all now economic persons: we have limited resources (incomes) and a very long list of things we would like to have.

Orthodox economic theory contains more than a set of beliefs about human nature. It is also an ideology justifying current economic organization, resource use, and the distribution of wealth. Not only do individuals prefer more to less, but those with more possessions are accorded higher status in market societies. To be "successful" is to have a higher income and a higher level of consumption. Moreover, those who are successful, so the underlying ideology tells us, are those who have proved their worth in the competitive market struggle. Economic theory not only describes how resources are allocated; it provides a justification for wealth, poverty, and exploitation.

The ultimate goal of a free-market economy is the efficient allocation of resources as defined by "Pareto optimality," a situation in which no further trading of economic goods can make one person better off without making someone else worse off. The starting point at which trade begins is not questioned, no matter how unequal the initial distribution of goods between trading partners. In essence, the Pareto definition of efficiency is a protection of the status quo.

The inequality of distribution of goods among individuals in a capitalist economy is justified according to the "marginal productivity theory of distribution." Workers are rewarded according to their contribution to total economic output. For example, if a firm hires one more worker and the value of the firm's output goes up by $100 per day, the daily wage of that worker should be $100. Those who add more to the total economic product of society should receive a greater share than those who add a smaller amount. Economists argue further that competition guarantees that wages will be equal to the value of the marginal product of labor. The ideological implication of marginal productivity theory is that in a competitive economy, all workers are paid what they deserve.

In the neoclassical economic theory of market exchange, the historical and social circumstances that enable one person to produce more than another are not considered. Inherited wealth, for example, gives a person access to more capital, and thus his or her marginal product will be higher than that of a person born into less privileged circumstances. In general, a person with more education—again, usually because of family circumstances—will have a higher marginal product and thus a higher income than will one who is less educated. Neoclassical theory sees individuals as isolated producers and isolated consumers of market goods, competing with one another. One's value as an individual is largely a function of economic success, of accumulating (and consuming) more wealth than does one's neighbor.

The view of human nature embedded in Western economic theory is an anomaly in human history. In fact, the basic organizing principle of our market economy—that humans are driven by greed and that more is always better than less—is a microscopically small minority view among the tens of thousands of cultures that have existed since *Homo sapiens* emerged some 200,000 years ago. Among the Hadza, for example, there are elaborate rules to ensure that all meat is equally shared. Hoarding, or even having a greater share than do others, is socially unacceptable. Apart from personal items, such as tools, weapons, or smoking pipes, there are sanctions against accumulating possessions. Further-

xviii   INTRODUCTION

more, because of the constant mobility of hunter-gatherers, possessions are a
nuisance. According to James Woodburn (see chapter 4), among the !Kung and
the Hadza, hoarding food when another person is hungry would be unthink-
able. The hunter-gatherer represents "uneconomic man."

In seeking paths toward environmental and social sustainability, we can
learn much about future possibilities by looking to the past. Hunter-gatherer
societies give us an opportunity to glimpse human nature in a much different
form, before it was informed by market relationships and modern economic
ideas. There may be socially constructed limits within the present framework
of Western industrial economy to cooperating, reducing consumption, and in
general living sustainably; but knowing that for 99 percent of human existence
these limits did not exist, it is impossible to conclude that there is something
"natural" about them. The mere existence, and in particular the success, of
hunter-gatherer societies proves that there are ways of organizing production
and distribution other than through markets.

A Brief Overview of Hunter-Gatherer Scholarship

The view of hunter-gatherers that dominated before the 1960s reflected notions of cultural evolution and progress embedded in the Western worldview.
In spite of modern technology and science and the extraordinary powers of
production they make possible, modern life is a struggle with scarcity, a battle
to make ends meet. The life of the hunter-gatherer, then, with none of today's
technological advantages in the battle to survive, must have been, in the words
of Thomas Hobbes, "nasty, brutish, and short." As Marshall Sahlins puts it,
"Having equipped the hunter with bourgeois impulses and paleolithic tools,
we judge his situation to be hopeless in advance." This view was reflected in
the pre-1960s anthropological literature. A quote by Robert Braidwood
(1957:122) is typical: "A man who spends his whole life following animals just
to kill them to eat, or moving from one berry patch to another, is really living
just like an animal himself."

The general view of hunter-gatherers as backward, brutish, and uncivilized
was shattered with the publication in 1968 of the book *Man the Hunter,* a collection of field studies of surviving hunter-gatherer societies. Hunter-gatherer
societies were shown to be generally well fed, egalitarian, ecologically sustainable, and socially and intellectually complex and to have an abundance of
leisure time. These characteristics were apparent in a variety of societies in a variety of physical environments: the !Kung bushmen of southern Africa, the
Australian Aborigines, the Hadza of Tanzania, the Pygmies of central Africa,
and the Inuit of northern Canada. The "affluence" of these societies is particularly remarkable given that the reason for their survival into modern times is

their location in what are widely considered some of the more inhospitable parts of the planet.

The model of hunter-gatherers that came to dominate in the 1960s was "neofunctionalism," that is, hunter-gatherers as ecologists (Bettinger 1980). Their behavior was described as (1) rational and adaptive, (2) group oriented, and (3) homeostatic. This line of analysis, an old one in anthropology, stresses the important links among society, technology, and the environment. It focuses on the adaptation of cultures through evolutionary selection. This line of thought has been criticized by a number of anthropologists, primarily because of its extreme adaptationist approach. Stressing the role of ecological adaptation as an explanation of cultural features can quickly lead to a "Panglossian" view that whatever trait is present in society exists because it has been "selected" by evolutionary forces.

In spite of its early excesses, the ecological adaptationist approach has provided valuable insights in numerous studies of hunter-gatherer societies (Lee 1969; Woodburn 1968) and simple agricultural (Rappaport 1968) societies. Another persistent criticism of evolutionary/ecological approaches is that they depend on group selection (Boehm 1997; Kelly 1995). This goes against the once prevailing view in biology that all natural selection takes place at the level of the individual or even at the level of the gene. However, in light of the ongoing revolution in evolutionary biology in which macroevolution (change through time based on selection of groups of individuals or even ecosystems) is increasingly accepted as one mechanism of evolutionary change, this criticism is no longer so telling as it once was.

In the 1980s, the research emphasis shifted to such subjects as optimal foraging strategies (Clark and Mangel 1986) and energy balances (Speth and Spielmann 1983). Much of this research involves the application of microeconomics, in particular cost-benefit analysis, to the problem of allocating time and effort in hunting and foraging economies. Not surprisingly, the results of these studies show that hunter-gatherers are quite rational in that they obtain particular food items with the least possible effort.

In the 1980s, there was increasing interest in the relationships between hunter-gatherers and agricultural societies and in the influence of the larger market economy on hunter-gatherer subsistence patterns. It was recognized that even relatively isolated hunter-gatherer populations have had decades or even centuries-long contact with neighboring agriculturalists. Interestingly, in spite of this contact, many hunter-gatherers shunned, and in fact continue to shun, agriculture. As a !Kung Bushman put it, "Why should we plant, when there are so many mongomongo nuts in the world?" (see chapter 2).

One of the most important insights refined in the 1980s was the development of the distinction between hunter-gatherer societies with storage and those without it (Testart 1982). James Woodburn and Alan Barnard make this distinction using the terms *immediate-return societies* and *delayed-return societies* (Woodburn 1982; Barnard and Woodburn 1988). Immediate-return societies are characterized by a lack of what economists call "fixed capital." Members of these societies live on day-to-day flows from hunting and gathering and have no elaborate means of collecting or storing food. Material technology is simple and accessible to all. Immediate-return societies are so unlike Western societies that it is difficult for us even to conceive how they function successfully, and for this reason they are particularly valuable in helping us to reassess our own way of viewing the world. All the assumptions economists make about economic man are absent in these societies. People in immediate-return societies are not acquisitive, self-centered cost-benefit calculators. In these societies, it can be most clearly seen that economic man as a universal human type is a fiction.

In the 1990s, an even greater appreciation emerged for the many important differences among various hunter-gatherer societies and the different roles of men and women in these societies. The division of labor along gender lines was critically examined. With the new emphasis on diversity in hunter-gatherer ways of life, a debate emerged as to whether hunter-gatherers should even be considered as a distinct category because of the great differences among nonagriculturalists (Burch and Ellanna 1994). This debate reflects not only the growing appreciation for the diversity of hunter-gatherer lifestyles but also an ideological division between anthropologists who view the hunter-gatherer way of life as different from that of economic man and those who argue that hunter-gatherers behave essentially as do members of modern market economies. An advocate of the latter approach, Robert Kelly, makes this clear: "In the daily activities of foragers, for the most part I now see costs and benefits of resources, caloric returns, differences in time allocation, opportunity costs, utility curves, and fitness benefits" (Kelly 1995:xiv). The economic rationality debate has raged among economists for more than a century, and it is interesting to see it replayed in the hunter-gatherer literature.

In spite of this inevitable and intellectually necessary questioning of categories and motives, the basic positive view of hunter-gatherers as the original affluent societies has held up well in the twenty-five years since the publication of Marshall Sahlins's now-classic book *Stone Age Economics*. Even among these well-studied groups, very little is known about how they lived before European contact. Even less can be said about their beliefs and attitudes about human existence and their place in nature. All such judgments have been filtered through Western urban eyes. In many cases, we can only guess about motives, appearances, and what is reality and what is illusion. In spite of the limits to our understanding, much can be learned from the information we have about hunting and gathering societies.

An Overview of the Issues

As an economist, the most important messages for me from these descriptions of hunter-gatherers are that (1) the economic notion of scarcity is largely a social construct, not an inherent property of human existence; (2) the separation of work from social life is not a necessary characteristic of economic production; (3) the linking of individual well-being to individual production is not a necessary characteristic of economic organization; (4) selfishness and acquisitiveness are not natural traits of our species; and (5) inequality based on class and gender is not a necessary characteristic of human society.

Scarcity

The notion of scarcity is largely a social construct, not an essential characteristic of human existence. Hunter-gatherers may be considered affluent because they achieve a balance between means and ends by wanting little. By contrast, the modern industrial system generates scarcity by creating unlimited wants. Consumers are addicted to a continual flow of consumer goods and feel continually deprived because addiction can never be satiated. In Sahlins's words, "Consumption is a double tragedy: what begins in inadequacy will end in deprivation" (see chapter 1). The modern worldwide addiction to material objects threatens our psychological well-being as well as our biophysical foundations. Although humans may not be naturally acquisitive, hunter-gatherers seem to be as susceptible to the seduction of modern consumerism as are the rest of us. How much of this is the result of the colonial mentality of a conquered people and how much arises from some basic human propensity is a critical question.

The Nature of Work

A second fact about hunter-gatherer life is that work is social and cooperative. Typically, immediate-return hunter-gatherers spend only three or four hours per day working at what we would call economic activities. This work involves hunting a large number of animal species and gathering a large variety of plant material. Field researchers express amazement at the amount of detailed knowledge hunter-gatherers possess about the characteristics and life histories of the plant and animal species on which they depend for survival. Work is integrated with rituals, socialization, and artistic expression to a degree unknown to most people in Western societies. The idea that work is drudgery whose only purpose is to enable people to live their "real" lives is not present in hunter-gatherer societies. The work-leisure trade-off discussed in economic textbooks is apparently absent there.

Production and Distribution

A third fact about hunter-gatherer economies also runs counter to the notion of economic man central to modern economic theory: no necessary connection exists between production by individuals and distribution to individuals. Economists have argued that sharing has an economically rational basis. The person with whom we share our catch today may feed us tomorrow when our luck or skill fails. In the traditional economic view, sharing is a kind of insurance policy that rationally spreads the risk of having nothing to eat. Sharing in hunter-gatherer societies, however, is much more profound than this. In many such societies, at least, there is no connection between who produces and who receives the economic output. According to James Woodburn (chapter 4), for example, some members of the Hadza of Tanzania do virtually no work for their entire lives. Many Hadza men gamble with spear points, and many are reluctant to hunt for fear of damaging their gambling "chips," yet these men continue to get their full share of the game animals killed. Interestingly, this lack of reciprocal behavior has also been observed among nonhuman predators such as lions. Disdain for those not engaged in productive activity is a culturally specific emotion.

The essence of the affluence of hunter-gatherers lies in one fundamental characteristic that is directly opposed to the ideological basis of modern capitalism: the absence of a link between individual production and individual economic security. Not only is the direct link between production and distribution a dominant characteristic of all non-hunter-gatherer societies, but it is also the very essence of the moral basis of modern capitalism. Again, the standard economic explanation of wages, profits, and rent (the marginal productivity theory of distribution) is that in a competitive economy, workers and owners of the means of production are paid according to what each contributes to total output. By concentrating on the "margin" or on incremental changes, it is possible to ignore the fact that the capital, technology, natural resource endowment, and knowledge that make all economic activity possible is the result of tens of thousands of years of human cultural evolution. Why should this collective productive power, accumulated over eons, be expropriated by a few individuals living at a particular point in time? To argue that it is "moral" and "natural" to distribute the product of economic activity based on each individual's incremental contribution to output is to ignore history and context and, evidently, to ignore human nature.

Ownership and Capital

Accounts by early European explorers and the anthropological accounts in this volume indicate that sharing and a lack of concern with ownership of personal possessions is a common characteristic of hunter-gatherer societies. The lack of private ownership of things also applies to the ownership of resources. James Woodburn (1968:50) writes:

> The Eastern Hadza assert no rights over land and its ungarnered resources. Any individual may live wherever he likes and may hunt animals, collect roots, berries, and honey and draw water anywhere in the Hadza country without any sort of restriction. Not only do the Hadza not parcel out their land and its resources among themselves, they do not even seek to restrict the land they occupy to members of their own tribe.

Attempts to characterize the relationship of some hunter-gatherers to the land as ownership may be a case of imposing Western concepts on people who have very different beliefs about relationships among people and between humans and nature. David Riches (1995) argues that the term *ownership* should be used only in cases in which people are observed denying others the right to use particular resources. The mere act of asking permission may be only a social convention expressing friendly intent and not an indication of "legal" control over a resource. Clearly, the institution of private property is not the only alternative in promoting efficient resource use.

The economist Nicholas Georgescu-Roegen (1971) emphasized the critical difference between living off stocks and living off flows. A *stock* is something that can be used at any rate; for example, a ton of coal can be burned as fuel in one day or over the course of several years. The term *flow* applies to something that can be used only at some limited rate. For example, a particular laborer may be able to dig 365 ditches per day for one year, but he or she cannot dig 365 ditches in one day. Whereas the growth of industrial economies is made possible by using the earth's stocks of nonrenewable natural resources such as fossil fuel, hunter-gatherers live off the flows of renewable biological resources and solar energy through their ecosystems. This fact is important to the egalitarian and cooperative nature of these societies. What economists call "capital stock" plays a minor role in immediate-return societies as a mediator between natural resources and final consumption.

To a large extent, hunter-gatherers depend only on their bodies and intelligence to produce their daily sustenance. Mobility is paramount, and physical capital is necessarily simple. Capital in a hunter-gatherer world is not a physical thing that can be manipulated and controlled but rather is knowledge that is shared and accessible to all. With this knowledge, hunter-gatherers can quickly construct their material culture. Colin Turnbull (1965:19) writes of the Pygmies of central Africa: "The materials for the making of shelter, clothing, and all other necessary items of material culture are all at hand at a moment's notice." Unlike the manufactured capital of industrial society, hunter-gatherer capital stock is knowledge, which is freely given and impossible to control for individual advantage. The lack of preoccupation with acquiring material goods gives hunter-gatherers the freedom to enjoy life. Most of a hunter-gatherer's life is spent not at a workplace, away from friends and family, but in talking, resting, sharing, and celebrating; in short, in being human. This is an ideal of modern Western society, expressed in the major religions and in popular culture, but it is largely unrealized.

Inequality

Finally, inequality is not a natural feature of human societies. As the readings in part I of this book make clear, immediate-return hunter-gatherer societies were "aggressively egalitarian" (see, chapter 4). These societies worked because of, not in spite of, the fact that power and authority were kept in check. Inequality as a result of human nature is another side of the cultural myth of economic man. The logic of economic rationality justifies as inevitable income differences based on class, race, or gender. Sometimes this justification is overt, but usually (and more dangerously), it is made through appeals to economic efficiency. A trade-off between economic growth and equity is a feature of most introductory economics textbooks. If Western society errs on the side of too much equity (so the story goes), the incentive to work is lost, production falls, and even the temporary beneficiaries of increased income equality end up worse off than before.

The hunter-gatherer literature shows that "rational economic behavior" is peculiar to market capitalism and is an embedded set of cultural beliefs, not an objective universal law of nature. The myth of economic man explains the organizing principle of contemporary capitalism, nothing more or less. It is no more rational than the myths that drive Hadza, Aborigine, or !Kung society. Just as the myth of economic man justifies the appropriation by a few of the human material culture that has evolved over millennia, so does it justify the appropriation and destruction of the natural world, the product of eons of evolution (Gowdy 1997).

What Can We Learn from Hunter-Gatherers?

Hunting and gathering societies were in ecological and social harmony to a degree unmatched in present times. This is interesting in itself, since humans lived as hunter-gatherers for almost the entire time our species has been on this planet. The same features that ensured environmental harmony also promoted an egalitarian social structure. These features were not based on deliberate cultivation of a higher ethical consciousness; they were embedded in the material characteristics of immediate-return economies. With the current population of the earth approaching 6 billion, we cannot return to a hunting and gathering way of life, barring a catastrophic collapse of the human population. We can, however, work to incorporate some of the features of hunter-gatherer societies that worked to promote ecological and social harmony. These include social security; living off renewable flows rather than exhaustible stocks; sexual equality; cultural and ecological diversity based on bioregionalism; and social rather than private capital.

Social Security. As the essays in this volume discuss, in immediate-return societies, every individual receives a share of the social product regardless of how much he or she has contributed to it. Social security can also play an important role in the sustainability of modern societies. Frances Moore Lappe and Rachel Schurman argue that social insurance in modern China has as much to do with the decline in birth rate as does the one-child policy (Gordon and Suzuki 1990:104). John Caldwell (1984) points to social security programs and old-age pensions as playing a decisive role in the reduction in population growth in Kerala (India) and Sri Lanka. He argues that when life is perceived to be secure, people do not need large families to ensure that they will be taken care of in old age.

Living Off Renewable Flows, Not Exhaustible Stocks. This is a primary recommendation of economists such as Nicholas Georgescu-Roegen (1977). Living off the flows of renewable resources not only promotes a sustainable economy but also may reduce the role of property as a means of obtaining power. Most important, living off flows breaks the vicious cycle of resource exhaustion, substitution, technological change, more resource exhaustion, and so on that seems to have been the pattern for human societies over the past ten thousand years or so.

In standard economic theory, the distinction between renewable and non-renewable resources is unimportant because of the assumption of universal substitutability, as embodied in the notion of "weak sustainability" (Pearce and Atkinson 1993). By this criterion for sustainability, it is permissible to cut down a rain forest (a form of what economists call "natural capital") if the monetary gain from doing so is invested for the benefit of future generations. The type of investment doesn't matter: it could be another forest, an automobile factory, or even an intangible investment. In standard economic theory (and in the market economy that theory describes), everything is reducible to a monetary value, and thus everything is substitutable. The distinction between stocks and flows disappears, as does the distinction between capital, labor, and natural resources. This way of looking at the world masks the fact that we are sacrificing for ephemeral economic gains the viability of resources on which our ultimate existence as a species depends.

Some ecological economists have called for a "strong sustainability" requirement. Renewable resources (such as forests and fisheries) should be used at a rate that is lower than their natural rate of regeneration, and nonrenewable resources (for example, fossil fuels) should be used at a rate lower than the rate of increase in technological improvements such as increased efficiency and the discovery of substitutes. Strong sustainability, unlike weak sustainability, recognizes that there are limits to substitution, but it is essentially only a modification of neoclassical economic theory, returning the factor "land" (meaning natural resources) to the standard list of primary economic inputs (land, labor, and capital). Hunter-gatherers had what Georgescu-Roegen called viable technologies: technologies that could perpetuate themselves indefinitely without using up irreplaceable stocks of natural resources.

Sexual Equality. Although the woman-as-gatherer, man-as-hunter distinction is evidently not as clear as was once believed, women in hunter-gatherer societies supplied the bulk of the food through gathering. This certainly contributed to the gender equality generally present in most hunter-gatherer societies. In the recent past, in cases in which hunter-gatherers have become agriculturalists, the status of women was sharply reduced. The low social status of women in many countries is frequently cited as a major contributor to explosive population growth (Jacobson 1987). Even in agricultural societies, women have played the dominant role in nurturing diversity and sustainability in ecological systems. Some of the most important ecopolitical movements, such as the Chipko movement in the Garhwal Himalaya, are led by women (Shiva 1993).

Cultural and Ecological Diversity Based on Bioregionalism. Hunters and gatherers occupied all the area of the earth populated by modern humans, and for the most part, they did so with sustainable technologies. The Inuit of northern North America and the Aborigines of the Australian deserts were able to live sustainably in climates in which industrial-society humans could not survive without a steady subsidy of resources from the outside. The hunting and gathering lifestyle represented a remarkable and varied response to different environmental conditions. For most of the more than 2 million years of human existence, a wide range of lifestyles and economic bases could be found in ecosystems from desert to tundra to rain forest. Such diversity is critical to the protection of natural systems. Vandana Shiva (1993:65) writes:

> Diversity is the characteristic of nature and the basis of ecological stability. Diverse ecosystems give rise to diverse life forms, and to diverse cultures. The co-evolution of cultures, life forms and habitats has conserved the biological diversity on this planet. Cultural diversity and biological diversity go hand in hand.

With a diversity of lifestyles, there is also a better chance for the human species to withstand shocks, climatic and otherwise. Warren Hern (1990) and Robert Allen (1977) have pointed out that the modern homogeneous world economy is particularly vulnerable to environmental or social disruption.

Social Versus Private Capital. The fact that the most important form of capital in hunting and gathering societies was common, readily shared knowledge meant that capital was public, not private. Even in complex hunter-gatherer cultures, capital equipment such as boats and nets were not private property as we know it. The provision of more public and less private capital is frequently recommended for our own economy—for example, public transportation instead of private automobiles, or public rental cabins in wilderness areas instead of private second homes.

Overview of the Book

The purpose of this book is threefold. The first motive is to bring together some of the classic articles on the few remaining immediate-return hunter-gatherer cultures—accounts of some of the "original affluent societies," as Marshall Sahlins first described them. Second, more recent and more theoretical papers assessing and extending the notion of the original affluent society are included to show how this conceptual understanding has held up in the years since the prevailing view of hunter-gathers changed so radically. Three issues in particular are highlighted: the separation of production from distribution, the status of women in preagricultural societies, and the ways in which the introduction of economic surpluses has affected social structure. Third, papers are included that evaluate hunter-gatherer societies in terms of what can be learned from them and applied to our present quest for environmental stability and social equality. This third motive is critical. The hunter-gatherer patterns of existence are not an irrelevant part of our cultural evolution. Humans lived as hunter-gatherers for almost our entire existence as a species. These societies had evidently solved, or avoided, problems that modern society seems incapable of seriously addressing. We have much to learn from the ways in which these societies successfully dealt with the problems of everyday survival, socialization, and ecological sustainability.

The modern age is increasingly characterized by despair. Human society seems out of control and on the brink of numerous irretrievable disasters. The interrelated issues of atmospheric change, global climate change, biodiversity loss, overpopulation, and social unrest threaten the very existence of our civilization, which most of us consider so superior to those earlier cultures from which ours evolved. It is somewhat comforting to realize that the blueprint for survival is contained within our cultural history. For most of the time humans have been on the planet, we have lived in harmony with the natural world and with one another. Our minds and cultures evolved under these conditions. Understanding how hunter-gatherer societies solved the basic problems of living within environmental constraints with a maximum of human freedom may give us a key to ensuring our biological and cultural long-term survival. If we fail in our search for a sustainable, egalitarian alternative to our present system, our future may well be that envisioned by Richard B. Lee and Irven DeVore thirty years ago in their introduction to *Man the Hunter:*

> To date, the hunting way of life has been the most successful and persistent adaptation man has ever achieved. Nor does this evaluation exclude the present precarious existence under the threat of nuclear annihilation and the population explosion. It is still an open question whether man will be able to survive the exceedingly complex and unstable ecological conditions he has created for himself. If he fails in this task, interplanetary archaeologists of the future will classify our planet as one in which a very long and stable period of small-scale hunting and gathering was followed by an apparently instantaneous efflorescence of technology and society leading rapidly to extinction. (Lee and DeVore 1968:3).

At the heart of this collection, I believe, are two ideas. The first is an (implicit or explicit) critique of the current world system, with its inequality and rapaciousness; the second is the hope of an alternative. As pointed out by Richard B. Lee in chapter 7, there is something still beyond the reach of the world socioeconomic system. In Lee's words, "The 'system' is powerful but not omnipotent." People are still able to choose different kinds of social systems. Like Voltaire's Dr. Pangloss, contemporary economics takes the extreme adaptationist view that whatever currently exists is best. Pangloss himself put this view most eloquently:

It is demonstrable that things cannot be otherwise than they are; for as all things have been created for some end, they must necessarily be created for the best end. Observe, for instance, the nose is formed for spectacles therefore we wear spectacles. The legs are visibly designed for stockings, accordingly we wear stockings. (Voltaire 1929:276)

This argument is also dominant among neoclassical economists, who use it to justify the alleged superiority of free-market outcomes (Gowdy 1992). Why would firms downsize if this were not economically rational and therefore the best thing for them to do? Why would gross income inequality exist if it were not necessary to encourage people to work harder? The very existence of an array of successful cultures that solved many of the problems we now see as intractable and inevitable gives hope that an egalitarian and environmentally sustainable human economy is possible. The world in which we live today is not the best of all possible worlds.

REFERENCES

Allen, R. 1977. "Towards a Primary Lifestyle." Pp. 313–29 in *Alternatives to Growth*, edited by D. Meadows. Cambridge: Cambridge University Press.

Barnard, A., and J. Woodburn. 1988. "Property, Power, and Ideology in Hunter-Gathering Societies: An Introduction." Pp. 4–31 in *Hunters and Gatherers*, vol. 2, *Property, Power, and Ideology,* edited by Tim Ingold, David Riches, and James Woodburn. Oxford: Berg.

Bettinger, R. 1980. "Explanatory/Predictive Models of Hunter-Gatherer Adaptation." *Advances in Archaeological Method and Theory* 3:189–255.

Boehm, C. 1997. "Impact of the Human Egalitarian Syndrome on Darwinian Selection Mechanics." *The American Naturalist* 150 (Supplement):S100–S121.

Braidwood, Robert J. 1952. *The Near East and the Foundations for Civilization.* Eugene: Oregon State System of Higher Education.

Burch, Ernest S., Jr., and Linda J. Ellanna, eds. 1994. *Key Issues in Hunter- Gatherer Research.* Oxford: Berg.

Caldwell, J. 1984. *Theory of Fertility Decline.* New York: Academic Press.

Clark, C. W., and M. Mangel. 1986. "The Evolutionary Advantages of Group Foraging." *Theoretical Population Biology* 30:45–75.

Georgescu-Roegen, Nicholas. 1971. *The Entropy Law and the Economic Process.* Cambridge, Mass.: Harvard University Press.

———. 1977. "Inequality, Limits, and Growth from a Bioeconomic Viewpoint." *Review of Social Economy* 37:361–365.

Gordon, A., and D. Suzuki. 1990. *A Matter of Survival.* Sydney: Allen and Unwin.

Gowdy, John. 1992. "Higher Selection Processes in Evolutionary Economic Change." *Journal of Evolutionary Economics* 2 (1):1–16.

———. 1997. "The Value of Biodiversity: Economy, Society, and Ecosystems." *Land Economics* 73:25–41.

Hern, W. 1990. "Why Are There So Many of Us? Description and Diagnosis of a Planetary Ecopathological Process." *Population and Environment* 12:9–42.

Jacobson, J. 1987. *Planning the Global Family*. Worldwatch Paper No. 80. Washington, D.C.: Worldwatch Institute.

Kelly, Robert. 1995. *The Foraging Spectrum: Diversity in Hunter-Gatherer Lifeways*. Washington, D.C.: Smithsonian Institution Press.

Lee, Richard B. 1969. "!Kung Bushman Subsistence: An Input-Output Analysis." Pp. 47–79 in *Environment and Cultural Behavior*, edited by Andrew P. Vayda. New York: Natural History Press.

Lee, Richard B. and Irven DeVore. 1968. Introduction to *Man the Hunter*. Chicago: Aldine.

Pearce, D., and G. Atkinson. 1993. "Capital Theory and the Measurement of Sustainable Development: An Indicator of Weak Sustainability." *Ecological Economics* 8:103–8.

Rappaport, Roy. 1968. *Pigs for the Ancestors*. New Haven, Conn.: Yale University Press.

Riches, David. 1995. "Hunter-Gatherer Structural Transformations." *Journal of the Royal Anthropological Institute* 1:679–701.

Shiva, Vandana. 1993. *Monocultures of the Mind*. London: Zed Books.

Speth, John, and Katherine Spielmann. 1983. "Energy Source, Protein Metabolism, and Hunter-Gatherer Subsistence Strategies." *Journal of Anthropological Archaeology* 2:1–31.

Testart, Alain. 1982. "The Significance of Food Storage Among Hunter-Gatherers: Residence Patterns, Population Densities, and Social Inequalities." *Current Anthropology* 23:523–37.

Turnbull, Colin. 1965. *The Mbuti Pygmies*. New York: Simon and Schuster.

Voltaire, François Marie Arouet de. 1929. *The Best of All Possible Worlds: Romances and Tales*. New York: Vanguard Press.

Woodburn, James. 1968. "An Introduction to Hadza Ecology." Pp. 49–55 in *Man the Hunter*, edited by Richard B. Lee and Irven DeVore. Chicago: Aldine.

———. 1982. "Egalitarian Societies." *Man* 17 (3):431–51.

FURTHER READING: A VERY SHORT LIST

Cultural Evolution

Johnson, Allen, and Timothy Earle. 1987. *The Evolution of Human Societies*. Stanford, Calif.: Stanford University Press.

Sanderson, Stephen. 1989. *Social Evolutionism: A Critical History*. New York: Basil Blackwell.

Steward, Julian. 1955. *Theory of Cultural Change*. Urbana: University of Illinois Press.

Tainter, Joseph. 1988. *The Collapse of Complex Societies*. New York: Cambridge University Press.

White, Leslie. 1959. *The Evolution of Culture*. New York: McGraw-Hill.

Cultural Materialism and Cultural Ecology

Harris, Marvin. 1978. *Cannibals and Kings*. New York: Random House.

———. 1979. *Cultural Materialism*. New York: Random House.

Rappaport, Roy. 1968. *Pigs for the Ancestors*. New Haven, Conn.: Yale University Press.

Sustainability

Daly, Herman, and John Cobb. 1989. *For the Common Good*. Boston: Beacon Press.

Gowdy, John. 1994. *Coevolutionary Economics*. Boston: Kluwer.

Jacobs, Michael. 1991. *The Green Economy*, London: Pluton Press.

Norgaard, Richard. 1994. *Development Betrayed: The End of Progress and the Coevolutionary Revisioning of the Future*. New York: Routledge.

Orr, David. 1994. *Earth in Mind*. Washington, D.C.: Island Press.

Hunter-Gatherer Diversity

Burch, Ernest S., Jr., and Linda J. Ellanna, eds. 1994. *Key Issues in Hunter-Gatherer Research*. Oxford: Berg.

Kelly, Robert. 1995. *The Foraging Spectrum: Diversity in Hunter-Gatherer Lifeways*. Washington, D.C.: Smithsonian Institution Press.

Economics and Society

Galbraith, John Kenneth. 1973. *Economics and the Public Purpose*. New York: Signet.

Georgescu-Roegen, Nicholas. 1971. *The Entropy Law and the Economic Process*. Cambridge, Mass.: Harvard University Press.

Heilbroner, Robert. 1994. *21st Century Capitalism*. New York: Norton.

Polanyi, Karl. 1944. *The Great Transformation*. Boston: Beacon Press.

LIMITED WANTS, UNLIMITED MEANS

PART 1

ORIGINAL
AFFLUENT SOCIETIES

The four chapters in Part I are representative of the revolution in the anthropology of hunter-gatherers that began in the 1960s. The information about hunter-gatherers contained therein directly challenges the universality of the myth of economic man. The first conference on hunter-gatherers, titled "Man the Hunter" and held at the University of Chicago in 1966, may be said to mark the beginning of a serious important scientific reassessment of these societies. The first two chapters were derived from papers presented at that conference. Chapter 1, Marshall Sahlins's "The Original Affluent Society," captured the imagination of the general public and also the spirit of the new way anthropologists were thinking about hunter-gatherers. In this provocative paper, Sahlins contrasts the traditional view of hunter-gatherer life as "nasty, brutish, and short" with the reality of societies that enjoyed abundant leisure time and whose material needs were easily satisfied. Most important, Sahlins spells out a simple yet revolutionary idea with profound implications for our turbulent times: scarcity is a social construct, not an inevitable condition of human existence.

Chapter 2, "What Hunters Do for a Living," from a paper presented at that first conference by Richard B. Lee, presents some detailed information about the !Kung, or San, of the southern African desert. Lee's chapter addresses the simple question, "How do hunters make a living?" The answer is, again, simple yet profound: they do so easily, ingeniously, and sustainably.

Chapter 3, Lorna Marshall's "Sharing, Talking, and Giving," first published in 1961, gives more detailed information about the social organization of !Kung society and how "sharing, talking, and giving" reinforce and are integrated with "economic" life. The difference between the possessive rationality of economic man and a society based on sharing, cooperation, and caring is striking. For example, trade with others, the Holy Grail of contemporary capitalism, is considered undignified and socially disruptive and is done only with outsiders.

Chapter 4, James Woodburn's "Egalitarian Societies," links social organization and ecological sustainability. Woodburn distinguishes immediate-return hunter-gatherer societies, which have a very simple technology, from delayed-return hunter-gatherer societies, which depend on capital equipment such as nets and traps. Woodburn characterizes immediate-return societies as "aggressively egalitarian." Some anthropologists argue that the differences between immediate-return and delayed return hunter-gatherer societies is more important than that between delayed-return hunter-gatherers and simple agriculturalists (see chapter 8). Apparently, even simple capital equipment can have a compromising effect on the egalitarian social structure of hunter-gatherers. A comparison of Marshall's account of !Kung social life with that in

John E. Yellen's description of a modern !Kung village in part III clearly illustrates this point.

Even the very limited introduction to hunter-gatherer societies given in part I of this volume shows the tapestry of possibilities of human social organization. The great economist Nicholas Georgescu-Roegen was fond of quoting Rudyard Kipling on this point:

> *There are nine and sixty ways of constructing tribal lays*
> *And-every-single-one-of-them-is-right!*

ONE

The Original Affluent Society

◆

Marshall Sahlins

If economics is the dismal science, the study of hunting and gathering economies must be its most advanced branch. Almost universally committed to the proposition that life was hard in the Paleolithic, our textbooks compete to convey a sense of impending doom, leaving one to wonder not only how hunters managed to live, but whether, after all, this was living? The specter of starvation stalks the stalker through these pages. His technical incompetence is said to enjoin continuous work just to survive, affording him neither respite nor surplus, hence not even the "leisure" to "build culture." Even so, for all his efforts, the hunter pulls the lowest grades in thermodynamics—less energy/capita/year than any other mode of production. And in treatises on economic development he is condemned to play the role of bad example: the so-called "subsistence economy."

The traditional wisdom is always refractory. One is forced to oppose it polemically, to phrase the necessary revisions dialectically: in fact, this was, when you come to examine it, the original affluent society. Paradoxical, that phrasing leads to another useful and unexpected conclusion. By the common understanding, an affluent society is one in which all the people's material wants are easily satisfied. To assert that the hunters are affluent is to deny then that the human condition is an ordained tragedy, with man the prisoner at hard labor of a perpetual disparity between his unlimited wants and his insufficient means.

For there are two possible courses to affluence. Wants may be "easily satisfied" either by producing much or desiring little. The familiar conception, the Galbraithean way, makes assumptions peculiarly appropriate to market economies: that man's wants are great, not to say infinite, whereas his means are limited, although improvable: thus, the gap between means and ends can be narrowed by industrial productivity, at least to the point that "urgent goods" become plentiful. But there is also a Zen road to affluence, departing from premises somewhat different from our own: that human material wants are finite and few, and technical means unchanging but on the whole adequate. Adopting the Zen strategy, a people can enjoy an unparalleled material plenty—with a low standard of living.

That, I think, describes the hunters. And it helps explain some of their more curious economic behavior: their "prodigality" for example—the inclination to consume at once all stocks on hand, as if they had it made. Free from market obsessions of scarcity, hunters' economic propensities may be more consistently predicated on abundance than our own. Destutt de Tracy, "fish-blooded bourgeois doctrinaire" though he might have been, at least compelled Marx's agreement on the observation that "in poor nations the people are comfortable," whereas in rich nations "they are generally poor."

This is not to deny that a preagricultural economy operates under serious constraints, but only to insist, on the evidence from modern hunters and gatherers, that a successful accommodation is usually made. After taking up the evidence, I shall return in the end to the real difficulties of hunting-gathering economy, none of which are correctly specified in current formulas of paleolithic poverty.

Sources of the Misconception

"Mere subsistence economy," "limited leisure save in exceptional circumstances," "incessant quest for food," "meager and relatively unreliable" natural resources, "absence of an economic surplus," "maximum energy from a maximum number of people"—so runs the fair average anthropological opinion of hunting and gathering.

> The aboriginal Australians are a classic example of a people whose economic resources are of the scantiest. In many places their habitat is even more severe than that of the Bushmen, although this is perhaps not quite true in the northern portion. . . . A tabulation of the foodstuffs which the aborigines of northwest central Queensland extract from the country they inhabit is instructive. . . . The variety in this list is impressive, but we must not be deceived into thinking that variety indicates plenty, for the available quantities of each element in it are so slight that only the most intense application makes survival possible. (Herskovits 1952:68–69)

Or again, in reference to South American hunters:

> The nomadic hunters and gatherers barely met minimum subsistence needs and often fell far short of them. Their population of 1 person

to 10 or 20 square miles reflects this. Constantly on the move in search of food, they clearly lacked the leisure hours for nonsubsistence activities of any significance, and they could transport little of what they might manufacture in spare moments. To them, adequacy of production meant physical survival, and they rarely had surplus of either products or time. (Steward and Faron 1959:60; cf. Clark 1953:27ff; Haury 1962:113; Hoebel 1958:188; Redfield 1953:5; White 1959)

But the traditional dismal view of the hunters' fix is also preanthropological and extra-anthropological, at once historical and referable to the larger economic context in which anthropology operates. It goes back to the time Adam Smith was writing, and probably to a time before anyone was writing.[1] Probably it was one of the first distinctly neolithic prejudices, an ideological appreciation of the hunter's capacity to exploit the earth's resources most congenial to the historic task of depriving him of the same. We must have inherited it with the seed of Jacob, which "spread abroad to the west, and to the east, and to the north," to the disadvantage of Esau who was the elder son and cunning hunter, but in a famous scene deprived of his birthright.

Current low opinions of the hunting-gathering economy need not be laid to neolithic ethnocentrism, however. Bourgeois ethnocentrism will do as well. The existing business economy, at every turn an ideological trap from which anthropological economics must escape, will promote the same dim conclusions about the hunting life.

Is it so paradoxical to contend that hunters have affluent economies, their absolute poverty notwithstanding? Modern capitalist societies, however richly endowed, dedicate themselves to the proposition of scarcity. Inadequacy of economic means is the first principle of the world's wealthiest peoples. The apparent material status of the economy seems to be no clue to its accomplishments; something has to be said for the mode of economic organization (cf. Polanyi 1947, 1957, 1959; Dalton 1961).

The market-industrial system institutes scarcity, in a manner completely unparalleled and to a degree nowhere else approximated. Where production and distribution are arranged through the behavior of prices, and all livelihoods depend on getting and spending, insufficiency of material means becomes the explicit, calculable starting point of all economic activity.[2] The entrepreneur is confronted with alternative investments of a finite capital, the worker (hopefully) with alternative choices of remunerative employ, and the consumer. . . . Consumption is a double tragedy: what begins in inadequacy will end in deprivation. Bringing together an international division of labor, the market makes available a dazzling array of products: all these Good Things within a man's reach—but never all within his grasp. Worse, in this game of consumer free choice, every acquisition is simultaneously a deprivation, for every purchase of something is a foregoing of something else, in general only marginally less desirable, and in some particulars more desirable, that could have been had instead. (The point is that if you buy one automobile, say a Plymouth, you cannot also have the Ford—and I judge from current television commercials that the deprivations entailed would be more than just material.)[3]

That sentence of "life at hard labor" was passed uniquely upon us. Scarcity is the judgment decreed by our economy—so also the axiom of our Economics: the application of scarce means against alternative ends to derive the most satisfaction possible under the circumstances. And it is precisely from this anxious vantage that we look back upon hunters. But if modern man, with all his technological advantages, still hasn't got the wherewithal, what chance has this naked savage with his puny bow and arrow? Having equipped the hunter with bourgeois impulses and paleolithic tools, we judge his situation hopeless in advance.[4]

Yet scarcity is not an intrinsic property of technical means. It is a relation between means and ends. We should entertain the empirical possibility that hunters are in business for their health, a finite objective, and that bow and arrow are adequate to that end.[5]

But still other ideas, these endemic in anthropological theory and ethnographic practice, have conspired to preclude any such understanding.

The anthropological disposition to exaggerate the economic inefficiency of hunters appears notably by way of invidious comparison with neolithic economies. Hunters, as Lowie put it blankly, "must work much harder in order to live than tillers and breeders" (1946:13). On this point evolutionary anthropology in particular found it congenial, even necessary theoretically, to adopt the usual tone of reproach. Ethnologists and archaeologists had become neolithic revolutionaries, and in their enthusiasm for the Revolution spared nothing denouncing the Old (Stone Age) Regime. Including some very old scandal. It was not the first time philosophers would relegate the earliest stage of humanity rather to nature than to culture. ("A man who spends his whole life following animals just to kill them to eat, or moving from one berry patch to another, is really living just like an animal himself" [Braidwood 1957:122].) The hunters thus downgraded, anthropology was free to extol the Neolithic Great Leap Forward: a main technological advance that brought about a "general availability of leisure through release from purely food-getting pursuits" (Braidwood 1952:5; cf. Boas 1940:285).

In an influential essay on "Energy and the Evolution of Culture," Leslie White explained that the neolithic generated a "great advance in cultural development . . . as a consequence of the great increase in the amount of energy harnessed and controlled per capita per year by means of the agricultural and pastoral arts" (1949:372). White further heightened the evolutionary contrast by specifying *human effort* as the principal energy source of paleolithic culture, as opposed to the *domesticated plant and animal resources* of neolithic culture. This determination of the energy sources at once permitted a precise low estimate of hunters' thermodynamic potential—that developed by the human body: "average power resources" of one-twentieth horsepower per capita (1949:369)—even as, by eliminating human effort from the cultural enterprise of the neolithic, it appeared that people had been liberated by some labor-saving device (domesticated plants and animals). But White's problematic is obviously misconceived. The principal mechanical energy available to both paleolithic and neolithic culture is that supplied by human beings, as transformed in both cases from plant and animal sources, so that, with negligible exceptions (the occasional direct use of nonhuman power), the amount of energy harnessed per capita per year is the same in paleolithic and neolithic economies—and fairly constant in human history until the advent of the industrial revolution.[6]

Another specifically anthropological source of paleolithic discontent develops in the field itself, from the context of European observation of existing hunters and gatherers, such as the native Australians, the Bushmen, the Ona, or the Yahgan. This ethnographic context tends to distort our understanding of the hunting-gathering economy in two ways.

First, it provides singular opportunities for naïveté. The remote and exotic environments that have become the cultural theater of modern hunters have an effect on Europeans most unfavorable to the latter's assessment of the former's plight. Marginal as the Australian or Kalahari desert is to agriculture, or to everyday European experience, it is a source of wonder to the untutored observer "how anybody could live in a place like this." The inference that the natives manage only to eke out a bare existence is apt to be reinforced by their marvelously varied diets (cf. Herskovits 1952, quoted above). Ordinarily including objects deemed repulsive and inedible by Europeans, the local cuisine lends itself to the supposition that the people are starving to death. Such a conclusion, of course, is more likely met in earlier than in later accounts, and in the journals of explorers or missionaries than in the monographs of anthropologists; but precisely because the explorers' reports are older and closer to the aboriginal condition, one reserves for them a certain respect.

Such respect obviously has to be accorded with discretion. Greater attention should be paid a man such as Sir George Grey (1841), whose expeditions in the 1830s included some of the poorer districts of western Australia, but whose unusually close attention to the local people obliged him to debunk his colleagues' communications on just this point of economic desperation. It is a mistake very commonly made, Grey wrote, to suppose that the native Australians "have small means of subsistence, or are at times greatly pressed for want of food." Many and "almost ludicrous" are the errors travellers have fallen into in this regard: "They lament in their journals that the unfortunate Aborigines should be reduced by famine to the miserable necessity of subsisting on certain sorts of food, which they have found near their huts; whereas, in many instances, the articles thus quoted by them are those which the natives most prize, and are really neither deficient in flavour nor nutritious qualities." To render palpable "the ignorance that has prevailed with regard to the habits and customs of this people when in their wild state," Grey provides one remarkable example, a citation from his fellow explorer, Captain Sturt, who, upon encountering a group of Aboriginals engaged in gathering large quantities of mimosa gum, deduced that the "'unfortunate creatures were reduced to the last extremity, and, being unable to procure any other nourishment, had been obliged to collect this mucilaginous.'" But, Sir George observes, the gum in question is a favorite article of food in the area, and when in season it affords the opportunity for large numbers of people to assemble and camp together, which otherwise they are unable to do. He concludes:

> Generally speaking, the natives live well; in some districts there may be at particular seasons of the year a deficiency of food, but if such is the case, these tracts are, at those times, deserted. It *is, however, utterly impossible for a traveller or even for a strange native to judge whether a district affords an abundance of food, or the contrary*... But in his own district a native is very differently situated; he knows exactly what it produces, the proper time at which the several articles are in season, and the readiest means of procuring them. According to these circumstances he regulates his visits to different portions of his hunting ground; *and I can only say that I have always found the greatest abundance in their huts*. (Grey 1841, vol. 2:259–62, emphasis mine; cf. Eyre 1845, vol. 2:244ff).[7]

In making this happy assessment, Sir George took special care to exclude the *lumpen-proletariat* aboriginals living in and about European towns (cf. Eyre 1845, vol. 2:250, 254–255). The exception is instructive. It evokes a second source of ethnographic misconceptions: the anthropology of hunters is largely an anachronistic study of ex-savages—an inquest into the corpse of one society, Grey once said, presided over by members of another.

The surviving food collectors, as a class, are displaced persons. They represent the paleolithic disenfranchised, occupying marginal haunts untypical of the mode of production: sanctuaries of an era, places so beyond the range of main centers of cultural advance as to be allowed some respite from the planetary march of cultural evolution, because they were characteristically poor beyond the interest and competence of more advanced economies. Leave aside the favorably situated food collectors, such as Northwest Coast Indians, about whose (comparative) well-being there is no dispute. The remaining hunters, barred from the better parts of the earth, first by agriculture, later by industrial economies, enjoy ecological opportunities something less than the later-paleolithic average.[8] "Moreover, the disruption accomplished in the past two centuries of European imperialism has been especially severe, to the extent that many of the ethnographic notices that constitute the anthropologist's stock in trade are adulterated culture goods. Even explorer and missionary accounts, apart from their ethnocentric misconstructions, may be speaking of afflicted economies (cf. Service 1962). The hunters of eastern Canada of whom we read in the *Jesuit Relations* were committed to the fur trade in the early seventeenth century. The environments of others were selectively stripped by Europeans before reliable report could be made of indigenous production: the Eskimo we know no longer hunt whales, the Bushmen have been deprived of game, the Shoshoni's piñon has been timbered and his hunting grounds grazed out by cattle.[9] If such peoples are now described as poverty-stricken, their resources "meager and unreliable," is this an indication of the aboriginal condition—or of the colonial duress?

The enormous implications (and problems) for evolutionary interpretation raised by this global retreat have only recently begun to evoke notice (Lee and DeVore 1968). The point of present importance is this: rather than a fair test of hunters' productive capacities, their current circumstances pose something of a supreme test. All the more extraordinary, then, the following reports of their performance.

"A Kind of Material Plenty"

Considering the poverty in which hunters and gatherers live in theory, it comes as a surprise that Bushmen who live in the Kalahari enjoy "a kind of material plenty," at least in the realm of everyday useful things, apart from food and water:

> As the !Kung come into more contact with Europeans—and this is already happening—they will feel sharply the lack of our things and will need and want more. It makes them feel inferior to be without clothes when they stand among strangers who are clothed. But in their own life and with their own artifacts *they were comparatively free from material pressures.* Except for food and water (important excep-

tions!) of which the Nyae Nyae !Kung have a sufficiency—but barely so, judging from the fact that all are thin though not emaciated—they all had what they needed or could make what they needed, for every man can and does make the things that men make and every woman the things that women make. . . . *They lived in a kind of material plenty* because they adapted the tools of their living to materials which lay in abundance around them and which were free for anyone to take (wood, reeds, bone for weapons and implements, fibers for cordage, grass for shelters), or to materials which were at least sufficient for the needs of the population. . . . The !Kung could always use more ostrich egg shells for beads to wear or trade with, but, as it is, enough are found for every woman to have a dozen or more shells for water containers—all she can carry—and a goodly number of bead ornaments. In their nomadic hunting-gathering life, travelling from one source of food to another through the seasons, always going back and forth between food and water, they carry their young children and their belongings. With plenty of most materials at hand to replace artifacts as required, the !Kung have not developed means of permanent storage and have not needed or wanted to encumber themselves with surpluses or duplicates. They do not even want to carry one of everything. They borrow what they do not own. With this ease, they have not hoarded, and the accumulation of objects has not become associated with status. (Marshall 1961:243–44, emphasis mine)

Analysis of hunter-gatherer production is usefully divided into two spheres, as Mrs. Marshall has done. Food and water are certainly "important exceptions," best reserved for separate and extended treatment. For the rest, the nonsubsistence sector, what is here said of the Bushmen applies in general and in detail to hunters from the Kalahari to Labrador—or to Tièrra del Fuego, where Gusinde reports of the Yahgan that their disinclination to own more than one copy of utensils frequently needed is "an indication of self-confidence." "Our Fuegians," he writes, "procure and make their implements with little effort" (1961:213).[10]

In the nonsubsistence sphere, the people's wants are generally easily satisfied. Such "material plenty" depends partly upon the ease of production, and that upon the simplicity of technology and democracy of property. Products are homespun: of stone, bone, wood, skin—materials such as "lay in abundance around them." As a rule, neither extraction of the raw material nor its working up take strenuous effort. Access to natural resources is typically direct—"free for anyone to take" even as possession of the necessary tools is general and knowledge of the required skills common. The division of labor is likewise simple, predominantly a division of labor by sex. Add in the liberal customs of sharing, for which hunters are properly famous, and all the people can usually participate in the going prosperity, such as it is.

But, of course, "such as it is": this "prosperity" depends as well upon an objectively low standard of living. It is critical that the customary quota of consumables (as well as the number of consumers) be culturally set at a modest point. A few people are pleased to consider a few easily-made things their good fortune: some meager pieces of clothing and rather fugitive housing in most climates;[11] plus a few ornaments, spare flints and sundry other items such as the "pieces of quartz, which native doctors have extracted from their patients" (Grey 1841, vol. 2:266); and, finally, the skin bags in which the faithful wife carries all this, "the wealth of the Australian savage" (p. 266).

For most hunters, such affluence without abundance in the nonsubsistence sphere need not be long debated. A more interesting question is why they are content with so few possessions—for it is with them a policy, a "matter of principle" as Gusinde says (1961:2), and not a misfortune.

Want not, lack not. But are hunters so undemanding of material goods because they are themselves enslaved by a food quest "demanding maximum energy from a maximum number of people," so that no time or effort remains for the provision of other comforts? Some ethnographers testify to the contrary that the food quest is so successful that half the time the people seem not to know what to do with themselves. On the other hand, *movement* is a condition of this success, more movement in some cases than others, but always enough to rapidly depreciate the satisfactions of property. Of the hunter it is truly said that his wealth is a burden. In his condition of life, goods can become "grievously oppressive," as Gusinde observes, and the more so the longer they are carried around. Certain food collectors do have canoes and a few have dog sleds, but most must carry themselves all the comforts they possess, and so only possess what they can comfortably carry themselves. Or perhaps only what the women can carry: the men are often left free to react to the sudden opportunity of the chase or the sudden necessity of defense. As Owen Lattimore wrote in a not too different context, "the pure nomad is the poor nomad." Mobility and property are in contradiction.

That wealth quickly becomes more of an encumbrance than a good thing is apparent even to the outsider. Laurens van der Post was caught in the contradiction as he prepared to make farewells to his wild Bushmen friends:

> This matter of presents gave us many an anxious moment. We were humiliated by the realization of how little there was we could give to the Bushmen. Almost everything seemed likely to make life more

difficult for them by adding to the litter and weight of their daily round. They themselves had practically no possessions: a loin strap, a skin blanket and a leather satchel. There was nothing that they could not assemble in one minute, wrap up in their blankets and carry on their shoulders for a journey of a thousand miles. They had no sense of possession. (1958:276)

A necessity so obvious to the casual visitor must be second nature to the people concerned. This modesty of material requirements is institutionalized: it becomes a positive cultural fact, expressed in a variety of economic arrangements. Lloyd Warner reports of the Murngin, for example, that portability is a decisive value in the local scheme of things. Small goods are in general better than big goods. In the final analysis "the relative ease of transportation of the article" will prevail, so far as determining its disposition, over its relative scarcity or labor cost. For the "ultimate value," Warner writes, "is freedom of movement." And to this "desire to be free from the burdens and responsibilities of objects which would interfere with the society's itinerant existence," Warner attributes the Murngin's "undeveloped sense of property," and their "lack of interest in developing their technological equipment" (1964: 136–137).

Here then is another economic "peculiarity"—I will not say it is general, and perhaps it is explained as well by faulty toilet training as by a trained disinterest in material accumulation: some hunters, at least, display a notable tendency to be sloppy about their possessions. They have the kind of nonchalance that would be appropriate to a people who have mastered the problems of production, even as it is maddening to a European:

They do not know how to take care of their belongings. No one dreams of putting them in order, folding them, drying or cleaning them, hanging them up, or putting them in a neat pile. If they are looking for some particular thing, they rummage carelessly through the hodgepodge of trifles in the little baskets. Larger objects that are piled up in a heap in the hut are dragged hither and yon with no regard for the damage that might be done them. The European observer has the impression that these [Yahgan] Indians place no value whatever on their utensils and that they have completely forgotten the effort it took to make them.[12] Actually, no one clings to his few goods and chattels which, as it is, are often and easily lost, but just as easily replaced. . . . The Indian does not even exercise care when he could conveniently do so. A European is likely to shake his head at the boundless indifference of these people who drag brand-new objects, precious clothing, fresh provisions, and valuable items through thick mud, or abandon them to their swift destruction by children and dogs. . . . Expensive things that are given them are treasured for a few hours, out of curiosity; after that they thoughtlessly let everything deteriorate in the mud and wet. The less they own, the more comfortable they can travel, and what is ruined they occasionally replace. Hence, they are completely indifferent to any material possessions. (Gusinde 1961:86–87)

The hunter, one is tempted to say, is "uneconomic man." At least as concerns nonsubsistence goods, he is the reverse of that standard caricature immortalized in any *General Principles of Economics,* page one. His wants are scarce and his means (in relation) plentiful. Consequently he is "comparatively free of material pressures," has "no sense of possession," shows "an undeveloped sense of property," is "completely indifferent to any material pressures," manifests a "lack of interest" in developing his technological equipment.

In this relation of hunters to worldly goods there is a neat and important point. From the internal perspective of the economy, it seems wrong to say that wants are "restricted," desires "restrained," or even that the notion of wealth is "limited." Such phrasings imply in advance an Economic Man and a struggle of the hunter against his own worse nature, which is finally then subdued by a cultural vow of poverty. The words imply the renunciation of an acquisitiveness that in reality was never developed, a suppression of desires that were never broached. Economic Man is a bourgeois construction—as Marcel Mauss said, "not behind us, but before, like the moral man." It is not that hunters and gatherers have curbed their materialistic "impulses"; they simply never made an institution of them. "Moreover, if it is a great blessing to be free from a great evil, our [Montagnais] Savages are happy; for the two tyrants who provide hell and torture for many of our Europeans, do not reign in their great forests,—I mean ambition and avarice. . . as they are contented with a mere living, not one of them gives himself to the Devil to acquire wealth" (LeJeune 1897:231).

We are inclined to think of hunters and gatherers as *poor* because they don't have anything; perhaps better to think of them for that reason as *free.* "Their extremely limited material possessions relieve them of all cares with regard to daily necessities and permit them to enjoy life" (Gusinde 1961:1).

Subsistence

When Herskovits was writing his *Economic Anthropology* (1952), it was common anthropological practice to take the Bushmen or the native Australians as "a classic illustration of a people whose economic resources are

of the scantiest," so precariously situated that "only the most intense application makes survival possible." Today the "classic" understanding can be fairly
reversed—on evidence largely from these two groups. A good case can be made
that hunters and gatherers work less than we do; and, rather than a continuous
travail, the food quest is intermittent, leisure abundant, and there is a greater
amount of sleep in the daytime per capita per year than in any other condition
of society.

Some of the substantiating evidence for Australia appears in early sources,
but we are fortunate especially to have now the quantitative materials collected
by the 1948 American–Australian Scientific Expedition to Arnhem Land.
Published in 1960, these startling data must provoke some review of the
Australian reportage going back for over a century, and perhaps revision of an
even longer period of anthropological thought. The key research was a temporal study of hunting and gathering by McCarthy and McArthur (1960),
coupled to McArthur's analysis of the nutritional outcome. Figures 1.1 and 1.2
summarize the principal production studies. These were short-run observations taken during nonceremonial periods. The record for Fish Creek (14 days)
is longer as well as more detailed than that for Hemple Bay (7 days). Only
adults' work has been reported, so far as I can tell. The diagrams incorporate

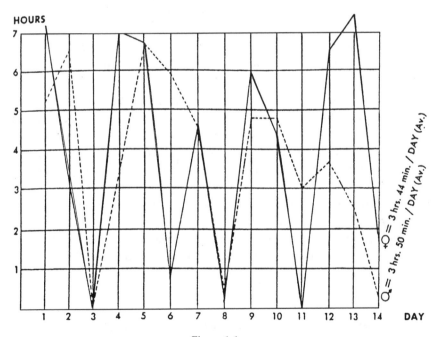

Figure 1.1
Hours per day in food-connected activities: Fish Creek group
(McCarthy and McArthur 1960).

information on hunting, plant collecting, preparing foods, and repairing weapons, as tabulated by the ethnographers. The people in both camps were free-ranging native Australians, living outside mission or other settlements during the period of study, although such was not necessarily their permanent or even their ordinary circumstance.[13]

One must have serious reservations about drawing general or historical inferences from the Arnhem Land data alone. Not only was the context less than pristine and the time of study too brief, but certain elements of the modern situation may have raised productivity above aboriginal levels: metal tools, for

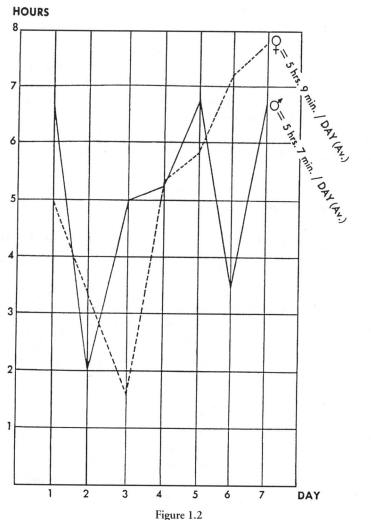

Figure 1.2
Hours per day in food-connected activities: Hemple Bay group
(McCarthy and McArthur 1960).

example, or the reduction of local pressure on food resources by depopulation. And our uncertainty seems rather doubled than neutralized by other current circumstances that, conversely, would lower economic efficiency: these semi-independent hunters, for instance, are probably not as skilled as their ancestors. For the moment, let us consider the Arnhem Land conclusions as experimental, potentially credible in the measure they are supported by other ethnographic or historic accounts.

The most obvious, immediate conclusion is that the people do not work hard. The average length of time per person per day put into the appropriation and preparation of food was four or five hours. Moreover, they do not work continuously. The subsistence quest was highly intermittent. It would stop for the time being when the people had procured enough for the time being, which left them plenty of time to spare. Clearly in subsistence as in other sectors of production, we have to do with an economy of specific, limited objectives. By hunting and gathering these objectives are apt to be irregularly accomplished, so the work pattern becomes correspondingly erratic. In the event, a third characteristic of hunting and gathering unimagined by the received wisdom: rather than straining to the limits of available labor and disposable resources, these Australians seem to *underuse* their objective economic possibilities.

> The quantity of food gathered in one day by any of these groups could in every instance have been increased. Although the search for food was, for the women, a job that went on day after day without relief [but see our Figures 1.1 and 1.2], they rested quite frequently, and did not spend all the hours of daylight searching for and preparing food. The nature of the men's food-gathering was more sporadic, and if they had a good catch one day they frequently rested the next. . . . Perhaps unconsciously they weigh the benefit of greater supplies of food against the effort involved in collecting it, perhaps they judge what they consider to be enough, and when that is collected they stop. (McArthur 1960:92)

It follows, fourthly, that the economy was not physically demanding. The investigators' daily journal indicates that the people pace themselves; only once is a hunter described as "utterly exhausted" (McCarthy and McArthur 1960:150ff). Neither did the Arnhem Landers themselves consider the task of subsistence onerous. "They certainly did not approach it as an unpleasant job to be got over as soon as possible, nor as a necessary evil to be postponed as long as possible" (McArthur 1960:92).[14] In this connection, and also in relation to their underuse of economic resources, it is noteworthy that the Arnhem

Land hunters seem not to have been content with a "bare existence." Like other Australians (cf. Worsley 1961:173), they become dissatisfied with an unvarying diet; some of their time appears to have gone into the provision of diversity over and above mere sufficiency (McCarthy and McArthur 1960:192).

In any case, the dietary intake of the Arnhem Land hunters was adequate—according to the standards of the National Research Council of America. Mean daily consumption per capita at Hemple Bay was 2,160 calories (only a 4 day period of observation), and at Fish Creek 2,130 calories (11 days). Table 1.1 indicates the mean daily consumption of various nutrients, calculated by McArthur in percentages of the NRCA recommended dietary allowances.

Finally, what does the Arnhem Land study say about the famous question of leisure? It seems that hunting and gathering can afford extraordinary relief from economic cares. The Fish Creek group maintained a virtually full-time craftsman, a man 35 or 40 years old, whose true specialty however seems to have been loafing:

> He did not go out hunting at all with the men, but one day he netted fish most vigorously. He occasionally went into the bush to get wild bees' nests. *Wilira* was an expert craftsman who repaired the spears and spear-throwers, made smoking-pipes and drone-tubes, and hafted a stone axe (on request) in a skillful manner; apart from these occupations he spent most of his time talking, eating and sleeping. (McCarthy and McArthur 1960:148)

Wilira was not altogether exceptional. Much of the time spared by the Arnhem Land hunters was literally spare time, consumed in rest and sleep (see Tables 1.2 and 1.3). The main alternative to work, changing off with it in a complementary way, was sleep:

> Apart from the time (mostly between definitive activities and during cooking periods) spent in general social intercourse, chatting, gossiping and so on, some hours of the daylight were also spent resting and sleeping. On the average, if the men were in camp, they usually

Table 1.1

Mean Daily Consumption as Percentage of Recommended Allowances (from McArthur 1960)

	Calories	Protein	Iron	Calcium	Ascorbic Acid
Hemple Bay	116	444	80	128	394
Fish Creek	104	544	33	355	47

Table 1.2
Daytime Rest and Sleep, Fish Creek Group
(Data from McCarthy and McArthur 1960)

Day	♂ Average	♀ Average
1	2'15"	2'45"
2	1'30"	1'0"
3	Most of the day	
4	Intermittent	
5	Intermittent and most of late afternoon	
6	Most of the day	
7	Several hours	
8	2'0"	2'0"
9	50"	50"
10	Afternoon	
11	Afternoon	
12	Intermittent, afternoon	
13	—	—
14	3'15"	3'15"

Table 1.3
Daytime Rest and Sleep, Hemple Bay
Group (Data from McCarthy and
McArthur 1960)

Day	♂ Average	♀ Average
1	—	45"
2	Most of the day	2'45"
3	1'0"	—
4	Intermittent	Intermittent
5	—	1'30"
6	Intermittent	Intermittent
7	Intermittent	Intermittent

slept after lunch from an hour to an hour and a half, or sometimes even more. Also after returning from fishing or hunting they usually had a sleep, either immediately after they arrived or whilst game was being cooked. At Hemple Bay the men slept if they returned early in the day but not if they reached camp after 4.00 p.m. When in camp all day they slept at odd times and always after lunch. The women, when out collecting in the forest, appeared to rest more frequently than the men. If in camp all day, they also slept at odd times, sometimes for long periods (McCarthy and McArthur, 1960:193).

The failure of Arnhem Landers to "build culture" is not strictly from want of time. It is from idle hands.

So much for the plight of hunters and gatherers in Arnhem Land. As for the Bushmen, economically likened to Australian hunters by Herskovits, two excellent recent reports by Richard Lee show their condition to be indeed the same (Lee 1968; 1969). Lee's research merits a special hearing not only because it concerns Bushmen, but specifically the Dobe section of !Kung Bushmen, adjacent to the Nyae Nyae about whose subsistence—in a context otherwise of "material plenty"—Mrs. Marshall expressed important reservations. The Dobe occupy an area of Botswana where !Kung Bushmen have been living for at least a hundred years, but have only just begun to suffer dislocation pressures. (Metal, however, has been available to the Dobe since 1880–90.) An intensive study was made of the subsistence production of a dry season camp with a population (41 people) near the mean of such settlements. The observations extended over four weeks during July and August 1964, a period of transition from more to less favorable seasons of the year, hence fairly representative, it seems, of average subsistence difficulties.

Despite a low annual rainfall (6 to 10 inches), Lee found in the Dobe area a "surprising abundance of vegetation." Food resources were "both varied and abundant," particularly the energy-rich mangetti nut—"so abundant that millions of the nuts rotted on the ground each year for want of picking" (all references in Lee 1969:59).[15] His reports on time spent in food-getting are remarkably close to the Arnhem Land observations. Table 1.4 summarizes Lee's data.

The Bushman figures imply that one man's labor in hunting and gathering will support four or five people. Taken at face value, Bushman food collecting is more efficient than French farming in the period up to World War II, when more than 20 percent of the population were engaged in feeding the rest. Confessedly, the comparison is misleading, but not as misleading as it is astonishing. In the total population of free-ranging Bushmen contacted by Lee, 61.3 percent (152 of 248) were effective food producers; the remainder were too young or too old to contribute importantly. In the particular camp under scrutiny, 65 percent were "effectives." Thus the ratio of food producers to the general population is actually 3 : 5 or 2 : 3. *But*, these 65 percent of the people "worked 36 percent of the time, and 35 percent of the people did not work at all"! (Lee 1969:67).

For each adult worker, this comes to about 2½ days' labor per week. ("In other words, each productive individual supported herself or himself and dependents and still had 3-1/2 to 5-1/2 days available for other activities.") A "day's work" was about 6 hours; hence the Dobe work week is approximately 15 hours, or an average of 2 hours 9 minutes per day. Even lower than the

Table 1.4
Summary of Dobe Bushmen Work Diary (from Lee 1969)

Week	Mean Group Size*	Man-Days of Consumption[†]	Man-Days of Work	Days of Work/ Week/Adult	Index of Subsistence Effort[‡]
1 (July 6–12)	25.6 (23–29)	179	37	2.3	.21
2 (July 13–19)	28.3 (23–37)	198	22	1.2	.11
3 (July 20–26)	34.3 (29–40)	240	42	1.9	.18
4 (July 27–Aug. 2)	35.6 (32–40)	249	77	3.2	.31
4-week totals	30.9	866	178	2.2	.21
Adjusted totals[§]	31.8	668	156	2.5	.23

* Group size shown in average and range. There is considerable short-term population fluctuation in Bushmen camps.

[†] Includes both children and adults, to give a combined total of days of provisioning required/week.

[‡] This index was constructed by Lee to illustrate the relation between consumption and the work required to produce it: S = W/C, where W = number of man-days of work, and C = man-days of consumption. Inverted, the formula would tell how many people could be supported by a day's work in subsistence.

[§] Week 2 was excluded from the final calculations because the investigator contributed some food to the camp on two days.

Arnhem Land norms, this figure however excludes cooking and the preparation of implements. All things considered, Bushmen subsistence labors are probably very close to those of native Australians.

Also like the Australians, the time Bushmen do not work in subsistence they pass in leisure or leisurely activity. One detects again that characteristic paleolithic rhythm of a day or two on, a day or two off—the latter passed desultorily in camp. Although food collecting is the primary productive activity, Lee writes, "the majority of the people's time (four to five days per week) is spent in other pursuits, such as resting in camp or visiting other camps" (1969:74):

> A woman gathers on one day enough food to feed her family for three days, and spends the rest of her time resting in camp, doing embroidery, visiting other camps, or entertaining visitors from other camps. For each day at home, kitchen routines, such as cooking, nut cracking, collecting firewood, and fetching water, occupy one to three hours of her time. This rhythm of steady work and steady leisure is maintained throughout the year. The hunters tend to work more frequently than the women, but their schedule is uneven. It is not unusual for a man to hunt avidly for a week and then do no hunting at all for two or three weeks. Since hunting is an unpredictable business and subject to magical control, hunters sometimes experience a run of bad luck and stop hunting for a month or longer. During these periods, visiting, entertaining, and especially dancing are the primary activities of men. (1968:37)

The daily per-capita subsistence yield for the Dobe Bushmen was 2,140 calories. However, taking into account body weight, normal activities, and the age-sex composition of the Dobe population, Lee estimates the people require only 1,975 calories per capita. Some of the surplus food probably went to the dogs, who ate what the people left over. "The conclusion can be drawn that the Bushmen do not lead a substandard existence on the edge of starvation as has been commonly supposed" (1969:73).

Taken in isolation, the Arnhem Land and Bushmen reports mount a disconcerting if not decisive attack on the entrenched theoretical position. Artificial in construction, the former study in particular is reasonably considered equivocal. But the testimony of the Arnhem Land expedition is echoed at many points by observations made elsewhere in Australia, as well as elsewhere in the hunting-gathering world. Much of the Australian evidence goes back to the nineteenth century, some of it to quite acute observers careful to make exception of the aboriginal come into relation with Europeans, for "his food supply is restricted, and . . . he is in many cases warned off from the waterholes which are the centers of his best hunting grounds" (Spencer and Gillen 1899:50).

The case is altogether clear for the well-watered areas of southeastern Australia. There the Aboriginals were favored with a supply of fish so abundant and easily procured that one squatter on the Victorian scene of the 1840s had to wonder "how that sage people managed to pass their time before my party came and taught them to smoke" (Curr 1965:109). Smoking at least solved the economic problem—nothing to do: "That accomplishment fairly acquired . . . matters went on flowingly, their leisure hours being divided between putting the pipe to its legitimate purpose and begging my tobacco." Somewhat more seriously, the old squatter did attempt an estimate of the amount of time spent in hunting and gathering by the people of the then Port Phillip's District. The women were away from the camp on gathering expeditions about six hours a day, "half of that time being loitered away in the shade or by the fire"; the men left for the hunt shortly after the women quit camp and returned around the same time (p. 118). Curr found the food thus acquired of "indifferent quality" although "readily procured," the six hours a day "abundantly sufficing" for that purpose; indeed the country "could have supported twice the number of Blacks we found in it" (p. 120). Very similar comments were made by another old-timer, Clement Hodgkinson, writing of an analogous environment in northeastern New South Wales. A few minutes' fishing would provide enough to feed "the whole tribe" (Hodgkinson 1845:223; cf. Hiatt 1965:103–4). "Indeed, throughout all the country along the eastern coast, the blacks have never suffered so much from scarcity of food as many commiserating writers have supposed" (Hodgkinson 1845:227).

But the people who occupied these more fertile sections of Australia, no-tably in the southeast, have not been incorporated in today's stereotype of an Aborigine. They were wiped out early.[16] The European's relation to such "Blackfellows" was one of conflict over the continent's riches; little time or in-clination was spared from the process of destruction for the luxury of contem-plation. In the event, ethnographic consciousness would only inherit the slim pickings: mainly interior groups, mainly desert people, mainly the Arunta. Not that the Arunta are all that bad off—ordinarily, "his life is by no means a miserable or a very hard one" (Spencer and Gillen 1899:7).[17] But the Central tribes should not be considered, in point of numbers or ecological adaptation, typical of native Australians (cf. Meggitt 1964). The following tableau of the indigenous economy provided by John Edward Eyre, who had traversed the south coast and penetrated the Flinders range as well as sojourned in the richer Murray district, has the right to be acknowledged at least as representative:

Throughout the greater portion of New Holland, where there do not happen to be European settlers, and invariably when fresh water can be permanently procured upon the surface, the native experiences no difficulty whatever in procuring food in abundance all the year round. It is true that the character of his diet varies with the changing seasons, and the formation of the country he inhabits; but it rarely happens that any season of the year, or any description of country does not yield him both animal and vegetable food. . . . Of these [chief] articles [of food], many are not only procurable in abundance, but in such vast quantities at the proper seasons, as to afford for a considerable length of time an ample means of subsistence to many hundreds of natives congregated at one place. . . . On many parts of the coast, and in the larger inland rivers, fish are obtained of a very fine description, and in great abundance. At Lake Victoria . . . I have seen six hundred natives encamped together, all of whom were living at the time upon fish procured from the lake, with the addition, perhaps, of the leaves of the mesembryanthemum. When I went amongst them I never perceived any scarcity in their camps. . . . At Moorunde, when the Murray annually inundates the flats, fresh-water cray-fish make their way to the surface of the ground . . . in such vast numbers that I have seen four hundred natives live upon them for weeks together, whilst the numbers spoiled or thrown away would have sustained four hundred more. . . . An unlimited supply of fish is also procurable at the Murray about the beginning of December. . . . The number [of fish] procured . . . in a few hours is incredible. . . . Another very favourite article of food, and equally abundant at a particular season of the year, in the eastern portion of the continent, is a species of moth which the natives procure from the cavities and hollows of the mountains in certain localities. . . . The tops, leaves, and stalks of a kind of cress, gathered at the proper season of the year . . . furnish a favourite, and inexhaustible, supply of food for an unlimited number of natives . . . There are many other articles of food among the natives, equally abundant and valuable as those I have enumerated. (Eyre 1845, vol. 2:250–54)

Both Eyre and Sir George Grey, whose sanguine view of the indigenous economy we have already noted ("I have always found the greatest abundance in their huts") left specific assessments, in hours per day, of the Australians' subsistence labors. (This in Grey's case would include inhabitants of quite undesirable parts of western Australia.) The testimony of these gentlemen and explorers accords very closely with the Arnhem Land averages obtained by McCarthy and McArthur. "In all ordinary seasons," wrote Grey (that is, when the people are not confined to their huts by bad weather), "they can obtain, *in two or three hours,* a sufficient supply of food for the day, but their usual custom is to roam indolently from spot to spot, lazily collecting it as they wander along" (1841, vol. 2:263; emphasis mine). Similarly, Eyre states: "In almost every part of the continent which I have visited, where the presence of Europeans, or their stock, has not limited, or destroyed their original means of subsistence, I have found that the natives could usually, in *three or four hours,* procure as much food as would last for the day, and that without fatigue or labour" (1845:254–55; emphasis mine).

The same discontinuity of subsistence of labor reported by McArthur and McCarthy, the pattern of alternating search and sleep, is repeated, further- more, in early and late observations from all over the continent (Eyre 1845, vol. 2:253–54; Bulmer, in Smyth 1878, vol. 1:142; Mathew 1910:84; Spencer and Gillen 1899:32; Hiatt 1965:103–4). Basedow took it as the general custom of the Aboriginal: "When his affairs are working harmoniously, game secured, and water available, the aboriginal makes his life as easy as possible; and he might to the outsider even appear lazy" (1925:116).[18]

Meanwhile, back in Africa the Hadza have been long enjoying a comparable ease, with a burden of subsistence occupations no more strenuous in hours per day than the Bushmen or the Australian Aboriginals (Woodburn 1968). Living in an area of "exceptional abundance" of animals and regular supplies of veg- etables (the vicinity of Lake Eyasi), Hadza men seem much more concerned with games of chance than with chances of game. During the long dry season especially, they pass the greater part of days on end in gambling, perhaps only to lose the metal-tipped arrows they need for big game hunting at other times. In any case, many men are "quite unprepared or unable to hunt big game even when they possess the necessary arrows." Only a small minority, Woodburn writes, are active hunters of large animals, and if women are generally more as- siduous at their vegetable collecting, still it is at a leisurely pace and without prolonged labor (cf. p. 51; Woodburn 1966). Despite this nonchalance, and an only limited economic cooperation, Hadza "nonetheless obtain sufficient food without undue effort." Woodburn offers this "very rough approximation" of subsistence-labor requirements: "Over the year as a whole probably an average of less than two hours a day is spent obtaining food" (Woodburn 1968:54).

Interesting that the Hadza, tutored by life and not by anthropology, reject the neolithic revolution in order to *keep* their leisure. Although surrounded by cultivators, they have until recently refused to take up agriculture themselves, "mainly on the grounds that this would involve too much hard work."[19] In this they are like the Bushmen, who respond to the neolithic question with another: "Why should we plant, when there are so many mongomongo nuts in the world?" (Lee 1968:33). Woodburn moreover did form the impression, although as yet unsubstantiated, that Hadza actually expend less energy, and probably less time, in obtaining subsistence than do neighboring cultivators of East Africa (1968:54).[20] To change continents but not contents, the fitful economic commitment of the South American hunter, too, could seem to the European outsider an incurable "natural disposition":

> . . . the Yamana are not capable of continuous, daily hard labor, much to the chagrin of European farmers and employers for whom they often work. Their work is more a matter of fits and starts, and in these occasional efforts they can develop considerable energy for a certain time. After that, however, they show a desire for an incalculably long rest period during which they lie about doing nothing, without showing great fatigue. . . . It is obvious that repeated irregularities of this kind make the European employer despair, but the Indian cannot help it. It is his natural disposition. (Gusinde 1961:27)[21]

The hunter's attitude towards farming introduces us, lastly, to a few particulars of the way they relate to the food quest. Once again we venture here into the internal realm of the economy, a realm sometimes subjective and always difficult to understand; where, moreover, hunters seem deliberately inclined to overtax our comprehension by customs so odd as to invite the extreme interpretation that either these people are fools or they really have nothing to worry about. The former would be a true logical deduction from the hunter's nonchalance, on the premise that his economic condition is truly exigent. On the other hand, if a livelihood is usually easily procured, if one can usually expect to succeed, then the people's seeming imprudence can no longer appear as such. Speaking to unique developments of the market economy, to its institutionalization of scarcity, Karl Polanyi said that our "animal dependence upon food has been bared and the naked fear of starvation permitted to run loose. Our humiliating enslavement to the material, which all human culture is designed to mitigate, was deliberately made more rigorous" (1947:115). But our problems are not theirs, the hunters and gatherers. Rather, a pristine affluence colors their economic arrangements, a trust in the abundance of nature's resources rather than despair at the inadequacy of human means. My point is that otherwise curious heathen devices become understandable by the people's confidence, a confidence which is the reasonable human attribute of a generally successful economy.[22]

Consider the hunter's chronic movements from camp to camp. This nomadism, often taken by us as a sign of a certain harassment, is undertaken by them with a certain abandon. The Aboriginals of Victoria, Smyth recounts, are as a rule "lazy travellers. *They have no motive to induce them to hasten their movements.* It is generally late in the morning before they start on their journey, and there are many interruptions by the way" (1878, vol. 1:125; emphasis mine). The good *Pere* Biard in his *Relation* of 1616, after a glowing description of the foods available in their season to the Micmac ("Never had Solomon his mansion better regulated and provided with food") goes on in the same tone:

> In order to thoroughly enjoy this, their lot, our foresters start off to their different places with as much pleasure as if they were going on a stroll or an excursion; they do this easily through the skillful use and great convenience of canoes . . . so rapidly sculled that, without any effort, in good weather you can make thirty or forty leagues a day; nevertheless we scarcely see these Savages posting along at this rate, for their days are all nothing but pastime. They are never in a hurry. Quite different from us, who can never do anything without hurry and worry. . . . (Biard 1897:81–85)

Certainly, hunters quit camp because food resources have given out in the vicinity. But to see in this nomadism merely a flight from starvation only perceives the half of it; one ignores the possibility that the people's expectations of greener pastures elsewhere are not usually disappointed. Consequently their wanderings, rather than anxious, take on all the qualities of a picnic outing on the Thames.

A more serious issue is presented by the frequent and exasperated observation of a certain "lack of foresight" among hunters and gatherers. Oriented forever in the present, without "the slightest thought of, or care for, what the morrow may bring" (Spencer and Gillen 1899:53), the hunter seems unwilling to husband supplies, incapable of a planned response to the doom surely awaiting him. He adopts instead a studied unconcern, which expresses itself in two complementary economic inclinations.

The first, prodigality: the propensity to eat right through all the food in the camp, even during objectively difficult times, "as if," LeJeune said of the Montagnais, "the game they were to hunt was shut up in a stable." Basedow wrote of native Australians, their motto "might be interpreted in words to the effect that while there is plenty for today never care about tomorrow. On this account an Aboriginal is inclined to make one feast of his supplies, in preference to a modest meal now and another by and by" (1925:116). LeJeune even saw his Montagnais carry such extravagance to the edge of disaster:

In the famine through which we passed, if my host took two, three, or four Beavers, immediately, whether it was day or night, they had a feast for all neighboring Savages. And if those people had captured something, they had one also at the same time; so that, on emerging from one feast, you went to another, and sometimes even to a third and a fourth. I told them that they did not manage well, and that it would be better to reserve these feasts for future days, and in doing this they would not be so pressed with hunger. They laughed at me. "Tomorrow" (they said) "we shall make another feast with what we shall capture." Yes, but more often they capture only cold and wind. (LeJeune 1897:281–83)

Sympathetic writers have tried to rationalize the apparent impracticality. Perhaps the people have been carried beyond reason by hunger: they are apt to gorge themselves on a kill because they have gone so long without meat—and for all they know they are likely to soon do so again. Or perhaps in making one feast of his supplies a man is responding to binding social obligations, to important imperatives of sharing. LeJeune's experience would confirm either view, but it also suggests a third. Or rather, the Montagnais have their own explanation. They are not worried by what the morrow may bring because as far as they are concerned it will bring more of the same: "another feast." Whatever the value of other interpretations, such self-confidence must be brought to bear on the supposed prodigality of hunters. More, it must have some objective basis, for if hunters and gatherers really favored gluttony over economic good sense, they would never have lived to become the prophets of this new religion.

A second and complementary inclination is merely prodigality's negative side: the failure to put by food surpluses, to develop food storage. For many hunters and gatherers, it appears, food storage cannot be proved technically impossible, nor is it certain that the people are unaware of the possibility (cf. Woodburn 1968:53). One must investigate instead what in the situation precludes the attempt. Gusinde asked this question, and for the Yahgan found the answer in the selfsame justifiable optimism. Storage would be "superfluous,"

because throughout the entire year and with almost limitless generosity the sea puts all kinds of animals at the disposal of the man who hunts and the woman who gathers. Storm or accident will deprive a family of these things for no more than a few days. Generally no one need reckon with the danger of hunger, and everyone almost anywhere finds an abundance of what he needs. Why then should anyone worry about food for the future! . . .

Basically our Fuegians know that they need not fear for the future, hence they do not pile up supplies. Year in and year out they can look forward to the next day, free of care. . . . (Gusinde 1961:336, 339)

Gusinde's explanation is probably good as far as it goes, but probably incomplete. A more complex and subtle economic calculus seems in play—realized however by a social arithmetic exceedingly simple. The advantages of food storage should be considered against the diminishing returns to collection within the compass of a confined locale. An uncontrollable tendency to lower the local carrying capacity is for hunters *au fond des choses:* a basic condition of their production and main cause of their movement. The potential drawback of storage is exactly that it engages the contradiction between wealth and mobility. It would anchor the camp to an area soon depleted of natural food supplies. Thus immobilized by their accumulated stocks, the people may suffer by comparison with a little hunting and gathering elsewhere, where nature has, so to speak, done considerable storage of her own—foods possibly more desirable in diversity as well as amount than men can put by. But this fine calculation—in any event probably symbolically impossible (cf. Codere 1968)—would be worked out in a much simpler binary opposition, set in social terms such as "love" and "hate." For as Richard Lee observes (1969:75), the technically neutral activity of food accumulation or storage is morally something else again, "hoarding." The efficient hunter who would accumulate supplies succeeds at the cost of his own esteem, or else he gives them away at the cost of his (superfluous) effort. As it works out, an attempt to stock up food may only reduce the overall output of a hunting band, for the have-nots will content themselves with staying in camp and living off the wherewithal amassed by the more prudent. Food storage, then, may be technically feasible, yet economically undesirable, and socially unachievable.

If food storage remains limited among hunters, their economic confidence, born of the ordinary times when all the people's wants are easily satisfied, becomes a permanent condition, carrying them laughing through periods that would try even a Jesuit's soul and worry him so that—as the Indians warn—he could become sick:

I saw them, in their hardships and in their labors, suffer with cheerfulness. . . . I found myself, with them, threatened with great suffering; they said to me, "We shall be sometimes two days, sometimes three, without eating, for lack of food; take courage, *Chihiné,* let thy soul be strong to endure suffering and hardship; keep thyself from being sad, otherwise thou wilt be sick; see how we do not cease to laugh, although we have little to eat." (LeJeune 1897:283; cf. Needham 1954:230)

Rethinking Hunters and Gatherers

> Constantly under pressure of want, and yet, by travelling, easily able
> to supply their wants, their lives lack neither excitement or pleasure.
> (Smyth 1878, vol. 1:123)

Clearly, the hunting-gathering economy has to be revaluated, both as to its
true accomplishments and its true limitations. The procedural fault of the received wisdom was to read from the material circumstances to the economic
structure, deducing the absolute difficulty of such a life from its absolute
poverty. But always the cultural design improvises dialectics on its relationship
to nature. Without escaping the ecological constraints, culture would negate
them, so that at once the system shows the impress of natural conditions and
the originality of a social response—in their poverty, abundance.

What are the real handicaps of the hunting-gathering *praxis?* Not "low productivity of labor," if existing examples mean anything. But the economy is seriously afflicted by the *imminence of diminishing returns.* Beginning in subsistence and spreading from there to every sector, an initial success seems only to
develop the probability that further efforts will yield smaller benefits. This describes the typical curve of food-getting within a particular locale. A modest
number of people usually sooner than later reduce the food resources within
convenient range of camp. Thereafter, they may stay on only by absorbing an
increase in real costs or a decline in real returns: rise in costs if the people
choose to search farther and farther afield, decline in returns if they are satisfied to live on the shorter supplies or inferior foods in easier reach. The solution, of course, is to go somewhere else. Thus the first and decisive contin-
gency of hunting-gathering: it requires movement to maintain production on
advantageous terms.

But this movement, more or less frequent in different circumstances, more
or less distant, merely transposes to other spheres of production the same diminishing returns of which it is born. The manufacture of tools, clothing,
utensils, or ornaments, however easily done, becomes senseless when these
begin to be more of a burden than a comfort. Utility falls quickly at the margin
of portability. The construction of substantial houses likewise becomes absurd
if they must soon be abandoned. Hence the hunter's very ascetic conceptions of
material welfare: an interest only in minimal equipment, if that; a valuation of
smaller things over bigger; a disinterest in acquiring two or more of most
goods; and the like. Ecological pressure assumes a rare form of concreteness
when it has to be shouldered. If the gross product is trimmed down in comparison with other economies, it is not the hunter's productivity that is at fault,
but his mobility.

Almost the same thing can be said of the demographic constraints of hunting-gathering. The same policy of *débarassment* is in play on the level of people, describable in similar terms and ascribable to similar causes. The terms are, cold-bloodedly: diminishing returns at the margin of portability, minimum necessary equipment, elimination of duplicates, and so forth—that is to say, infanticide, senilicide, sexual continence for the duration of the nursing period, etc., practices for which many food-collecting peoples are well known. The presumption that such devices are due to an inability to support more people is probably true—if "support" is understood in the sense of carrying them rather than feeding them. The people eliminated, as hunters sometimes sadly tell, are precisely those who cannot effectively transport themselves, who would hinder the movement of family and camp. Hunters may be obliged to handle people and goods in parallel ways, the draconic population policy an expression of the same ecology as the ascetic economy. More, these tactics of demographic restraint again form part of a larger policy for counteracting diminishing returns in subsistence. A local group becomes vulnerable to diminishing returns—so to a greater velocity of movement, or else to fission—in proportion to its size (other things equal). Insofar as the people would keep the advantage in local production, and maintain a certain physical and social stability, their Malthusian practices are just cruelly consistent. Modern hunters and gatherers, working their notably inferior environments, pass most of the year in very small groups widely spaced out. But rather than the sign of underproduction, the wages of poverty, this demographic pattern is better understood as the cost of living well.

Hunting and gathering has all the strengths of its weaknesses. Periodic movement and restraint in wealth and population are at once imperatives of the economic practice and creative adaptations, the kinds of necessities of which virtues are made. Precisely in such a framework, affluence becomes possible. Mobility and moderation put hunters' ends within range of their technical means. An undeveloped mode of production is thus rendered highly effective. The hunter's life is not as difficult as it looks from the outside. In some ways the economy reflects dire ecology, but it is also a complete inversion.

Reports on hunters and gatherers of the ethnological present—specifically on those in marginal environments—suggest a mean of three to five hours per adult worker per day in food production. Hunters keep banker's hours, notably less than modern industrial workers (unionized), who would surely settle for a 21–35-hour week. An interesting comparison is also posed by recent studies of labor costs among agriculturists of neolithic type. For example, the average adult Hanunoo, man or woman, spends 1,200 hours per year in swidden cultivation (Conklin 1957:151); which is to say, a mean of three hours twenty minutes per day. Yet this figure does not include food gathering, animal raising, cooking, and other direct subsistence efforts of these Philippine tribesmen.

Comparable data are beginning to appear in reports on other primitive agriculturalists from many parts of the world. The conclusion is put conservatively when put negatively: hunters and gatherers need not work longer getting food than do primitive cultivators. Extrapolating from ethnography to prehistory, one may say as much for the neolithic as John Stuart Mill said of all labor-saving devices, that never was one invented that saved anyone a minute's labor. The neolithic saw no particular improvement over the paleolithic in the amount of time required per capita for the production of subsistence; probably, with the advent of agriculture, people had to work harder.

There is nothing either to the convention that hunters and gatherers can enjoy little leisure from tasks of sheer survival. By this, the evolutionary inadequacies of the paleolithic are customarily explained, while for the provision of leisure the neolithic is roundly congratulated. But the traditional formulas might be truer if reversed: the amount of work (per capita) increases with the evolution of culture, and the amount of leisure decreases. Hunters' subsistence labors are characteristically intermittent, a day on and a day off, and modern hunters at least tend to employ their time off in such activities as daytime sleep. In the tropical habitats occupied by many of these existing hunters, plant collecting is more reliable than hunting itself. Therefore, the women, who do the collecting, work rather more regularly than the men, and provide the greater part of the food supply. Man's work is often done. On the other hand, it is likely to be highly erratic, unpredictably required; if men lack leisure, it is then in the Enlightenment sense rather than the literal. When Condorcet attributed the hunter's unprogressive condition to want of "the leisure in which he can indulge in thought and enrich his understanding with new combinations of ideas," he also recognized that the economy was a "necessary cycle of extreme activity and total idleness." Apparently what the hunter needed was the assured leisure of an aristocratic *philosophe*.

Hunters and gatherers maintain a sanguine view of their economic state despite the hardships they sometimes know. It may be that they sometimes know hardships because of the sanguine views they maintain of their economic state. Perhaps their confidence only encourages prodigality to the extent the camp falls casualty to the first untoward circumstance. In alleging this is an affluent economy, therefore, I do not deny that certain hunters have moments of difficulty. Some do find it "almost inconceivable" for a man to die of hunger, or even to fail to satisfy his hunger for more than a day or two (Woodburn 1968:52). But others, especially certain very peripheral hunters spread out in small groups across an environment of extremes, are exposed periodically to the kind of inclemency that interdicts travel or access to game. They suffer—although perhaps only fractionally, the shortage affecting particular immobilized families rather than the society as a whole (cf. Gusinde 1961:306–7).

Still, granting this vulnerability, and allowing the most poorly situated modern hunters into comparison, it would be difficult to prove that privation is distinctly characteristic of the hunter-gatherers. Food shortage is not the indicative property of this mode of production as opposed to others; it does not mark off hunters and gatherers as a class or a general evolutionary stage. Lowie asks:

> But what of the herders on a simple plane whose maintenance is periodically jeopardized by plagues—who, like some Lapp bands of the nineteenth century, were obliged to fall back on fishing? What of the primitive peasants who clear and till without compensation of the soil, exhaust one plot and pass on to the next, and are threatened with famine at every drought? Are they any more in control of misfortune caused by natural conditions than the hunter-gatherer? (1938:286)

Above all, what about the world today? One-third to one-half of humanity are said to go to bed hungry every night. In the Old Stone Age the fraction must have been much smaller. *This* is the era of hunger unprecedented. Now, in the time of the greatest technical power, is starvation an institution. Reverse another venerable formula: the amount of hunger increases relatively and absolutely with the evolution of culture.

This paradox is my whole point. Hunters and gatherers have by force of circumstances an objectively low standard of living. But taken as their *objective*, and given their adequate means of production, all the people's material wants usually can be easily satisfied. The evolution of economy has known, then, two contradictory movements: enriching but at the same time impoverishing, appropriating in relation to nature but expropriating in relation to man. The progressive aspect is, of course, technological. It has been celebrated in many ways: as an increase in the amount of need-serving goods and services, an increase in the amount of energy harnessed to the service of culture, an increase in productivity, an increase in division of labor, and increased freedom from environmental control. Taken in a certain sense, the last is especially useful for understanding the earliest stages of technical advance. Agriculture not only raised society above the distribution of natural food resources, it allowed neolithic communities to maintain high degrees of social order where the requirements of human existence were absent from the natural order. Enough food could be harvested in some seasons to sustain the people while no food would grow at all; the consequent stability of social life was critical for its material enlargement. Culture went on then from triumph to triumph, in a kind of progressive contravention of the biological law of the minimum, until it proved it could support human life in outer space—where even gravity and oxygen were naturally lacking.

Other men were dying of hunger in the market places of Asia. It has been an evolution of structures as well as technologies, and in that respect like the mythical road where for every step the traveller advances his destination recedes by two. The structures have been political as well as economic, of power as well as property. They developed first within societies, increasingly now between societies. No doubt these structures have been functional, necessary organizations of the technical development, but within the communities they have thus helped to enrich they would discriminate in the distribution of wealth and differentiate in the style of life. The world's most primitive people have few possessions, *but they are not poor.* Poverty is not a certain small amount of goods, nor is it just a relation between means and ends; above all it is a relation between people. Poverty is a social status. As such it is the invention of civilization. It has grown with civilization, at once as an invidious distinction between classes and more importantly as a tributary relation—that can render agrarian peasants more susceptible to natural catastrophes than any winter camp of Alaskan Eskimo.

All the preceding discussion takes the liberty of reading modern hunters historically, as an evolutionary base line. This liberty should not be lightly granted. Are marginal hunters such as the Bushmen of the Kalahari any more representative of the paleolithic condition than the Indians of California or the Northwest Coast? Perhaps not. Perhaps also Bushmen of the Kalahari are not even representative of marginal hunters. The great majority of surviving hunter-gatherers lead a life curiously decapitated and extremely lazy by comparison with the other few. The other few are very different. The Murngin, for example: "The first impression that any stranger must receive in a fully functioning group in Eastern Arnhem Land is of industry. . . .

"And he must be impressed with the fact that with the exception of very young children . . . there is no idleness" (Thomson 1949a:33–34). There is nothing to indicate that the problems of livelihood are more difficult for these people than for other hunters (cf. Thomson 1949b). The incentives of their unusual industry lie elsewhere: in "an elaborate and exacting ceremonial life," specifically in an elaborate ceremonial exchange cycle that bestows prestige on craftsmanship and trade (Thomson 1949a:26, 28, 34ff, 87 passim). Most other hunters have no such concerns. Their existence is comparatively colorless, fixed singularly on eating with gusto and digesting at leisure. The cultural orientation is not Dionysian or Apollonian, but "gastric," as Julian Steward said of the Shoshoni. Then again it may be Dionysian, that is, Bacchanalian: "Eating among the Savages is like drinking among the drunkards of Europe. Those dry and ever-thirsty souls would willingly end their lives in a tub of malmsey, and the Savages in a pot full of meat; those over there talk only of drinking, and these here only of eating" (LeJeune 1897:249).

It is as if the superstructures of these societies had been eroded, leaving only the bare subsistence rock, and since production itself is readily accomplished, the people have plenty of time to perch there and talk about it. I must raise the possibility that the ethnography of hunters and gatherers is largely a record of incomplete cultures. Fragile cycles of ritual and exchange may have disappeared without trace, lost in the earliest stages of colonialism, when the intergroup relations they mediated were attacked and confounded. If so, the "original" affluent society will have to be rethought again for its originality, and the evolutionary schemes once more revised. Still this much history can always be rescued from existing hunters: the "economic problem" is easily solvable by paleolithic techniques. But then, it was not until culture neared the height of its material achievements that it erected a shrine to the Unattainable: *Infinite Needs.*

NOTES

1. At least to the time Lucretius was writing (Harris 1968:26–27).
2. On the historically particular requisites of such calculation, see Codere 1968, (especially pp. 574–75).
3. For the complementary institutionalization of "scarcity" in the conditions of capitalist production, see Gorz 1967:37–38.
4. It deserves mention that contemporary European-Marxist theory is often in accord with bourgeois economics on the poverty of the primitive. Cf. Boukharine 1967; Mandel 1962, vol. 1; and the economic history manual used at Lumumba University (listed in bibliography as "Anonymous, n.d.").
5. Elman Service for a very long time almost alone among ethnologists stood out against that traditional view of the penury of hunters. The present paper owes great inspiration to his remarks on the leisure of the Arunta (1963:9), as well as to personal conversations with him.
6. The evident fault of White's evolutionary law is the use of "per capita" measures. Neolithic societies in the main harness a *greater total amount of energy* than pre-agricultural communities because of the greater number of energy-delivering humans sustained by domestication. This overall rise in the social product, however, is not necessarily effected by an increased productivity of labor—which in White's view also accompanied the neolithic revolution. Ethnological data now in hand (see text *infra*) raise the possibility that simple agricultural regimes are not more efficient thermodynamically than hunting and gathering—that is, in energy yield per unit of human labor. In the same vein, some archaeology in recent years has tended to privilege stability of settlement over productivity of labor in explanation of the neolithic advance (cf. Braidwood and Wiley 1962).
7. For a similar comment, referring to missionary misinterpretation of curing by blood consumption in eastern Australia, see Hodgkinson 1845:227.
8. Conditions of primitive hunting peoples must not he judged, as Carl Sauer notes, "'from their modern survivors, now restricted to the most meager regions of the earth, such as the interior of Australia, the American Great Basin, and the Arctic

tundra and taiga. The areas of early occupation were abounding in food'" (cited in Clark and Haswell 1964:23).

9. Through the prison of acculturation one glimpses what hunting and gathering might have been like in a decent environment from Alexander Henry's account of his bountiful sojourn as a Chippewa in northern Michigan: see Quimby 1962.

10. Turnbull similarly notes of Congo Pygmies: "The materials for the making of shelter, clothing, and all other necessary items of material culture are all at hand at a moment's notice." And he has no reservations either about subsistence: "Throughout the year, without fail, there is an abundant supply of game and vegetable foods" (1965:18).

11. Certain food collectors not lately known for their architectural achievements seem to have built more substantial dwellings before being put on the run by Europeans. See Smythe 1871, vol. 1:125–8.

12. But recall Gusinde's comment: "Our Fuegians procure and make their implements with little effort" (1961:213).

13. Fish Creek was an inland camp in western Arnhem Land consisting of six adult males and three adult females. Hemple Bay was a coastal occupation on Groote Eylandt; there were four adult males, four adult females, and five juveniles and infants in the camp. Fish Creek was investigated at the end of the dry season, when the supply of vegetable foods was low; kangaroo hunting was rewarding, although the animals became increasingly wary under steady stalking. At Hemple Bay, vegetable foods were plentiful; the fishing was variable but on the whole good by comparison with other coastal camps visited by the expedition. The resource base at Hemple Bay was richer than at Fish Creek. The greater time put into food-getting at Hemple Bay may reflect, then the support of five children. On the other hand, the Fish Creek group did maintain a virtually full-time specialist, and part of the difference in hours worked may represent a normal coastal-inland variation. In inland hunting, good things often come in large packages hence, one day's work may yield two day's sustenance. A fishing-gathering regime perhaps produces smaller if steadier returns, enjoining somewhat longer and more regular efforts.

14. At least some Australians, the Yir-Yiront, make no linguistic differentiation between work and play (Sharp 1958:6).

15. This appreciation of local resources is all the more remarkable considering that Lee's ethnographic work was done in the second and third years of "one of the most severe droughts in South Africa's history" (1968:39; 1969:73 n.).

16. As were the Tasmanians, of whom Bonwick wrote: "The Aborigines were never in want of food; though Mrs. Somerville has ventured to say of them in her 'Physical Geography' that they were 'truly miserable in a country where the means of existence were so scanty.' Dr. Jeannent, once Protector, writes: 'They must have been superabundantly supplied, and have required little exertion or industry to support themselves'"(Bonwick 1870:14).

17. This by way of contrast to other tribes deeper in the Central Australian Desert, and specifically under "ordinary circumstances," not the times of long-continued drought when "he has to suffer privation" (Spencer and Gillen 1899:7).

18. Basedow goes on to excuse the people's idleness on the grounds of overeating, then to excuse the overeating on the grounds of the periods of hunger natives suffer, which he further explains by the droughts Australia is heir to, the effects of which have been exacerbated by the white man's exploitation of the country.

19. This phrase appears in a paper by Woodburn distributed to the Wenner-Gren symposium on "Man the Hunter," although it is only elliptically repeated in the published account (1968:55). I hope I do not commit an indiscretion or an inaccuracy citing it here.

20. "Agriculture is in fact the first example of servile labor in the history of man. According to biblical tradition, the first criminal, Cain, is a farmer" (Lafargue 1911 [1883]:11 n.)

It is notable too that the agricultural neighbors of both Bushmen and Hadza are quick to resort to the more dependable hunting-gathering life come drought and threat of famine (Woodburn 1968:54; Lee 1968:39–40).

21. This common distaste for prolonged labor manifested by recently primitive peoples under European employ, a distaste not restricted to ex-hunters, might have alerted anthropology to the fact that the traditional economy had known only modest objectives, so within reach as to allow an extraordinary disengagement, considerable "relief from the mere problem of getting a living."

The hunting economy may also be commonly underrated for its presumed inability to support specialist production. Cf. Sharp 1934–35:37; Radcliffe-Brown 1948:43; Spencer 1959:155, 196, 251; Lothrup 1928:71; Stewart 1938:44. If there is not specialization, at any rate it is clearly for lack of a "market," not for lack of time.

22. At the same time that the bourgeois ideology of scarcity was let loose, with the inevitable effect of downgrading an earlier culture, it searched and found in nature the ideal model to follow if man (or at least the workingman) was ever to better his unhappy lot: the ant, the industrious ant. In this the ideology may have been as mistaken as in its view of hunters. The following appeared in the *Ann Arbor News,* January 27, 1971, under the head, "Two Scientists Claim Ants a Little Lazy": Palm Springs, Calif. (AP)—"Ants aren't all they are reported [reputed?] to be," say Drs. George and Jeanette Wheeler.

"The husband–wife researchers have devoted years to studying the creatures, heroes of fables on industriousness.

"'Whenever we view an anthill we get the impression of a tremendous amount of activity, but that is merely because there are so many ants and they all look alike," the Wheelers concluded.

"'The individual ants spend a great deal of time just loafing. And, worse than that, the worker ants, who are all females, spend a lot of time primping.'"

REFERENCES

Basedow, Herbert, 1925. *The Australian Aboriginal.* Adelaide, Australia: Preece.

Biard, le Pere Pierre, 1897. "Relation of New France, of Its Lands, Nature of the Country, and of Its Inhabitants . . . ," in R. G. Thwaites (ed.), *The Jesuit*

Relations and Allied Documents, Vol. 3. Cleveland: Burrows (First French edition, 1616).

Boas, Franz, 1940. *Race, Language and Culture.* New York: Free Press.

Bonwick, James, 1870. *Daily Life and Origin of the Tasmanians.* London: Low and Merston.

Boukharine, N., 1967. *La Theorie du materialism historique.* Paris: Editions Anthropos (First Russian edition, 1921).

Braidwood, Robert J., 1952. *The Near East and the Foundations for Civilization.* Eugene: Oregon State System of Higher Education.

Braidwood, Robert J., 1957. *Prehistoric Men,* 3rd ed. Chicago Natural History Museum Popular Series, Anthropology, Number 37.

Braidwood, Robert J., and Gordon R. Wiley (eds.), 1962. *Courses Toward Urban Life.* Chicago: Aldine.

Clark, Colin, and Margaret Haswell, 1964. *The Economics of Subsistence Agriculture.* London: Macmillan.

Clark, Graham, 1953. *From Savagery to Civilization.* New York: Schuman.

Codere, Helen, 1968. "Money-Exchange Systems and a Theory of Money," *Man* (n.s.) 3:557–77.

Conklin, Harold C., 1957. *Hanunoo Agriculture.* Rome: Food and Agriculture Organization of the United Nations.

Curr, E. M., 1965. *Recollections of Squatting in Victoria, Then Called the Port Phillip District, from 1841–1851.* (First edition, 1883.) Melbourne: At the University Press.

Dalton, George, 1961. "Economic Theory and Primitive Society," *American Anthropologist* 63:1–25.

Eyre, Edward John, 1845. *Journals of Expeditions of Discovery into Central Australia, and Overland from Adelaide to King George's Sound, in the Years 1940–41.* 2 Vols. London: Boone.

Gorz, Andre, 1967. *Le socialisme difficile.* Paris: Seuil.

Grey, Sir George, 1841. *Journals of Two Expeditions of Discovery in North-West and Western Australia, During the Years 1837, 38, and 39.* 2 Vols. London: Boone.

Gusinde, Martin, 1961. *The Yamana.* 5 Vols. New Haven, Conn.: Human Relations Area Files (German edition, 1931).

Harris, Marvin, 1968. *The Rise of Anthropological Theory.* New York: Thomas Y. Crowell.

Haury, Emil W., 1962. The Greater American Southwest," in J. Braidwood and G. R. Willey (eds.), *Courses Toward Urban Life.* Chicago: Aldine.

Herskovits, Melville J., 1952. *Economic Anthropology.* New York: Knopf.

Hiatt, L., 1965. *Kinship and Conflict.* Canberra: Australian National University.

Hodgkinson, Clement, 1845. *Australian from Port Macquarie to Moreton Bay, with Descriptions of the Natives.* London: Boone.

Hoebel, E. Adamson, 1958. *Man in the Primitive World.* 2nd ed. New York: McGraw-Hill.

Lafargue, Paul, 1911 [1883]. *The Right to Be Lazy.* Chicago: Kerr (First French edition, 1883).

Lee, Richard, 1968. "What Hunters Do for a Living, or, How to Make Out on Scarce Resources," in R. Lee and I. DeVore (eds.), *Man the Hunter*. Chicago: Aldine.

Lee, Richard, 1969. "!Kung Bushman Subsistence: An Input-Output Analysis," in A. Vayde (ed.), *Environment and Cultural Behavior.* Garden City, N.Y.: Natural History Press.

Lee, Richard B., and Irven DeVore (eds.), 1968. *Man the Hunter.* Chicago: Aldine.

LeJeune, le Pere Paul, 1897. "Relation of What Occurred in New France in the Year 1634," in R. G. Thwaites (ed.), *The Jesuit Relations and Allied Documents*, Vol. 6. Cleveland: Burrows (First French edition, 1635).

Lothrup, Samuel K., 1928. *The Indians of Tierra del Fuego.* New York: Museum of the American Indian, Heye Foundation.

Lowie, Robert H., 1938. "Subsistence," in F. Boas (ed.), *General Anthropology.* Boston: Heath.

Lowie, Robert H., 1946. *An Introduction to Cultural Anthropology.* 2nd ed. New York: Rinehart.

McArthur, Margaret, 1960. "Food Consumption and Dietary Levels of Groups of Aborigines Living on Naturally Occurring Foods," in C. P. Mountford (ed.), *Records of the Australian-American Scientific Expedition to Arnhem Land*, Vol. 2: *Anthropology and Nutrition.* Melbourne: Melbourne University Press.

McCarthy, Frederick D., and Margaret McArthur, 1960. "The Food Quest and the Time Factor in Aboriginal Economic Life," in C. P. Mountford (ed.), *Records of the Australian-American Scientific Expedition to Arnhem Land*, Vol. 2: *Anthropology and Nutrition.* Melbourne: Melbourne University Press.

Mandel, Ernest, 1962. *Traite d'économie Marxist.* 2 Vols. Paris: Julliard.

Marshall, Lorna, 1961. "Sharing, Talking, and Giving: Relief of Social Tensions Among !Kung Bushmen," *Africa* 31:231–49.

Mathew, John, 1910. *Two Representative Tribes of Queensland.* London: Unwin.

Mauss, Marcel, 1966. "Essai sur le don: Forme et raison de l'échange dans les sociétés archaïques," in *Sociologie et anthropologie.* (First published 1923–24 in L'Année Sociologique.) Paris: Universitaires de France.

Meggitt, Mervyn, 1964. "Indigenous Forms of Government Among the Australian Aborigines," Bijdragen tot de Taal-, Land-, en Volkenkunde 120:163–80.

Needham, Rodney, 1954. "Siriono and Penan: A Test of Some Hypotheses," *Southwestern Journal of Anthropology*, 10:228–32.

Polanyi, Karl, 1947. "Our Obsolete Market Mentality," *Commentary* 3:109–17.

Polanyi, Karl, 1957. "The Economy as Instituted Process," in K. Polanyi, C. Arensberg, and H. Pearson (eds.), *Trade and Market in the Early Empires.* Glencoe: Free Press.

Polanyi, Karl, 1959. "Anthropology and Economic Theory," in M. Fried (ed.), *Readings in Anthropology.* Vol. 2. New York: Crowell.

Quimby, George I. 1962. "A Year with a Chippewa Family, 1763–1764, *Ethnohistory* 9:217–39.

Radcliffe-Brown, A. R., 1948. *The Andaman Islanders.* Glencoe: Free Press (First edition 1922).

Redfield, Robert, 1953. *The Primitive World and Its Transformations.* Ithaca, N.Y.: Cornell University Press.

Service, Elman R., 1962. *Primitive Social Organization.* New York: Random House.

Service, Elman R., 1963. *Profiles in Ethnology.* New York: Harper & Row.

Sharp, Lauriston, 1934–35. "Ritual Life and Economics of the Yir-Yiront of Cape York Peninsula," *Oceania* 5:19–42.

Sharp, Lauriston, 1958. "People without Politics," in V. F. Ray (ed.), *Systems of Political Control and Bureaucracy in Human Societies.* American Ethnological Society. Seattle: University of Washington Press.

Smyth, R. Brough, 1878. *The Aborigines of Victoria.* 2 Vols. Melbourne: Government Printer.

Spencer, Baldwin, and F. J. Gillen. 1899. *The Native Tribes of Central Australia.* London: Macmillan.

Spencer, Robert F., 1959. *The North Alaskan Eskimo: A Study of Ecology and Society.* Smithsonian Institution Bureau of American Ethnology Bulletin 171. Washington, D.C.: U.S. Government Printing Office.

Stewart, Julian, 1938. *Basin-Plateau Aboriginal Sociopolitical Groups.* Smithsonian Institution Bureau of American Ethnology Bulletin 120. Washington, D.C.: U.S. Government Printing Office.

Steward, Julian H., and Louis C. Faron. 1959. *Native Peoples of South America.* New York: McGraw-Hill.

Thomson, Donald F., 1949a. *Economic Structure and the Ceremonial Exchange Cycle in Arnhem Land.* Melbourne: Macmillan.

Thomson, Donald F., 1949b. "Arnhen Land: Explorations Among an Unknown People," *The Geographical Journal* 113:1–8; 114:54–67.

Turnbull, Colin, 1965. *Wayward Servants.* Garden City, N.Y.: Natural History Press.

van der Post, Laurens, 1958. *The Lost World of the Kalahari.* New York: Morrow.

Warner, W. Lloyd, 1964. *A Black Civilization* (Harper "Torchbook" from the edition of 1958; first edition 1937). New York: Harper & Row.

White, Leslie A., 1949. *The Science of Culture.* New York: Farrar, Strauss.

White, Leslie A., 1959. *The Evolution of Culture.* New York: McGraw-Hill.

Woodburn, James (Director), 1966. "The Hadza" (film available from the anthropological director, Department of Anthropology, London School of Economics).

Woodburn, James, 1968. "An Introduction to Hadza Ecology," in R. Lee and I. DeVore (eds.), *Man the Hunter.* Chicago: Aldine.

Worsley, Peter M., 1961. "The Utilization of Food Resources by the Australian Aboriginal Tribe," *Acta Ethnographica* 10:153–90.

TWO

What Hunters Do for a Living, or, How to Make Out on Scarce Resources

◆

Richard B. Lee

The current anthropological view of hunter-gatherer subsistence rests on two questionable assumptions. First is the notion that these peoples are primarily dependent on the hunting of game animals, and second is the assumption that their way of life is generally a precarious and arduous struggle for existence.

Recent data on living hunter-gatherers (Meggitt 1964b; Service 1966; and papers in this volume) show a radically different picture. We have learned that in many societies, plant and marine resources are far more important than are game animals in the diet. More important, it is becoming clear that, with a few conspicuous exceptions, the hunter-gatherer subsistence base is at least routine and reliable and at best surprisingly abundant. Anthropologists have consistently tended to underestimate the viability of even those "marginal isolates" of hunting peoples that have been available to ethnographers.

The purpose of this paper is to analyze the food-getting activities of one such "marginal" people, the !Kung Bushmen of the Kalahari Desert. Three related questions are posed: How do the Bushmen make a living? How easy or difficult is it for them to do this? What kinds of evidence are necessary to measure and evaluate the precariousness or security of a way of life? And after the relevant data are presented, two further questions are asked: What makes this security of life possible? To what extent are the Bushmen typical of hunter-gatherers in general?

Bushman Subsistence

The !Kung Bushmen of Botswana are an apt case for analysis.[1] They inhabit the semi-arid northwest region of the Kalahari Desert. With only six to nine

Reprinted with permission from: Lee, Richard B., and Irven DeVore, *Man the Hunter* (New York: Aldine de Gruyter). Copyright © 1968 by the Wenner-Gren Foundation for Anthropological Research.

inches of rainfall per year, this is, by any account, a marginal environment for human habitation. In fact, it is precisely the unattractiveness of their homeland that has kept the !Kung isolated from extensive contact with their agricultural and pastoral neighbors.

Field work was carried out in the Dobe area, a line of eight permanent waterholes near the South-West Africa border and 125 miles south of the Okavango River. The population of the Dobe area consists of 466 Bushmen, including 379 permanent residents living in independent camps or associated with Bantu cattle posts, as well as 87 seasonal visitors. The Bushmen share the area with some 340 Bantu pastoralists largely of the Herero and Tswana tribes. The ethnographic present refers to the period of field work: October 1963–January 1965.

The Bushmen living in independent camps lack firearms, livestock, and agriculture. Apart from occasional visits to the Herero for milk, these !Kung are entirely dependent upon hunting and gathering for their subsistence. Politically they are under the nominal authority of the Tswana headman, although they pay no taxes and receive very few government services. European presence amounts to one overnight government patrol every six to eight weeks. Although Dobe-area !Kung have had some contact with outsiders since the 1880's, the majority of them continue to hunt and gather because there is no viable alternative locally available to them.[2]

Each of the fourteen independent camps is associated with one of the permanent waterholes. During the dry season (May–October) the entire population is clustered around these wells. Table 2.1 shows the numbers at each well at the end of the 1964 dry season. Two wells had no camp resident and one large well supported five camps. The number of camps at each well and the size of each camp changed frequently during the course of the year. The "camp" is an open aggregate of cooperating persons which changes in size and composition from day to day. Therefore, I have avoided the term "band" in describing the !Kung Bushman living groups.[3]

Each waterhole has a hinterland lying within a six-mile radius which is regularly exploited for vegetable and animal foods. These areas are not territories in the zoological sense, since they are not defended against outsiders. Rather they constitute the resources that lie within a convenient walking distance of a waterhole. The camp is a self-sufficient subsistence unit. The members move out each day to hunt and gather, and return in the evening to pool the collected foods in such a way that every person present receives an equitable share. Trade in foodstuffs between camps is minimal; personnel do move freely from camp to camp, however. The net effect is of a population constantly in motion. On the average, an individual spends a third of his time living only with close rel-

Table 2.1
Numbers and Distribution of Resident Bushmen and Bantu by Waterhole*

Name of Waterhole	No. of Camps	Population of Camps	Other Bushmen	Total Bushmen	Bantu
Dobe	2	37	—	37	—
!angwa	1	16	23	39	84
Bate	2	30	12	42	21
!ubi	1	19	—	19	65
!gose	3	52	9	61	18
/ai/ai	5	94	13	107	67
!xabe	—	—	8	8	12
Mahopa	—	—	23	23	73
Totail	14	248	88	336	340

*Figures do not include 130 Bushmen outside area on the date of census.

atives, a third visiting other camps, and a third entertaining visitors from other camps.

Because of the strong emphasis on sharing, and the frequency of movement, surplus accumulation of storable plant foods and dried meat is kept to a minimum. There is rarely more than two or three days' supply of food on hand in a camp at any time. The result of this lack of surplus is that a constant subsistence effort must be maintained throughout the year. Unlike agriculturalists who work hard during the planting and harvesting seasons and undergo "seasonal unemployment" for several months, the Bushmen hunter-gatherers collect food every third or fourth day throughout the year.

Vegetable foods comprise from 60–80 per cent of the total diet by weight, and collecting involves two or three days of work per woman per week. The men also collect plants and small animals but their major contribution to the diet is the hunting of medium and large game. The men are conscientious but not particularly successful hunters; although men's and women's work input is roughly equivalent in terms of man-days of effort, the women provide two to three times as much food by weight as the men.

Table 2.2 summarizes the seasonal activity cycle observed among the Dobe-area !Kung in 1964. For the greater part of the year, food is locally abundant and easily collected. It is only during the end of the dry season in September and October, when desirable foods have been eaten out in the immediate vicinity of the waterholes, that the people have to plan longer hikes of 10–15 miles and carry their own water to those areas where the mongongo nut is still available. The important point is that food is a constant, but distance required to reach food is a variable; it is short in the summer, fall, and early winter, and reaches its maximum in the spring.

Table 2.2
The Bushman Annual Round

	Jan.	Feb.	Mar.	April	May	June	July	Aug.	Sept.	Oct.	Nov.	Dec.
Season		Summer Rains		Autumn Dry			Winter Dry			Spring Dry		First Rains
Availability of water		Temporary summer pools everywhere		Large summer pools			Permanent waterholes only					Summer pools developing
Group Moves		Widely dispersed at summer pools			At large summer pools		All population restricted to permanent waterholes					Moving out to summer pools
Men's Subsistence Activities		1. Hunting with bow, arrows, and dogs (Year-round) 2. Running down immatures 3. Some gathering (Year-round)						Trapping small game in snares			Running down newborn animals	
Women's Subsistence Activities		1. Gathering of mongongo nuts (Year-round) 2. Fruits, berries, melons					Roots, bulbs, resins				Roots, leafy greens	
Ritual Activities				Dancing, trance performances, and ritual curing (Year-round)	Boys' initiation*							†
Relative Subsistence Hardship		Water-food distance minimal					Increasing distance from water to food				Water-food distance minimal	

* Held once every five years; none in 1963–64.

† New Year's: Bushmen join the celebrations of their missionized Bantu neighbors.

This analysis attempts to provide quantitative measures of subsistence status including data on the following topics: abundance and variety of resources, diet selectivity, range size and population density, the composition of the work force, the ratio of work to leisure time, and the caloric and protein levels in the diet. The value of quantitative data is that they can be used comparatively and also may be useful in archeological reconstruction. In addition, one can avoid the pitfalls of subjective and qualitative impressions; for example, statements about food "anxiety" have proven to be difficult to generalize across cultures (see Holmberg 1950; and Needham's critique [1954]).

Abundance and Variety of Resources

It is impossible to define "abundance" of resources absolutely. However, one index of *relative* abundance is whether or not a population exhausts all the food available from a given area. By this criterion, the habitat of the Dobe-area Bushmen is abundant in naturally occurring foods. By far the most important food is the mongongo (mangetti) nut (*Ricinodendron rautanenii* Schinz). Although tens of thousands of pounds of these nuts are harvested and eaten each year, thousands more rot on the ground each year for want of picking.

The mongongo nut, because of its abundance and reliability, alone accounts for 50 per cent of the vegetable diet by weight. In this respect it resembles a cultivated staple crop such as maize or rice. Nutritionally it is even more remarkable, for it contains five times the calories and ten times the proteins per cooked unit of the cereal crops. The average daily per capita consumption of 300 nuts yields about 1,260 calories and 56 grams of protein. This modest portion, weighing only about 7.5 ounces, contains the caloric equivalent of 2.5 pounds of cooked rice and the protein equivalent of 14 ounces of lean beef (Watt and Merrill 1963).

Furthermore the mongongo nut is drought resistant and it will still be abundant in the dry years when cultivated crops may fail. The extremely hard outer shell protects the inner kernel from rot and allows the nuts to be harvested for up to twelve months after they have fallen to the ground. A diet based on mongongo nuts is in fact more reliable than one based on cultivated foods, and it is not surprising, therefore, that when a Bushman was asked why he hadn't taken to agriculture he replied: "Why should we plant, when there are so many mongongo nuts in the world?"

Apart from the mongongo, the Bushmen have available 84 other species of edible food plants, including 29 species of fruits, berries, and melons and 30 species of roots and bulbs. The existence of this variety allows for a wide range of alternatives in subsistence strategy. During the summer months the Bushmen have no problem other than to choose among the tastiest and most easily collected foods. Many species, which are quite edible but less attractive, are bypassed, so that gathering never exhausts *all* the available plant foods of an area. During the dry season the diet becomes much more eclectic and the many species of roots, bulbs, and edible resins make an important contribution. It is this broad base that provides an essential margin of safety during the end of the dry season when the mongongo nut forests are difficult to reach. In addition, it is likely that these rarely utilized species provide important nutritional and mineral trace elements that may be lacking in the more popular foods.

Diet Selectivity

If the Bushmen were living close to the "starvation" level, then one would expect them to exploit every available source of nutrition. That their life is well above this level is indicated by the data in Table 2.3. Here all the edible plant species are arranged in classes according to the frequency with which they were observed to be eaten. It should be noted that although there are some 85 species available, about 90 per cent of the vegetable diet by weight is drawn from only 23 species. In other words, 75 per cent of the listed species provide only 10 per cent of the food value.

In their meat-eating habits, the Bushmen show a similar selectivity. Of the 223 local species of animals known and named by the Bushmen, 54 species are classified as edible, and of these only 17 species were hunted on a regular basis.[4] Only a handful of the dozens of edible species of small mammals, birds, reptiles, and insects that occur locally are regarded as food. Such animals as rodents, snakes, lizards, termites, and grasshoppers, which in the literature are included in the Bushman dietary (Schapera 1930), are despised by the Bushmen of the Dobe area.

Range Size and Population Density

The necessity to travel long distances, the high frequency of moves, and the maintenance of populations at low densities are also features commonly associated with the hunting and gathering way of life. Density estimates for hunters in western North America and Australia have ranged from 3 persons/square mile to as low as 1 person/100 square miles (Kroeber 1939; Radcliffe-Brown 1930). In 1963–65, the resident and visiting Bushmen were observed to utilize an area of about 1,000 square miles during the course of the annual round for an effective population density of 41 persons/100 square miles. Within this area, however, the amount of ground covered by members of an individual camp was surprisingly small. A day's round-trip of twelve miles serves to define a "core" area six miles in radius surrounding each water point. By fanning out in all directions from their well, the members of a camp can gain access to the food resources of well over 100 square miles of territory

Table 2.3. !Kung Bushman Plant Foods

Food Class	Fruit and Nut	Bean and Root	Fruit and Stalk	Root, Bulb	Fruit, Berry, Melon	Resin	Leaves	Seed, Bean	Total number of species in class	Estimated contribution by weight to vegetable diet	Estimated contribution of each species
Primary Eaten daily throughout year (mongongo nut)	1	—	—	—	—	—	—	—	1	c. 50	c. 50*
II. Major Eaten daily in season	1	1	1	1	4	—	—	—	8	c. 25	c. 3 †
III. Minor Eaten several times per week in season	—	—	—	7	3	2	2	—	14	c. 15	c. 1
IV. Supplementary Eaten when classes I–III locally unavailable	—	—	—	9	12	10	1	—	32	c. 7	c. 0.2
V. Rare Eaten several times per year	—	—	—	9	4	—	—	—	13	c. 3	c. 0.1 ‡
VI. Problematic Edible but not observed to be eaten	—	—	—	4	6	4	1	2	17	nil	nil
Total Species	2	1	1	30	29	16	4	2	85	100	—

* 1 species constitutes 50 per cent of the vegetable diet by weight.   † 23 species constitute 90 per cent of the vegetable diet by weight.
‡ 62 species constitute the remaining 10 percent of the diet.

within a two-hour hike. Except for a few weeks each year, areas lying beyond this six-mile radius are rarely utilized, even though they are no less rich in plants and game than are the core areas.

Although the Bushmen move their camps frequently (five or six times a year) they do not move them very far. A rainy season camp in the nut forests is rarely more than ten or twelve miles from the home waterhole, and often new campsites are occupied only a few hundred yards away from the previous one. By these criteria, the Bushmen do not lead a free-ranging nomadic way of life. For example, they do not undertake long marches of 30 to 100 miles to get food, since this task can be readily fulfilled within a day's walk of home base. When such long marches do occur they are invariably for visiting, trading, and marriage arrangements, and should not be confused with the normal routine of subsistence.

Demographic Factors

Another indicator of the harshness of a way of life is the age at which people die. Ever since Hobbes characterized life in the state of nature as "nasty, brutish and short," the assumption has been that hunting and gathering is so rigorous that members of such societies are rapidly worn out and meet an early death. Silberbauer, for example, says of the Gwi Bushmen of the central Kalahari that "life expectancy . . . is difficult to calculate, but I do not believe that many live beyond 45" (1965:17). And Coon has said of the hunters in general:

> The practice of abandoning the hopelessly ill and aged has been ob-
> served in many parts of the world. It is always done by people living
> in poor environments where it is necessary to move about frequently
> to obtain food, where food is scarce, and transportation difficult. . . .
> Among peoples who are forced to live in this way the oldest genera-
> tion, the generation of individuals who have passed their physical
> peak, is reduced in numbers and influence. There is no body of elders
> to hand on tradition and control the affairs of younger men and
> women, and no formal system of age grading. (1948:55)

The !Kung Bushmen of the Dobe area flatly contradict this view. In a total population of 466, no fewer than 46 individuals (17 men and 29 women) were determined to be over 60 years of age, a proportion that compares favorably to the percentage of elderly in industrialized populations.

The aged hold a respected position in Bushman society and are the effective leaders of the camps. Senilicide is extremely rare. Long after their productive years have passed, the old people are fed and cared for by their children and grandchildren. The blind, the senile, and the crippled are respected for the special ritual and technical skills they possess. For instance, the four elders at !gose waterhole were totally or partially blind, but this handicap did not prevent their active participation in decision making and ritual curing.

Another significant feature of the composition of the work force is the late assumption of adult responsibility by the adolescents. Young people are not expected to provide food regularly until they are married. Girls typically marry between the ages of 15 and 20, and boys about five years later, so that it is not unusual to find healthy, active teenagers visiting from camp to camp while their older relatives provide food for them.

As a result, the people in the age group 20–60 support a surprisingly large percentage of nonproductive young and old people. About 40 per cent of the population in camps contribute little to the food supplies. This allocation of work to young and middle-aged adults allows for a relatively carefree childhood and adolescence and a relatively unstrenuous old age.

Leisure and Work

Another important index of ease or difficulty of subsistence is the amount of time devoted to the food quest.[5] Hunting has usually been regarded by social scientists as a way of life in which merely keeping alive is so formidable a task that members of such societies lack the leisure time necessary to "build culture."[6] The !Kung Bushmen would appear to conform to the rule, for as Lorna Marshall says:

> It is vividly apparent that among the !Kung Bushmen, ethos, or "the spirit which actuates manners and customs," is survival. Their time and energies are almost wholly given to this task, for life in their environment requires that they spend their days mainly in procuring food. (1965:247)

It is certainly true that getting food is the most important single activity in Bushman life. However this statement would apply equally well to small-scale agricultural and pastoral societies too. How much time is *actually* devoted to the food quest is fortunately an empirical question. And an analysis of the work effort of the Dobe Bushmen shows some unexpected results. From July 6 to August 2, 1964, I recorded all the daily activities of the Bushmen living at the Dobe waterhole. Because of the coming and going of visitors, the camp population fluctuated in size day by day, from a low of 23 to a high of 40, with a mean of 31.8 persons. Each day some of the adult members of the camp went out to hunt and/or gather while others stayed home or went visiting. The daily recording of all personnel on hand made it possible to calculate the number of man-days of work as a percentage of total number of man-days of consumption.

Although the Bushmen do not organize their activities on the basis of a seven-day week, I have divided the data this way to make them more intelligible. The work-week was calculated to show how many days out of seven each adult spent in subsistence activities (Table 2.4, Column 7). Week II has been eliminated from the totals since the investigator contributed food. In week I, the people spent an average of 2.3 days in subsistence activities, in week III, 1.9 days, and in week IV, 3.2 days. In all, the adults of the Dobe camp worked about two and a half days a week. Since the average working day was about six hours long, the fact emerges that !Kung Bushmen of Dobe, despite their harsh environment, devote from twelve to nineteen hours a week to getting food. Even the hardest working individual in the camp, a man named ≠oma who went out hunting on sixteen of the 28 days, spent a maximum of 32 hours a week in the food quest.

Because the Bushmen do not amass a surplus of foods, there are no seasons of exceptionally intensive activities such as planting and harvesting, and no seasons of unemployment. The level of work observed is an accurate reflection of the effort required to meet the immediate caloric needs of the group. This work diary covers the mid-winter dry season, a period when food is neither at its most plentiful nor at its scarcest levels, and the diary documents the transition from better to worse conditions (see Table 2.2). During the fourth week the gatherers were making overnight trips to camps in the mongongo nut forests seven to ten miles distant from the waterhole. These longer trips account for the rise in the level of work, from twelve or thirteen to nineteen hours per week.

If food getting occupies such a small proportion of a Bushman's waking hours, then how *do* people allocate their time? A woman gathers on one day enough food to feed her family for three days, and spends the rest of her time resting in camp, doing embroidery, visiting other camps, or entertaining visitors from other camps. For each day at home, kitchen routines, such as cooking, nut cracking, collecting firewood, and fetching water, occupy one to three hours of her time. This rhythm of steady work and steady leisure is maintained throughout the year.

The hunters tend to work more frequently than the women, but their schedule is uneven. It is not unusual for a man to hunt avidly for a week and then do no hunting at all for two or three weeks. Since hunting is an unpredictable business and subject to magical control, hunters sometimes experience a run of bad luck and stop hunting for a month or longer. During these periods, visiting, entertaining, and especially dancing are the primary activities of men. (Unlike the Hadza, gambling is only a minor leisure activity.)

Table 2.4. Summary of Dobe Work Diary

Week	(1) Mean Group Size	(2) Adult-Days	(3) Child-Days	(4) Total Man-Days of Consumption	(5) Man-Days of Work	(6) Meat (lbs.)	(7) Average Work Week / Adult	(8) Index of Subsistence Effort
I (July 6–12)	25.6 (23–29)	114	65	179	37	104	2.3	.21
II (July 13–19)	28.3 (23–27)	125	73	198	22	80	1.2	.11
III (July 20–26)	34.3 (29–40)	156	84	240	42	177	1.9	.18
IV (July 27–Aug. 2)	35.6 (32–40)	167	82	249	77	129	3.2	.31
4-wk. Total	30.9	562	304	866	178	490	2.2	.21
Adjusted Total*	31.8	437	231	668	156	410	2.5	.23

* See text.

KEY: Column 1: Mean group size = (total man-days of consumption) / 7
Column 7: Work week = the number of work days per adult per week.
Column 8: Index of Subsistence Effort = (man-days of work) / (man-days of consumption) (e.g., in Week I, the value of "S" = .21, i.e., 21 days of work/100 days of consumption or 1 work day produces food for 5 consumption days).

The trance-dance is the focus of Bushman ritual life; over 50 per cent of the men have trained as trance-performers and regularly enter trance during the course of the all-night dances. At some camps, trance-dances occur as frequently as two or three times a week and those who have entered trances the night before rarely go out hunting the following day. Accounts of Bushman trance performances have been published in Lorna Marshall (1962) and Lee (1967). In a camp with five or more hunters, there are usually two or three who are actively hunting and several others who are inactive. The net effect is to phase the hunting and nonhunting so that a fairly steady supply of meat is brought into a camp.

Caloric Returns

Is the modest work effort of the Bushmen sufficient to provide the calories necessary to maintain the health of the population? Or have the !Kung, in common with some agricultural peoples (see Richards 1939), adjusted to a permanently substandard nutritional level?

During my field work I did not encounter any cases of kwashiorkor, the most common nutritional disease in the children of African agricultural societies. However, without medical examinations, it is impossible to exclude the possibility that subclinical signs of malnutrition existed.[7]

Another measure of nutritional adequacy is the average consumption of calories and proteins per person per day. The estimate for the Bushmen is based on observations of the weights of foods of known composition that were brought into Dobe camp on each day of the study period. The per-capita figure is obtained by dividing the total weight of foodstuffs by the total number of persons in the camp. These results are set out in detail elsewhere (Lee, in press) and can only be summarized here. During the study period 410 pounds of meat were brought in by the hunters of the Dobe camp, for a daily share of nine ounces of meat per person. About 700 pounds of vegetable foods were gathered and consumed during the same period. Table 2.5 sets out the calories and proteins available per capita in the !Kung Bushman dietary from meat, mongongo nuts, and other vegetable sources.

This output of 2,140 calories and 93.1 grams of protein per person per day may be compared with the Recommended Daily Allowances (RDA) for persons of the small size and stature but vigorous activity regime of the !Kung Bushmen. The RDA for Bushmen can be estimated at 1,975 calories and 60 grams of protein per person per day (Taylor and Pye 1966: 45–48, 463). Thus it is apparent that food output exceeds energy requirements by 165 calories and 33 grams of protein. One can tentatively conclude that even a modest subsistence effort of two or three days' work per week is enough to provide an adequate diet for the !Kung Bushmen.

Table 2.5
Caloric and Protein Levels in the !Kung Bushman Dietary, July–August, 1964

Class of Food	Percentage Contribution to Diet by Weight	Per-Capita Consumption		Calories per person per day	Percentage Caloric Contribution of Meat and Vegetables
		Weight in grams	Protein in grams		
Meat	37	230	34.5	690	33
Mongongo nuts	33	210	56.7	1,260	
Other Vegetable Foods	30	190	1.9	190	67
Total All Sources	100	630	93.1	2,140	100

The Scarcity of Bushman Life

I have attempted to evaluate the subsistence base of one contemporary hunter-gatherer society living in a marginal environment. The !Kung Bushmen have available to them some relatively abundant high-quality foods, and they do not have to walk very far or work very hard to get them. Furthermore this modest work effort provides sufficient calories to support not only the active adults, but also a large number of middle-aged and elderly people. The Bushmen do not have to press their youngsters into the service of the food quest, nor do they have to dispose of the oldsters after they have ceased to be productive.

The evidence presented assumes an added significance because this security of life was observed during the third year of one of the most severe droughts in South Africa's history. Most of the 576,000 people of Botswana are pastoralists and agriculturalists. After the crops had failed three years in succession and over 100,000 head of cattle had died on the range for lack of water, the World Food Program of the United Nations instituted a famine relief program which has grown to include 180,000 people, over 30 per cent of the population (Government of Botswana 1966). This program did not touch the Dobe area in the isolated northwest corner of the country and the Herero and Tswana women there were able to feed their families only by joining the Bushman women to forage for wild foods. Thus the natural plant resources of the Dobe area were carrying a higher proportion of population than would be the case in years when the Bantu harvested crops. Yet this added pressure on the land did not seem to adversely affect the Bushmen.

In one sense it was unfortunate that the period of my field work happened to coincide with the drought, since I was unable to witness a "typical" annual subsistence cycle. However, in another sense, the coincidence was a lucky one, for the drought put the Bushmen and their subsistence system to the acid test and, in terms of adaptation to scarce resources, they passed with flying colors. One can postulate that their subsistence base would be even more substantial during years of higher rainfall.

What are the crucial factors that make this way of life possible? I suggest that the primary factor is the Bushmen's strong emphasis on vegetable food sources. Although hunting involves a great deal of effort and prestige, plant foods provide from 60–80 per cent of the annual diet by weight. Meat has come to be regarded as a special treat; when available, it is welcomed as a break from the routine of vegetable foods, but it is never depended upon as a staple. No one ever goes hungry when hunting fails.

The reason for this emphasis is not hard to find. Vegetable foods, are abundant, sedentary, and predictable. They grow in the same place year after year, and the gatherer is guaranteed a day's return of food for a day's expenditure of energy. Game animals, by contrast, are scarce, mobile, unpredictable, and difficult to catch. A hunter has no guarantee of success and may in fact go for days or weeks without killing a large mammal. During the study period, there were eleven men in the Dobe camp, of whom four did no hunting at all. The seven active men spent a total 78 man-days hunting, and this work input yielded eighteen animals killed, or one kill for every four man-days of hunting. The probability of any one hunter making a kill on a given day was 0.23. By contrast, the probability of a woman finding plant food on a given day was 1.00. In other words, hunting and gathering are not equally felicitous subsistence alternatives.

Consider the productivity per man-hour of the two kinds of subsistence activities. One man-hour of hunting produces about 100 edible calories, and of gathering, 240 calories. Gathering is thus seen to be 2.4 times more productive than hunting. In short, hunting is a *high-risk, low-return* subsistence activity, while gathering is a *low-risk, high-return* subsistence activity.

It is not at all contradictory that the hunting complex holds a central place in the Bushman ethos and that meat is valued more highly than vegetable foods (Marshall 1960). Analogously, steak is valued more highly than potatoes in the food preferences of our own society. In both situations the meat is more "costly" than the vegetable food. In the Bushman case, the cost of food can be measured in terms of time and energy expended. By this standard, 1,000 calories of meat "costs" ten man-hours, while the "cost" of 1,000 calories of vegetable foods is only four man-hours. Further, it is to be expected that the less predictable, more expensive food source would have a greater accretion of myth and ritual built up around it than would the routine staples of life, which rarely if ever fail.

Eskimo–Bushman Comparisons

Were the Bushmen to be deprived of their vegetable food sources, their life would become much more arduous and precarious. This lack of plant foods, in fact, is precisely the situation among the Netsilik Eskimo, reported by Balikci (1968). The Netsilik and other Central Arctic peoples are perhaps unique in the almost total absence of vegetable foods in their diet. This factor, in combination with the great cyclical variation in the numbers and distribution of Arctic fauna, makes Eskimo life the most precarious human adaptation on earth. In effect, *the kinds of animals that are "luxury goods" to many hunters and gatherers, are to the Eskimos, the absolute necessities of life.* However, even this view should not be exaggerated, since most of the Eskimos in historic times have lived south of the Arctic Circle (Laughlin, 1968) and many of the Eskimos at all latitudes have depended primarily on fishing, which is a much more reliable source of food than is the hunting of land and sea mammals.

What Hunters Do for a Living: A Comparative Study

I have discussed how the !Kung Bushmen are able to manage on the scarce resources of their inhospitable environment. The essence of their successful strategy seems to be that while they depend primarily on the more stable and abundant food sources (vegetables in their case), they are nevertheless willing to devote considerable energy to the less reliable and more highly valued food sources such as medium and large mammals. The steady but modest input of work by the women provides the former, and the more intensive labors of the men provide the latter. It would be theoretically possible for the Bushmen to survive entirely on vegetable foods, but life would be boring indeed without the excitement of meat feasts. The totality of their subsistence activities thus represents an outcome of two individual goals; the first is the desire to live well with adequate leisure time, and the second is the desire to enjoy the rewards, both social and nutritional, afforded by the killing of game. In short, *the Bushmen of the Dobe area eat as much vegetable food as they need, and as much meat as they can.*

It seems reasonable that a similar kind of subsistence strategy would be characteristic of hunters and gatherers in general. Wherever two or more kinds of natural foods are available, one would predict that the population exploiting them would emphasize the more reliable source. We would also expect, however, that the people would not neglect the alternative means of subsistence. The general view offered here is that gathering activities, for plants and shellfish, should be the most productive of food for hunting and gathering man, followed by fishing, where this source is available. The hunting of mammals is the least re liable source of food and should be generally less important than either gathering or fishing.

In order to test this hypothesis, a sample of 58 societies was drawn from the *Ethnographic Atlas* (Murdock 1967). The basis for inclusion in the sample was a 100 per cent dependence on hunting, gathering, and fishing for subsistence as rated in Column 7–11 of the *Atlas* (Murdock 1967:154–55). These 58 societies are plotted in Figures 2.1 and 2.2 and are listed in Tables 2.7 and 2.8 of the Appendix to this article.[8, 9*]

The *Ethnographic Atlas* coding discusses "Subsistence Economy" as follows:

> A set of five digits indicates the estimated relative dependence of the society on each of the five major types of subsistence activity. The first digit refers to the gathering of wild plants and small land fauna; the second, to hunting, including trapping and fowling; the third, to fishing, including shell fishing and the pursuit of large aquatic animals; the fourth, to animal husbandry; the fifth, to agriculture. (Murdock 1967:154–55)

Two changes have been made in the definitions of subsistence. First, the participants at the symposium on Man the Hunter agreed that the "pursuit of large aquatic animals" is more properly classified under hunting than under fishing. Similarly, it was recommended that shellfishing should be classified under gathering, not fishing. These suggestions have been followed and the definitions now read: *Gathering*—collecting of wild plants, small land fauna and shellfish; *Hunting*—pursuit of land and sea mammals; *Fishing*—obtaining of fish by any technique. In 25 cases, the subsistence scores have been changed in light of these definitions and after consulting ethnographic sources.[10]

In Tables 2.9 and 2.10 of the Appendix to this article,* the percentage dependence on gathering, hunting, and fishing, and the most important single source of food for each society, are presented. Such scores can be at best only rough approximations; however, the results are so striking that the use of these scores seems justified. In the Old World and, South American sample of 24 societies, sixteen depend on gathering, five on fishing, while only three depend primarily on mammal hunting: the Yukaghir of northeast Asia, and the Ona and Shiriana of South America. In the North American sample, thirteen societies have primary dependence on gathering, thirteen on fishing, and eight on hunting. Thus for the world as a whole, half of the societies (29 cases) emphasize gathering, one-third (18 cases) fishing, and the remaining one-sixth (11 cases) hunting.

*Note that the Appendix mentioned is not reproduced in this collection but can be found in the original publication.

On this evidence, the "hunting" way of life appears to be in the minority. The result serves to underline the point made earlier that mammal hunting is the least reliable of the subsistence sources, and one would expect few societies to place primary dependence on it. As will be shown, most of the societies that rely primarily on mammals do so because their particular habitats offer no viable alternative subsistence strategy.

The Relation of Latitude to Subsistence

The peoples we have classified as "hunters" apparently depend for most of their subsistence on sources *other* than meat, namely, wild plants, shellfish and fish. In fact the present sample over-emphasizes the incidence of hunting and fishing since some three-fifths of the cases (34/58) are drawn from North America (north of the Rio Grande), a region which lies entirely within the temperate and arctic zones. Since the abundance and species variety of edible plants decreases as one moves out of the tropical and temperate zones, and approaches zero in the arctic, it is essential that the incidence of hunting, gathering, and fishing be related to latitude.

Table 2.6 shows the relative importance of gathering, hunting, and fishing within each of seven latitude divisions. Hunting appears as the dominant mode of subsistence *only* in the highest latitudes (60 or more degrees from the equator). In the arctic, hunting is primary in six of the eight societies. In the cool to cold temperate latitudes, 40 to 59 degrees from the equator, fishing is the dominant mode, appearing as primary in 14 out of 22 cases. In the warm-temperate, subtropical, and tropical latitudes, zero to 39 degrees from the equator, gathering is by far the dominant mode of subsistence, appearing as primary in 25 of the 28 cases.

For modern hunters, at any rate, it seems legitimate to predict a hunting emphasis only in the arctic, a fishing emphasis in the mid-high latitudes, and a gathering emphasis in the rest of the world.[11]

The Importance of Hunting

Although hunting is rarely the primary source of food, it does make a remarkably stable contribution to the diet. Fishing appears to be dispensable in the tropics, and a number of northern peoples manage to do without gathered foods, but, with a single exception, *all* societies at all latitudes derive at least 20 per cent of their diet from the hunting of mammals. Latitude appears to make little difference in the amount of hunting that people do. Except for the highest latitudes, where hunting contributes over half of the diet in many

Table 2.6
Primary Subsistence Source by Latitude

Degrees from the Equator	Primary Subsistence Source			
	Gathering	Hunting	Fishing	Total
More than 60°	—	6	2	8
50°–59°	—	1	9	10
40°–49°	4	3	5	12
30°–39°	9	—	—	9
20°–29°	7	—	1	8
10°–19°	5	—	1	6
0°–9°	4	1	—	5
World	29	11	18	58

cases, hunted foods almost everywhere else constitute 20 to 45 per cent of the diet. In fact, the mean, the median, and the mode for hunting all converge on a figure of 35 per cent for hunter-gatherers at all latitudes. This percentage of meat corresponds closely to the 37 per cent noted in the diet of the !Kung Bushmen of the Dobe area. It is evident that the !Kung, far from being an aberrant case, are entirely typical of the hunters in general in the amount of meat they consume.

Conclusions

Three points ought to be stressed. First, life in the state of nature is not necessarily nasty, brutish, and short. The Dobe-area Bushmen live well today on wild plants and meat, in spite of the fact that they are confined to the least productive portion of the range in which Bushman peoples were formerly found. It is likely that an even more substantial subsistence base would have been characteristic of these hunters and gatherers in the past, when they had the pick of African habitats to choose from.

Second, the basis of Bushman diet is derived from sources other than meat. This emphasis makes good ecological sense to the !Kung Bushmen and appears to be a common feature among hunters and gatherers in general. Since a 30 to 40 per cent input of meat is such a consistent target for modern hunters in a variety of habitats, is it not reasonable to postulate a similar percentage for prehistoric hunters? Certainly the absence of plant remains on archeological sites is by itself not sufficient evidence for the absence of gathering. Recently abandoned Bushman campsites show a similar absence of vegetable remains, although this paper has clearly shown that plant foods comprise over 60 per cent of the actual diet.

Finally, one gets the impression that hunting societies have been chosen by ethnologists to illustrate a dominant theme, such as the extreme importance of environment in the molding of certain cultures. Such a theme can be best exemplified by cases in which the technology is simple and/or the environment is harsh. This emphasis on the dramatic may have been pedagogically useful, but unfortunately it has led to the assumption that a precarious hunting subsistence base was characteristic of all cultures in the Pleistocene. This view of both modern and ancient hunters ought to be reconsidered. Specifically I am suggesting a shift in focus away from the dramatic and unusual cases, and toward a consideration of hunting and gathering as a persistent and well-adapted way of life.

NOTES

1. These data are based on fifteen months of field research from October 1963, to January 1965. I would like to thank the National Science Foundation (U.S.) for its generous financial support. This paper has been substantially revised since being presented at the symposium on Man the Hunter.

2. The Nyae Nyae !Kung Bushmen studied by Lorna Marshall (1957, 1960, 1965) have been involved in a settlement scheme instituted by the South African government. Although closely related to the Nyae Nyae !Kung, the Dobe !Kung across the border in Botswana have not participated in the scheme.

3. Bushman group structure is discussed in more detail in Lee (1965:38–53; 1968).

4. Listed in order of their importance, the principal species in the diet are: wart hog, kudu, duiker, steenbok, gemsbok, wildebeeste, springhare, porcupine, ant bear, hare, guinea fowl, francolin (two species), korhaan, tortoise, and python.

5. This and the following topic are discussed in greater detail in Lee, "!Kung Bushman Subsistence: An Input-Output Analysis" (1969).

6. Lenski, for example, in a recent review of the subject, states: "Unlike the members of hunting and gathering societies [the horticulturalists] are not compelled to spend most of their working hours in the search for food and other necessities of life, but are able to use more of their time in other ways" 1966:121). Sahlins (1968) offers a counter-argument to this view.

7. During future field work with the !Kung Bushmen, a professional pediatrician and nutritionist are planning to examine children and adults as part of a general study of hunter-gatherer health and nutrition sponsored by the U.S. National Institutes of Health and the Wenner-Gren Foundation for Anthropological Research.

8. Two societies, the Gwi Bushmen and the Walbiri of Australia, were not coded by the *Ethnographic Atlas*. Their subsistence base was scored after consulting the original ethnographies (for the Gwi, Silberbauer 1965; for the Walbiri, Meggitt 1962, 1964a).

9. In order to make more valid comparisons, I have excluded from the sample

mounted hunters with guns such as the Plains Indians, and casual agriculturalists such as the Gê and Siriono. Twenty-four societies are drawn from Africa, Asia, Australia, and South America. This number includes practically all of the cases that fit the definition. North America alone, with 137 hunting societies, contains over 80 per cent of the 165 hunting societies listed in the *Ethnographic Atlas*. The sampling procedure used here was to choose randomly one case from each of the 34 "clusters" of North American hunter-gatherers.

10. For their useful suggestions, my thanks go to Donald Lathrap, Robin Ridington, George Silberbauer, Hitoshi Watanabe, and James Woodburn. Special thanks are due to Wayne Suttles for his advice on Pacific coast subsistence.

11. When severity of winter is plotted against subsistence choices, a similar picture emerges. Hunting is primary in three of the five societies in very cold climates (annual temperature less than 32° F.); fishing is primary in 10 of the 17 societies in cold climates (32°–50° F.); and gathering is primary in 27 of the 36 societies in mild to hot climates (over 50° F.).

REFERENCES

Balikci, Asen, 1968. "The Netsilik Eskimos: Adaptive Processes." Chapter 8 in *Man the Hunter*, R. Lee and I. DeVore (eds.), Chicago: Aldine, pp. 78–82.

Botswana, Government of. 1966. Republic of Botswana fact sheet. Gabarone, Botswana.

Coon, Carleton S., 1948. *Reader in General Anthropology*. New York: Henry Holt.

Holmberg, Allan R., 1950. *Nomads of the Long Bow: The Siriono of Eastern Bolivia*. Smithsonian Institution, Publications of the Institute of Social Anthropology, no. 10.

Kroeber, A. L., 1939. *Cultural and Natural Areas of Native North America*. University of California Publications in American Archaeology and Ethnology (Berkeley), 38.

Laughlin, William, 1968. "The Demography of Hunters: An Eskimo Example." Chapter 25 in *Man the Hunter*, R. Lee and I. DeVore (eds.), Chicago: Aldine, pp. 241–43.

Lee, Richard B., 1965. *Subsistence Ecology of !Kung Bushmen*. Unpublished doctoral dissertation, University of California, Berkeley.

Lee, Richard, B., 1967. "The Sociology of Bushman Trance Performances." In Raymond Prince (ed.), *Trance and Possession States*. Montreal: McGill University Press.

Lee, Richard, 1969. "!Kung Bushman Subsistence: An Input-Output Analysis." In A. Vayde (ed.), *Environment and Cultural Behavior*. Garden City, N.Y.: Natural History Press.

Lee, Richard B., et al. 1968. "Analysis of Group Composition," Chapter 17c in *Man and the Hunter*, R. Lee and I. DeVore(eds.) Chicago: Aldine, pp. 150–155.

Lenski, Gerhard, 1966. *Power and Privilege: A Theory of Social Stratification*. New York: McGraw-Hill.

Marshall, Lorna K., 1957. "The Kin Terminology System of the !Kung Bushmen." *Africa* 27:1–25

Marshall, Lorna K., 1960. "!Kung Bushmen Bands." *Africa* 30:325–55.

Marshall, Lorna K., 1962. "!Kung Bushmen Religious Beliefs." *Africa* 32:221–52

Marshall, Lorna K., 1965. "The !Kung Bushmen of the Kalahari Desert." In James Gibbs (ed.), *Peoples of Africa.* New York: Holt, Rinehart, and Winston.

Meggitt, M. J., 1962. *Desert People: A Study of the Walbiri Aborigines of Central Australia.* Sydney: Angus and Robertson.

Meggitt, M. J., 1964a. "Indigenous Forms of Government Among the Australian Aborigines." *Bijdragen tot de Taal-, Land-, en Volkenkunde* 120:163–80.

Meggitt, M. J., 1964b. "Pre-industrial Man in the Tropical Environment: Aboriginal Food-Gatherers of Tropical Australia." *Proceedings and Papers of the Ninth Technical Meeting,* I.U.C.N., Nairobi, Kenya, 1963. Morges (Vaud), Switzerland: International Union for the Conservation of Nature and Natural Resources.

Murdock, George Peter, 1967. "The Ethnographic Atlas: A Summary." *Ethnology* 6 (2).

Needham, Rodney, 1954. "Siriono and Penan: A Test of Some Hypotheses." *Southwestern Journal of Anthropology* 10 (3):228–32.

Radcliffe-Brown, A. R., 1930. "Former Numbers and Distribution of the Australian Aborigines." *Official Yearbook of the Commonwealth of Australia* 23:671–96.

Richards, Audrey I., 1939. *Land, Labour and Diet in Northern Rhodesia.* London: Oxford University Press.

Sahlins, Marshall, 1968. "Notes on the Original Affluent Society." In *Man the Hunter,* R. Lee and I. DeVore (eds.), Chicago: Aldine, pp. 86–88.

Schapera, Isaac, 1930. *The Khoisan Peoples of South Africa: Bushmen and Hottentots.* London: Routledge and Kegan Paul.

Service, Elman R., 1966. *The Hunters.* Englewood Cliffs, N.J.: Prentice-Hall.

Silberbauer, G. B., 1965. *Report to the Government of Bechuanaland on the Bushman Survey.* Gaberones, Bechuanaland: Government of Bechuanaland.

Taylor, Clara M., and Pye, Orrea F., 1966. *Foundations of Nutrition.* (6th ed.). New York: Macmillan.

Watt, Bernice K., and Merrill, Annabel L., 1963. *Composition of Foods: Raw, Processed, Prepared.* Agricultural Handbook no. 8. U.S. Department of Agriculture, Agricultural Research Service.

THREE

Sharing, Talking, and Giving: Relief of Social Tensions Among the !Kung

◆

Lorna Marshall

This chapter describes customs practiced by the !Kung which help them to avoid situations that are likely to arouse ill will and hostility among individuals within bands and between bands. My observations were made among !Kung in the Nyae Nyae area in Namibia (South West Africa). Two customs which I consider to be especially important and which I describe in detail are meat-sharing and gift-giving. I discuss also the ways in which mannerliness, the custom of talking out grievances, the customs of borrowing and lending and of not stealing function to prevent tension from building up dangerously between members of a group and help to bring about peaceful relationships.

The common human needs for cooperation and companionship are particularly apparent among the !Kung. An individual never lives alone nor does a single nuclear family live alone. All live in bands composed of several families joined by consanguineous or affinal bonds. The arduous hunting-gathering life would be insupportable for a single person or a single nuclear family without the cooperation and companionship of the larger group. Moreover, in this society, the ownership of the resources of plant foods and waterholes and the utilization of them are organized through the band structure, and individuals have rights to the resources through their band affiliation.[1] Thus, the !Kung are dependent for their living on belonging to a band. They must belong; they can live no other way. They are also extremely dependent emotionally on the sense of belonging and on companionship. Separation and loneliness are unendurable to them. I believe their wanting to belong and be near is actually visible in the way families cluster together in an encampment and in the way they sit huddled together, often touching someone, shoulder against shoulder, ankle across ankle. Security and comfort for them lie in their belonging to their group, free from the threat of rejection and hostility.

Their security and comfort must be achieved side-by-side with self-interest and much jealous watchfulness. Altruism, kindness, sympathy, or genuine generosity were not qualities that I observed often in their behavior. However, these qualities were not entirely lacking, especially between parents and offspring, between siblings, and between spouses. One mother carried her sick adult daughter on her back for three days in searing summer heat for us to give her medicine. N/haka carried her lame son, Lame ≠Gau, for years. Gau clucked and fussed over his second wife, Hwan//ka, when she was sick. When !'Ku had a baby, her sister, /Ti!kai, gathered food for her for five days. On the other hand, people do not generally help each other. They laugh when the lame man, !Xəm, falls down and do not help him up. !'Ku's jealous eyes were like those of a viper when we gave more attention to her husband, ≠Toma, than to her on one occasion because he was much more ill than she. And, in the extreme, there was a report from the 1958 Marshall expedition of an instance of apparently callous indifference in one band on the part of some young relatives to a dying, old, childless woman, an old aunt, when her sister with whom she lived had died.

Occasions when tempers have got out of control are remembered with awe. The deadly poisoned arrows are always at hand. Men have killed each other with them in quarrels—though rarely—and the !Kung fear fighting with a conscious and active fear. They speak about it often. Any expression of discord ("bad words") makes them uneasy. Their desire to avoid both hostility and rejection leads them to conform in high degree to the unspoken social laws. I think that most !Kung cannot bear the sense of rejection that even mild disapproval makes them feel. If they do deviate, they usually yield readily to expressed group opinion and reform their ways. They also conform strictly to certain specific useful customs that are instruments for avoiding discord.

Talking and Talks

I mention talking as an aid to peaceful social relations because it is so very much a part of the daily experience of the !Kung, and because I believe it usefully serves three particular functions. It keeps up good, open communication among the members of the band; through its constantly flowing expression it is a salutary outlet for emotions; and it serves as the principal sanction in social discipline. Songs are also used for social discipline. The !Kung say that a song composed specifically about someone's behavior and sung to express disapproval, perhaps from the deepest shadow of the encampment at night, is a very effective means of bringing people who deviate back into the pattern of approved behavior. Nevertheless, during our observations, songs were not used as much as talking. If people disapprove of an individual's behavior, they may criticize him or her directly, usually putting a question, "Why do you do that?," or they may gossip a bit or make oblique hints. In the more intense instances what I call a talk may ensue.

The !Kung are the most loquacious people I know. Conversation in a !Kung encampment is a constant sound like the sound of a brook, and as low and lapping, except for shrieks of laughter. People cluster together in little groups during the day, talking, perhaps making artifacts at the same time. At night, families talk late by their fires, or visit at other family fires with their children between their knees or in their arms if the wind is cold.

There always seems to be plenty to talk about. People tell about events with much detail and repetition and discuss the comings and goings of their relatives and friends and make plans. Their greatest preoccupation and the subject they talk about most often, I think, is food. The men's imaginations turn to hunting. They converse musingly, as though enjoying a sort of daydream together, about past hunts, telling over and over where game was found and who killed it. They wonder where the game is at present, and say what fat bucks they hope to kill. They also plan their next hunts with practicality. Women (who, incidentally, do not seem to me to talk as much as men in !Kung society) gave me the impression of talking more about who gave or did not give them food and their anxieties about not having food. They spoke to me about women who were remembered for being especially quick and able gatherers, but they did not have pleasurable satisfaction in remembering their hot, monotonous, arduous days of digging and picking and trudging home with their heavy loads.

Another frequent subject of conversation is gift-giving. Men and women speak of the persons to whom they have given or propose to give gifts. They express satisfaction or dissatisfaction with what they have received. If someone has delayed unexpectedly long in making a return gift, the people discuss this. One man was excused by his friends because his wife, they said, had got things into her hands and made him poor, so that he now had nothing suitable to give. Sometimes, on the other hand, people were blamed for being ungenerous ("far-hearted") or not very capable in managing their lives, and no one defended them for these defects or asked others to have patience with them. The experiences of daily life are a further topic of conversation. While a person speaks, the listeners are in vibrant response, repeating the phrases and interposing a contrapuntal "eh." "Yesterday," "eh," "at Deboragu," "eh," "I saw Old /"Xashe." "You saw Old /"Xashe," "eh, eh." "He said that he had seen the great python under the bank." "EH!" "The python!" "He wants us," "eh, eh, eh," "to help him catch it." The "ehs" overlap and coincide with the phrase, and the people so often all talk at once that one wonders how anyone knows what the speaker has said.

Bursts of laughter accompany the conversations. Sometimes the !Kung laugh mildly with what we would call a sense of humor about people and events; often they shriek and howl as though laughter were an outlet for tension. They laugh at mishaps that happen to other people, like the lions eating up someone else's meat, and shriek over particularly telling and insulting sexual sallies in the joking relationships. Individual singing of lyrical songs accompanied by the //gwashi (pluriarc), snatches of ritual music, the playing of rhythmical games, or the ritual curing dances occupy the evenings as well, but mostly the evening hours are spent in talk.

As far as we know, only two general subjects are avoided in conversation. Men and women do not discuss sexual matters openly together except as they make jokes in the joking relationship. The !Kung avoid speaking the names of the gods aloud and do not converse about the gods for fear of attracting their attention and perhaps their displeasure.

A talk differs from a conversation or an arranged, purposeful discussion. It flares spontaneously, I believe from stress, when something is going on in which people are seriously concerned and in disagreement. I think that no formalities regulate it. Anyone who has something he wants to say joins in. People take sides and express opinions, accusing and denying, or defending persons involved. I witnessed one such talk only, in 1952. It occurred over a gift-giving episode at the time of N!ai's betrothal and involved persons in Bands 1 and 2 who were settled near together at the time. Hwan//ka, the mother of /"Xontah, N!ai's betrothed, had diverted a gift—a knife—that people thought was making its way to K"xau, the present husband of N!ai's mother. Instead of giving it to him at the time when an exchange of gifts was in order, she gave it to one of her relatives. N!ai's mother's sister, !'Ku, sitting at her own fire, began the talk. She let it be known what she thought of Hwan//ka, in a loud voice, a startling contrast to the usual low flow of talk. /Ti!kai, N'ai's mother, sitting with her shoulder pressed against her sister's, joined in. People went to sit at each other's fires, forming little groups who agreed and supported each other. From where they sat, but not all at once and not in an excited babble, they made their remarks clearly, with quite long pauses between. Some expressed themselves in agreement with !'Ku as she recounted Hwan//ka's faults and deviations, past and present. Hwan//ka's family and friends, who had moved to sit near her, denied the accusations from time to time, but did not talk as much or as loudly as !'Ku. Hwan//ka muttered or was silent. !'Ku said she disapproved of her sister's daughter marrying the son of such a woman but would reconsider her position if Hwan//ka gave the expected gift to K"xau. The talk lasted about twenty minutes. At that point Hwan//ka got up and walked away, and the talk subsided to !'Ku's mutterings and others' low conversation. In a few days Hwan//ka gave K"xau a present, not the gift in question, but one which satisfied K"xau, and, as they said, "they all started again in peace."

There is a third form of verbal expression which might be called a "shout" rather than a "talk," but as far as I know the !Kung have no special name for it. It is a verbal explosion. Fate receives the heat of the remarks in a "shout."

We were present on two such occasions, one in 1952, the other in 1953. Both occurred in response to the burning of shelters. In both instances little children, whose mothers had taken their eyes off them for a few minutes, had picked up burning sticks from the fire, had dropped them on the soft, dry, bedding grass in the shelters, and, at the first burst of flame, had sensibly run outside unscathed. On the first occasion, the two children, who were about three years old, were frightened and were soothed and comforted by their mothers and other relatives. They were not scolded. On the second occasion, Hwan//ka, the two-year-old granddaughter of Old ≠Toma and /Tɔm, had set fire to her grandparents' shelter. She was not apparently frightened at all and was found placidly chewing her grandfather's well-toasted sandal. She was not scolded either.

What was especially interesting was the behavior of the people. On both occasions they rushed to the burning shelters, emitting all at once, in extremely loud, excited voices, volcanic eruptions of words. The men made most of the noise, but the women were also talking excitedly. No one tried to do anything, nor could they, for the grass shelters burned like the fiery furnace. I asked the interpreters to stand close to one person at a time and try to hear what he said. People were telling where they had been when the fire started, why they had not got there sooner. They shouted that mothers should not take their eyes off their children, that the children might have been burned. They lamented the objects which had been destroyed—all in the greatest din I have ever heard humans produce out of themselves. It went on for about eight or ten minutes in bursts, then tapered off for another ten. While Old ≠Toma's shelter was burning, he and his wife, /Tɔm, the great maker of beads, sat on one side weeping. After the shouting had subsided, a dozen or more people set about looking for Old ≠Toma's knife blade and arrow points and picking up what beads they could find for /Tɔm in the cooling ashes. The two instances of "shouts" provided examples of the vehemence which vocal expression can have and vividly illustrated the !Kung way of venting emotion in words.

There is still another kind of talk, not conversation, that I consider to be an outlet for tension and anxiety. We happened to hear it only in relation to anxiety about food and do not know if other concerns sometimes find expression in this way. It occurs in varying degrees of intensity. It is a repeating of something over and over and over again. For instance, whether it is actually so or not, someone may be reiterating that he has no food or that no one has given him food. The remarks are made in the presence of other individuals, but the other individuals do not respond in the manner of a discussion or conversation. In an extreme instance we saw a woman visitor go into a sort of trance and say over and over for perhaps half an hour or so in ≠Toma's presence that he had not given her as much meat as was her due. It was not said like an accusation. It was said as though he were not there. I had the eerie feeling that I was present in someone else's dream. ≠Toma did not argue or oppose her. He continued doing whatever he was doing and let her go on.

All these ways of talking, I believe, aid the !Kung in maintaining their peaceful social relations. Getting things out in words keeps everyone in touch with what others are thinking and feeling, releases tensions, and prevents pressures from building up until they burst out in aggressive acts.

Aspects of Good Manners

In !Kung society good manners require that, when !Kung meet other !Kung who are strangers, all the men should lay down their weapons and approach each other unarmed. The first time ≠Toma approached us, he paused about thirty or forty feet away from us, laid down his bow, arrows, and assegai (spear) on the ground, and walked toward us unarmed. After we were accepted and given !Kung names, we were no longer strangers and we never observed the practice again.

Good manners require that visitors be received courteously and asked to sit by the fire. The woman whose fire it is may welcome the visitor by taking a pinch of the sweet smelling *sā* powder, which she carries in a little tortoise shell hung from her neck, and sprinkling it on the visitor's head in a line from the top of the head to the forehead.

Good manners in eating express restraint. A person does not reveal eagerness or take more than a modest share. When a visitor comes to the fire of a family which is preparing food or eating, he should sit at a little distance, not to seem importunate, and wait to be asked to share. On several occasions we gave small gifts of corned beef to be shared with a group. The person who received the food from us would take only a mouthful. Once an old man who received the meat first only licked his fingers. The lump of food would be passed from one to another. Each would take a modest bite. The last person often got the most. I found it moving to see so much restraint about taking food among people who are all thin and often hungry, for whom food is a source of constant anxiety. We observed no unmannerly behavior and no cheating and no encroachment about food. Although informants said that quarrels had occurred occasionally in the past between members of a band over the time to go to gather certain plant foods, and although we observed expressions of dissatisfaction, no quarrels of any kind arose over food during our observations.

The polite way to receive food, or any gift, is to hold out both hands and have the food or other gift placed in them. To reach out with one hand suggests grabbing to the !Kung. Food may be placed also in front of the person who is to receive it.

Good manners in general should be inoffensive. Any behavior which is likely to stir up trouble is regarded with apprehension and disapproval by the !Kung. In view of this, the joking relationship has its interesting side. Men and women who have the joking relationship insult each other in a facetious way and also point out actual faults or remark on actual episodes which embarrass a person. Everyone joins in the uproarious, derisive laughter. All this is joking and one should not take offense. The !Kung say this teaches young persons to keep their tempers.

In contrast to the joking is their care in other aspects of conduct to avoid giving offense. ≠Toma said, for instance, that if he were forming a hunting party and a man whom he did not want asked to join him, he would be careful to refuse indirectly by making some excuse and would try not to offend the man.

Gossip which can stir up trouble is discouraged. People do gossip but usually discreetly, in low voices, with near and trusted relatives and friends. It is best to mind one's own business, they say.

People are expected to control their tempers, and they do so to a remarkable degree. If they are angry, aggrieved, or frustrated, they tend to mope rather than to become aggressive, expressing their feelings in low mutters to their close relatives and friends. ≠Toma told us that he had lost his temper twice when he was a young man and on one occasion had knocked his father down. On the other he had pushed his wife into hot ashes. It had so frightened him to realize that he could lose control of himself and behave in this violent way that, he said, he had not lost his temper since.

Meat-sharing

The !Kung custom of sharing meat helps to keep stress and hostility over food at a low intensity. The practical value of using up the meat when it is fresh is obvious to all, and the !Kung are fully aware of the enormous social value of the sharing custom. The fear of hunger is mitigated: the person with whom one shares will share in turn when he gets meat; people are sustained by a web of mutual obligation. If there is hunger, it is commonly shared. There are no distinct haves and have-nots. One is not alone.

To have a concept of the potential stress and jealousy that meat-sharing mitigates in !Kung society, one has only to imagine one family eating meat and others not, when they are settled only ten or fifteen feet apart in a firelit encampment, and there are no walls for privacy. The desert does not hide secret killing and eating because actions are printed in its sands for all to read. The idea of eating alone and not sharing is shocking to the !Kung. It makes them shriek with an uneasy laughter. Lions could do that, they say, not men.

Small animals, the size of duikers or smaller, and birds belong to the man who shoots or snares them. Tortoises, lizards, grasshoppers, and snakes are picked up incidentally and belong to the person who picks them up. That person may share his find only with his or her immediate family or with others as he or she chooses, in the way plant foods are shared. ≠Toma says that if he has only a small creature, he and his family eat a meal and give a little to anyone who happens to be nearby at the time.

The custom of meat-sharing applies to the big animals which are deliberately hunted by hunting parties. In the Nyae Nyae area they were eland, kudu, gemsbok, wildebeest, hartebeest, springbok, warthog, and ostrich. Buffalo were found less commonly. The Nyae Nyae hunters sometimes managed to shoot the wary giraffe but only occasionally. All the above-mentioned animals weigh hundreds of pounds; a large bull eland may weigh a ton. It is the meat of these animals that is distributed according to custom and is shared by all present in the encampment.

The composition of the hunting party is not a matter of strict convention or of anxious concern. Whoever the hunters are, the meat is shared and everyone profits. The men are free to organize their hunting parties as they like. No categories of consanguineous kin or affines are prohibited from hunting together, whether or not they have the joking relationship or practice the sitting and speaking avoidances. Men from different bands may hunt together.

A father has authority over his sons and sons-in-law and could ask them to go hunting or to accompany him and would expect them to obey. Otherwise, participation in a hunting party is voluntary. Any man may instigate a hunt and may ask others to join. No one is formally in command of a party unless he is the father with his sons or sons-in-law, but often an informal kind of leadership develops out of skill and judgment. The men fall in with the plans and suggestions of the best hunter or reach agreement among themselves somehow.

Hunting parties are usually composed of from two to four or five men. One hunter alone would be at a disadvantage in many ways. Ordinarily, the !Kung do not form large parties. Small parties hunting in different directions have much more chance of finding game than one large single party has.

When the kill is made, the hunters have the prerogative of eating the liver on the spot and may eat more of the meat until their hunger is satisfied. If they are far from the band, they may eat the parts that are especially perishable or most awkward to carry, like the head, and they sometimes eat the cherished marrow. They then carry the animal to the band in its parts, bones and all, or, if the animal is very big, they leave most of the bones and cut the meat into strips. The strips dry to biltong quickly and thus are preserved before they decay, and they can be hung on carrying-sticks[2] and transported more easily than big chunks. The blood is carried in bags made of the stomach or bladder.

The gall bladder and testicles are discarded at the kill. Eventually the picked bones and horns are thrown away. (The !Kung make only a few artifacts of bone and horn; the artifacts last a long time and seldom need replacing.) Sinews are kept for making cord. The hide would be skinned off whole and tanned, if it were suitable for a kaross and someone wanted a new kaross at the time. Otherwise, the hide is dried, pounded up, and eaten. Hides are actually quite tasty. Feet are picked of every tissue; gristle is dried and pounded. Soft parts, such as the fetus, udder, heart, lungs, brains, and blood, are often given to old people with poor teeth. Intestines are enjoyed and desired by all. The meat of the rump, back, chest, and neck is highly appreciated. Nothing is wasted; all is distributed.

The owner of the animal is the owner of the first arrow to be effectively shot into the animal so that it penetrates enough for its poison to work. That person is responsible for the distribution. The owner may or may not be one of the hunters.

Hunters have arrows which they acquire in three different ways. Each man makes arrows for himself, shaping the points (usually now of metal, but still possibly of bone or wood) with some slight distinction so that he will know them from the arrows of other men. Secondly, arrows are given as gifts. The man, who made the arrow or had himself acquired it as a gift, may give it to someone else, either a man or a woman, consanguineous kin, affine, or friend. Thirdly, people lend arrows to one another. The status of the arrow plays its part in the distribution of the animal killed with it. There is much giving and lending of arrows. The society seems to want to extinguish in every way possible the concept of the meat belonging to the hunter.

A hunter chooses which arrow he will use. The owner of the arrow—who ipso facto owns the animal—may therefore be the hunter himself, who has chosen to use an arrow he made or one that was given him, or he may be a person who lent the arrow to the hunter.

There may be several hunters in the hunting party and several arrows in the animal, but this seems to cause no confusion or conflict. Every arrow is known, of course. The hunters see which first penetrates effectively so that its poison could account for the kill. But I think that often it is arranged beforehand who will own the animal. A man asking another to accompany him might say, "Come and help me get a buck." Or "Old Gau lent me an arrow and asked me to hunt for him. You come too."

I think there is little or no dissension as to who owned the animal because it is not a cause for great stress; each hunter gets a share of the meat anyway. I think also that a man wants sometimes to be the owner of the meat in order to start the distribution off in the direction of his own relatives, but that one is also content sometimes not to have the onus of the main distribution.

If the animal is large, the hunters cut it up at the kill. If the whole animal is to be cut up in the encampment, any of the men may participate in the butchering. They cut the animal in a customary way each time—all know how to do it, all are skilled. If the owner of the animal is a man, he would probably work at butchering himself; and the hunters would probably help, but not necessarily so. Others might do this work. Women do not participate in butchering an animal, and we did not see any assist in carrying the meat around in the distribution even though we saw women carry meat at other times.

The first distribution the owner makes is to the hunters and to the giver of the arrow, if the arrow was not one the owner made himself. The meat, always uncooked in the first distribution, is given on the bone unless the animal is so large that the meat has been cut into strips at the kill.

In a second distribution, the several persons who got meat in the first distribution cut up their shares and distribute them further. This meat also is given uncooked. The amounts depend on the number of persons involved, but should be as much as the giver can manage. In the second distribution, close kinship is the factor that sets the pattern of the giving. Certain obligations are compulsory. A man's first obligation at this point, we were told, is to give to his wife's parents. He must give to them the best he has in as generous portions as he can, while still fulfilling other primary obligations, which are to his own parents, his spouse, and his offspring. He keeps a portion for himself at this time and from it gives to his siblings, to his wife's siblings if they are present, and to other relatives and friends who are there; possibly he gives only in small quantities by then.

Everyone who receives meat gives again, in another wave of sharing, to his or her parents, parents-in-law, spouse, offspring, siblings, and others. The meat may be cooked and the quantities small.

Visitors, even though they are not close relatives, are given meat by the people whom they are visiting. This social rule is strongly felt. Visitors may receive small quantities of cooked meat, which is like being asked to dinner.

Name-relatives often receive generous portions of meat because they have the same name as the giver or because their names associate them with his close kin, but this seems to be more a favor than an absolute rule. ≠Toma said there were far too many men named ≠Toma for him to give them special consideration.

The result of the distribution is that everybody gets some meat.

In the later waves of sharing, when the primary distribution and primary kinship obligations have been fulfilled, the giving of meat from one's own portion has the quality of gift-giving. !Kung society requires at this point only that a person should give with reasonable generosity in proportion to what he has received and not keep more than an equitable amount for himself. Then the person who has received a gift of meat must give a reciprocal gift some time in the future. Band affiliation imposes no pattern on this giving. Except that the hunters are customarily given a forequarter or a hindquarter, no rule prescribes that any particular part of the animal must be given to any particular person or to any category of kin or affine. People give different parts of the meat and different amounts, this time to some, next time to others, more generously or less generously according to their own reasons. We are certain that the motives are the same as in gift-giving in general: to measure up to what is expected of them, to make friendly gestures, to win favor, to repay past favors and obligations, and to enmesh others in future obligation. I am sure that when feelings of genuine generosity and real friendliness exist, they would also be expressed by giving.

The distribution of an eland which was killed by K'xau Beard of Band 2 will serve as an example of the way meat was shared on one occasion. (On every occasion, the amounts given and the parts given would differ, and the first recipients would vary.) More than a hundred !Kung were present at Gausha at the time of the hunt. Both /Gausha bands (Bands 1 and 2) were present. Bands 3, 4, and 7 and a sprinkling of people from other bands were visiting.

The hunting party was composed of four men: K''xau Beard, with //Kau, his first wife's brother, and /Twi, his own brother, both of whom lived with him in Band 2. N!aishe, his brother-in-law, who was visiting at the time, joined the party.

The party had hunted for eight days without success in heat so exhausting that they had to lie covered with sand through the middle part of the day.

/Twi was the first to see the eland. It was a huge one. As /Twi had been asked by his brother to come and help on the hunt, he told his brother where the eland was and did not shoot at it himself.

Two boys joined the men to track the eland after it was shot. The party tracked it for three days and then found it dead from the poison. They cut up the meat and brought it to the encampment at /Gausha, which was two days' travel away. The hunt had lasted thirteen days in all.

K"xau Beard was himself the owner of the arrow. The arrow had been given by one person to another five times. /Gau Music of Band 1, who had made it, gave it to his sister, /"Xoishe, who gave it to her husband, ≠Gau of Band 3. He gave it to his brother, K"xau, also of Band 3, who gave it to his wife , /Ti!kai. /Ti!kai gave it to K"xau Beard, her brother, who shot the eland with it and who was responsible for the distribution of the meat.

K"xau Beard first gave meat to the hunters who helped him, as was the custom. To N!aishe he gave a forequarter and to //Kau a forequarter and the head. (The hunters usually received a forequarter or hindquarter or an equivalent amount. The head was an extra gift.) The two boys who helped track got nothing because their fathers would give them some, we were told. To our astonishment, /Twi was given nothing. K"xau Beard explained that his brother would eat from his pot. (Actually he might eat more in this way as he would not have to share the cooked meat with anyone but his wife and child.)

K"xau Beard's sister, /Ti!kai, who had given him the arrow, received the meat of the back and throat and the intestines.

K"xau Beard kept the meat of the neck for himself. Continuing the distribution, he gave the rest of the meat as follows:

To his first wife, //Kushe, he gave both hindquarters, the meat of the chest, the lungs, part of the liver, and one hind foot. To his mother he gave the meat of the belly and one hind foot. To his sister, //Kushe, and to /Tasa, the wife of his brother, /Twi, he gave one front foot each.

The amount given to his first wife was enormous. In addition to giving to her co-wife, also named //Kushe, and to her children and her co-wife's children, she gave a large portion of meat to her parents, who lived with them in Band 2. (On other occasions the man had given directly to his wife's parents—not through his wife.) When the meat was cut up, //Kushe gave to her father, Old ≠Toma, four bundles of strips of boneless raw meat (it was somewhat dried by then). There were about ten or twelve strips to a bundle, about 76 cm to 92 cm long. We guessed the weight of this gift to be about 27 to 32 kg. She gave meat also to her two younger brothers, /Gau and /"Xontah. (Her other brother, //Kau who had been one of the hunters, had got his share from K"xau Beard.) She gave to her co-wife's father, ≠Gau of Band 4, and to old /"Xashe of Band 4, her co-wife's MoFa. She then gave to six other persons, all in Band 1. They were: her cousin, Old Gau (her FaSiSo); his two daughters; two other cousins (FaSiDas), /Ti!kai and !'Ku; and !'Ku's husband, ≠Toma.

The giving of raw meat went on. Old ≠Toma gave to eighteen people: his wife; six affines; three consanguineous kin; two name-relatives (that is, a visitor whose father's name was ≠Toma, and Old /Gasa, whose deceased husband's name was ≠Toma); and six other persons. Telling us the reasons for giving to the last six, whose consanguineous or affinal connections (if any) with Old ≠Toma were so remote we did not bother to trace them, he said of one, "He is an old man whom I like in my heart," and of another, "He was hungry for meat." In the end Old ≠Toma gave some of the meat back to his daughter, //Kushe.

/Ti!kai of Band 3, the giver of the arrow, gave raw meat to six persons: her husband's mother; his brother and his two sisters (all in Band 2); a visitor who was her HuSiHuBr; and her mother's brother in the visiting Band 7.

Persons who had by this time received substantial amounts of raw meat began giving to others. We recorded sixty-three gifts of raw meat. Doubtless there were more. After the raw meat was given, individuals shared their portions, cooked or raw, with parents, offspring, spouses, and others.

Meat is not habitually cooked and eaten as a family meal among the !Kung. When an individual receives a portion of meat, he owns it outright for himself. He may give and share it further as he wishes, but it never becomes family or group property. The men, women, and children may cook their pieces when and as they wish, often roasting bits in the coals and hot ashes and eating them alone at odd times. Or someone may start a big pot boiling, and several people will bring their pieces to put into it at the same time, each taking his own piece out when it is cooked.

The sense of possessing one's own piece personally is, I believe, very important to the !Kung. It gives one the responsibility of choosing when to eat one's meat and struggling with hunger as best one can when it is finished, without occasion or excuse for blaming others for eating more than their share.

It has often been reported that when San have plenty of meat, they gorge themselves until they can hardly walk. We have seen the Nyae Nyae !Kung eat hearty meals of meat when they have been long without, but nothing more than we considered a normal amount. They hang meat in the bushes to dry and can keep it for some time. It is not uncommon for them to eat quite sparingly and save bits for a coming journey or against a future day of hunger.

The !Kung are quite conscious of the value of meat-sharing and they talk about it, especially about the benefit of the mutual obligation it entails. The idea of sharing is deeply implanted and very successfully imposes its restraints. To keep meat without sharing is one of the things that just is not done.

Gift-giving

The custom of gift-giving, in my opinion, comes second only to meat-sharing in aiding the !Kung to avoid jealousy and ill will and to develop friendly relations. !Kung society puts considerable emphasis on gift-giving. Almost everything a person has may have been given to him and may be passed on to others in time. The !Kung make their artifacts, on the whole, of durable material and take good care of them. The objects may last for generations, moving in a slow current among the people. The dealings in gift-giving are only between individuals, but they are numerous and provide occasion, perhaps more than any one other activity does, for visits which bring groups of people together.

We gave cowrie shells as parting gifts in 1951 to the women in Band 1, the band which first sponsored us and with which we stayed on each expedition wherever they were. When providing ourselves with gifts for the !Kung on our first expedition, we had had to guess as best we could what would appeal to them. The idea of cowrie shells came from seeing in museums so many West African objects encrusted with the shells. We thought the !Kung might like them as a novelty and bought a supply from a New York shell dealer. They came from the Pacific, and we amused ourselves imagining future archaeologists finding them in !Kung sites in the Kalahari, to their bewilderment. We carefully observed that there were no cowrie shells among the !Kung ornaments before we gave them. We gave to each woman enough for a short necklace, one large brown shell and twenty smaller gray ones. In 1952, there was hardly a cowrie shell to be found in Band 1. They had been given to relatives and friends, and they appeared not as whole necklaces but in ones and twos in people's ornaments to the edges of the area.

The !Kung have not developed special objects to use as gifts. Nor have they invested ordinary objects with special gift significance. What they give each other are the common artifacts and materials of everyday life. However, among those, some are more highly valued than others, as one would expect. I gathered that relative scarcity of material was a factor and that objects were appreciated for their beauty, workmanship, and appropriate size (a wide headband is better than a narrow one). People took an interest in remembering to whom an object had been given in the recent past, but the !Kung, who are present-oriented, do not place special value upon antiquity as such or systematically hold the distant past in mind.

The !Kung decorate their artifacts very little. (They have developed music and dancing but not the plastic or pictorial arts.) However, they delight in ornaments with which to adorn themselves. The most highly valued are the traditional ornaments of ostrich-eggshell beads, especially the wide headbands and the necklaces of five or six strings of beads that reach to the navel—the measurement of a good necklace. The creamy white of the shells is particularly becoming to the yellow-brown skin of the !Kung and is a relief from the monotonous gray-brown of the karosses that the women wear. The !Kung also like ornaments made with European beads of all colors, though white is preferred. They like all beads, any beads, we were told; K"xau Beard said that the only thing they do not like about beads is scarcity of them.

They value artifacts that take time and care to make: the musical instrument (pluriarc) called //gwashi; a well-shaped wooden bowl; a long string of dance rattles. They also value metal implements and pots; these they obtain by trade.

The !Kung do not trade among themselves. They consider the procedure undignified and avoid it because it is too likely to stir up bad feelings. They trade with the Bantu, however, in the border country settlements of western Botswana. The !Kung offer well-tanned antelope hides and ostrich-eggshell beads. For these they obtain tobacco; beads; knives; axes; malleable metal for making arrowpoints and assegai blades; and occasional files and chisels, fire-strikers, and pots.

The odds are with the Bantu in the trading. Big, aggressive, and determined to have what they want, they easily intimidate the !Kung. Several !Kung informants said that they tried not to trade with Herero if it was possible to avoid it because, although the Tawana were hard bargainers, the Herero were worse. /Twi of Band 1, a mild man, said he had been forced by a Herero, one whom he was afraid to anger, to trade the shirt and pants we had given him as a parting gift in 1952 for a small enamel pan and a little cup. /Ti!kai had more gumption. A Herero at the beginning of a negotiation with him brought out a good-sized pile of tobacco but took from it only a pinch when it was time to pay. /Ti!kai picked up the object he was trading and ran off. ≠Toma said with amused exaggeration that "a very good Herero, a respectable one, will give a handful of tobacco for five cured steinbok skins. A bad Herero will give a pipeful" (he showed the size of his fingernail) "for three skins." The Tawana values are a little better. A well-tanned gemsbok hide brings a pile of tobacco about 36 cm in diameter and about 10 cm high. The values vary. Some that were reported to us were three duiker or steinbok skins for a good-sized knife, five strings of ostrich-eggshell beads for an assegai.

The !Kung have become dependent on metal, especially knives, axes, and arrowpoints. They have been able to trade enough for every man to have these implements. They could, however, exist without them and do still use a few bone and wood arrowpoints, as it is poison, not penetrating power, that makes their arrows deadly. The pots are Ovambo or Okavango pottery (the !Kung make no pottery themselves) or European ironware. The !Kung like to have a pot around to borrow sometimes; not everyone wants to carry one. They cook mostly in hot ashes. More for their novelty, I thought, than for their worth, the !Kung trade also for old oddments of cloth garments (they weave neither cloth nor mats), pieces of blankets, basins, and so forth—things they do not really need but like to have.

Tobacco they need "to make the heart feel better." Oddly enough for these passionate smokers, tobacco is not given as much emphasis in gift-giving as one might expect. They do make gifts of tobacco, but when anyone lights a pipe he passes it around anyway; all present drag smoke into their lungs until they almost faint, and it does not seem to matter much who owned the tobacco.

Eland fat is a very highly valued gift. An eland provides so much fat that people can afford to be a little luxurious. They rub it on themselves and on their implements, and they eat it. ≠Toma said that when he had eland fat to give, he took shrewd note of certain objects he might like to have and gave their owners especially generous gifts of fat.

Real property and the resources of plant foods and waterholes are not owned by individuals and cannot be given away. However, meat, once it is distributed after the hunt, and plant foods, once they are gathered, become private property and may be given. Artifacts are privately owned by the individual man, woman, or child, as outrightly owned if received as a gift as if made by the individual. The !Kung borrow and lend a great deal—in itself this is one of the ways they support each other and aid themselves in maintaining social solidarity—but this does not blur the clarity of ownership. Each object acquires some markings of its own from the maker and from usage. It is easy for the !Kung, with their highly developed powers of observation and visual memory, to keep track of the commonest objects, know the ownership, and remember the history of the gifts.

As far as we know, no rules of avoidance govern the objects given to any category of person. For instance, although women, especially when menstruating, should not touch hunting weapons lest the hunter's powers be weakened, they may own arrows that are given to them.

The gifts vary in quantity. One which /Ti!kai gave to ≠Toma was considered generous. It was a fine ostrich-eggshell headband, three ostrich eggshells, and a well-tanned duiker skin as soft as suede. Another generous gift consisted of a knife, an assegai, and a triple string of traded white European beads. Often gifts were less. The feelings persons have for each other, the degree of their past indebtedness, what they happen to possess and can give determine the generosity of the gift.

The acquisition, per se, of the objects is seldom, I believe, of primary importance to most individuals in gift-giving—that is, if the objects are their own artifacts. As the !Kung come into more contact with Europeans—and this is already happening—they will feel sharply the lack of our things and will need and want more. It makes them feel inferior to be without clothes when they stand among strangers who are clothed. But in their own life and with their own artifacts, they are comparatively free from both material want and pressures to acquire. Except for food and water (important exceptions!), with which the Nyae Nyae !Kung are in balance, but I believe barely so, they all had what they needed, or they could make what they needed. Every man can and does make the things that men make, and every woman the things that women make. No one was dependent upon acquiring objects by gift-giving.

The !Kung live in a kind of material plenty because they have adapted the tools of their living to materials which lie in abundance around them and are free for anyone to take (wood, reeds, bone for weapons and implements; fibers for cordage; grass for shelters), or to materials which are at least sufficient in quantity to satisfy the needs of the population. The Nyae Nyae !Kung have hides enough for garments and bags; they keep extra hides for when they need them for new garments or when they want them for trade; otherwise they eat them. The !Kung can always use more ostrich eggshells for beads to wear or trade, but enough are found, at least, for every woman to have eight or ten shells for water-containers—all she can carry—and a goodly number of bead ornaments.

In their nomadic hunting-gathering life, traveling from one source of food to another through the seasons, always going back and forth between food and water, they carry their young children and all their belongings. With plenty of most materials at hand to replace artifacts as required, the !Kung have not needed or wanted to encumber themselves with duplicates or surpluses. They do not even want to carry one of everything. They borrow what they do not own. I believe for these reasons they have not developed permanent storage, have not hoarded, and the accumulation of objects has not become associated with admirable status. Instead of keeping things, they use them as gifts to express generosity and friendly intent, and to put people under obligation to make return tokens of friendship. Even more specifically in my opinion, they mitigate jealousy and envy, to which the !Kung are prone, by passing on to others objects that might be coveted.

Except, as ≠Toma said, that it would be surprising to see a man give a present to a woman who was not related to him (and vice versa I imagine), anyone may give to anyone. Degree or kind of consanguinity or affinity, having the joking relationship or lacking it, impose no requirements or restrictions. We did hear people say, however, that the *k'xau n!a* of a band may feel that he should lean well to the generous side in his giving, for this position focuses a little extra attention on him, and he wants whatever attention he attracts not to be envious. Someone remarked that this could keep such a man poor.

The times of giving are determined almost entirely by the individual's convenience. The !Kung do not know their birthdays or anniversaries and have no special days of the year which they mark by giving gifts. Gifts are required by convention on only three ritual occasions. The type or quantity of the gift is not patterned, but the gift should be generous. The occasions are (1) betrothals and (2) weddings, when the parents exchange gifts and give to the young couple, and (3) the ritual of a baby's first haircut, when the *!ku n!a,* the person for whom the baby is named, should give him a fine present.

Relatives give to young people with the idea of setting them up in life. K"xau Beard gave an assegai and a kaross to his FaSiSo, saying it was his duty to see that the boy got some things because among the boy's relatives he was the most able to do so. The boy's father was very old, he explained, and did not have many possessions. People expect to wait a long time for young people to make return gifts.

The two rigid requirements in gift-giving are that one must not refuse a proffered gift and that one must give in return. Demi said that even if he might prefer not to be obligated to someone, he would accept and prepare to make his return gift. If a gift were to be refused, he continued, the giver would be terribly angry. He would say, "Something is very wrong here." This could involve whole groups in tensions, bad words, taking sides—even a talk might occur—just what the !Kung do not want. Demi said it does not happen: a !Kung never refuses a gift. (I thought of our Christmas giving and how one would feel if one's Christmas gift were refused.) And a !Kung does not fail to give in return. ≠Toma said that would be "neglecting friendship." A person would know that others thought him "far-hearted" and "this would worry him."

In reciprocating, one does not give the same object back again but something of comparable value. The interval of time between receiving and reciprocating varies from a few weeks to a few years. Propriety requires that there be no unseemly haste. The giving must not look like trading.

Incidentally, we were not included by the !Kung in their gift-giving patterns. They gave us a few things spontaneously which they thought we would enjoy—python meat for instance—but did not feel obligated to reciprocate for every gift we gave them.

Asking for a first-time gift or asking that a return gift be made after due time has elapsed is within the rules of propriety. People prefer that others give in return without being asked, but ≠Toma says he does not hesitate to ask if a gift is long overdue. If a person wants a particular object, he may ask for it. Asking is also a means by which people play upon each other's feelings. One can test a friendship in this way. One can give vent to jealousy or satisfy it by acquiring some object. And one can make someone else uncomfortable. I thought that /Ti!kai (an intelligent man, but very touchy, self-centered, and—with us—uncooperative) used to ask for gifts in order to play with anger, arousing it for the sake of feeling it, as children do with fear, playing witches in the dark. His remarks one day indicated a mingling of feelings and purposes. He told us that one may ask for anything. He did, he said. He would go to a person's fire and sit and ask. (I could imagine him with his black, glancing eyes, sitting and asking!) He would ask usually for only one or two things, but if a person had a lot, he might ask for more. He said he was almost never refused. However, if a man had only one pot and /Ti!kai asked for it, the man might say, "I am not refusing but it is the only pot I have. If I get another, you may come for this one. I am very sorry but this is the only pot I have." /Ti!kai said this would not make him angry unless he were refused too many times. To be refused too many times would make a person very angry. But, said /Ti!kai, he himself did not tire of people asking him for gifts. Asking, he claimed, "formed a love" between people. It meant "he still loves me, that is why he is asking." At least it formed a communication of some sort between people, I thought.

I have stressed the mitigation of envy and jealousy as the important value of gift-giving. !Kung informants stressed more the value of making a friendly gesture even if it is only a token gesture. It puts people under the obligation of making a friendly gesture in return. People are quite conscious of this and speak about it. Demi said, "The worst thing is not giving gifts. If people do not like each other, but one gives a gift, and the other must accept; this brings a peace between them. We give to one another always. We give what we have. This is the way we live together."

Absence of Stealing

One day, when I wanted to talk with a group of informants about what the !Kung considered to be a wrongdoing, I began with /Ti!kai. He said promptly, "Making crooked arrows and fighting," but could not think of anything else that was a wrongdoing. Informants had previously said that not sharing food would be the worst thing they could think of. Others had mentioned that the breaking of the incest and menstruation prohibitions would be very wrong, and that girls should not sit in immodest postures. No one seemed to think lying was very serious wrongdoing, and no one mentioned stealing. I finally asked directly and K"xau replied meditatively they had not thought to mention stealing because they did not steal.

We had heard of a man who took honey from a tree, honey which had been found and marked and was therefore owned by someone else. He was killed for it by the furious owner. That was the only episode of stealing that we discovered.

The !Kung stole nothing from us. Even when we went away on trips leaving several bands of !Kung settled around our camp site, we left our supplies and equipment unlocked, in the open or in our tents, with confidence that nothing would be stolen. Things that we lost or forgot in the !Kung encampment were returned to us, even two cigarettes in a crumpled package.

Stealing without being discovered is practically impossible in !Kung life because the !Kung know everybody's footprints and every object. Respect for ownership is strong. But, apart from that, /Ti!kai said, "Stealing would cause nothing but trouble. It might cause fighting."

Conclusion

During seventeen and a half months of field work with the Nyae Nyae !Kung (with Bands 1 and 2 and many visitors, usually about sixty to seventy-five persons), I personally saw only four flare-ups of discord and heard about three others which occurred in neighboring bands during that period. All were resolved before they became serious quarrels. Of the seven, four were flare-ups of sexual jealousy. Another was the talk about Hwan//ka's gift. Two were minor disagreements about going somewhere. On one occasion, K"xau Beard coerced his young second wife into going with him when she wanted to stay visiting her parents. He coerced her swiftly and decisively by snatching her baby from her arms and walking off with him. In a flash the wife ran a few steps and hit him on the head with her digging stick, then she went around in a circle, stamping her feet in great, high stamps like an enraged samurai in a Japanese print, then she followed her husband. On another occasion, /Ti!kai gave his brother a shove for refusing to accompany him. None of the conflicts concerned food.

On a later expedition, in another year, John Marshall witnessed three serious quarrels.[3] Anger flared more hotly than in the episodes I saw. One of those quarrels was about food. It was a dispute about the possession of an animal that had been killed. Another was about a marital matter, another about the failure of a curer to come to cure a sick child when he was asked. All three quarrels were resolved by talks. Vehement talking it was, but it stopped short of physical fighting.

I consider that the incidence of quarrels is low among the !Kung, that they manage very well to avoid physical violence when tensions are high and anger flares, and that they also manage well to keep tension from reaching the point of breaking into open hostility. They avoid arousing envy, jealousy, and ill will; and, to a notable extent, they cohere and achieve the comfort and security which they so desire in human relations.

NOTES

1. This chapter was originally published in *Africa* 31:3 (July 1961), 231–249. It is republished here with the kind permission of the International African Institute. The second paragraph of the essay is partially rewritten for greater clarity. The sentence marked with this note is especially changed. It formally read: "Moreover, in this society the ownership of resources of food and water is organized through the headmen of bands and individuals have rights to these resources by being members of a band connected to the headman by some near or remote kin or affinal bond." I feel that the statement needs explanation, especially the word headman. However, since this paragraph is not the place to explain it, I prefer to take the sentence out to make instead the more general statement that the ownership of resources is organized through the band structure, and to give brief explanation of the former sentence in this note. The head of a band is called k" xau n!a, "big owner." He does not own the resources personally or exclusively as !Kung own their artifacts. He symbolizes the ownership for the band and gives the ownership continuity.

2. Slabs of meat are cut into strips in the following manner: an incision is made across the slab from the edge, say the right edge, an inch or two down from the top of the slab; the incision is stopped shortly before it reaches the left edge. An inch or two below it another incision is begun, this time at the left edge; it is stopped shortly before it reaches the right edge; and so on. Held at the top, the slab cut in this way unfolds into a zigzag strip, about one to two inches wide.

3. This paragraph, mentioning the three additional quarrels that John Marshall witnessed and filmed, is an addition to the paper.

Egalitarian Societies

◆

James Woodburn

In a work published after his death, Malinowski made the splendidly forth-right declaration that 'authority is the very essence of social organisation' (1960:61). I am going to talk about a type of social organisation, not under-stood in Malinowski's day, in which individuals have no real authority over each other. This lecture is about certain societies in which there is the closest approximation to equality known in any human societies and about the basis for that equality. I have chosen to use the term 'egalitarian' to describe these societies of near-equals because the term directly suggests that the 'equality' that is present is not neutral, the mere absence of inequality or hierarchy, but is *asserted*. The term 'egality', from which 'egalitarian' is derived, was intro-duced into English with its present meaning in a poem by Tennyson in 1864 to suggest politically assertive equality of the French variety.[1] Even today 'egal-itarian' carries with it echoes of revolution, of fervour for equality in opposi-tion to elaborate structures of inequality. But politically assertive egalitari-anism is, of course, not found only in hierarchical systems under challenge and in their successor regimes. It is equally characteristic of many systems without direct experience of elaborate instituted hierarchy. Yet it may still seem surprising at first that equality should be asserted in certain very simply organised contemporary hunting and gathering societies which I am going to talk about, and in which, one might think, equality would simply be taken for granted.

In these societies equalities of power, equalities of wealth and equalities of prestige or rank are not merely sought but are, with certain limited exceptions, genuinely realised. But, the evidence suggests, they are never unchallenged. People are well aware of the possibility that individuals or groups within their own egalitarian societies may try to acquire more wealth, to assert more power

Malinowski Memorial Lecture for 1981, given at the London School of Economics and Political Science on May 5th. *Man* (N.S.) 17, 431–51. Reprinted with permission of the Royal Anthropological Institute of Great Britain and Ireland. Copyright © 1982 by the Royal Anthropological Institute.

or to claim more status than other people, and are vigilant in seeking to prevent or to limit this. The verbal rhetoric of equality may or may not be elaborated but actions speak loudly: equality is repeatedly acted out, publicly demonstrated, in opposition to possible inequality.

It is noteworthy that although very many societies are in some sense egalitarian, those in which inequalities are at their minimum depend on hunting and gathering for their subsistence. For reasons which I shall seek to explain, only the hunting and gathering way of life permits so great an emphasis on equality. But there is, of course, no question of the equality being a simple product of the hunting and gathering way of life. Many hunter-gatherers have social systems in which there is very marked inequality of one sort or another, sometimes far more marked than the inequalities in certain simple agricultural or nomadic pastoral societies.

In a number of recent papers (Woodburn 1978, 1979, 1980), I have sought to classify hunting and gathering societies—that is societies in which people obtain their food from wild products by hunting wild animals, by fishing and by gathering wild roots, fruits and the honey of wild bees[2]—into two major categories, those with immediate-return systems and those with delayed-return systems.

Immediate-return systems have the following basic characteristics. People obtain a direct and immediate return from their labour. They go out hunting or gathering and eat the food obtained the same day or casually over the days that follow. Food is neither elaborately processed nor stored. They use relatively simple, portable, utilitarian, easily acquired, replaceable tools and weapons made with real skill but not involving a great deal of labour.

Delayed-return systems, in contrast, have the following characteristics. People hold rights over valued assets of some sort, which either represent a yield, a return for labour applied over time or, if not, are held and managed in a way which resembles and has similar social implications to delayed yields on labour. In delayed-return hunting and gathering systems these assets are of four main types, which may occur separately but are more commonly found in combination with one another and are mutually reinforcing:

1. Valuable technical facilities used in production: boats, nets, artificial weirs, stockades, pit-traps, beehives and other such artefacts which are a product of considerable labour and from which a food yield is obtained gradually over a period of months or years.

2. Processed and stored food or materials usually in fixed dwellings.

3. Wild products which have themselves been improved or increased by human labour: wild herds which are culled selectively, wild food-producing plants which have been tended and so on.

4. Assets in the form of rights held by men over their female kin who are then bestowed in marriage on other men.

In principle all farming systems, unless based on wage or slave labour, must be delayed-return for those doing the work, since the yield on the labour put into crop-growing or herding domestic animals is only obtained months or years later. Of course in all delayed-return systems there is some immediate-return activity, but it is usually rather restricted and may be treated as low-status activity. Among hunting and gathering societies, the available information suggests that both immediate-return systems and delayed-return systems are common. Most are surprisingly easily classified into one or the other category, but there are some which cause difficulties, as is inevitable with any simple binary distinction.[3]

Delayed-return systems in all their variety (for almost all human societies are of this type) have basic implications for social relationships and social groupings: they depend for their effective operation on a set of ordered, differentiated, jurally-defined relationships through which crucial goods and services are transmitted. They imply binding commitments and dependencies between people. For an individual to secure the yield from his labour or to manage his assets, he depends on others. The farmer, for example, will almost invariably pool his labour with others—at least with a spouse and usually during the labour peaks of the agricultural cycle with several others—but, equally important, he depends on others for the protection of his growing crops, of his use rights to the land on which they are growing and of the yield when he obtains and stores it.[4] While it would, in principle, be possible to imagine situations in which individuals *on their own*, invested substantial amounts of labour over time *on their own*, protected the asset in which the labour was invested *on their own*, and then secured and managed the yields *on their own*, in practice this seems almost never to occur.

Until quite recently most anthropological research has been conducted in relatively small-scale, delayed-return, pastoral, agricultural and hunting and gathering societies and here we find the familiar kinship commitments and dependencies; lineages, clans and other kinship groups; marriages in which women are bestowed in marriage by men on other men; marriage alliances between groups. Immediate-return systems have only recently begun to be properly investigated and hence their social arrangements are still relatively unfamiliar. Societies which fall into this category include the Mbuti Pygmies of Zaire (Turnbull 1965; 1966); the !Kung Bushmen (San) of Botswana and Namibia (Lee 1979; Marshall 1976; Lee and DeVore 1976; Wiessner 1977); the Pandaram and Paliyan of south India (Morris 1975; Gardner 1980); the Batek Negritos of Malaysia (K. M. Endicott 1974, 1979; K. L. Endicott 1979) and the Hadza of Tanzania (Woodburn 1968a, 1968b, 1970, 1972) among whom my own fieldwork was conducted and about whom I can talk with most confidence.[5] Most of my illustrations will be drawn from material on the Hadza and the !Kung.

The characteristics of these immediate-return systems I have spelt out in some detail elsewhere. Here all I intend is an outline sufficient to provide a background for my discussion of how these societies promote equality. The social organisation of these societies has the following basic characteristics:

1. Social groupings are flexible and constantly changing in composition.

2. Individuals have a choice of whom they associate with in residence, in the food quest, in trade and exchange, in ritual contexts.

3. People are not dependent on *specific* other people for access to basic requirements.

4. Relationships between people, whether relationships of kinship or other relationships, stress sharing and mutuality but do not involve long-term binding commitments and dependencies of the sort that are so familiar in delayed-return systems.

I should stress, as I have before (Woodburn 1980:111), that I am not seeking to reduce social organisation in hunter-gatherer or other societies to no more than a mere epiphenomenon of technology, the work process and the rules governing the control of assets. All I am saying is this: in a delayed-return system there must be organisation having the very general characteristics I have outlined. The *particular* form the organisation will take cannot be predicted, nor can one say that the organisation exists in order to control and apportion these assets because, once in existence, the organisation will be used in a variety of ways, which will include the control and apportionment of assets, but which are not otherwise determined. In societies without delayed yields and assets, we do not find delayed-return social organisation.

All the six immediate-return systems listed are egalitarian, profoundly egalitarian, though not all quite in the same way or to the same extent; delayed-return systems are far more variable, but to the best of my knowledge not one of them is egalitarian to nearly the same extent as any one of the immediate-return systems. There is no doubt that, whatever else I may be defining by these categories, I certainly am marking off one set of societies that resemble one another in their realisation of a remarkable degree of equality.

What is perhaps surprising is that these societies systematically eliminate distinctions—other than those between the sexes—of wealth, of power and of status. There is here no disconnection between wealth, power and status, no tolerance of inequalities in one of these dimensions any more than in the others. I have exempted relations between men and women from this sweeping assertion. In fact normal relationships between men and women are quite variable in these societies, although in all of them women have far more independence than is usual in delayed-return systems. But since I have talked specifically about male-female relations (1978), I have decided to leave them out of the discussion today. In the present article, all the general statements I make about relationships should be taken unless otherwise stated as referring only to adult males.

Let us now see how these systems operate in practice.

Mobility and Flexibility

In all these six societies nomadism is fundamental. There are no fixed dwellings, fixed base camps, fixed stores, fixed hunting or fishing apparatus—such as stockades or weirs—or fixed ritual sites to constrain movements. People live in small camp units containing usually a dozen or two people and moving frequently.

These small nomadic camp units are associated with particular areas, usually described in the literature as territories, large enough to provide for subsistence requirements during the annual cycle. Each area at any one time will usually contain one or more camps: camp size and the number of camps vary seasonally. In some cases rights are asserted over its natural resources by the people most closely associated with the area. There is variation between these societies in the extent to which such rights are asserted, but what seems clear is that in every case individuals have full rights of access to camps in several of these areas and there is no question of tightly defined groups monopolising the resources of their areas and excluding outsiders. People can and do move from one camp to another and from one area to another, either temporarily or permanently and without economic penalty. Lee describes how the composition of !Kung camps which usually contain between ten and thirty individuals changes from day to day. Intercamp visiting is, he says, the main source of this fluctuation, but each year about 13 per cent. of the population makes a permanent residential shift from one camp to another. Another 35 per cent. divides its period of residence equally among two or three different camps which may or may not be within the same area (1979:54).

For the Hadza the situation is relatively simple. Like the !Kung, individual Hadza identify strongly with particular areas but, unlike the !Kung, Hadza do not assert rights to the areas with which they are associated. Anyone may live, hunt and gather wherever he or she likes without restriction—both within the area with which he or she is mainly associated and anywhere else in Hadza country. The camp units in which people live are not fixed entities: there is constant movement in and out while a camp remains at one site: when the site is changed people may move together to one or more new sites or all or some may choose to move to an existing camp elsewhere. There are continuities in the composition of these local groupings but none which seriously limit individual freedom of movement (Woodburn 1968b, 1972).

In all these societies nomadic movement of all types, both within and outside the local area, is apparently not seen as a burdensome necessity but positively as something healthy and desirable in itself. I have discussed elsewhere (Woodburn 1972) how neither the frequency nor the spatial patterning of Hadza moves can be interpreted in terms of ecological factors alone, although probably such flexible movement does, among other things, rapidly accomplish a rational distribution of people in relation to resources available at any particular time. What it also does is to allow people to segregate themselves easily from those with whom they are in conflict, without economic penalty and without sacrificing any other vital interests. Most important of all for the present discussion is the way that such arrangements are subversive for the development of authority. Individuals are not bound to fixed areas, to fixed assets or to fixed resources. They are able to move away without difficulty and at a moment's notice from constraint which others may seek to impose on them and such possibility of movement is a powerful levelling mechanism, positively valued like other levelling mechanisms in these societies.

Access to Means of Coercion

Another important factor in this context is the access which all males have to weapons among the !Kung, Hadza, Mbuti and Batek. Hunting weapons are lethal not just for game animals but also for people. There are serious dangers in antagonising someone: he might choose simply to move away but if he feels a strong sense of grievance that his rights have been encroached upon he could respond with violence. Lee gives a number of important case histories of !Kung murders showing clearly that there are contexts in which individuals are prepared to use their poisoned arrows (1979:370–400). Hadza recognise not just the danger of open public violence, where at least retaliation may be possible, but also the hazard of being shot when asleep in camp at night or being ambushed when out hunting alone in the bush (Woodburn 1979:252).[6] Effective protection against ambush is impossible. Those of you who have seen the film about the Hadza which I was involved in making (Woodburn and Hudson 1966) may remember Salida, the successful hunter of an impala in the film and of very many other animals in ordinary life. He is now dead and is believed by the Hadza to have died in such an ambush. Only his bones were found. The Hadza had theories about who the murderer might be but there was much uncertainty; the cause of the conflict is said to have been a dispute over a woman.[7]

No action was taken. The important point in all this is that, with such lethal weapons available to all men, with the possibility of using them for murder undetected, with the likelihood that even if detected no action will be taken,[8] with the knowledge that such weapons have indeed been used for murder in the past, the dangers of conflict between men over claims not only to women but more generally to wealth, to power or to prestige are well understood.

Yet there have been instances over the years of Hadza men who have in spite of the apparent risks demonstrated that they are not averse to attempting to dominate other Hadza, to order them about, to take their wives or to plunder their possessions. What is striking is that these instances are typically backed by coercive powers derived *from outside Hadza society* and have only been effective to the extent that such men have been able to override the crucial limiting mechanisms—the mobility of the victims and their individual capacity to retaliate—which would in normal circumstances be sufficient to prevent such predation (Woodburn 1979:262–64).

In normal circumstances the possession by all men, however physically weak, cowardly, unskilled or socially inept, of the means to kill secretly anyone perceived as a threat to their own well-being not only limits predation and exploitation; it also acts directly as a powerful levelling mechanism. Inequalities of wealth, power and prestige are a potential source of envy and resentment and can be dangerous for holders where means of effective protection are lacking.

What we have here is direct and immediate access to social control, access which is not mediated through formal institutions or through relationships with other people. It is directly analogous to, and matched by, the direct and immediate access, again not normally mediated through formal institutions or through relationships with other people, which people have to food and other resources.

Access to Food and Other Resources

I have already discussed how, within the general pattern of nomadic movement, individuals are able to avoid constraint by their freedom to detach themselves from others at a moment's notice without economic or other penalty. But let us now look more closely at the rights which individuals enjoy without which such action would not be practicable. What are an individual's entitlements to food and other resources and how are these entitlements taken up?

In all these societies individuals have direct access, limited by the division of labour between the sexes, to the ungarnered resources of their country. Whatever the system of territorial rights, in practice in their own areas and in other areas with which they have ties, people have free and equal access to wild foods and water; to all the various raw materials they need for making shelters, tools, weapons and ornaments; to whatever wild resources they use, processed or unprocessed, for trade.

Among the !Kung each area and its resources are used both by a core of men and women with long-standing associations with the area, who identify with it rather than with other areas, and by a wide range of other people who have come from other areas, some temporarily and some more permanently, and who are in most cases linked to one or more of the core members or other residents by a kinship or affinal tie (Marshall 1976; Lee 1979). Anyone with such a link who comes to live with the people of the area cannot, in practice, be refused full access to its resources provided that he or she observes certain minimal rules of politeness. As Marshall explains, newcomers share equally while they live there. No core member or anyone else has the right to withhold resources from the newcomer or to take a larger share (1976:189).

Among the !Kung, this relative freedom of access operates in spite of the fact that people long associated with an area claim to be 'owners' *(k"ausi)* of it and in particular of its plant and water resources. The !Kung notion of 'ownership' is clearly a broad one and seems here to mean association with, involvement in, identification with the area rather than narrow possession of it. Lee tells us that the usual term for a hunter in !Kung is *!gaik"au,* for which he gives the literal translation 'hunt owner' (1979:206). This suggests that the term *k"au* ('owner') can indicate association and not just possession. In general in these societies, and even among the !Kung where land rights might at first sight appear to be important in constraining movement and access, what association with a particular locality seems usually to provide is a means of identifying oneself and others, a way of mapping out social relations spatially, rather than a set of exclusive rights. Among the Hadza, people identify strongly with their own areas but place far more emphasis than the !Kung do on an individual's rights of access to resources everywhere, both in his own area and elsewhere.

The boundaries of Hadza areas are, as one would expect from what has already been said, undefined: in effect there are no boundaries (Woodburn 1968b:104). According to Marshall, !Kung boundaries between areas are rather closely defined in localities where important wild plants can be gathered (1976:187–88). Lee subsequently suggests that at least in the region where he worked, territories are not clearly defined or bounded even in relation to plant foods: he tells us that he believes 'the !Kung *consciously* strive to maintain a boundaryless universe because this is the best way to operate as hunter-gatherers in a world where group size and resources vary from year to year' (1979:335). If there were a rather rigid principle of recruitment to local groups combined with rather rigid boundaries between the areas used by local groups, material inequalities between local groups would inevitably develop as populations and resources fluctuated through time. Double flexibility—over group boundaries and territorial boundaries—obviously limits, in a bad year, the dangers of local food shortages or of destructive over-exploitation of sources of wild food. But given the low population density and the limited pressure on resources even in bad years I think it would be appropriate to give less attention to the nutritional benefits of all this flexibility in very rare times of crisis and to stress its day-to-day significance as a levelling mechanism.

Not just among the !Kung but generally in these societies, this double flexibility directly limits the development of local variation in wealth or in standard of living. If in one area people are eating better than in another, or obtaining food more easily than in another, then, other things being equal, movement of people, coupled perhaps with adjustment of boundaries, is likely over time to tend to even out such unacceptable discrepancies.

The direct and immediate access to food and to other resources which people enjoy is important in other ways. Without seeking permission, obtaining instruction, or being recognised as qualified (except by sex), individuals in these societies can set about obtaining their own requirements as they think fit. They need considerable knowledge and skill but this is freely available to all who are of the appropriate sex and is not, in general, transmitted by formal (or even informal) instruction: rather it is learnt by participation and emulation. In most, but not all, of these societies neither kinship status nor age is used as a qualification to obtain access to particular hunting and gathering skills or equipment.[9] A Hadza boy who wishes to try to hunt large game with bow and poisoned arrows can do so without restriction as soon as he wishes to do so and is able to make or obtain the necessary arrows. More important still, any person—man, woman or child—who seeks to obtain his or her requirements either individually or in association with others can do so without entering into commitments to and dependencies on kin, affines or contractual partners. Adults of either sex can readily, if they choose, obtain enough food to feed themselves adequately and are, in spite of the rules of the division of labour, *potentially* autonomous. It is not rare, at least among the Hadza, to find individuals, usually males, living entirely on their own as hermits for long periods. Of course in practice people living within the community do not live simply on self-acquired food: there are pooling and sharing practices, some of them very important, which I shall describe separately. What matters here is the lack of *dependence* on sharing or pooling of resources: a Hadza woman out gathering with other women will consume much of the proceeds on the spot and, out of what she brings back to camp, little, if any, may go to her husband. Similarly a Hadza man out hunting will expect to feed himself by picking and

eating berries and by consuming any small animal he may kill. Only food
surpluses cross the sexual boundary. The Hadza are perhaps an extreme instance: in some other immediate-return societies much more food is used socially—is brought back to camp and consumed jointly by people of both sexes.
Only among the net-hunting Mbuti (as distinct from the archer Mbuti) does
co-ordinated activity provide a substantial amount of food and even in this instance many sources of food are available to and obtained by individuals.

The net-hunting Mbuti apparently gather wild fruits and roots in a manner
not very different from the Hadza (Turnbull 1966:166–68). But hunting is a
co-operative venture: women and children drive game animals, large and
small, into a semi-circle of nets set up by the men. The yield is shared out
among the various participants as soon as they return to camp (1966: 157–58).
I must stress that this co-operation in the hunt is of a very specific sort. Within
the rather broad limits set by the optimal numbers for an efficient hunt
(1966:154), anyone who is present may participate according to his or her sex
role and is entitled to a proportion of the yield. There is no commitment to
participate and no basis for exclusion from participation. Each hunt is complete in itself and participation today apparently carries no obligation to par-
ticipe tomorrow. This is fundamentally different from cooperation in any agricultural system where the members of the productive group are not an *ad hoc*
aggregation but are a set of people bound by more enduring ties of kinship or
of contract.

What I want to stress here in this lack of dependence on specific others is
the implication for authority and, most obviously, for domestic authority. The
process of production is not in general controlled and directed by the household head or, if it is, the control is not authoritarian and is better described as
limited co-ordination by consent. Indeed among the Hadza I would say there
are no household heads (Woodburn 1968b:109). Older children and young
unmarried adults in these societies are not dependent on the senior generation
for access to property, to food or to resources though they may receive some
property, food and resources from them. Among both Hadza and !Kung, children do relatively little work and what they do is done at their choice rather
than under parental direction. Neither the parent-child nexus, nor the relationship between generations more generally, provides either a model or a
training ground for relationships of authority and dependency; indeed they
provide an alternative model for and training in personal decision-making and
in the possibilities of self-reliance, in sharing but not dependency on sharing.

The point can perhaps be made most clear if a simple contrast is drawn
with some agricultural and pastoral societies living in south eastern Africa.
Using detailed ethnographic evidence on the Southern Bantu, Richards long
ago drew attention to the importance of access to food and other resources for

an understanding of inequality: she stressed how, in the absence of other valuables, possession or control of food is singularly important as a means of differentiating one member of the community from another and as a source of power (1932:89). The authority of a man as household head over his unmarried sons, both immature and adult, his right to direct their labour and to demand obedience and respect from them is linked with

> the father's possession and control over the food supply—the cattleherd and their produce, and in general, the grain supply too. The head of the family is . . . bound to support his sons . . . The receipt of food marks the dependence of the child on the father . . . Unless he can earn money [in employment], . . . he simply cannot acquire food except from his parents' hands . . . one woman alone—his mother, or her substitute—must cook [it for him]. His dependence is thus displayed concretely by the receipt of actual food . . . (1932:77)

In immediate-return hunting and gathering societies the household head has no comparable role as real or symbolic provider, as the source of most good things. It is, I am sure, not accidental that neither !Kung nor Hadza usually place much emphasis on formal meal times. A great deal of food is eaten informally throughout the day (Lee 1979:199). Marshall records that 'Meat is not habitually cooked and eaten as a family meal among the !Kung . . . The men, women, and children may cook their pieces when and as they wish, often roasting bits in the coals and hot ashes and eating them alone at odd times' (1976:302).

Sharing

The genuine equality of opportunity that individuals enjoy in their access to resources, limited only by the division of labour between the sexes, does not, of course, ensure equality of yield. The quantities of all the various items which individuals obtain, either on their own or jointly with other people, vary greatly depending on skill, on luck, on persistence, on capacity to work and on other factors. It is at this point that the most crucial controls on the development of inequality come into action.

The principal occasions in which individuals in these societies are brought into association with valued assets which could be accumulated or distributed to build status are when large game animals are killed. And it is then that the most elaborate formal rules dissociating the hunter from his kill and denying him the privileges of ownership are brought to bear. Levelling mechanisms come into operation precisely at the point where the potential for the devel-

opment of inequalities of wealth, power and prestige is greatest. Among the
Hadza and the !Kung hunting success among adult men seems to be very variable. A high proportion of animals are killed by a small proportion of men
(Lee 1979:242–44). Techniques for drying meat and converting it into relatively lightweight stores of biltong are known. Yet successful individual
hunters are specifically denied the opportunity to make effective use of their
kills to build wealth and prestige or to attract dependents. Lee has reported
how !Kung are expected to be self-deprecating about their hunting successes;
boasting is met with scorn (1979:243–46). Turnbull (1966:183) tells us that
'some [Mbuti] men, because of exceptional hunting skill, may come to resent
it when their views are disregarded, but if they try to force those views they are
very promptly subjected to ridicule'. A Hadza returning to camp having shot
a large animal is expected to exercise restraint. He sits down quietly with the
other men and allows the blood on his arrow shaft to speak for him. If the
animal has only been wounded, the name of the species may not be mentioned
directly: the effect of uttering its name would, Hadza believe, allow it to recover from the arrow poison and escape. Special respectful terms must be used
and there should be a minimum of comment. Similarly, to talk of a dead
animal before it has been dismembered is believed to put at risk the animal's
fat which the Hadza value more highly than lean meat. One effect of these
rules is, certainly, to deny to the hunter praise which he might otherwise
expect to receive.[10]

For the !Kung the owner of the first arrow to hit the animal effectively is the
owner of the kill with the right to distribute it. Arrow-lending is common and
the owner of the arrow is often someone other than the hunter himself. Lee explains that meat distribution brings prestige but it also brings the risk of accusations of stinginess or improper behaviour if the distribution is not to everybody's liking (1979:247–48). So hunters are not reluctant to hunt sometimes
with someone else's arrow and to pass over the responsibility for distributing
the kill to him. When discussing this practice Marshall suggests that 'the society seems to want to extinguish in every way possible the concept of the meat
belonging to the hunter' (1976:297).

The meat of the kill is widely shared within the camp unit. Among the
Hadza the best portions (which differ depending on which species has been
killed) belong to the initiated men and may not under any circumstances be
eaten by the hunter on his own. For the Hadza this would be a particularly
heinous offence which would be likely to result in violence towards the hunter;
it would also, Hadza believe, cause him to become seriously ill and perhaps
even die. The hunter's rights to the initiated men's meat are identical to those
of each of other initiated men: the meat must be eaten in secret by the initiated
men as a group until it is finished. The rest of the meat is described as people's
meat and is distributed first at the kill site among those who have come to

carry in the meat, then back at camp it is distributed among those who remained behind and then, finally, when it is cooked, it is consumed by those who happen to be present and not simply by the person or the family grouping to whom the meat was allocated. The hunter himself will often not be involved in dismembering the carcass and in distributing the meat but he and his wife's mother and father, if they are present, will receive substantial shares. Among the !Kung the meat is distributed and redistributed in waves of sharing through the camp: everyone receives a share.

It has often been suggested that meat-sharing is simply a labour-saving form of storage. The hunter surrenders his rights to much of his kill in order to secure rights over parts of the kills of other hunters in future. There are problems with this formulation: as I have already mentioned, hunting success is unequal. Donors often remain on balance donors and may not receive anything like an equivalent return. Entitlement does not depend in any way on donation. Some men who are regular recipients never themselves contribute. Instead of seeing the arrangement as being in the interest of the donor, I think we should be clear that it is imposed on the donor by the community. Instead of seeing the transaction as a form of reciprocal exchange, I would suggest we treat it as analogous to taxation on incomes of the successful in our own society. The successful pay more than the less successful and are obliged to do so. They are not able to establish greater claims in future through having paid more tax and do not derive much prestige from having contributed more to the tax pool than they have withdrawn from it in benefits. The analogy may sound rather crude: certainly the hunter derives more prestige from contributing an animal than any taxpayer does from paying his taxes, but it does bring out the important fact that we are dealing here with a socially imposed levelling mechanism and not a mere practical convenience for the hunter.

Vegetable foods, which are less highly valued and which are obtained more easily and more predictably and in amounts which correspond more closely to the needs of the gatherers, are less widely shared but are not narrowly reserved for each gatherer and her immediate family. Among the Hadza it would be out of the question for a woman to hoard food while others are hungry. Sharing rights for pregnant women are particularly emphasised by the Hadza: they have the right to ask anyone for food at any time and are believed to be at risk if they are refused.

Sanctions on the Accumulation of Personal Possessions

Clothing, tools, weapons, smoking pipes, bead ornaments and other similar objects are personally held and owned. At least in the case of the three African societies, they are in general *relatively* simple objects, made with skill but not elaborately styled or decorated and not vested with any special significance.

They can be made or obtained without great difficulty. Rules of inheritance are flexible and no one depends on receiving such objects either by inheritance or by formal transmission from close kin of the previous generation during their lifetime.

Everywhere we find that there are sanctions against accumulation. This cannot be explained, as so many writers have mistakenly suggested, simply in practical terms: nomadic people who have to carry everything they possess are concerned that their possessions should be readily portable so that they can be carried with ease when the time comes to move camp, but sanctions against accumulation go far beyond meeting this requirement and apply even to the lightest objects such as beads, arrowheads or supplies of arrow poison.

The Transmission of Possessions Between People

Hadza use a distinctive method for transmitting such personally owned objects between people which has profound consequences for their relationships. In any large camp men spend most of their time gambling with one another, far more time than is spent obtaining food. They gamble mainly for metal-headed hunting arrows, both poisoned and non-poisoned, but are also able to stake knives, axes, beads, smoking pipes, cloth and even occasionally a container of honey which can be used in trade. A few personally owned objects cannot be staked, because, Hadza say, they are not sufficiently valuable. These are a man's hunting bow, his non-poisoned arrows without metal heads used for hunting birds and small animals, and his leather bag used for carrying his pipes and tobacco, arrowheads and other odds and ends. Those objects excluded from gambling share two characteristics: first, they maintain a man's capacity to feed and protect himself and secondly, they are made from materials available in every part of the country. In contrast many of the objects used in gambling are made, at least in part, of materials not available in every part of the country. For example, poisoned arrows incorporate a head made from scrap metal obtained in trade from non-Hadza, poison which is made from the sap of one tree or the seeds of another which are local in their distribution and entirely absent from large areas of the country, and, if possible, a lightweight shaft of a particular species of shrub even more restricted in its range. Stone smoking pipes are made from a type of soapstone which is again only found in certain localities.

The game involves tossing a handful of bark discs against a tree and reading the result which depends on which way up the various discs fall. Basically it is a game of chance and players have relatively little opportunity of influencing the result. Skill in throwing does play some part but the effect is reduced by banning the winner of the previous throw from acting as thrower next time.

In the course of a day in a large dry-season camp there will usually be hundreds of contests each one involving the transfer of a piece of property from the loser or losers to the winner. During the day many objects pass through competitors' hands, but as the game is a game of chance the randomising effect means that they will usually end the day without a substantial net gain or loss. If the player ends the day with some winnings, usually they will include some objects he wants to keep and use. He restakes objects he does not want and keeps back, as far as he can, objects he wants. From time to time people do gain substantial winnings and are then subject to great pressure to continue to compete so that other competitors can win back their lost possessions. Often winners, in an attempt to keep their winnings intact for longer than would otherwise be possible, move to another camp, but they are then usually followed by some of the other competitors. I can recall only one instance of a man who succeeded in keeping most of his winnings for a period of as long as a few weeks and he was a quite exceptional person who withstood the pressures on him and rationed his subsequent play whenever he won.

I have discussed Hadza gambling at greater length than might at first seem justified because its effects are so important. It is the major means by which scarce and local objects are circulated throughout the country: much inter-camp visiting is stimulated by gambling and winnings are constantly on the move. Objects such as stone pipes which are made in one part of the country circulate out to other areas where they are withdrawn from the game and put to use.

This circulation is accomplished, then, not through some form of exchange which would bind participants to one another in potentially unequal relationships of kinship or contract. The transactions are neutralised and depersonalised by being passed through the game. Even close kin and affines gamble with each other and the game acts against any development of one-way flows and dependency in relationships between them.

Individual effort, craft skill and, particularly, the skill of trading with outsiders are quite variable. The attraction of gambling mobilises effort and skill but distributes its proceeds at random in a way which subverts the accumulation of individual wealth by the hard-working or by the skilled. It further subverts any tendency to regional differentiation within Hadza country based on valuable local resources which are in demand in other areas. It is paradoxical that a game based on the desire to win and, in a sense, to accumulate should operate so directly against the possibility of systematic accumulation. Its levelling effect is very powerful.

!Kung transmit personal possessions in a quite different way which has far less levelling potential. Each !Kung enters into formal exchange partnerships known as *hxaro*, with a number of other people with whom systematic exchanges of personal possessions and of hospitality take place. Far from subverting relationships as Hadza gambling does, these exchanges create ties involving some mutual commitment. However, they seem to be organized in ways which stress the equal relationship between partners and provide little opportunity for property accumulation or the development of patron-client type relations between partners (Wiessner 1977). Marshall shows how the gifts are simple tokens of generosity and friendly intent. The trivial debts incurred are quite unlike the binding jural obligations at the centre of delayed-return systems. And as Marshall says, 'no one was dependent on obtaining objects by gift giving' (1976:308).

Both among the !Kung and among the Hadza individuals with any objects for which they appear to have no immediate need are under the greatest pressure to give them up and many possessions are given away almost as soon as they are obtained and usually, I think, without any expectation of return.[11] Among the Hadza the attitude to property often seems very casual. I well remember early on in my fieldwork being pressed very strongly to give people hoop iron to make arrowheads: I obtained the iron with some difficulty, gave out a piece to each man in the camp and was rather affronted when I discovered that, because I had given out more than could immediately be used, some of it had simply been thrown away. Limitations on the uses to which property can be put, especially if no gambling is going on at the time, in a context in which saving and accumulation are so actively discouraged and pressure for *de facto* equality of wealth is so great, mean that people often seem to place surprisingly little value both on their own and on other people's possessions.

Leadership and Decision Making

In these societies there are either no leaders at all or leaders who are very elaborately constrained to prevent them from exercising authority or using their influence to acquire wealth or prestige.[12] A Hadza camp at any particular time is often known by the name of a well-known man then living in it (for example, *ets'a ma Durugida*—Durugida's camp). But this indicates only that the man is well enough known for his name to be a useful label, and not that he acts as either a leader or a representative of the camp (Woodburn 1968b:105). Hadza decisions are essentially individual ones: even when matters such as the timing of a camp move or the choice of a new site are to be decided, there are no leaders whose responsibility it is to take the decisions or to guide people towards some general agreement. Sporadic discussion about moving does occur but usually it takes the form of announcements by some individual men that they are going to move and where they are going to move to. Other men will often defer a decision about whether to stay, whether to accompany those who are moving, or whether to move elsewhere, until the move actually begins. Certainly some, particularly older men with large families who are often those after whom camps are named, are likely to have more influence on the outcome than others and to precipitate by their individual decisions the movement of an entire camp or segment of a camp. But I would not describe them as leaders (Woodburn 1979:253).

The !Kung also name camps after individuals, whom Lee describes as leaders but leaders with a very limited role. 'In group discussions these people may speak out more than others, may be deferred to by others, and one gets the feeling that their opinions hold a bit more weight than the opinions of other discussants' (1979:343). What is particularly striking is that personal qualities suggesting that a !Kung individual is ambitious for power or wealth exclude such a person from the possibility of leadership.

> None is arrogant, overbearing, boastful, or aloof. In !Kung terms these traits absolutely disqualify a person as a leader and may engender even stronger forms of ostracism . . . Another trait emphatically not found among traditional camp leaders is a desire for wealth or acquisitiveness . . . Whatever their personal influence over group decisions, they never translate this into more wealth or more leisure time than other group members have (1979:345) . . . Their accumulation of material goods is never more, and is often much less, than the average accumulation of the other households in their camp. (1979:457)

Leaders should ideally be 'modest in demeanor, generous to a fault, and egalitarian . . .' (1979:350). Leaders such as these pose no threat to egalitarian values and indeed could be said to display and reinforce egalitarianism.

These are, of course, not the only contexts in which equality is expressed and levelling mechanisms operate: to do justice to the subject it would be necessary to go much further and in particular to explore the expression of egalitarianism in religious belief and practice. But I think I have said enough to show that we have here the application of a rigorously systematic principle: in these societies the ability of individuals to attach and to detach themselves at will from groupings and from relationships, to resist the imposition of authority by force, to use resources freely without reference to other people, to share as equals in game meat brought into camp, to obtain personal possessions without entering into dependent relationships—all these bring about one central aspect of this specific form of egalitarianism. *What it above all does is to disengage people from property, from the potentiality in property rights for creating dependency.* I think it is probable that this specialised development can only be realised without

impoverishment in societies with a simple hunting and gathering economy because elsewhere this degree of disengagement from property would damage the
operation of the economy. Indeed the indications are that this development is
intrinsic, a necessary component of immediate-return economies which occurs
only in such economies.

It is time that I discussed very briefly how these societies compare with
others that have been described as egalitarian. Of course we are all familiar
with the application of the term to those modern complex societies, including
our own, in which egalitarian sentiments are commonly expressed in political
discourse. But let us leave these aside. Anthropologists, at least those con-
ducting research outside Europe, have more commonly used the term as a
simple synonym for acephalous societies, societies without rulers, societies
without formal political offices. Delayed-return systems within this category,
in contrast to the immediate-return systems which I have been discussing in
some detail, are egalitarian in a very different sense. To generalise about so
wide and variable a category is not really satisfactory but a few obvious points
can be made: first, the community of political equals is usually a community of
property-holding household heads whose relations with their wives and female
kin and with their junior male kinsmen within the household are far from
equal. Intergenerational inequality and especially the inequality of holder and
heir is usually stressed. The household head has the right and the duty to
maintain and control the assets held by the household and to direct the labour
of its members.

Equality between household heads is in many of these systems only a
starting-point, a qualification to compete in a strenuous competition for
wealth, power and prestige. Writing about Papua New Guinea, Forge (1972:
533) tells us that 'to be equal and stay equal is an extremely onerous task requiring continual vigilance and effort. Keeping up with the Joneses may be
hard work, but keeping up with all other adult males of a community is incomparably harder. The principal mechanism by which equality is maintained
is equal exchange of things of the same class or of identical things. Basically all
presentations of this type are challenges to prove equality.' The outcome of
such challenges is striking inequality. Writing about the same area Burridge
tells us what happens to the casualties. 'Rubbish-men', as impoverished people
are called,

> were men who had either opted out of the status competition, or who
> habitually failed to meet their obligations. Often, they lived on the
> fringes of a settlement, between the village proper and the forest or
> bush outside: a placement which reflected their position in the moral
> order. Because they had failed to meet their obligations, or were un-

able or had chosen not to participate in the process whereby proper men were supposed to demonstrate their moral nature, they hardly rated as men, were not fully moral beings in the locally recognized sense. Treated with a charitable contempt which they accepted with resigned equanimity, rubbish-men were generally left to their own devices, working by and for themselves at a markedly lower level of subsistence than others. (1975:95)

This type of competitive equality contrasts dramatically with the non-competitive equality of the systems I have been describing. There equality does not have to be earned or displayed, in fact should not be displayed, but is intrinsically present as an entitlement of all men. There are no casualties of the principle of equality among the Hadza[13] or the !Kung, none of whose moral worth is destroyed by poor economic performance or lack of personal competitiveness. Egalitarianism is asserted as an automatic entitlement which does not have to be validated.

New Guinea is something of an extreme instance but even the less aggressive egalitarianism of east African pastoral societies, whose members do not engage in the competitive displays of wealth so characteristic of New Guinea, are still highly competitive in comparison with the !Kung and the Hadza and have far more in common socially with New Guinea than they do with these hunter-gatherers. There are marked differences in wealth in cattle and in standard of living. They too have casualties. Household heads who through bad management or bad luck lose all or most of their herd, lose at the same time the essential qualification for equality with herdowners. They have then to work as low-status clients or else move out of the pastoral economy.

Burnham has recently discussed what he describes as the structural conservatism of nomadic pastoral societies (1979:349–60). In a valuable paper he argues that fluidity of local grouping and spatial mobility are remarkably resistant to change. They promote egalitarianism and greatly inhibit the development of both political centralisation and class stratification. Within sub-Saharan African nomadic pastoral societies such centralisation and stratification have emerged only in situations of conquest and/or substantial sedentarisation.

I would argue that the nomadic hunting and gathering societies I have discussed are even more profoundly conservative. Fluidity of local grouping and spatial mobility, here combined with and reinforced by a set of distinctive egalitarian practices which disengage people from property, inhibit not only political change but any form of intensification of the economy. There is no easy transition from non-competitive egalitarianism to competitive egalitarianism.

Lee has described the difficulties some !Kung have encountered in their efforts to live by agriculture and by keeping domestic animals (1979:409–14). The difficulties are not technical ones: some individual !Kung have for years worked for neighbouring farmers and have become knowledgeable about farming techniques. The overwhelming difficulties lie in the egalitarian levelling mechanisms. There is no way that farming can be carried on without some accumulation, without stores of grain and of agricultural tools, and the major difficulty for the few individual !Kung who wish to make a real effort to farm is not that they themselves are unable to exercise self-restraint and to build up their stocks but that they are unable to restrain their kin and affines from coming to eat the harvested grain. Exactly the same has occurred again and again in the Hadza government-run settlements. Almost everybody understands basic agricultural techniques and almost everybody is prepared to carry out some cultivation. But those few who apply their labour systematically and skilfully and obtain a good crop have found that their fields are raided by other Hadza even before the grain is harvested, and once it has been harvested those with grain in store are under relentless pressure to share it with other Hadza rather than to ration its use so that it will last until the next harvest is obtained. In the face of such obstacles, even the successful farmer is likely to give up. If it is so difficult for these egalitarian hunter-gatherers to take up agriculture nowadays with so many pressures on them to settle, it is even less likely that they would have been able to convert to agriculture in the past.[14] I have suggested elsewhere that if we are to understand the development of agriculture from hunting and gathering, we ought to look at delayed-return hunter-gatherers who have the values and the organisation to facilitate the transition.

To end I should like to return briefly again to the nature of equality in these systems and its association with certain other values. Are people in these societies, who are relatively free from want and free from many of the forms of competition which are so evident in other societies, humane, altruistic and caring towards those who are not able to care for themselves? The answer is not simple but it is possible to say a little. In delayed-return systems people are bound to their close kin and to certain other associates in relationships which commonly involve the constant exchange of goods and services in fulfilment of obligations of one sort or another. People are committed to one another both in the sense that they have material obligations to one another and in the wider sense that they accept a measure of responsibility for one another. The potentiality for autonomy and the limitation of obligations to *specific* other people—as opposed to the generalised obligation to share—certainly seem to reduce the sense of commitment that people feel to others, at least in the Hadza instance where the movement of goods between people is so often de-personalised by the gambling game. There are instances in which the Hadza have abandoned the seriously ill when they moved camp, leaving them with their possessions and with food and water but knowing that they were unlikely to be able to provide for themselves. I was very surprised by the neglect of a previously popular grandmother in one of the settlements when she became senile and I think it less likely that this would have occurred within a household of one of the neighbouring agricultural societies. I have to allow, though, for the fact that the total number of instances of neglect or abandonment that have come to my attention is small and that such instances are more public among the Hadza than they are in societies where they can occur behind closed doors.

In another respect I can report with more confidence. Hadza society is open. People who are able to associate themselves at will with whatever area and whatever camp they choose do not impose social boundaries between themselves and others. There is no basis for exclusion. I think this is best brought out by their treatment of lepers. Among neighbouring sedentary societies lepers are not able to participate effectively in social life and are commonly ostracised or even expelled (these days usually to a leprosarium). There are a very small number of Hadza lepers who appear to be treated exactly like everyone else although the Hadza are very well aware of the dire consequences of the disease and the fact that it can be transmitted from one person to another. The principle is entirely clear. It is not that the Hadza are particularly sympathetic or humane towards lepers, who may well be mercilessly teased about their clumsiness: the principle is that Hadza society is open and there is simply no basis for exclusion. Equality is, in a sense, generalised by them to all mankind but, sadly, few of the rest of mankind, so enmeshed in property relations, would be willing to extend parity of esteem to hunter-gatherers who treat property with such a lack of seriousness.

NOTES

1. The term was used earlier with a different meaning (Murray et al. 1970).
2. In some, people obtain part of their food from wild products and part directly in exchange for wild products.
3. In using this simple, indeed over-simplified, dichotomous categorization into immediate-return and delayed-return systems, I should stress that it is designed as an initial, rough-and-ready basis for looking at what seem to be crucial variables for understanding social organisation. The job of specifying them more precisely and of disentangling their implications is still to come if it is accepted that the timing of yields on labour is significant for social organisation. I recognise, of course, that the four types of assets listed for delayed-return systems are qualitatively different and certainly do not have identical implications for social organisation though they do, it seems to me, have enough in common for it to be useful to group them together initially. I recognise too that some yields are part-immediate and part-delayed, that some immediate yields are much more immediate than others and that some delayed yields are much more delayed than others. I

also recognise not only that there is always some immediate-return activity in delayed-return systems (most strikingly in the case of Australian Aboriginal societies) but also that there is some delayed-return activity in immediate-return systems. In taking the matter further, the valuable comments of the following colleagues will be taken into account: Andrade 1979; Dodd 1980; Firth pers. comm. 1981; Ingold 1980; Ndagala pers. comm. 1981; Wiessner 1980.

4. If some undemanding agricultural crop is grown in an area where land is plentiful, if it does not require systematic application of labour over time and if it is unsuitable for storage, then this dependency may be small and the organisational requirements more limited.

5. I have listed here only a few of the more relevant references. Additional references to these societies are given in Woodburn 1980.

6. Out of the twenty-two !Kung homicides which Lee records, seventeen occurred during spontaneous open public violence while five were the result of premeditated sneak attacks (1979:382). Ambushes are possibly less likely to occur among the !Kung where 'a person's footprints are as well known as his face' (Marshall 1976:188). Hadza are expert trackers but are usually not able to recognise one another's footprints.

7. The murdered man was a rather aggressive character and had in the past been involved in disputes about women. Years earlier he himself had made threats in my presence that he would kill a man—not his suspected assailant—whom he accused of committing adultery with his wife.

8. Among the !Kung some killings lead to retaliatory killings, others do not. According to Lee's figures, four killings led to retaliatory killings (some of them multiple) while seven did not (1979:389).

9. Mbuti are an exception here: for them age distinctions are of some importance in the work process (Turnbull 1966).

10. I am not, of course, suggesting that this is the main significance of such rules.

11. The unremitting demands Hadza make on one another are highly conspicuous and often go beyond asking for things for which the owner has no immediate need. A man who obtains a ball of tobacco, a shirt or a cloth by trading with or begging from non-Hadza is unlikely to keep it for long unless he is very determined and willing to make himself unpopular. He will be asked for it endlessly. The pressures on outsiders (including anthropologists) to give away their possessions is equally great. Lee writes of how he was repelled by the !Kung's 'nagging demands for gifts, demands that grow more insistent the more we give' (1979:458).

12. I leave aside leaders imposed on these societies by outsiders or who derive their power from links with outsiders (Lee 1979:348–50; Woodburn 1979:261–64).

13. As I mention at the end of this article, there are casualties of one sort: the seriously ill, the senile and others unable to care for themselves and to claim equality, may not be well treated.

14. In an important recent article Cashdan discusses the contrast between equality among the !Kung and inequality (especially in wealth) among the //Gana, a Central Kalahari population derived from mixed marriages between immigrant

Bakgalagadi men and San (Bushman) women. The //Gana supplement their basic hunting and gathering subsistence with some farming. They are nomadic but from a home base. She attributes //Gana inequality not to the development of any formal organisation of inequality but to 'the inevitable result of the *lifting* of the constraints that produce strict egalitarianism among other Kalahari hunter-gatherers' (1980:119–20). I differ from her in believing that egalitarian values, so deeply built into traditional hunting and gathering systems in the area, would be unlikely to be so easily shed were it not for the fact that the community is of mixed origin and drew part of its membership from people with experience of farming and delayed-return.

REFERENCES

Andrade, J. 1979. The economic, social and cosmological dimensions of the preoccupation with short-term ends in three hunting and gathering societies: the Mbuti Pygmies of Zaire, the !Kung San of Namibia and Botswana, and the Netsilik Eskimos of Northern Canada. Thesis, University of London.

Burnham, P. 1979. Spatial mobility and political centralisation in pastoral societies. In *Pastoral production and society: proceedings of the international meeting on nomadic pastoralism, Paris, 1–3 December 1976*. Cambridge: Univ. Press.

Burridge, K. O. L. 1975. The Melanesian manager. In *Studies in social anthropology: essays in memory of E. E. Evans-Pritchard by his former Oxford colleagues* (eds) J. H. M. Beattie and R. G. Lienhardt. Oxford: Clarendon Press.

Cashdan, E. A. 1980. Egalitarianism among hunters and gatherers. *Am. Anthrop.* 82, 116–20.

Dodd, R. 1980. Ritual and the maintenance of internal co-operation among the Baka hunters and gatherers. In *2nd international conference on hunting and gathering societies, 19 to 24 September 1980*. Quebec: Université Laval, Département d'Anthropologie.

Endicott, K. L. 1979. Batek Negrito sex roles. Thesis, Australian National University.

Endicott, K. M. 1974. Batek Negrito economy and social organisation. Thesis, Harvard University.

———. 1979. *Batek Negrito religion: the world-view and rituals of a hunting and gathering people of peninsular Malaysia*. Oxford: Clarendon Press.

Forge, A. 1972. The golden fleece. *Man* (N.S.) 7, 527–40

Gardner, P. M. 1972. The Paliyans. In *Hunters and gatherers today* (ed) M. G. Bicchieri. New York: Holt, Rinehart & Winston.

Ingold, T. 1980. The principle of individual autonomy and the collective appropriation of nature. In *2nd international conference on hunting and gathering societies, 19 to 24 September 1980*. Quebec: Université Laval, Département d'Anthropologie.

Lee, R. B. 1979. *The !Kung San: men, women, and work in a foraging society*. Cambridge: Univ. Press.

———. and I. DeVore (eds) 1976. *Kalahari hunter-gatherers: studies of the !Kung San and their neighbors*. Cambridge, Mass.: Harvard Univ. Press.

Malinowski, B. 1960. *A scientific theory of culture.* New York: Oxford Univ. Press.

Marshall, L. 1976. *The !Kung of Nyae Nyae.* Cambridge, Mass.: Harvard Univ. Press.

Morris, B. 1975. An analysis of the economy and social organisation of the Malapantaram, a South Indian hunting and gathering people. Thesis, University of London.

Murray, J. A. H. et al. (eds) 1970. *The Oxford English dictionary.* Oxford: Clarendon Press.

Richards, A. I. 1932. *Hunger and work in a savage tribe: a functional study of nutrition among the Southern Bantu.* London: Routledge.

Turnbull, C. M. 1965. *The Mbuti Pygmies: an ethnographic survey* (Anthrop. Papers Am. Mus. Nat. Hist. 50: 3). New York: American Museum of Natural History.

———— 1966. *Wayward servants: the two worlds of the African Pygmies.* London: Eyre & Spottiswoode.

Wiessner, P. 1977. Hxaro: a regional system of reciprocity for reducing risk among the !Kung San. Thesis, University of Michigan.

———— 1980. History and continuity in !Kung San reciprocal relationships. In *2nd international conference on hunting and gathering societies, 19 to 24 September 1980.* Quebec: Université Laval, Département d'Anthropologie.

Woodburn, J. C. 1968a. An introduction to Hadza ecology. In *Man the hunter* (eds) R. B. Lee and I. DeVore. Chicago: Aldine.

———— 1968b. Stability and flexibility in Hadza residential groupings. In *Man the hunter* R. B. Lee and I. DeVore. Chicago: Aldine.

———— 1970. *Hunters and gatherers: the material culture of the nomadic Hadza.* London: The British Museum.

———— 1972. Ecology, nomadic movement and the composition of the local group among hunters and gatherers: an East African example and its implications. In *Man, settlement and urbanism* (eds) P. J. Ucko, R. Tringham and G. W. Dimbleby. London: Duckworth.

———— 1978. Sex roles and the division of labour in hunting and gathering societies. Paper presented at the first international conference on hunting and gathering societies. Paris, June 1978.

———— 1979. Minimal politics: the political organisation of the Hadza of North Tanzania. In *Politics in leadership: a comparative perspective* (eds) W. A. Shack and P. S. Cohen. Oxford: Clarendon Press.

———— 1980. Hunters and gatherers today and reconstruction of the past. In *Soviet and Western anthropology* (ed) E. Gellner. London: Duckworth.

———— and S. Hudson. 1966. *The Hadza: the food quest of an East African hunting and gathering tribe.* (16 mm. film.)

• PART II •

THE ORIGINAL
AFFLUENT SOCIETY:
ASSESSMENT AND EXTENSIONS

The first chapter in part II, "Beyond 'The Original Affluent Society,'" Nurit Bird-David's reassessment of Marshall Sahlins's original contribution, evaluates the criticism of the earlier work on hunter-gatherers, including its limited sample size. According to Bird-David, Sahlins's essential message has held up well. In fact, she takes the original affluence hypothesis even further than did Sahlins:

> [John Kenneth Galbraith's] main argument was that the way to the really affluent society lies in an ideological disengagement between production and economic security and between production and income. These ideas are precisely the ideas which are embodied in the cosmic economy of sharing. In respect to their cultural ideas, therefore, hunter-gatherers with immediate-return systems constitute the original affluent society in a more comprehensive sense than Sahlins envisaged. (p. 133–134)

Why is this so? Incredible as it may seem, immediate-return hunter-gatherers, living what people of the industrial age would call an impoverished material life, were more economically secure than are most of us today. Furthermore, because of industrial societies' linking of production with distribution, we are the most economically insecure during the most vulnerable periods of life, that is, during childhood and old age, when we cannot produce.

Chapter 6, Eleanor Leacock's "Women's Status in Egalitarian Society," points out that ideological and cultural blinders make it difficult for modern observers to fathom the "separate but equal" status of women in hunter-gatherer societies. Leacock prefers the word *autonomous* to *egalitarian*, meaning that women held decision-making power over their own lives to the same extent as men did over theirs. A central argument of Leacock's chapter is that power relations depend on access to, or control of, wealth. She criticizes the tendency of commentators to see "incipient patterns" of hierarchies in places where they may not occur:

> From band to tribe, tribe to chiefdom, chiefdom to state, the development of decision-making processes is seen quantitatively as progressive change toward Western forms of power and control. Fundamental qualitative distinctions between egalitarian and class societies are lost. A hierarchical view of sex roles fits easily into the scheme. That sex roles exist is, after all, a human universal, and to assume that any difference between the sexes necessarily involves hierarchy is seen, not as ethnocentrism but as common sense.

Chapter 7, "Art, Science, or Politics," Richard B. Lee's second work in this volume is a recent critical appraisal of the state of hunter-gatherer studies, including the "revisionist critique," which essentially denies the existence of hunter-gatherers as a category. Lee argues, as he did almost three decades before, that what sets hunter-gatherers apart is their ability to thrive materially and culturally while severely limiting the concentration of wealth and power. Lee's chapter surveys the subtleties of hunter-gatherer societies and highlights the most important controversies of the past three decades. Among these are (1) hunter-gatherers and the evolution of human behavior, (2) optimal foraging strategies, (3) gender issues, (4) worldviews, and (5) hunter-gatherers in history and prehistory. Lee also makes an important point about the accelerated destruction of the lifeways of traditional peoples during the past two decades and the importance of this to recent (1980s and 1990s) interpretations (and misinterpretations) of earlier fieldwork. At the end of his chapter (p. 184) Lee gets to the heart of the matter: "When anthropologists look at hunter-gatherers they are seeking . . . a vision of human life and human possibilities without the pomp and glory, but also without the misery and inequity of state and class society."

Chapter 8, "The Future of Hunter-Gatherer Research," by Ernest S. Burch, Jr., may be seen as a companion piece to Lee's "Art, Science, or Politics?" Burch discusses the practical, conceptual, and methodological problems facing researchers of hunter-gatherer societies brought about by the assimilation, acculturation, and outright genocide of the world's small-scale societies. Burch argues that the most definitive distinction of small-scale societies is not between foragers and agriculturalists but between immediate-return and delayed return societies. According to Burch (p. 210), "Immediate-return or 'generalized' hunter-gatherer societies are so unlike all others that, as Birdsell (1973:338) once noted, it is difficult even for anthropologists who have not personally experienced one to conceive how they can exist; it is almost impossible for nonanthropologists to do so."

FIVE

Beyond "The Original Affluent Society": A Culturalist Reformulation[1]

◆

Nurit Bird-David

The idea of "the original affluent society" was first presented during the 1966 "Man the Hunter" conference, which laid the foundations for the anthropological study of modern hunter-gatherers. The participants—social anthropologists, archaeologists, human biologists, ecologists, and demographers—were struck by the brief contribution of Marshall Sahlins, a nonspecialist invited discussant, in response to their papers (Sahlins 1968a). Sahlins later produced a much longer essay on the idea for *Les temps modernes* (1968b), and this became the basis for the first chapter of his *Stone Age Economics* (1972). The book was a highly controversial text on tribal societies, and the essay itself—which proposed, essentially, that the hunting-and-gathering way of life provided unparalleled affluence for its followers—became notorious both inside and outside anthropology. It was hotly debated by scholars from a broad spectrum of disciplines that shared an interest in the evolution of human society. It has since become the representative text on hunter-gatherers in introductory courses (see, e.g., Cole 1988) and appears on the reading lists of most anthropology departments. Despite their initial enthusiasm, however, up to the 1980s specialists gave Sahlins's essay little serious or direct attention. It was rarely challenged or further explored through empirical research. It is fair to say, in fact, that in their research—as opposed to their teaching—many anthropologists made an effort to ignore it.

The explanation for the fate of "The Original Affluent Society" during this period is complex. The general interest in it no doubt reflected our symbolic and ideological needs and our (Western) construction of the prehistoric past. Furthermore, the essay was timely in dispelling certain inadequate conceptions

Reprinted by permission of the publisher from *Current Anthropology*, Volume 33, Number 1, February 1992. Copyright © by The Wenner-Gren Foundation for Anthropological Research.

of "primitive" economic life and disclosing anthropologists' ethnocentric biases. Beyond this, it marked the inception of modern hunter-gatherer research and constituted certification of its legitimacy. Above all, most specialists, and many other scholars as well, recognized, if only intuitively, that Sahlins "had a point." We sensed that he had touched on something essential to the hunting-and gathering way of life, although—and this is the problem—we did not know quite what it was.

The ambivalence of specialists had to do with gaps between data and conclusions. Intended to provoke as well as to document, the essay soared beyond conventional scientific discourse, appealing directly to Western fantasies about work, happiness, and freedom. It offered, as a result, a peculiar synthesis of theory and data, insight and banality, breadth of view and gimmicky wit, all so craftily blended together as to make it extraordinarily resistant to analysis. Had specialists attempted to engage with Sahlins's essay in the years immediately following its publication, they would have encountered three problems in particular.

First, despite the paucity of reliable data, Sahlins drew quantitative and pseudo-quantitative conclusions concerning hunter-gatherers' work ("a mean of three to five hours per adult worker per day in food production" (1972:34) and leisure ("a greater amount of sleep in the day time per capita than in any other condition of society" [p.14]). In addition to the anecdotal observations—perceptive in their own terms—of explorers and missionaries he relied upon three professional studies. Two of these had been undertaken in the course of a 1948 American–Australian expedition in Arnhem Land by McCarthy and McArthur (1960)—the first a nutritionist, the second an anthropologist. The third, a remarkable and pioneering work on the Dobe !Kung by Lee (1968, 1969), was influenced as much by Lee's evolutionary objective as by his actual fieldwork experience, which only in subsequent years came to include a more rounded study of the !Kung way of life. These case studies provided samples too small to be statistically meaningful: they concerned 13 and 9 individuals in the two Arnhem Land camps and an average of about 30 individuals in the Dobe !Kung camp, studied for one, two, and three weeks, respectively.[2] Nor were Sahlins's conclusions capable of further testing. It is difficult enough to study "work time" among time—illiterate peoples who scatter across rough terrain as they go hunting and gathering, singly or in small groups, not only for need but for leisure, let alone to construct a comparable parameter for other peoples that pursue activities of an entirely different kind.

Second, Sahlins integrated into the argument concepts which specialists would have found difficult to use in economic analysis at that time. How could they address in analysis and pursue in the context of fieldwork suggestions that hunter-gatherers follow the "Zen way" to affluence or that "a pristine affluence colors their economic arrangements, a trust in the abundance of nature's resources rather than despair at the inadequacy of human means" (1972:29)?

Finally, and most important, although Sahlins acknowledged the difficulties involved in studying contemporary peoples as descendants or representatives of prehistoric hunter-gatherers, in discussing evolutionary processes of the macro-time scale, he projected ethnographic observations of the micro-time scale—which left much to be desired. Extraordinary as it now seems, a close examination of the published sources, McCarthy and McArthur (1960) and McArthur (1960), shows that even the nine adults who constituted the Fish Creek group were in fact encountered in a missionary station and invited to participate in an "experiment" (McArthur 1960:91). Not only that, but they "became so tired of the diet, the greater part of which was animal food, that on 12 October, the fifth day of the survey, two of the men walked into Oenpelli to get flour and rice." Luckily, they acquiesced to the researchers' wishes and "willingly handed over these foods until the conclusion of the experiment"—and so "the quantitative survey was continued" (McCarthy and McArthur 1960:147). As for Lee's early quantitative study, while it was more sophisticated and less contrived, it nevertheless focussed on a selected group that represented 58 per cent of the 425 !Kung counted in the Dobe area in 1964—the others were involved in other activities or did not stay for the four-week survey (Lee 1969:52–54) and Lee later found that even these selected people had previously been working for wages and had occasionally grown their food (1979:409; 1976:18).

In short, "The Original Affluent Society," in spite of its importance, remained too complex for straightforward examination by students of modern hunter-gatherers for many years after its publication. It thus became a kind of a sacred text. It was left-untouched and unapproached, and there evolved an oral tradition, passed down from teacher to student, which gave it an acceptable meaning (see Barnard and Woodburn 1988:11–12). We continued to include it in our reading lists, as much for its historical importance as for that "something" which we felt it had and also because we had nothing better to offer. Occasionally a (bright) student would exclaim, "The king is naked!" but we considered it a king even if indecently dressed.

Recently, however, ecologically oriented specialists have taken up the essay and, drawing on advances made during the intervening years in both fieldwork and theory, read it as a hypothesis to be tested by means of empirical research (e.g., Hayden 1981; Hawkes and O'Connell 1981; Hawkes et al. 1985; Gould 1982; Hill et al. 1985; Headland 1987; Smith 1987). A major session was devoted to their work at the recent Sixth International Conference on Hunting and Gathering Societies in Fairbanks, Alaska. Making use of quantitative data collected within research projects informed by optimal foraging theory

(Winterhalder and Smith 1981), these specialists have focussed mainly on hunter-gatherers' work time. They have reported that Sahlins's argument does not apply universally, because some peoples—for example, the Ache, the Alyawara, the Agta, and even the !Kung (see esp. Hawkes and O'Connell 1981; Headland 1987; Hill et al. 1985; Hayden 1981; Lee 1979:278)—work on average at least six hours a day. They have argued that the studies Sahlins used were not universally representative (a charge which can be made against virtually any anthropological work) and, moreover, that they take account neither of the societies concerned at large nor of the full seasonal cycle, let alone of irregular ecological changes. They have also addressed the construction of the parameter "work time" and argued that it is misleading because it does not include time devoted to constructing and maintaining tools, the preparation of food, child care, and the informal exchange of information. While most of these scholars have challenged "The Original Affluent Society" on these grounds, some have concentrated on Sahlins's idea of "limited wants," reframing it within evolutionary-ecological theory (e.g., Hawkes et al. 1985; Smith 1987; Winterhalder 1990) and asking whether "limited needs" had any ecological rationale in terms of optimal foraging theory ("time minimizing," "opportunity maximizing," and "energy maximizing").

Twenty-five years after the idea was introduced, it is indeed time to revisit "The Original Affluent Society." Yet it is not enough to pick up components of the argument such as "work time" and "limited needs" and pursue them piecemeal. To understand what Sahlins was trying to get at, we must first penetrate the essay analytically and strip the argument of its rhetorical and polemical excesses. This is the first objective of this paper. The second objective is to offer an up-to-date culturally oriented analysis of hunter-gatherers' work and material welfare. In recent years a culturalist method of economic analysis (following Gudeman 1986) has developed, and its application to the study of hunter-gatherer economy has already begun (see Bird-David 1990). Drawing on culturally oriented data, new and old, concerning three groups—the Nayaka of South India, the Mbuti of Central Africa, and the Batek of Malaysia—I will argue that Sahlins's argument, duly updated and reconceptualized, does indeed hold.

I will, however, confine myself to the modern dimension of "The Original Affluent Society," leaving the evolutionary dimension to be pursued separately at a different analytical level of abstraction and with due care for the massive problems involved. The recent debate on the status of modern hunter-gatherers (e.g., Solway and Lee 1990; Wilmsen and Denbow 1991), which I have addressed elsewhere (Bird-David 1988, n.d.), lies outside the concern of the present paper, since it does not deal with how the modern peoples in question have come to be the way they are—through evolution or as a result of colonialism.

An Analysis of "The Original Affluent Society"

Along with all other observers of modern hunter-gatherers, Sahlins was struck by what he described as their "peculiar" economic behaviour. In his terms, they have only a few possessions, which can be manufactured easily from materials which lie in abundance around them, and display a notable tendency to be careless about them and to lack interest in developing their technological equipment. Lack of foresight is apparent in "their propensity to eat right through all the food in the camp, even during objectively difficult times," and in their "failure to put by food surpluses and develop food storage" (pp. 30–31). Many of these features have since been combined by Woodburn in a single construct, "the immediate-return system" (1980, 1982, 1988).

In "The Original Affluent Society" Sahlins intended to offer a culture-specific explanation of this "peculiar" economic behaviour. Referring to the formalist/substantivist controversy of the 1960s, he set himself against the use of "ready-made models of orthodox Economics, especially the 'microeconomics' taken as universally valid and applicable grosso modo to primitive societies" (1972:xi). He expressed, instead, a commitment to "a culturalist study that as a matter of principle does honour to different societies for what they are" (p. xi) and to a view of the economy as "a category of culture rather than behaviour" (p. xii). Any lingering uncertainty about his theoretical position is dispelled by *Culture and Practical Reason* (1976), where he argued for an economic analysis that takes into consideration peoples' cultural constructions of the material world and challenged the assumption that there is an economic sphere which is regulated by practical reason. Interestingly, he specifically criticized analyses which present a "naturalization of the hunter-gatherer economy" and concern themselves with the "naturalistic ordering of culture" instead of "the cultural order of nature" (1976:100).

What he did in "The Original Affluent Society" was, however, precisely the reverse of his intention: he discussed hunter-gatherers' work in terms of practical reason and ecological constraints and analyzed their economy with none other than a microeconomic model focussing on individuals' optimal, rational behaviour. He argued, in fact, that the imminence of diminishing returns shaped the hunter-gatherer economy, first imposing mobility and then enforcing prodigality (pp. 31–33). "Hunters and gatherers," he concluded, ignoring their culture altogether, "have *by force of circumstances* an objectively low standard of living" (p. 37, emphasis added).

How did this happen? It was not for lack of trying. Sahlins offered two promising cultural propositions. The first was that affluence is a culture-specific relation between material wants and means and that hunter-gatherers achieve it by reducing their material wants through cultural processes: "Want not, lack not.") This would have been a good starting point from which to explore the ideas of hunter-gatherers in relation to their economic conduct and thereby to provide a culturalist framework for understanding their economic arrangements. But Sahlins did not pursue it, in part because of lack of relevant data and conceptual apparatus and in part, unfortunately, because he sacrificed the issue to wit and glossed this proposition as the "Zen way." In so doing, he diverted attention from the hunter-gatherers' own ideas, since, needless to say, "honour(ing) different societies for what they are" means projecting upon them neither Western nor Zen ideas.

Sahlins's second cultural proposition was, essentially, that hunter-gatherers have confidence in their environment and that their economic conduct makes sense in relation to that confidence. In "Notes on the Original Affluent Society" he put this boldly, arguing that "a certain confidence, at least in many cases, attends their economic attitudes and decisions. The way they dispose of food on hand, for example—as if they had it made" (1968a:86). Notably, most of the speakers in the discussion that followed (1968a:89–92) addressed their comments to this proposition, designated by one of them as the "thesis of confidence in the yield of the morrow" (Helm 1968:89). Although they discussed it in a preliminary way, in impressionistic terms, and did not find it equally applicable to all cases, the consensus was that this proposition did apply to peoples whose economies were later to be characterized as "immediate-return systems" and in restricted ways to other groups as well.

When Sahlins made the same point again in "The Original Affluent Society," however, he added a qualifier which brought to an end the interest he and others had shown in this proposition. He wrote: "My point is that the otherwise curious heathen devices become understandable by the people's confidence, a confidence which is the reasonable human attribute of a generally successful economy" (p. 29, emphasis added). He later indicated that by "successful economy" he meant gaining a livelihood while retaining a low ratio of work time to leisure time. While the initial proposition could clearly have led to a culture-sensitive analysis—because confidence in the natural environment reflects cultural representations as much as objective, ecological conditions—this addition reduced it to a practical reason and prepared the way for the ecological proposition.

Sahlins did not, I think, go back on the explanatory importance of hunter-gatherers' confidence in their environment. He simply laid his bet on another proposition which he had come to believe would make his case more strongly.

Reputed to be central and crucial to "The Original Affluent Society," this proposition was that hunter-gatherers work an average of three to five hours per adult per day. In retrospect, and taking into account the recent work discussed briefly above, it is clear that he bet on the weaker horse. However, even in the essay itself one can see how the illusion evolved and, moreover, that this proposition is not a necessary condition for Sahlins's argument.

Pre-1968 theory had explained hunter-gatherers' economic dispositions in terms of their unrelenting quest for food. Sahlins's attack on this theory was what made his essay historically important, but he addressed it only to pave the way for his own. It would have been sufficient for that purpose to point out— in a general way, and, without going into the problematic statistics—that what were then new and exceptionally rich empirical findings conclusively showed that hunter-gatherers did not work relentlessly. (This would also have confirmed the impressions of attentive travellers and missionaries.) However, Sahlins chose a more polemical and dramatic approach, and as a result, while he debunked the old theory sensationally, he lost control of his own.

He overprocessed the ecologically oriented quantitative data from the aforementioned studies and in the course of that adopted the analytical construct of "work time"—a modern Western construct par excellence that is meaningful within the ecological paradigm but not in a culturalist study. Moreover, with the zeal of the newly converted, he further quantified the quantitative measures of work time that, with considerable caution, Lee and McArthur and McCarthy had provided and so arrived at estimates of "four or five hours" (in the case of the Arnhem Land Aborigines [p. 17] and "an average of 2 hours and 9 minutes per day" (in the case of the Dobe !Kung [p. 21]. The simplistic reduction of the data to these two figures was unfortunate, because when he then turned to his other sources he found in them suggestive comparable estimates: "two or three hours," "three or four hours," and "an average of less than two hours a day" (p. 26, citing Grey 1841, vol. 2:263; Eyre 1845:254–55; Woodburn 1968:54). He himself was aware that the estimates were "very rough," but—lo and behold!—they were similar to each other and to the estimates just mentioned. (Sahlins further highlighted the similarity by printing the estimates in boldface.) These were similar enough, in any case, for scholars who had just discovered what has been called the "magic number" in hunter-gatherer studies—the 25-strong hunter-gatherer band—and suggested a second magic number, "a mean of three to five hours" of work per adult worker per day.

This seeming fact was sufficient for Sahlins's case: if they worked so little, they indeed enjoyed unparalleled affluence. Furthermore, it made the cultural propositions simple corollaries of this fact: if hunter-gatherers could gain an adequate livelihood by working so little it was obvious that they could easily get what they wanted and did not want more than they could easily get, and, furthermore, it was obvious ("reasonable") that they had confidence in their environment. Thus, Sahlins centered his concluding theory on the ecological proposition, which should not have been offered (since there was neither sufficient evidence nor any theoretical need for it), and abandoned the cultural propositions.

It is as a result of this that he provided a theory of *abundance with cost* (owing to ecological dictates) when he had set out to offer the opposite, a theory of *affluence without abundance* (owing to cultural influences). His theory was, in Winterhalder's terms, "the neoclassical formulation preceded by a minus sign" (1990:498) a neat formula in the best formalist fashion that lacked culture-sensitive depth. Worst of all, the whole argument came to appear doubtful in the light of subsequent work because the ecological proposition upon which it rested had been called into question. I would argue, however, that in drawing attention to the explanatory power of hunter-gatherers' trust in their environment, Sahlins did point the way towards a culturally oriented theory of hunter-gatherers' economic behaviour. He was on the threshold of what can now be pursued by using the culturalist method of economic analysis.

The Cosmic Economy of Sharing

No one can seriously suppose either that all modern hunter-gatherers will be the same or that any point needs to be made of this. It seems, however, that not only do hunter-gatherers with immediate-return systems share the economic features which perplexed Sahlins (whilst other modern hunter-gatherers differ from them in various ways) but at least some of them view their natural environments in a similar way: they have, in Gudeman's (1986) terms, very similar primary metaphors. These metaphors are drawn from their social institutions and constitute the cores of the metaphorical models that Gudeman has called local economic models. I shall move on to discuss these metaphorical models and then show that this ethnographic material provides substance for Sahlins's cultural propositions, a basis on which to refine them, and, in addition (and as Sahlins suspected), a means of making sense of these hunter-gatherers' economic behaviour.

I began to explore the primary metaphors of hunter-gatherers with immediate-return systems in an earlier paper (Bird-David 1990), where I examined one metaphorical model—the giving environment—in relation to patterns of exchange and ownership in the context of a contrast between the South Indian Nayaka and their shifting-cultivator neighbours the Bette and Mullu Kurumbas. Here I discuss a closely related metaphorical model—the cosmic economy of sharing—in relation to subsistence activities in the context of a comparison between the Nayaka and two other groups with immediate-return systems, the Mbuti of Zaire and the Batek of Malaysia. Each group has animistic notions which attribute life and consciousness to natural phenomena, including the forest itself and parts of it such as hilltops, tall trees, and river sources. I shall examine the way in which they construct their relationship with these agents—at once natural and human-like—by looking eclectically at their ritual and myth and their everyday discourse and conduct and by paying special attention to the metaphors which they use. Four features in particular are prominent:

First, the natural (human-like) agencies socialize with the hunter-gatherers. The Mbuti *molimo* festival, for example, is, in fact, precisely about this: the Forest visits the Mbuti camp, plays music, and sings with the people (Turnbull 1961). The Batek similarly say that the supernatural spirits, called *hala'*, "come to earth merely for the pleasure of sharing a good singing session with the Batek." During the fruit season, Batek frequently sing for—and with—the natural spirits (Endicott 1979:219). The Nayaka confine the merriment of a communal get-together with the natural agencies to a festival normally held once a year. However, throughout this festival, which lasts 24 hours, they converse, dance, sing, eat, and even share cigarettes with natural-cum-ancestral spirits, which they invoke by shamanistic performances.

Second, the natural agencies give food and gifts to everyone, regardless of specific kinship ties or prior reciprocal obligations. The Mbuti, for example, explicitly say that "the forest gives them . . . food and shelter, warmth and clothing" (Turnbull 1976 [1965]:253; 1978:165). They view game, honey, and other natural foods as "gifts" (Turnbull 1976 [1965]:161, 180, 277; 1961:61, 237). The Batek, according to their origin stories, hold that the *hala'* created most of the plants and animals especially for the Batek (Endicott 1979:54–55, 72) and now demand nothing in return, not even (with a few exceptions) sacrifices or offerings (p. 219). According to some versions, some *hala'* even turned themselves into the plants and animals that the Batek eat (p. 67). The *hala'*, the Batek say, keep large quantities of fruit blossoms in their abodes, "like goods on a shop shelf" (p. 44), and release the fruit in season, "freely bestowing their bounties" (p. 219).

Third, the people regard themselves as "children of" the forest, the term connoting generic ties rather than simply bonds of emotion and care. For example, not only do Mbuti often refer to the forest as "father" and "mother" (Turnbull 1976 [1965]:252; cf. Mosko 1987) and say that it "gives them . . . affection" 1965:253) but also they describe it as the source of all spiritual matter and power, including the vital essence of people's lives *(pepo)* (Turnbull 1976 [1965]:247, 252). They describe the forest as a "womb" (Turnbull

1978:167, 215; 1983:30, 32, 44) which plays a part in the conception and de-velopment of a Mbuti foetus (Turnbull 1978:165, 167–70; 1976 [1965]:178; cf. Mosko 1987:899). In a similar vein, although from the opposite perspec-tive, the Nayaka not only refer to natural agencies (especially hilltops and large rock formations) by the terms *dod appa* (big father) and *dod awa* (big mother) and to themselves correspondingly by the terms *maga(n)* and *maga(l)* (male and female children) but also say that dead Nayaka become one with the forest spirits. They do not exclude their own immediate forefathers, and further-more, they perform secondary mortuary rituals to help their deceased relatives join the forest spirits. The Batek also address the end point of the life-cycle, though they depict a two-stage transformation. They say that the spirits of their dead relatives first go to the land of the dead, where superhuman friends and relatives transform them into superhumans and teach them the skills and songs of the *hala'*; thereupon they become *hala'* and move to the *hala'* place (Endicott 1979:111–15, 219).

Finally, these groups not only depict their ties with the natural agencies as ties of sharing between relatives but also explain experiences which could be seen to be at odds with this cultural representation in its own terms, as tem-porary, accidental, and remediable exceptions. The Mbuti, for example, say that mishaps occur when the forest is asleep. Then they have to awaken it by singing and "draw the forest's attention to the immediate needs of its children" (Turnbull 1961:87; 1976 [1965]:257). The Batek even go in for a preventive measure and believe that as long as they sing, the *hala'*, who like the songs, will send food in abundance (Endicott 1979:54, 56, 219). The Nayaka explain mishaps in another way, though they too effectively relocate the volition out-side the natural agencies. They maintain that the natural agencies are generi-cally benign but, interestingly, "people from far away," through sorcery, have affected them. Nevertheless, as for the Mbuti, it is simple enough for Nayaka to restore the order of goodness. Through divination they make it known that the natural agencies are not at fault, and the natural agencies turn back into their normal, benign selves.[3]

While we will never know for certain how Nayaka, Mbuti, or Batek relate to their environments, it is clear enough that the metaphor of sharing provides an important clue to it. Drawn from the institution of sharing so common in these hunter-gatherers' social life, it is a primary metaphor which can help us to loosen slightly the bonds of our own Western ways of viewing the world. Whereas we commonly construct nature in mechanistic terms, for them nature seems to be a set of agencies, simultaneously natural and human-like. Further-more, they do not inscribe into the nature of things a division between the nat-ural agencies and themselves as we do with our "nature:culture" dichotomy. They view their world as an integrated entity. While many other non-Western peoples view the world in this fashion, it seems that hunter-gatherers with im-mediate-return systems distinctively view their ties with the natural agencies in terms of visiting and sharing relationships. We can say that their world—according to the metaphorical template carried by the image of sharing—is a cosmic system of sharing which embraces both human-to-human and nature-to-human sharing. The two kinds of sharing are constituents of a cosmic economy of sharing.

Hunting and Gathering as Aspects of the Cosmic Economy of Sharing

The culture-specific dimensions of hunting and gathering can be brought into relief by examining them through the metaphorical model of the cosmic economy of sharing. Within it, they are constructed as acts of nature-to-human sharing which stimulate further acts of sharing in the world.[4] During the past 20 years, we have learnt a great deal about hunter-gatherers' human-to-human sharing. We have learnt that sharing is a social event which demonstrates relatedness, affection, and concern. In economic terms, the value of sharing often lies in its occurrence—in that it secures recurrence—rather than in the value of the resources involved in the particular transaction. Verbally, agents praise generosity in general and generous individuals in particular, but at the same time, in what has come to be called demand sharing (see Bird-David 1990; Peterson 1988), they moan excessively about their poverty and needs. Practically, would-be-recipients request what they *see* in the possession of others and do not request them to produce what they do not appear to have. With these aspects of sharing in mind, we can see that these hunter-gatherers do indeed engage with their natural environments as with sharing partners in at least four ways.

First, as in the case of human-to-human sharing, they care about going on forays just as they do about the value of their products. For example, on some days they collect items of no immediate use and of no great value, and, having collected something, return to the camp, even in the middle of the day. A concern with the activity itself—as much as, and sometimes more than, with its yield—is even more conspicuous when people engage temporarily in other subsistence activities. They continue to go on expeditions in the forest every now and then, even though they often collect little or nothing at all and could do without it. When they forage in the forest, they feel that they are in touch with the natural agencies. The Batek, for example, "feel they are being brought closer to the *hala'*" (Endicott 1979:67). The Mbuti experience a communion with the forest in that "the moment of killing . . . [is] . . . a moment of intense compassion and reverence" (Turnbull 1976 [1965]:161). In some of their stories, the Nayaka even tell of encounters with their supernatural relatives during the course of gathering. According to one story, for example, a woman dug up roots and came upon an elongated stone (the Nayaka point out that it resembles the human body in its shape and refer to it as *kalu* [deity]. She brought the stone to the hamlet (where it still is) and placed it with the other items, including other stones as well as personal mementoes of deceased relatives, that are ceremonially entertained and fed once a year.

Second, like sharing, hunting and gathering are social events and contexts for socializing. The Batek, for example, do not "view work as a burden. . . . Most men and women approach their economic activities enthusiastically" (K. L. Endicott 1980:650). "Women often go fishing with their children as a way of filling an hour or two after other work has been completed" (p. 634). They often say when they go that "they are tired of sitting around camp" and when they return that "they were just playing around at fishing" (Endicott 1979:21). Nayaka families often walk in the forest, each on its own, at a slow, indulgent pace. While picking up usable items, they observe what has happened since last they were there, what has blossomed and what has wilted, and talk about it in a leisurely way. Mbuti approach their hunting in a similar way, as is vividly evident in the following example (which is especially interesting in that it is provided by an ecologically oriented ethnographer [see Hart and Hart 1986], who is here describing a hunt for commercial ends): "The overall pace of the hunt is so leisurely that old people and mothers with infants may join. Between casts of the nets, the hunters regroup . . . to share tobacco or snacks of fruit and nuts gathered along the way . . . to flirt and visit, to play with babies" (Hart 1978:337).

Third, as in human-to-human sharing, seeing constitutes a crucial moment in hunting and gathering activities.[5] These hunter-gatherers tend to appropriate what they see rather than to search for something they want. They often set off from their huts with no particular sense of what they want to acquire in mind and collect what they happen to see on their way. Moreover, although it is impossible to see far ahead in the forest, they often do not even plan their route, instead going in the direction which seems best at the time. Again, they rarely request the natural agencies to produce more resources. They use, for example, very few if any magical means to try to improve their luck in hunting, fishing, and other endeavours (Endicott 1979:22). Seeing also establishes right of first access to resources in the forest, and this is particularly noticeable with respect to certain valued resources—for instance, certain kinds of honey—which can be collected repeatedly in the same place. The individual who first sees the tree on which it is annually found owns the tree, which means that he has the right to initiate the collection expedition.

Finally, echoing demand sharing in the human realm, these hunter-gatherers both praise the goodness and generosity of the natural agencies and (regardless of what they actually have) frequently complain of hunger and other insatiable needs. During their 24-hour shamanistic sessions, the Nayaka, for example, repeatedly do both. Similarly, the Mbuti complain of food shortage, although they also frequently sing to the goodness of the forest as they walk in it and as they hunt and gather alone and in groups (Turnbull 1976 [1965]:167, 256; 1961:57, 79; 1978:164). As in human-to-human sharing, complaints and praise are but complementary idioms in an economic discourse premised on giving (see Bird-David 1990).

From this ethnographic glimpse of hunter-gatherers with immediate-return systems it appears that the metaphor of sharing is a clue both to their views of their environment and to their action within it. Recent theory—from diverse perspectives—indeed shows that cognition (concepts, especially metaphorical ones, and percepts) is interrelated with action (Lakoff and Johnson 1980; Gibson 1979, 1982; Ingold 1989), and this is, of course, in harmony with our own most commonplace experience. For example, our use of the metaphor "a dog is a friend" indicates that through close interaction with the dog we have come to perceive and approach it as a friend. Even when we represent the dog as an animal, in the course of what Marx called the life activity we engage with the dog as our friend and express this in various ways in our conduct and discourse.

The primary metaphor of "sharing" is thus a concept with which we can make sense of the hunter-gatherers' economic arrangements (Gudeman 1986) and, moreover, a metaphorical concept by which *they* make sense of their environment, one that guides their action within it. Through their close interaction with the environment they have come to perceive it, and act with it, as with a friend, a relative, a parent who shares resources with them. Though in certain contexts they talk about aspects of their environment in "knowledge of" terms, for the most part in the course of their life activity they normally engage with it as if they were in a sharing relationship.

The metaphor "the natural environment is a sharing partner" thus constitutes an analytical tool (to be used with caution, in awareness of the inevitable uncertainty of our own authorship, continually checked and refined as we use it) to examine the issues which Sahlins raises in "The Original Affluent Society." For example, how do hunter-gatherers with immediate-return systems construct their needs vis-à-vis their environment in culture-specific terms? Do they trust their environment, and in what culture-specific sense? How does this metaphor make sense of their seemingly "peculiar" economic behaviour?

Rewriting Sahlins's Cultural Propositions

Do hunter-gatherers have "confidence in the yield of the morrow"? Being keen observers of nature's vicissitudes and ecological variations, hunter-gatherers with immediate-return systems are as cognizant of uncertainties in the "yield of the morrow" as we are, and probably more so. They have experienced periods of hardship in the past and know only too well that such periods may recur. Nevertheless, as in a sharing relationship, although they do not know—and know that they cannot know—what the natural environment will provide, they are confident that under normal conditions it will give them food. Moreover, irrespective of what they obtain in any particular hunting and gathering event—in any momentary episode of the life-long engagement of sharing—the very fact that they have obtained something in their eyes reaffirms their relationship with the natural agencies and therefore secures the recurrence of sharing. In a sense, then, they do have "confidence in the yield of the morrow"—a confidence born of the view that the environment is morally bound to share food and other material resources with them and that under normal conditions it will.

There is a certain truth in Sahlins's suggestion that hunter-gatherers have "limited needs," although it is empirically—not merely theoretically—inaccurate to say that they restrict their material desires in the way that Zen believers do. True, they are not interested in possessions and do not go to a great deal of bother to obtain and accumulate them. However, it is equally apparent that they delight in abundance when circumstances afford it and that they consume ostentatiously what they have. Furthermore, to quote Barnard and Woodburn (1988:12), their "demand for food and other goods from anthropologists, as well as from members of their own societies, is very great, indeed at times almost insatiable." Although these observations seem contradictory, they make sense given that these peoples construct their material requirements from their natural environment—and also, in many ways, from their social environment—in the way in which they construct their demands in a sharing relationship. They culturally construct their needs as the want of a share. Therefore, they require of their environment what they see when they see it and do not request it to produce more. But at the same time they enjoy and exhaust what they have obtained, however much it is, and persist in their demands for shares, irrespective of what they already have. They thus restrict their material wants, but in the way in which one does within a sharing relationship.

Not only food but also technological means are constructed as objects which are shared between the environment and people. This means that they are also regarded as items which can be appropriated from the environment, used without effecting modifications, and then returned to it, directly or via other people. As Woodburn has pointed out, these people often pick up tools just before, and for, the imminent collection of a resource and then leave them behind. They do not concern themselves with developing their technological equipment, although, if the environment provides sophisticated equipment, such as a gun or a Land Rover, they will readily use it, while showing the same remarkable (but not "peculiar") disposition to be careless about it. Their expertise has come to be the sophisticated use of the material means which the environment provides.

With one critical proviso, there is also value in Sahlins's suggestion that hunter-gatherers' economic dispositions are predicated on abundance. The proviso is that "abundance" is an assumption of their economic model—homologous with and opposite to the assumption of scarcity in Western economic models. In non-extreme situations, irrespective of what we have, the assumption of scarcity has a bearing upon our decisions, choices, and actions. In the case of these hunter-gatherers, the assumption of abundance has the same function. It is consistent with their view of the natural environment as a sharing partner, which implies that as human agents appropriate their shares they secure further sharing. The assumption of scarcity is consistent with Westerners' mechanistic view of the natural environment, which implies that in the course of time, as human agents use up resources, the total stock is depleted.

In conclusion, then, Sahlins suggested that hunter-gatherers follow the "Zen way" to affluence, which presupposes that "human material wants are few and finite, and technical means unchanging, but on the whole adequate" (1972:2). This way contrasts, he argued, with the modern Western one (the "Galbraithian way"), whose assumptions are appropriate to market economies—"that man's wants are great, not to say infinite, whereas his means are limited, although improveable." Hunter-gatherers with immediate-return systems in fact follow a third way—the "sharing way"—to affluence. Their way is based on assumptions appropriate to their sharing economy—that material wants are linked with material means which are available for sharing. (They want a share of however much is available.)

Further, Sahlins observed that in the Western market economy "all economic activity starts from a position of shortage. . . . one's resources are insufficient to the possible uses and satisfactions' (1968a:86). In this respect, the hunter-gatherers' case is the reverse. All economic activity starts from a position of affluence (affluence as a premise). One expects to obtain sufficient resources—at times of abundance even in excess of possible uses and satisfactions.

Finally, Sahlins wrote that "otherwise curious heathen devices become understandable by the people's confidence" (1972:29) and that hunter-gatherers behave "as if they had it made" (1968a:86). He was right on both points—if read to say that just as Westerners' behaviour is understandable in relation to their assumption of shortage, so hunter-gatherers behaviour is understandable in relation to their assumption of affluence. Moreover, just as we analyze, even predict, Westerners' behaviour by presuming that they behave as if they did not have enough, so we can analyze, even predict, hunter-gatherers' behaviour by presuming that they behave as if they had it made.

Towards New Ecological Propositions

In terms of the cosmic economy of sharing, then, the "peculiar" economic behaviour of hunter-gatherers with immediate-return systems makes sense. Moreover, reconceptualized in this way, Sahlins's cultural propositions hold. But the reader is likely to ask: under what ecological conditions can people maintain, and live by, such an economic model? Furthermore, do they in fact have abundant resources, or do they merely think that they do? These are our questions, framed within our models; the people in question would not ask them. Nevertheless, most of our colleagues in the world of learning and in policy-making circles—let alone most students of hunter-gathering peoples—think in Western terms. We therefore have to address these questions, especially since Sahlins's implicit assumption that hunter-gatherers' confidence in the environment is explained by abundance (albeit under conditions of enforced mobility and prodigality) does not hold.

Unfortunately, much as we might want to explore the ecological dimension of these hunter-gatherers' cultural-economic system in their own terms, we cannot do so. In the case of the farmers of the eastern Andes, Gudeman and Rivera (1990) have shown that Westerners, and even certain Western economists, can engage in direct conversation with the local people, but this is possible only because of the close affinity between the local model, the folk Western model, and the model of certain Western economists (they argue for a historical link dating to the Iberian conquest of the Americas). In the case of the hunter-gatherers, in contrast, there is a fundamental disjuncture between the Western and the local model: the terms of each exclude the other. While the Western model presupposes a detached observer concerned with an inanimate nature, the local one presupposes an actor personally involved with an animate natural environment (see Ingold 1989).

However, as I have shown above, the local model relates experientially to action and, moreover, to the same physical reality—the natural environment—with which we are concerned. Therefore, although we cannot translate their experience into our terms, we can come to understand it (see Lakoff 1987, chap. 17) by finding a new way of looking at the natural environment. We need to create a new metaphor of our own and use it as an imaginative cognitive model. Ideally, this metaphor will evoke the way in which these hunter-gatherers relate to their environments in terms equivalent to their own. From such a metaphor we should be able to deduce new, testable propositions and gain novel perspectives on their economy.

I think that there is a metaphor which fills the bill, and it involves the Western institution of the bank. Not only is it the major institution of exchange in the Western economy, and therefore equivalent to sharing, but we draw on it metaphorically, just as the hunter-gatherers draw on sharing, when we are dealing with resources which, for us, are ambiguously placed between the animate and the inanimate (we have, for example, blood banks and semen banks).

Furthermore, the bank is a system which is both concerned with the circulation and use of resources and founded on trust. Individuals save resources for future need, but instead of keeping their valued resources privately they deposit them in the bank, in trust, so that when the time comes they will be able to repossess either them or their exact equivalent instantaneously. For the most part, however, these resources are meanwhile accessible to the public for gainful use, on the basis of the statistical fact that at any given time only a fraction of the savers will claim their deposits. Now, the hunter-gatherers not only have trust in their natural environment and regard its resources as their due shares but, indeed, also make intermittent claims on those shares. They engage in occasional opportunistic pursuit of other subsistence activities (for example, labouring for their neighbours) and frequently shift between these and hunting and gathering (see Bird-David n.d.). Moreover, the bank is a system which can only work if people do not withdraw proceeds from it in order to hoard or circulate them within restricted, private circles. This is precisely the case among the hunter-gatherers and is, after all, what the social institution of sharing is all about. It seems, therefore, that the metaphor "nature is a bank" captures the essence of these hunter-gatherers' engagement with the natural environment while embodying the material basis as well as the cultural aspect of their economy.

Among the many possible propositions which can be deduced from this metaphorical model, there is one which is relevant to the question of the ecological foundations of the local economic model. This is that the hunter-gatherers can maintain their trust in the natural environment—and a successful economy—even when the natural environment cannot, in fact, provide sufficient resources for everyone simultaneously. This hypothesis may seem paradoxical, but it is no more so than the case of the Western bank (see Samuelson 1951:323). The crucial ecological condition may be, as it is in the banking system, a minimum threshold of resources which corresponds to the fraction of the group that is likely to make claims on its shares instantaneously. To explore this possibility, we will need to move away from the goose-chase study of "near pure" hunter-gatherers and look instead at the temporal and idiosyncratic structures of hunting and gathering in the heterogeneous groups that we encounter. We will need to find out what portion of the group pursues foraging at any given period of time, how frequently individuals within the community shift between subsistence activities, and how often they hunt and gather. We may then be able to work out the minimum ecological threshold for a successful economy premised on trust in the natural environment. There is a related proposition of which we must be aware: this kind of economy can collapse as a result of a breakdown of confidence even when there is no crucial decline in the level of natural resources. The history of banking systems provides examples of this, and we may find also hunter-gatherer cases.

The second question, and the more intriguing one, concerns the extent to which these hunter-gatherers' cultural-economic system generates wealth. Does the fact that they view their environment as rich make it richer? Ecologically oriented scholars have already explored the proposition that sharing—human-to-human sharing—constitutes a kind of collective insurance against unpredictable natural fluctuations and argued that it safeguards individuals from poverty (e.g., Wiessner 1982; Cashdan 1985; Smith 1988; Gould 1982). They have not, however, gone far enough. They ignore both a fundamental part of the ecological equation and the way in which the actors themselves view their environment. Since these scholars view natural resources as an independent variable, they take into account neither the stochastic link between past human use and present level of natural resources nor the fact that, like money in a bank, natural resources left in nature can grow.

The metaphorical model "nature is a bank" implies a more complex development of their proposition, namely, that sharing constitutes an insurance scheme which also involves investment in a banking system. Not only does it safeguard individuals from unpredictable troubles but also it increases their resources. The simpler way in which this may happen can be best explained by an example drawn from a non-monetary banking system. For instance, with the blood bank each individual protects himself by giving blood when he can and receives blood when he needs it. However, the total volume of blood in the bank meanwhile increases as well, because what may not have been a resource before now becomes one. For example, blood which may have been the wrong type for one's friends and relatives becomes a usable resource once it is deposited in the bank. We need to explore whether these hunter-gatherers' economy works in a similar way. For instance, does the general sharing of large game generate wealth because a large amount which would have been wasted on one's own friends and close relatives stretches farther when it is divided among all members of the group?

The second and more complex way in which a banking system generates wealth can be illustrated by our monetary banking system, in which money in fact generates more money. The folk explanation is simple enough: we say that money grows, and, noticeably, we ourselves use the metaphor "money in the bank is like a plant in nature." The technical explanation is complicated and lies in the paradoxical nature of circulation and ownership in this system (put simply, it has to do with the fact that for each pound sterling in the bank, there are about four individuals who simultaneously own it and use it). We need to explore the ways in which this may happen within these hunter-gatherers' economic system. The sharing of large game, for example, may also generate wealth in an additional way: recipients of meat are likely to postpone hunting, since they have had a share and since they are confident that meat is secured in the bank of nature until they need it, meanwhile allowing more time for natural increase. I suspect that if we examine the temporal and idiosyncratic patterns of foraging, as well as patterns of ownership and circulation, with these aspects of the banking system in mind, we will find that in many other ways these hunter-gatherers' economic system, premised on trust in the natural environment, does generate wealth. Sahlins summarized his case by the catch phrase "Want not, lack not." It may well be, however, that the hunter-gatherers' case is "Think rich, be rich."

Conclusions

The fundamental flaw in "The Original Affluent Society" was Sahlins's conflation of cultural and ecological perspectives. As shown here, however, this problem can be resolved, and the relevant empirical studies then show that Sahlins did indeed "have a point"; his essay is a king that could—and should—be scientifically reclothed. The evocative title of his essay was inspired by John Kenneth Galbraith's *The Affluent Society* (1969 [1958]). It is ironic that Galbraith in fact emphasized the impact of ideas on the economy, arguing—in a mirror image of what I have argued for the hunter-gatherers in question—that the assumption of scarcity continues to influence economic conduct in the increasingly wealthy West and thereby acts to preserve poverty. The irony is doubled, for in the second edition of his book Galbraith criticized those who misread his argument and overrated his point on the shortening of work hours. His main argument was that the way to the really affluent society lies in an ideological disengagement between production and economic security and between production and income. These ideas are precisely the ideas which are embodied in the cosmic economy of sharing. In respect to their cultural ideas, therefore, hunter-gatherers with immediate-return systems constitute the original affluent society in a more comprehensive sense than Sahlins envisaged.

NOTES

1. My thanks go to Barbara Bodenhorn, Ernest Gellner, Keith Hart, Caroline Humphrey, Tim Ingold, Marilyn Strathern, and James Woodburn for comments on the early version of the paper and to Alan Barnard, Harvey Feit, Stephen Gudeman, and Richard Lee for their support of the earlier paper in which I began to explore these ideas.
2. Lee's output-input study was carried out over a period of four weeks, but he excluded one week during which his own contribution to subsistence effort was too great to be overlooked.
3. In the case of extreme and lingering problems, it is believed that a local Nayaka has interfered with the natural agencies and has made them harmful. There is a more elaborate way of addressing this problem.
4. It should also be useful to look at hunting and gathering from the perspective of the sociology of work, which since the 1950s has gone well beyond the examination of work as labour.
5. Among the !Kung and some northern hunters individuals "see" game in divinatory dreams and then set out to get it, or they "see" where it will be best to go foraging (e.g., Lee 1979; Tanner 1979).

REFERENCES

BARNARD A., AND J. WOODBURN. 1988. "Introduction," in *Hunters and gatherers*, vol. 2, *Property, power, and ideology*. Edited by T. Ingold, D. Riches, and J. Woodburn, pp. 4–31. Oxford: Berg.

BIRD-DAVID, N. 1988. "Hunter-gatherers and other people: A re-examination," in *Hunters and Gatherers*, vol. 1, *History, evolution, and Social Change*. Edited by T. Ingold, D. Riches, and J. Woodburn. Oxford: Berg.

———. 1990. "The giving environment: Another perspective on the economic system of gatherer-hunters." *Current Anthropology* 31:183–96.

———. n.d. Beyond "Man the Hunter": Hunter-gatherers between nature and nation. *Man*. In press.

CASHDAN, E. 1985. Coping with risk: Reciprocity among the Basarwa of northern Botswana. *Man* 20:454-74.

COLE, J. B. Editor. 1988. *Anthropology for the nineties: Introductory readings*. New York: Free Press.

ENDICOTT, K. 1979. *Batek Negrito religion: The world view and rituals of a hunting and gathering people of peninsular Malaysia*. Oxford: Clarendon Press.

ENDICOTT, K. L. 1980. Batek Negrito sex roles: Behaviour and ideology.

Paper presented at the Second International Conference on Hunting and Gathering Societies, Quebec, Canada.

EYRE, E. J. 1845. *Journals of expeditions of discovery into Central Australia, and overland from Adelaide to King George's Sound, in the years 1840–41.* 2 vols. London: Boone.

GALBRAITH, J. K. 1969 (1958). *The affluent society.* Harmondsworth: Penguin.

GIBSON, J. J. 1979. *The ecological approach to visual perception.* Boston: Houghton Mifflin.

———. 1982. *Reasons for realism: Selected essays of James J. Gibson.* Edited by E. Reed and R. J. Jones. Hillsdale: Lawrence Erlbaum.

GOULD, R. 1982. "To have and have not: The ecology of sharing among hunter-gatherers," in *Resource managers: North American and Australian hunter-gatherers.* Edited by N. Williams and E. Hunn. Boulder: Westview.

GREY, SIR GEORGE. 1841. *Journals of two expeditions of discovery in north west and western Australia during the years 1837, 38 and 39.* 2 vols. London: Boone.

GUDEMAN, S. 1986. *Economics as culture: Models and metaphors of livelihood.* London: Routledge and Kegan Paul.

GUDEMAN, S., AND A. RIVERA. 1990. *Conversations in Colombia.* Cambridge: Cambridge University Press.

HART, J. A. 1978. From subsistence to market: A case study of the Mbuti net hunters. *Human Ecology* 6:325–53.

HART, T. B., AND J. A. HART. 1986. The ecological basis of hunter-gatherer subsistence in African rain forests: The Mbuti of Western Zaire. *Human Ecology* 14:29–55.

HAYDEN, B. 1981. "Subsistence and ecological adaptations of modern hunter/gatherers," in *Omnivorous primates: Gathering and hunting in human evolution.* Edited by Robert S. Harding and Geza Teleki, pp. 344–421. New York: Columbia University Press.

HAWKES, K., AND JAMES F. O'CONNELL. 1981. Affluent hunters? Some comments in light of the Alyawara case. *American Anthropologist* 84:622–26.

HAWKES, K., JAMES F. O'CONNELL, KIM HILL, AND ERIC L. CHARNOV. 1985. How much is enough? Hunters and limited needs. *Ethology and Sociobiology* 6:3–15.

HEADLAND, T. N. 1987. The wild yam question: How well could independent hunter-gatherers live in a tropical rain forest ecosystem? *Human Ecology* 15:463–91.

HELM, J. 1968. "Comment on 'Does hunting bring happiness?'" in *Man the Hunter.* Edited by R. Lee and I. DeVore, p. 89. Chicago: Aldine.

HILL, K., H. KAPLAN, K. HAWKES, AND A. M. HURTADO. 1985. Men's time allocation to subsistence work among the Ache of eastern Paraguay. *Human Ecology* 13:29–47.

INGOLD, T. 1989. Culture and the perception of the environment. Paper presented at the Sixth EIDOS Workshop on Cultural Understanding of the Environment, London, June.

KEMP, WILLIAM B. 1971. The flow of energy in a hunting society. *Scientific American* 225(3):105–15 [GWW]

LAKOFF, G. 1987. *Women, fire, and dangerous things: What categories reveal about the mind.* Chicago: University of Chicago Press.

LAKOFF, G., AND M. JOHNSON. 1980. *Metaphors we live by.* Chicago: University of Chicago Press.

LAUGHLIN, WILLIAM S. 1968. "Hunting: An integrating biobehavior system and its evolutionary importance," in *Man the hunter.* Edited by R. B. Lee and I. DeVore, pp. 304-20. Chicago: Aldine. (ESB)

LEE, R. B. 1968. "What hunters do for a living; or, How to make out on scarce resources," In *Man the hunter.* Edited by R. B. Lee and I. DeVore. Chicago: Aldine.

———. 1969. "!Kung Bushman subsistence: An input-output analysis," in *Environment and cultural behavior.* Edited by A. P. Vayda, pp. 47–79. New York: Natural History Press.

———. 1979. *The !Kung San: Men, women, and work in a foraging society.* New York: Cambridge University Press.

McARTHUR, M. 1960. "Food consumption and dietary levels of groups of Aborigines living on naturally occuring foods," in *Records of the American-Australian Scientific Expedition to Arnhem Land,* vol. 2, *Anthropology and nutrition.* Edited by C. P. Mountford. Melbourne: Melbourne University Press.

McCARTHY, F. D., AND M. McARTHUR. 1960. "The food quest and the time factor in aboriginal economic life," in *Records of the American-Australian Scientific Expedition to Arnhem Land,* vol. 2 *Anthropology and nutrition.* Edited by C. P. Mountford. Melbourne: Melbourne University Press.

MOSKO, M. 1987. The symbols of "Forest": A structural analysis of Mbuti culture and social organization. *American Anthropologist* 89:896–913.

PETERSON, N. 1988. Reciprocity and the demand for generosity. Paper presented at the Fourth International Conference on Hunting and Gathering Societies, London.

SAHLINS, M. 1968a. "Notes on the original affluent society," in *Man the hunter.* Edited by R. B. Lee and I. DeVore, pp. 85– 89. Chicago: Aldine.

———. 1968b. La première société d'abondance. *Les temps modernes* no. 268, pp. 641–80.

———. 1972. *Stone Age Economics.* Chicago: Aldine.

———. 1976. *Culture and practical reason.* Chicago: University of Chicago Press.

SAMUELSON, P. A. 1951. *Economics: An introductory analysis.* New York: McGraw-Hill.

SMITH, E. A. 1987. On fitness maximization, limited needs, and hunter-gatherer time allocation. *Ethnology and Sociobiology* 8:73–85.

————. 1988. "Risk and uncertainty in the 'original affluent society': Evolutionary ecology of resource-sharing and land tenure" in *Hunters and gatherers*, vol. 1, *History, evolution, and social change*. Edited by T. Ingold, D. Riches, and J. Woodburn. Oxford: Berg.

SOLWAY, J., AND R. B. LEE. 1990. Foragers, genuine or spurious? Situating the Kalahari San in history. *Current Anthropology* 31:109–46.

TANNER, A. 1979. *Bringing home animals: Religious ideology and mode of production of the Mistassini Cree hunters*. London: Hurst.

TURNBULL, C. M. 1961. *The forest people: A study of the Pygmies of the Congo*. New York: Simon and Schuster.

————. 1976 (1965). *Wayward servants: The two worlds of the African Pygmies*. Westport: Greenwood Press.

————. 1978. "The politics of non-aggression (Zaire)," in *Learning non-aggression: The experience of non-literate societies."* Edited by A. Montagu, pp. 161–222. Oxford: Oxford University Press.

————. 1983. *The Mbuti Pygmies: Change and adaptation*. Holt, Rinehart and Winston.

WIESSNER, P. 1982. "Risk, reciprocity, and social influence on !Kung San economics," in *Politics and history in band societies*. Edited by E. Leacock and R. Lee. Cambridge: Cambridge University Press.

WILMSEN, E., AND J. DENBOW. 1991. Paradigmatic history of San-speaking peoples and current attempts at revision. *Current Anthropology* 31:489–524.

WINTERHALDER, B. 1990. "An ecological explanation for limited effort foraging," the *Sixth International Conference on Hunter-Gatherers. Fairbanks, Alaska, May 1990 (precirculated Papers and Abstracts)*, vol. 1, pp. 489–503.

WINTERHALDER, B., AND E. A. SMITH. Editor. 1981. *Hunter-gatherer foraging strategies*. Chicago: University of Chicago Press.

WOODBURN, J. 1980. "Hunters and gatherers today and reconstruction of the past," in *Soviet and Western anthropology*. Edited by E. Gellner. London: Duckworth.

————. 1982. Egalitarian societies. *Man* 17:431–45.

————. 1988. "African hunter-gatherer social organization: Is it best understood as a product of encapsulation?" in *Hunters and gatherers*, vol. 1, *History, evolution, and social change*. Edited by T. Ingold, D. Riches, and J. Woodburn, pp. 31–64. Oxford: Berg.

Women's Status in Egalitarian Society: Implications for Social Evolution[1]

◆

Eleanor Leacock

The analysis of women's status in egalitarian society is inseparable from the analysis of egalitarian social-economic structure as a whole, and concepts based on the hierarchical structure of our society distort both. I shall argue that the tendency to attribute to band societies the relations of power and property characteristic of our own obscures the qualitatively different relations that obtained when ties of economic dependency linked the individual directly with the group as a whole, when public and private spheres were not dichotomized, and when decisions were made by and large by those who would be carrying them out. I shall attempt to show that a historical approach and an avoidance of ethnocentric phraseology in the study of such societies reveals that their egalitarianism applied as fully to women as to men. Further, I shall point out that this is a fact of great importance to the understanding of social evolution.

Demonstrating that women's status in egalitarian society was qualitatively different from that in our own presents problems at several levels. First, the societies studied by anthropologists are virtually all in some measure incorporated into world economic and political systems that oppress women, and most have been involved in these larger systems for centuries. Anthropologists know this historical reality well, but commonly ignore it when making generalizations about preclass social-economic systems.

A second problem follows from the selectivity of research. Too many questions about women have not been asked, or not of the right people, and gaps in ethnographic reports are too readily filled with clichés. To handle women's participation in a given society with brief remarks about food preparation and

This essay originally appeared in *Current Anthropology*, Volume 19, No. 2, June 1978. It was subsequently reprinted in *Current Anthropology*, Volume 33, Supplement, 1992. It is reprinted here from the 1992 version, with permission from the publisher. Copyright © 1978 by The Wenner-Gren Foundation for Anthropological Research.

child care has until very recently met the requirements for adequate ethnography. Hence a once-over-lightly of cross-cultural data can readily affirm the virtual universality of the Western ideal for women's status. Ethnocentric interpretation contributes to this affirmation. Women are commonly stated or implied to hold low status in one or another society without benefit of empirical documentation. Casual statements about menstrual blood as polluting and as contributing to women's inferior status may be made without linguistic or other supporting data to demonstrate that this familiarly Western attitude of repugnance actually obtains in the culture under discussion.

A further problem for the analysis of women's status in egalitarian society is theoretical. That women were autonomous in egalitarian society—that is, that they held decision-making power over their own lives and activities to the same extent that men did over theirs—cannot be understood unless the nature of individual autonomy in general in such society is clear. (I prefer the term "autonomy" to "equality," for equality connotes rights and opportunity specific to class society and confuses similarity with equity. Strictly speaking, who can be, or wants to be, "equal" to anyone else?) Non-class-based societies are usually not seen as qualitatively different from those that are class-organized when it comes to processes of leadership and decision making. Differences are seen as purely quantitative, and the possibility that altogether different sets of relationships from those involving economic power might be operating in non-class society is not followed through. Instead, as a result of intellectual habits that stem from Platonic metaphysical traditions, universalistic categories are set up on the basis of individual behavior and are named, counted, described, or otherwise reified by the failure to move on to a discovery of the social-economic processes that lie behind them.

It is difficult to apply the principle that all reality involves interacting processes, and not interacting "essences" or things. Respects may be paid to the concepts of process and conflict, which may then be reified as well. Since these reified concepts are derived from our own culture, it is no accident that hierarchical patterns similar to our own are found to be "incipient" wherever they are not well established. From band to tribe, tribe to chiefdom, chiefdom to state, the development of decision-making processes is seen quantitatively as progressive change toward Western forms of power and control. Fundamental qualitative distinctions between egalitarian and class societies are lost. A hierarchical view of sex roles fits easily into the scheme. That sex roles exist is, after all, a human universal, and to assume that any difference between the sexes necessarily involves hierarchy is seen, not as ethnocentrism, but as common sense.

The reification of the concept "tribe," pointed out by Fried (1968, 1975), affords a good example of what I mean. Fried argues that insofar as tribes exist as culturally and territorially bounded and politically integrated groupings of bands or villages, they are the creatures of colonial relations. However, for want of a clear conception as to what might replace it, the term "tribe" continues in use and fosters the misconception that egalitarian peoples were organized in closed territorially defined units, uniformly obeying the mandates of custom and controlled by the authority, weak though it might be, of a chief and/or council. The structure is not merely "cold"; it is positively frozen. In reality, people were far more cosmopolitan than the term "tribesmen" suggests. They moved about, traded and negotiated, and constantly chose among the various alternatives for action.

In relation to the study of sex roles, the core of tribal structure is commonly seen in terms of unilineal agnatic systems that represent formal, jural authority, as counterposed to the "familial" sphere of influence accorded to women. The polarization of public male authority and private female influence is taken as a given of the human condition. Thereby areas in which women exercised socially recognized authority are obscured or downgraded. The reality of the distinction between unilineal and segmenting kinship systems has recently been questioned on the basis of comparison of Melanesian and African data (Barnes 1971; Keesing 1971). It is my contention that the public-private dichotomy is similarly inadequate for understanding societies that are (or were) not structured along class lines. Instead, insofar as social processes of the precolonial world can be reconstructed, the delineation and opposition of public and private spheres can be seen as emergent in many culture areas, where individual families were becoming more or less competitive units in conflict with the communality of family-bands or kin groups. Furthermore, the complex of processes involved, concerning specialization, exchange, and the expenditure of labor on land, together constituted initial steps toward class differentiation. Although the accidents of history caused these processes to become thoroughly entangled with colonial relations throughout the world, some of their essential outlines can still be defined through ethnohistorical research and comparative analysis.

In the case of foraging societies, the control women exercised over their own lives and activities is widely, if not fully, accepted as ethnographic fact. However, assumptions of a somehow lower status and deferential stance toward "dominant" men are made by most writers on the subject. The very existence of different roles for females and males is seen as sufficient explanation, given women's responsibility for childbearing and suckling. The possibility that women and men could be "separate but equal" is seldom considered, albeit not surprisingly, since it seems to tally with the adjuration to women in our society to appreciate the advantages of the liabilities maternity here incurs. That an equal status for women could be interwoven with childbearing is a notion that has only begun to be empirically examined (Draper 1975).

My point is that concepts of band organization must be reexamined if the nature of women's autonomy in foraging societies is to be understood. To describe the band as "familistic" (Service 1966:8) or "only a simple association of families" (Sahlins 1961:324) may serve in a rough-and-ready way to convey something of the nonhierarchical and informal character of social-economic life among foragers, but it implies a universal "family" to be at the core of all society. Such a view of the band, whether implicit or explicit, leaves no alternative than for sex roles in band society to present a glimmer of what was to develop in class society. It implies historical evolution to be a continuum in which social forms become quantitatively more and more like those we experience, rather than to be constituted by a series of qualitative transformations, in the course of which relations between the sexes could have become altogether different.

To argue the point of sexual egalitarianism, then, involves a combination of theoretical and empirical reexamination. In the following pages, I shall give several examples of what I think is called for. The materials are everywhere at hand; they form the corpus of the ethnographic record.

The Band

As a student of the Montagnais-Naskapi people of the Labrador Peninsula, some 25 years ago, I looked at changing relations to the land and its resources among hunters turned fur-trappers and traders. At that time I confronted the fact that the band as then conceived (Speck 1926:277–78)—a rather neat entity, with a leader, a name, and a more or less bounded territory—had simply not existed in the past. Missionaries, traders, and government representatives alike bemoaned its absence and did what they could to bring it into existence, while the fur trade itself exerted its inevitable influence. "It would be wrong to infer . . . that increasing dependence on trade has acted to destroy formerly stable social groups," I wrote at that time. Instead, "changes brought about by the fur trade have led to more stable bands with greater formal organization" (Leacock 1954:20). The *Jesuit Relations,* when analyzed in detail, reveal the 17th-century Montagnais-Naskapi band to have been, not a loose collection of families, but a seasonal coalition of smaller groups that hunted cooperatively through most of the winter. These groups, in turn, were made up of several lodge groups that stayed together when they could, but separated when it was necessary to cover wider ranges for hunting. The lodge groups of several families, not individual families, were the basic social-economic units (Leacock 1969; Rogers 1972:133).

Among foraging peoples, seasonal patterns of aggregation and dispersal vary according to the ecological features of different areas and the specific technologies employed to exploit them (Cox 1973; Damas 1969). However, that aggregates of several families operate as basic social-economic units which coalesce with and separate from other such units remains constant. These aggregates are highly flexible. Congeniality as well as viable age and sex ratios are fundamental to their makeup; kin ties are important but do not rule out friendships; and when formal kinship is important, as in Australia, the focus is on categorical relationships that define expectations for reciprocity, rather than on genealogical linkages that define status prerogatives. ·

Distinctions between bands of this sort and bands as they have come to exist may seem slight, but in fact they are profound. The modern band consists of loosely grouped nuclear families that are economically dependent to one extent or another on trade or work outside of the group or on some governmental allowance or missionary provisioning. Therefore the modern band has a chief or leader of some sort to represent its corporate interests in negotiations with governmental, business, or missionary personnel, or individual men, who are accepted by outsiders as heads of nuclear families, take on this role. As an inevitable concomitant of dependence on political and economic relations outside the group, a public domain becomes defined, if but hazily, as counterposed to a private "familial" sphere. Furthermore, the public domain, associated with men, is either the economically and politically more significant one or is rapidly becoming so.

Decision Making in Foraging Society

What is hard to grasp about the structure of the egalitarian band is that leadership as we conceive it is not merely "weak" or "incipient," as is commonly stated, but irrelevant. The very phrases "informal" and "unstable" that are typically applied to band society imply a groping for the "formality" and "stability" of the band as we comfortably construe it and hinder the interpretation of the qualitatively different organizational form, of enormous resiliency, effectiveness, and stability, that preceded the modern band. The fact that consensus, freely arrived at, within and among multifamily units was both essential to everyday living and possible has implications that we do not usually confront. Individual autonomy was a necessity, and autonomy as a valued principle persists to a striking degree among the descendants of hunter/gatherers. It was linked with a way of life that called for great individual initiative and decisiveness along with the ability to be extremely sensitive to the feelings of lodge-mates. I suggest that personal autonomy was concomitant with the direct dependence of each individual on the group as a whole. Decision making in this context calls for concepts other than ours of leader and led, dominant and deferent, no matter how loosely these are seen to apply.

In egalitarian band society, food and other necessities were procured or manufactured by all able-bodied adults and were directly distributed by their producers (or occasionally, perhaps, by a parallel band member, ritualizing the sharing principle). It is common knowledge that there was no differential access to resources through private land ownership and no specialization of labor beyond that by sex, hence no market system to intervene in the direct relationship between production and distribution. It is not generally recognized, however, that *the direct relation between production and consumption was intimately connected with the dispersal of authority*. Unless some form of control over resources enables persons with authority to withhold them from others, authority is not authority as we know it. Individual prestige and influence must continually validate themselves in daily life, through the wisdom and ability to contribute to group well-being. The tragically bizarre forms personal violence can take among foraging peoples whose economy has been thoroughly and abruptly disrupted, as described recently for the Ik by Turnbull (1972) and for the central and western Australians of an earlier period by Bates (1938), do not vitiate this principle; the bitter quality of collective suicide they portray only underlines it.

The basic principle of egalitarian band society was that people made decisions about the activities for which they were responsible. Consensus was reached within whatever group would be carrying out a collective activity. Infringements upon the rights of others were negotiated by the parties concerned. Men and women, when defined as interest groups according to the sexual division of labor, arbitrated or acted upon differences in "public" ways, such as when women would hold council among the 17th-century Montagnais-Naskapi to consider the problem of a lazy man, or would bring a male ceremony to an early conclusion among the Pitjandjara of west-central Australia because they were having to walk too far for food and were ready to move (Tindale 1972:244–45). The negotiation of marriages for young people would seem to be an exception to the principle of autonomy in those societies in which it occurred. However, not only did young people generally have a say in the matter (Lee 1972:358), but divorce was easy and at the desire of either partner.

The dispersal of authority in band societies means that the public-private or jural-familial dichotomy, so important in hierarchically organized society, is not relevant. In keeping with common analytic practice of setting up quantitatively conceived categories for comparative purposes, it could be argued that decisions made by one or several individuals are more private, while decisions that affect larger numbers are more public, and decision-making processes could be tallied and weighted accordingly. My point is that analysis along any such lines continues to mystify actual decision-making processes in egalitarian societies by conceptualizing them in terms of authority and dependence patterns characteristic of our own society.

The Status of Women

With regard to the autonomy of women, nothing in the structure of egalitarian band societies necessitated special deference to men. There were no economic and social liabilities that bound women to be more sensitive to men's needs and feelings than vice versa. This was even true in hunting societies, where women did not furnish a major share of the food. The record of 17th-century Montagnais-Naskapi life in the *Jesuit Relations* makes this clear. Disputes and quarrels among spouses were virtually nonexistent, Le Jeune reported, since each sex carried out its own activities without "meddling" in those of the other. Le Jeune deplored the fact that the Montagnais "imagine that they ought by right of birth, to enjoy the liberty of wild ass colts, rendering no homage to any one whomsoever." Noting that women had "great power," he expressed his disapproval of the fact that men had no apparent inclination to make their wives "obey" them or to enjoin sexual fidelity upon them. He lectured the Indians on this failing, reporting in one instance, "I told him then that he was the master, and that in France women do not rule their husbands." Le Jeune was also distressed by the sharp and ribald joking and teasing into which women entered along with the men. "Their language has the foul odor of the sewers," he wrote. The *Relations* reflect the program of the Jesuits to "civilize" the Indians, and during the course of the 17th century they attempted to introduce principles of formal authority, lectured the people about obeying newly elected chiefs, and introduced disciplinary measures in the effort to enforce male authority upon women. No data are more illustrative of the distance between hierarchical and egalitarian forms of organization than the Jesuit account of these efforts (Leacock 1975, 1977; Leacock and Goodman 1977).

Nonetheless, runs the argument for universal female subservience to men, the hunt and war, male domains, are associated with power and prestige to the disadvantages of women. What about this assumption?

Answers are at several levels. First, it is necessary to modify the exaggerations of male as hunter and warrior. Women did some individual hunting, as will be discussed below for the Ojibwa, and they participated in hunting drives that were often of great importance. Men did a lot of non-hunting. Warfare was minimal or nonexistent. The association of hunting, war, and masculine assertiveness is not found among hunter/gatherers except, in a limited way, in Australia. Instead, it characterizes horticultural societies in certain areas, notably Melanesia and the Amazon lowlands.

It is also necessary to reexamine the idea that these male activities were in the past more prestigious than the creation of new human beings. I am sympathetic to the scepticism with which women may view the argument that their gift of fertility was as highly valued as or more highly valued than anything men did. Women are too commonly told today to be content with the wondrous ability to give birth and with the presumed propensity for "motherhood" as defined in saccharine terms. They correctly read such exhortations as saying, "Do not fight for a change in status." However, the fact that childbearing is associated with women's present oppression does not mean this was the case in earlier social forms. To the extent that hunting and warring (or, more accurately, sporadic raiding, where it existed) were areas of male ritualization, they were just that: areas of male ritualization. To a greater or lesser extent women participated in the rituals, while to a greater or lesser extent they were also involved in ritual elaborations of generative power, either along with men or separately. To presume the greater importance of male than female participants, or casually to accept the statements to this effect of latter-day male informants, is to miss the basic function of dichotomized sex-symbolism in egalitarian society. Dichotomization made it possible to ritualize the reciprocal roles of females and males that sustained the group. As ranking began to develop, it became a means of asserting male dominance, and with the full-scale development of classes sex ideologies reinforced inequalities that were basic to exploitative structures.

Much is made of Australian Aboriginal society in arguments for universal deference of women toward men. The data need ethnohistorical review, since the vast changes that have taken place in Australia over the last two centuries cannot be ignored in the consideration of ritual life and of male brutality toward women. Disease, outright genocidal practices, and expulsion from their lands reduced the population of native Australians to its lowest point in the 1930s, after which the cessation of direct genocide, the mission distribution of foods, and the control of infant mortality began to permit a population increase. The concomitant intensification of ceremonial life is described as follows by Godelier (1973:13, translation mine):[2]

> This ... phenomenon, of a politico-religious order, of course expresses the desire of these groups to reaffirm their cultural identity and to resist the destructive pressures of the process of domination and acculturation they are undergoing, which has robbed them of their land and subjected their ancient religious and political practices to erosion and systematic extirpation.

Thus ceremonial elaboration was oriented toward renewed ethnic identification, in the context of oppression. Furthermore, on the reserves, the economic autonomy of women vis-à-vis men was undercut by handouts to men defined as heads of families and by the sporadic opportunities for wage labor open to men. To assume that recent ritual data reflect aboriginal Australian symbolic structures as if unchanged is to be guilty of freezing these people in some timeless "traditional culture" that does not change or develop, but only becomes lost; it is to rob them of their history. Even in their day, Spencer and Gillen (1968:443) noted the probable decline in women's ceremonial participation among the Arunta.

Allusions to male brutality toward women are common for Australia. Not all violence can be blamed on European colonialism, to be sure, yet it is crass ethnocentrism, if not outright racism, to assume that the grim brutality of Europeans toward the Australians they were literally seeking to exterminate was without profound effect. A common response to defeat is to turn hostility inward. The process is reversed when people acquire the political understanding and organizational strength to confront the source of their problems, as has recently been happening among Australian Aborigines.

References to women of recent times fighting back publicly in a spirited style, occasionally going after their husbands with both tongue and fighting club, and publicly haranguing both men and women bespeak a persisting tradition of autonomy (Kaberry 1939:25–26, 181). In relation to "those reciprocal rights and duties that are recognized to be inherent in marriage," Kaberry writes (pp. 142–43):

> I, personally, have seen too many women attack their husbands with a tomahawk or even their own boomerangs, to feel that they are invariably the victims of ill treatment. A man may perhaps try to beat his wife if she has not brought in sufficient food, but I never saw a wife stand by in submission to receive punishment for her culpable conduct. In the quarrel she might even strike the first blow, and if she were clearly in danger of being seriously hurt, then one of the bystanders might intervene, in fact always did within my experience.

Nor did the man's greater strength tell in such a struggle, for the wife "will pack up her goods and chattels and move to the camp of a relative . . . till the loss of an economic partner . . . brings the man to his senses and he attempts a reconciliation" (p. 143). Kaberry concludes that the point to stress about this indispensability of a woman's economic contribution is "not only her great importance in economics, but also her power to utilize this to her own advantage in other spheres of marital life."

A further point also needs stressing: such quarrels are not, as they may first appear, structurally at the same level as similar quarrels in our society. In our case, reciprocity in marital rights and duties is defined in the terms of a social order in which subsistence is gained through paid wage labor, while women supply socially essential but unpaid services within a household. A dichotomy between "public" labor and "private" household service masks the household "slavery" of women. In all societies, women use the resources available to them to manipulate their situation to their advantage as best they can, but they are in a qualitatively different position, structurally, in our society from that in societies where what has been called the "household economy" is the *entire* economy. References to the autonomy of women when it comes to making decisions about their own lives are common for such societies. Concomitant autonomy of attitude is pointed out by Kaberry, again, for the Kimberley peoples: "The women, as far as I could judge from their attitudes," she writes, "remained regrettably profane in their attitude towards the men." To be sure, they much admired the younger men as they paraded in their ceremonial finery, but "the praise uttered was in terms that suggested that the spectators regarded the men as potential lovers, and not as individuals near unto gods" (p. 230). In summary, Kaberry argues that "there can be no question of identifying the sacred inheritance of the tribe only with the men's ceremonies. Those of the women belong to it also" (p. 277). As for concepts of "pollution," she says, "the women with regard to the men's rituals are profane and uninitiated; the men with regard to the women's ritual are profane and uninitiated" (p. 277).

The record on women's autonomy and lack of special deference among the 17th-century Montagnais-Naskapi is unambiguous. Yet this was a society in which the hunt was overwhelmingly important. Women manufactured clothing and other necessities, but furnished much less food than was the usual case with hunter/gatherers. In the 17th century, women as well as men were shamans, although this is apparently no longer remembered. As powerful shamans, they might exhort men to battle. Men held certain special feasts to do with hunting from which women were excluded. Similarly, men were excluded from women's feasts about which we know nothing but that they were held. When a man needed more than public teasing to ensure his good conduct, or in times of crisis, women held their own councils. In relation to warfare, anything but dominance-deference behavior is indicated. In historic times, raids were carried on against the Iroquois, who were expanding their territories in search of furs. The fury with which women would enjoin men to do battle and the hideous and protracted intricacies of the torture of captives in which they took the initiative boggle the mind. Getting back at the Iroquois for killing their menfolk was central, however, not "hailing the conquering hero."

Errors, Crude and Subtle

Despite this evidence, relative male dominance and female deference is a constant theme in the ethnographic record. The extent to which data can be skewed by a nonhistorical approach that overlooks centuries-old directions of change and by ethnocentric interpretation based on assumptions about public-prestigious males versus private-deferent females becomes apparent when we consider the following two descriptions of hunting society.

In one, women are extremely self-sufficient and independent and "much more versatile than men." They take much pride and interest in their work, especially in the skills of leatherwork and porcupine or quill embroidery. "Girls are urged to do work of such quality that it will excite envy and admiration." The prestige of a good worker spreads fast, and others seek her out to learn from or obtain some of her work. Men listen in on women's discussions in order to hear about "gifted women" they might wish to seek in marriage. Women also gain "public recognition" as midwives and as herbal doctors (also a male occupation). Some women become so interested that "they trade with individuals in distant groups . . . to secure herbs that are not indigenous." They achieve renown as runners or participants in other sports, where they at times compete with, and may win over, men, and occasionally in warfare, where "a girl who qualifies as a warrior is considered as a warrior, and not as a queer girl," by her male colleagues. Women compose songs and dances that may become popular and pass down through the generations, and they make fine masks used in important bear ceremonials.

Young girls often accompany their fathers on hunting trips, so they commonly learn men's as well as women's skills. There are more variations in women's lives than in men's, and many women at some time in their lives support themselves by hunting, in mother-daughter, sister-sister, or grandmother-daughter pairs. Some support disabled husbands for a while in this way. If need be, women who are resourceful can make their own canoes. On the whole, "women who adopt men's work are characteristically resourceful and untroubled." Women actively pursue, choose, and desert husbands or lovers, or choose to remain unmarried for long periods of time. Too open, casual, or disruptive promiscuity is frowned upon, and there is some feeling against an unmarried girl's having a baby. However, should she or the child's father not wish to marry, a woman with a child has little trouble finding a husband if she wants one.

Women have visions that bring them supernatural powers more easily than do men; visions have to be induced in boys through isolation and repeated fasting. Elder women spend long hours in winter evenings telling stories about women, some factual, some semihistorical, and some legendary.

By contrast, the second description deals with a hunting society in which women are "inferior" and lack "distinct training," in which the generalization is made "that any man is intrinsically and vastly superior to any woman," and in which women are taught to be "recipients of male favors, economic and sexual, and are supposed to be ignored by men." Men's activities are widely spoken of and publicized, while women's tasks are "unpublished"; the "mythology occupies itself with the pursuits and rewards of men." "Artistic women—in marked contrast to gifted men—are given no title nor are they regarded with the awe that indicates general respect." Instead, women "fall into the role of onlookers who watch and admire[men] with bated breath." "No individual woman is distinctive" in the world of men, and although women "discuss the merits of their work just as men do the merits of theirs, . . . these discussions and boasts are not formal, as the men's are; they belong to the level of gossip." A double standard with regard to sex is enjoined on women. Attention is paid to the adolescent activities of boys, while girls, at their first menses, are isolated as full of "maleficent power."

The latter society sounds quite familiar, but one may wonder about the first. The trick is that the two accounts not only describe the same people, but are taken, selectively, from the same monograph, *The Ojibwa Woman*, by Ruth Landes (1938:viii, 5, 11, 18–19, 23–25, 42, 128–32, 136, 140, 180). I regret being critical of a study that offers full documentation of women's activities and interests, but Landes has undermined her own contribution to the understanding of sex roles in a hunting society through the downgrading of women that is built into unexamined and ethnocentric phraseology.

Unacknowledged contradictions abound in her account. Landes is clear and unequivocal about the resourcefulness of women and the fact that they are allowed greater latitude in their activities than men, but then ascribes this to "the general atmosphere of cultural indifference which surrounds them" and "the sketchy and negatively phrased ideals with which tradition makes a pretense of providing them" (p. 181). In another context, however, she speaks of women who "become self-conscious in terms of their work" and "develop a self-respect which finds satisfaction in the recognition accorded it." She calls this bringing "men's motivations into women's work" and pursuing "feminine occupations as a masculine careerist would" (pp. 154–55). Women are "not trained to these attitudes" of competitive striving and shame in defeat while learning female skills, Landes writes, but learn them in games where the emphases "are the same for boys and girls, for men and women," and both "feel that their self-respect hangs upon the outcome of the game" (pp. 23, 27, 155). Yet in another context, she states, "girls are urged to do work of such quality that it will excite admiration and envy (p. 19). Furthermore, in the context of case examples of renowned women, Landes makes a non-sex-linked statement about abilities, writing that "individual differences in ability are clearly recognized by the people, and include such careful distinctions as that of small ability hitched to great ambition, or that of potentially great ability confined by small ambition" (p. 27).

Girls, Landes writes, are given "protectlve" names like "Shining of the Thunderbird," while boys are given names with more "vocational promise" like "Crashing Thunder" (p. 13). Then she writes, without comment, of the shaman "Thunder Woman" (pp. 29, 37), of the woman warrior "Chief Earth Woman" (p. 141), and of "Iron Woman," a shaman who was taught by her "medicine" father and her grandfather and who defeated "even the best men players" at games of chance and skill (pp. 26–27, 62–63, 137).

The basic division of labor, Landes writes, "is in the assignment to the men of hunting and securing raw materials, and the assignment to the women of manufacturing the raw materials" (pp. 130–31). Men's work is less varied than women's, "but it is appraised culturally as infinitely more interesting and honorable" (p. 131). 'Women's work is conventionally ignored" by men (p. 18). How, then, does Landes handle the interest shown in women's work by both women and men? She writes that "excellence of handiwork excites the *informal* attention of women as widely as the boy's talent in hunting excites the attention of men" (pp. 18–19, italics added); that a man may brag of his wife's handiwork, which "had led him to walk many miles" to claim her, *"in an unguarded moment"* (p. 11, italics added); and that men learn about gifted workers that they might want to seek in marriage "from *eavesdropping* upon the *chatter* of their own women folk"(p. 19, italics added). The "private" and less prestigious world of women thus having been established, Landes later implies another common stereotype—that of women as "passive" vis-à-vis men in relation to sex: "Men seem to be more articulate than women about love. It is men who are said to be proud of their wives, not women of their husbands . . ."(p. 120).

I am not suggesting that Landes did not record statements from both men and women about the greater importance of men's work, as well as statements to the contrary. In fact, when she was in the field, men's work *was* more important. The reciprocity of the sexual division of labor had long since given way to considerable dependence upon trade goods. "Since the advent of the traders," Landes writes, "Ojibwa men have learned how to barter. They trade furs and meat which they have secured in hunting, and since the men, rather than the women, possessed the materials desired by the Whites, they became the traders" (p. 134). She describes the men returning from the post and showing "the results of their trade; ammunition, weapons, traps and tobacco for themselves; yard print, ribbons and beads for the women and children; candy, fruit, whiskey for all" (p. 17). The fact that women remained as autonomous as they did among the Ojibwa was apparently related to the fact that hunting continued to be the main source of food and women could and did often support themselves and their families by hunting. Furthermore, "Today [1932–1933], when rice and berries and maple sugar are commanding some White attention, the women also are learning to function as dealers" (p. 134).

Landes's downgrading of women's status among the Ojibwa, in the face of her own evidence to the contrary, flows in part from contradictions due to the changes taking place in women's social-economic position[3] and in part from her lack of a critical and historical orientation toward her material. Nonetheless, Landes deserves credit for making available such full material on women that explicit criticism of her work is possible.

Iroquois materials offer similar contradictions. Horticultural but still egalitarian, Iroquois society of the 17th and 18th centuries is well known for the high status of its women. Lands were handed down in matrilineages, and the matrons managed the economic affairs of the communal "long houses," arranged marriages, nominated and deposed the sachems of the intertribal council, and participated in equal numbers with men as influential "Keepers of the Faith." Postmarital residence was uxorilocal, and a woman could divorce a man who did not please her with little ceremony, sending him back to his own family. Women's value was expressed in the fact that a murdered woman called for twice the compensation of a murdered man.

Yet one can have one's choice among contradictory statements about the status of Iroquois women. In the early 18th century, Lafitau wrote of Iroquois women (or perhaps of the similar Huron), "all real authority is vested in them. . . . They are the soul of the Councils, the arbiters of peace and of war" (Brown 1970:153). On the other hand, there is the more commonly quoted sentence of none other than Morgan himself: "The Indian regarded woman as the inferior, the dependent, and the servant of man, and from nature and habit, she actually considered herself to be so" (1954:315; cited, for example, in Goldberg 1973:40, 58, 241; Divale 1976:202).

The contrast between the two generalizations is partly a matter of the period. Morgan was working with Iroquois informants in the 19th century, when the long house was but a memory and the Iroquois lived in nuclear families largely supported by wage-earning men. Morgan, however, later quoted Rev. A. Wright on the high position of women among the Seneca: "The women were the great power among the clans, as everywhere else. They did not hesitate, when occasion required, to 'knock off the horns,' as it was technically called, from the head of a chief and send him back to the ranks of the warriors" (1974:464).

During the period between the *League of the Iroquois* and *Ancient Society*, Morgan was developing his thinking on human social evolution and on the decline in women's relative status with the advent of "civilization." "The mother-right and gyneocracy among the Iroquois . . . is not overdrawn," he wrote later. "We may see in this an ancient phase of human life which has had a wide presence in the tribes of mankind. . . . Not until after civilization had begun among the Greeks, and gentile society was superseded by political society, was the influence of the old order of society overthrown" (1965:66). With monogamy, the woman "was now isolated from her gentile kindred, living in the separate and exclusive house of her husband. Her new condition tended to subvert and destroy the power and influence which descent in the female line and the joint-tenement houses had created" (p. 128).

Yet this is not the end of the matter, for Morgan continued (p. 128):

> But this influence of the woman did not reach outward to the affairs of the gens, phratry, or tribe, but seems to have commenced and ended with the household. This view is quite consistent with the life of patient drudgery and of general subordination to the husband which the Iroquois wife cheerfully accepted as the portion of her sex.

The question is how such a characterization squares with the description of Wright, who lived many years with the Seneca (Morgan 1965:65-66):

> Usually, the female portion ruled the house, and were doubtless clannish enough about it. The stores were in common; but woe to the luckless husband or lover who was too shiftless to do his share of the providing. No matter how many children, or whatever goods he might have in the house, he might at any time be ordered to pick up his blanket and budge; and after such orders it would not be healthful for him to disobey; the house would be too hot for him; and unless saved by the intercession of some aunt or grandmother, he must retreat to his own clan.

An explanation comes readily to mind in terms of the familiar discrepancy between ideal and real wifely roles in our society. Ideally, the wife is the patient and cheerful "helpmeet" in an entrepreneurial nuclear family. A common reality, behind an acceptable public façade, may be a frustrated wife bolstering up, manipulating, and dominating an emotionally dependent husband. Hence an assumption of male dominance as a cultural ideal and the "henpecked husband" as an alternative reality in societies where women's private "power" is constrained by exclusion from public authority is projected into much ethnography. Furthermore, variations on the theme can be observed in erstwhile egalitarian societies in which trade, various forms of sharecropping, wage work, or outright slavery have been important in recent times. These economic relations transform household collectives that were largely controlled by women and that took communal responsibility for raising children; women and children become dependent upon individual men. However, when the previous structures of such societies are reconstructed and the range of decisions made by women is considered, women's autonomous and public role emerges. Their status was not as literal "equals" of men (a point that has caused much confusion), but as what they were—female persons, with their own rights, duties, and responsibilities, which were complementary to and in no way secondary to those of men.

Women's status in Iroquois society was not based on their economic contribution per se. Women make an essential economic contribution in all societies, but their status depends on how this contribution is structured. The issue is whether they control the conditions of their work and the dispensation of the goods they produce. In egalitarian societies, women are limited by the same technological and ecological considerations as men are, but there is no socially defined group that directs their activities. Brown (1970) documents this point for the Iroquois, and its ramifications have been explored by other researchers (Caulfield 1977; Sanday 1974; Sacks 1975; Schlegel 1977).

Iroquois matrons preserved, stored, and dispensed the corn, meat, fish, berries, squashes, and fats that were buried in special pits or kept in the long house. Brown notes (p. 162) that women's control over the dispensation of the foods they produced, and meat as well, gave them the de facto power to veto declarations of war and to intervene in order to bring about peace: "By supplying the essential provisions for male activities—the hunt, the warpath, and the Council—they were able to control these to some degree." Women also guarded the "tribal public treasure" kept in the long house, the wampum, quill and feather work, and furs—the latter, I would add, new forms of wealth that would be their undoing. The point to be stressed is that this was "household management" of an altogether different order from management of the nuclear or extended family in patriarchal societies. In the latter, women may cajole, manipulate, or browbeat men, but always behind the public facade; in the former case, *"household management was itself the management of the 'public' economy."*

The point that household management had a public character in egalitarian society was made by Engels (1972:137); it was not understood by Morgan. Like most anthropologists today, Morgan saw the status of women in Iroquois society as qualitatively different from what it later became.

Indeed, to pursue Morgan's views on Iroquois women is interesting. Despite his contribution to the understanding of historical factors underlying women's changing status, his *League of the Iroquois* is hardly free of derogatory innuendos with regard to them. From reading the *League* alone, one would not know that the matrons nominated the sachems, and their role as providers is dispensed with in the statement that "the warrior despised the toil of husbandry and held all labor beneath him" (1954:320), although Morgan elsewhere refers to how hard the men worked at hunting. Ignoring women's agriculture, he writes as if the Iroquois were primarily hunters. Without the influence of cities, he states, Iroquois institutions "would have lasted until the people had abandoned the hunter state; until they had given up the chase for agriculture, the arts of war for those of industry" (p. 132). When he describes women's formal participation in tribal affairs, he writes, "Such was the spirit of the Iroquois system of government, that the influence of the inferior chiefs, the warriors, and *even* of the women would make itself felt" (p. 66, italics added); and "If a band of warriors became interested in the passing question, they held a council apart, and having given it full consideration, appointed an orator to communicate their views to the sachems. . . . In like manner would the chiefs, and *even* the women proceed" (p. 101, italics added).

Richards (1957) argues that "the aboriginal matriarchy pictured by Lafitau, Morgan, and Hewitt was . . . a mistake" and that the status of Iroquois women had increased by 1784, the beginning of reservation life. Her documentation reveals, however, not an increase in status, but a change from the informality of a fully egalitarian society to the formalization of powers necessary for handling a new and complicated set of political and economic conditions.

Richards takes up two of women's formal powers, the right to dispose of war captives and the right to decide about marriage. On the basis of incidents in the *Jesuit Relations* and other early sources, she concludes (p. 40) that there was "a gradual increase in the decision making power of the women and a corresponding loss by the men" as a "product of a long continued contact situation." Richards presents eleven incidents pertaining to the disposition of war captives, eight between 1637 and 1655, one in 1724, and two in 1781. She states (p. 38) that "women in the early period had little if any decision making power," that later they shared power with the men in their families, subject to acceptance by the captors of the prisoner and the council, and that later still "they were able to intervene and even actually instigate the capture of an individual though it was still necessary to complete the formality of obtaining council approval." However, among the eight cases in the first period, several indicate the active and successful intervention by a woman on behalf of a captive, concluded with the formal presentation of wampum to the council, and there is an instance in which a woman insists on the death of a captive given her to replace her dead brother, in spite of the council's wish to the contrary.

True, in no case do women exercise power equivalent to that held by bodies of men in patriarchal class-based societies. Instead, the cases illustrate the flexibility of decision-making processes characteristic of egalitarian societies. The captors, the council, and interested individuals all had a say in the disposition of captives, and individual women or men apparently won or lost according to the depth of their conviction and the persuasiveness with which they presented their case. What is of significance to the present line of argument is that in all instances, scattered as they are over time and among different Iroquois peoples, women operated formally and publicly in their own interest, with ceremonial gift giving, use of the arts of rhetoric, and other public display. Richards (p. 41) quotes Radisson's report of his return from a war foray; his adoptive mother, he says, "comes to meet me, leaping and singing. . . . Shee takes the woman slave that I had and would not that any should medle with her. But my brother's prisoner was burned ye same day." Radisson's mother had first claimed him in the following fashion: "The old woman followed me, speaking aloud, whom they answered with a loud ho, then shee tooke her girdle and about me she tyed it, so brought me to her cottage."

In relation to marriage decisions in the earlier period, Richards cites several examples in which matrons did not have the clear-cut power to decide on spouses for their sons and daughters. However, the early records instead indicate that young women lived in dormitories, took lovers, experimented with trial marriages, and made the decisions about whom they were going to marry, albeit with the advice and formal recognition of their parents. Cartier wrote of this "very bad" custom for the girls, who "after they are of an age to marry . . . are all put into a common house, abandoned to everybody who desires them until they have found their match" (Richards 1957:42). Other early accounts report both parents as involved in selecting spouses for their children, but girls as having the right to reject a suitor after trying him out (pp. 40, 43). Marriage arrangements were apparently flexible and included both polygyny and polyandry.

The fact that matrons' powers over disposition of war captives and over marriage became more clear-cut with the formalization of the Iroquois constitution betokens not an increase in power, but a formal recognition of prestige and influence that had long operated. With relation to marriage, in a society where consensus was essential, the young were *influenced* rather than *ordered* by their elders with regard to the conduct of their personal lives. However, the formal codification of women's social position took place in a situation in which their autonomy was already undermined. The subsequent history of the Iroquois polity involved a temporary strengthening of the "public sphere" represented by the confederacy at the point at which it was being supplanted by colonial rule. The long-house communities were replaced by settlements of nuclear family units; what remained were some of the interpersonal styles and traditions of cooperation and personal autonomy.

Transition

Like the Iroquois, societies around the world have been transformed by the economic system that emerged in Europe in what Wallerstein terms "the 'long' sixteenth century" of 1450–1640 (1974:406–7). Unfortunately, this fact has been obscured in anthropology by the practice of separating the "internal" functioning of societies from their total economic and political contexts, in order to reconstruct supposedly "traditional" cultures through deletion of "modern" involvements. Wallerstein's article is not specifically directed at anthropologists, but his criticism of ahistorical methods (p. 389) is apt: "The crucial issue when comparing 'stages' is to determine the units of which the 'stages' are synchronic portraits (or 'ideal types'). . . . And the fundamental error of ahistorical social science (including ahistorical versions of Marxism) is to reify parts of the totality into such units and then to compare reified structures." To be effective in the interpretation of history, stages must be of total social systems.

Wallerstein distinguishes social systems as "minisystems" or "world-systems." A mini-system is "an entity that has within it a complete division of labor, and a single cultural framework," such as "are found only in very simple agricultural or hunting and gathering societies" (p. 390). He continues: "Such mini-systems no longer exist in the world. Furthermore, there were fewer in the past than is often asserted, since any such system that became tied to an empire by the payment of tribute as 'protection costs' ceased by that fact to be a 'system,' no longer having a self-contained division of labor." Other factors that have been undermining the self-contained division of labor of mini-systems for centuries are trade, involvement in raiding or being raided for slaves (in the New World as well as in Africa), taxation of various kinds (often as an incentive to wage work), and wage labor, often entailing men's absence from home villages for long periods. In all cases, missionizing played an important role in urging people toward an individualized work ethic and a nuclear family form. Since mini-systems no longer exist, says Wallerstein, social analysis must take into account that "the only kind of social system is a world-system, . . . a unit with a single division of labor and multiple cultural systems." This world-system is "the capitalist world economy."

Recognition of this fact has serious implications for the cross-cultural study of women, since involvements with a developing capitalist world economy have had profound effects on their relation to the production and distribution of basic group needs, hence to sources of decision-making power. The practice of stacking contemporary peoples in "historical" layers—as hunter/gatherers, simple agriculturalists, and advanced agriculturalists with domestication—does, it is true, yield some insight into the nature of women's decline in status, since a people's involvement in the world-system starts within each "layer" from a different basis. Furthermore, cultural traditions can be remarkably strong, and people can wage stiff battles for those they value. Hence the method of comparing near-contemporary cultures can be used with care to suggest historical trends (see, e.g., Sacks 1976). However, socioeconomic systems separated from the economic and political constraints that in part define them cannot be treated as direct representations of sex-role definitions in contrasting societies.

Two recent books, *Woman, Culture, and Society* (Rosaldo and Lamphere 1974) and *Women and Men* (Friedl 1975), share an ahistorical orientation and assume from recent and contemporary evidence the universality of male dominance and the cultural devaluation of women. The assumption is neither documented nor argued on the basis of ethnohistorical materials. Instead, 19th-century concepts of matriarchal power—incorrectly ascribed to Marx and Engels (Friedl 1975:4) or Morgan (Rosaldo and Lamphere 1974:2)—are cited briefly as inadequate, and the alternative of women's equal prestige and autonomy in egalitarian societies is given but passing reference and subsequently ignored (Friedl 1975:4–7; Rosaldo and Lamphere 1974:3). Yet the authors eschew simplistic psychobiological explanations for an assumed universal male dominance and see the structure of women's position as critical to relative subordination or autonomy in different facets of cultural life, making for an open-ended future according to structural changes.

Friedl offers thoughtful discussions of women's participation in the production and control of food and goods in a variety of cultures, but with no reference to the fact that both ethnohistorical and recent materials indicate a general decline in women's control with the advent of trade (certain notable exceptions do not pertain to the peoples she describes). Rosaldo and Lamphere (1974:9) write of the papers in their book that they "establish that women's role in social processes is far greater than has previously been recognized" and that they show that "women, like men, are social actors who work in structured ways to achieve desired ends" and who "have a good deal more power than conventional theorists have assumed." However, they reveal their entrapment in the anthropological ethos that sees contemporary Third World peoples as virtually unchanged representatives of the past in stating (p. 14) that "the papers . . . do not, on the whole, address questions concerning female roles today." With the exception of a paper on the 19th-century Mende of Sierra Leone, the empirical papers do treat "female roles today"—among the Igbo and Ijaw of Nigeria, the Mbum Kpau of Tchad, the Javanese and other Indonesian groups, Lake Atitlán villagers in Guatemala, and people of rural Montenegro, pre- and postrevolutionary China, and urban black communities in the United States. By what fiat are such peoples removed from the world of today?

The upshot of an ahistorical perspective is to see giving birth and suckling as in and of themselves furnishing the basis for a presumed past subordination, though subject to change in the future. Since the division of labor by sex was central to the evolution of cultural life, it is easy to fall into the trap; women bear children; the early division of labor is related to this fact, as is women's present subordination; hence there has been a quantitative but not a qualitative shift in women's status relative to men, which took place as egalitarian social forms were transmuted into hierarchical ones. The structural implications of the fact that, when labor is not specialized beyond the division by sex, goods are completely shared within a band or village collective are ignored, as is the concomitant control by every member of the group over the distribution of the resources and products that each acquires or manufactures. Thereby the source of transformation in women's status is bypassed: the development of trade and specialization to the point that relations of dependence emerge outside of the band, village, or kin collective, undermine individual control and personal autonomy, and lay the basis for hierarchy.

Brown (1970) contrasts the public control exercised by Iroquois women, based on their responsibility for the collective household and its stores, with women's loss of such control, and concomitant loss of status, among the centralized and hierarchical Bemba. In comparative studies, Sacks (1975) and Sanday (1974) affirm the relationship between control of production and distribution by women and their "public" participation and status. Goldhamer (1973) shows the variability in women's control over the products of their labor in the New Guinea highlands and the significance of these variations to their status.

For example, among the Mae Enga women are reponsible for the daily allocation of their produce, but "men retain the 'right and duty' involved in the important distribution of pigs, pork, and produce—for prestation, trade and debt-payments" (Goldhamer 1973:6). By contrast, among the Tor of West Irian, "men say that it is women's total control over the food supply that affords them the 'exceptionally high position' that prevails throughout the district" (p. 10). Food presentation may be a "public" or political act or a private service, according to the structural setting. Among the Tor, as among the Iroquois of the past, women's dispensation of food to strangers is a public act; it sets the stage for the reception of newcomers. "The women's expressed attitude toward strangers coming into the villages determines how they will be received by the men" (p. 10). By contrast, Bemba women dispense food as a family service that redounds to the husband's stature and enjoins obligations to him on the part of the recipients in the same way as does chiefly extending of hospitality. Among the Mae Enga, women's labor furnishes produce that is consumed by the pigs which are distributed in political negotiations by men.

The relatively higher status of women among the Iroquois and Tor, where they control their work and its distribution, than among the Mae Enga and especially the Bemba, where they do not, suggests that preliminary phases in the process of class development did in fact accompany women's decline in status, as Engels originally proposed. The link between women's reduced status, on the one hand, and the growth of private property and economic classes, on the other, was in Engels's view the emergence of the individual family as an independent economic unit. Taking shape within and subverting the former collective economy, the family as an economic unit transformed women's work from public production to private household service. The critical development that triggered the change was the specialization of labor that increasingly replaced the production of goods for use by the production of commodities for exchange and set up economic relationships that lay beyond the control of the producers.

Commodity production, Engels (1972:233) wrote, "undermines the collectivity of production and appropriation" and "elevates appropriation by individuals into the general rule," thereby setting in motion "incorporeal alien powers" that rise up against the producers. The seeds of private property and class exploitation are planted, and the single family as an economic property-owning and inheriting unit develops within and destroys the collective. "The division of labor within the family . . . remained the same; and yet it now turned the previous domestic relation upside down simply because the division of labor outside the family had changed" (p. 221). Instead of carrying out public responsibilities in the band or village collective within which goods were distributed, women became dependent on men as the producers of commercially relevant goods. In the context of the individual family, "the woman was degraded and reduced to servitude, . . . a mere instrument for the production of children" (p. 121).

Engels described the process as unfolding through the domestication of animals in the ancient East and the exchange of cattle, which were cared for, and hence came to be owned, by men. Since unequal control over resources and subjugation by class and by sex developed in very different ecological settings in many parts of the world prior to, as well as within, the period of European colonialism, it is important to separate Engels's statement on women's subjugation from the specific context of his discussion. The processes associated with the transformation of goods produced for use to "commodities," produced for future exchange, then become apparent in all world areas. These are: specialization of labor in connection with trade, and warfare to ensure or control trade; intensive work on agricultural land and unequal access to or privatization of prime lands; differences in economic status expressed in categories of "slaves," "rubbish men," perpetual youth, and the like; competition among lineage groups, within which the individual family as an economic unit begins to take shape; the institutionalization of "political" functions connected with warfare and property as separate from "social" functions and the dichotomiza-

tion of "public" and "private" spheres; and the institutionalization and ideological rationalization of male superiority.

Summary

I have argued that the structure of egalitarian society has been misunderstood
as a result of the failure to recognize women's participation in such society as
public and autonomous. To conceptualize hunting/gathering bands as loose
collections of nuclear families, in which women are bound by dyadic relations
of dependency to individual men, projects onto hunter/gatherers the dimensions of our own social structure. Such a concept implies a teleological and unilineal view of social evolution, whereby our society is seen as the full expression of relations that have been present in all society. Ethnohistorical and
conceptual reinterpretation of women's roles in hunting/gathering societies reveals that qualitatively different relationships obtained. The band as a whole
was the basic economic unit; individuals distributed their own produce; property did not exist as a foundation for individual authority; and decisions were
on the whole made by those who would be carrying them out.

Failure to appreciate the structure of egalitarian relations renders more difficult the problem of unravelling the complex processes that initiated class and
state formation. Ethnohistorical research indicates that in precolonial horticultural societies where egalitarianism still prevailed, women continued to
function publicly in making economic and social decisions, often through
councils that mediated their reciprocal relations with men. The comparison of
such societies with those characterized by differences in rank and wealth indicates that the main concomitant of women's oppression originally outlined by
Engels is indeed found cross-culturally. The transmutation of production for
consumption to production of commodities for exchange (usually along with
intensive work on land as a commodity for future use) begins to take direct
control of their produce out of the hands of the producers and to create new
economic ties that undermine the collectivity of the joint households. Women
begin to lose control of their production, and the sexual division of labor related to their childbearing ability becomes the basis for their oppression as private dispensers of services in individual households. The process is by no
means simple, automatic, or rapid, and where women retain some economic
autonomy as traders they retain as well a relatively high status. In West Africa
women were organized to maintain and protect their rights well into the development of economic classes and political states.

The documentation and analysis of women's social roles, then, show that
family relations in preclass societies were not merely incipient forms of our

own. Social evolution has not been unilineal and quantitative. It has entailed profound qualitative changes in the relations between women and men.

NOTES

1. This paper is based on one originally given at the 73d annual meeting of the American Anthropological Association, Mexico City, November 1974.
2. "Ce . . . phenomène, d'ordre politico-réligíeux, traduit bien entendu la volunté de ces groupes de réaffirmer leur identité culturelle et de résister aux pressions déstructrices du procés de domination et d'acculturation qu'elles subissent, que les a privés de leur terre et soumet leurs anciennes pratiques réligieuses et politiques a un travail d'erosion et d'extirpation systematique."
3. For studies of comparable changes in women's status, cf. Hamamsy (1957) and Leacock (1955).

REFERENCES

Barnes, John A. 1971. "African models in the New Guinea highlands," in *Melanesia: Readings on a culture area.* Edited by L. L. Langness and John C. Weschler. Scranton: Chandler.

Bates, Daisy. 1938. *The passing of the Aborigines: A lifetime spent among the natives of Australia.* London: Murray.

Brown, Judith K. 1970. Economic organization and the position of women among the Iroquois. *Ethnohistory* 17:151–67.

Caulfield, Mina Davis. 1977. Universal sex oppression? A critique from Marxist anthropology. *Catalyst,* nos. 10–11:60–77.

Cox, Bruce. Editor. 1973. *Cultural ecology: Readings on the Canadian Indians and Eskimos.* Toronto: McClelland and Stewart.

Damas, David. 1969. *Contributions to anthropology: Band societies.* National Museums of Canada Bulletin 28.

Divale, William Tulio. 1976. Female status and cultural evolution: A study in ethnographic bias. *Behavior Science Research* 11:169–211.

Draper, Patricia. 1975. "!Kung women: Contrasts in sexual egalitarianism in foraging and sedentary contexts," in *Toward an anthropology of women.* Edited by Rayna R. Reiter. New York: Monthly Review Press.

Engels, Frederick. 1972. *The origin of the family, private property and the state.* New York: International.

Fried, Morton H. 1968. "On the concepts of 'tribe' and 'tribal society.'" *Proceedings of the 1967 Annual Spring Meeting, American Ethnological Society,* pp. 3–20.

———. 1975. *The notion of tribe.* Menlo Park, Calif.: Cummings.

Friedl, Ernestine. 1975. *Women and men: An anthropologist's view.* New York: Holt, Rinehart and Winston.

Godelier, Maurice. 1973. Modes de production, rapports de parenté et structures démographiques. *La Pensée,* December, pp. 8–31.

Goldberg, Steven. 1973. *The inevitability of patriarchy.* New York: Morrow.

Goldhamer, Florence Kalm. 1973. The "misfit" of role and status for the New Guinea Highlands woman. Paper read at the 72d annual meeting of the American Anthropological Association.

Hamamsy, Laila Shukry. 1957. The role of women in a changing Navajo society. *American Anthropologist* 59:101–11.

Kaberry, Phyllis M. 1939. *Aboriginal woman, sacred and profane.* London: Routledge.

Keesing, Roger M. 1971. "Shrines, ancestors, and cognatic descent: The Kwaio and Tallensi," in *Melanesia: Readings on a culture area.* Edited by L. L. Langness and John C. Weschler. Scranton: Chandler.

Landes, Ruth. 1938. *The Ojibwa woman.* New York: Columbia University Press.

Leacock, Eleanor. 1954. *The Montagnais "hunting territory" and the fur trade.* American Anthropological Association Memoir 78.

———. 1955. Matrilocality in a simple hunting economy (Montagnais-Naskapi). *Southwestern Journal of Anthropology* 11:31–47.

———. 1969. "The Naskapi band," in *Contributions to anthropology: Band societies.* Edited by David Damas. National Museums of Canada Bulletin 228.

———. 1975. "Class, commodity, and the status of women," in *Women cross-culturally: Change and challenge.* Edited by Ruby Rohrlich-Leavitt. The Hague: Mouton.

———. 1977. "Women in egalitarian society," in *Becoming visible: Women in European history.* Edited by Renate Bridenthal and Claudia Koonz. Boston: Houghton Mifflin.

Leacock, Eleanor, and Jacqueline Goodman. 1977. Montagnais marriage and the Jesuits in the 17th century. *Western Canadian Journal of Anthropology.*

Lee, Richard B. 1972. "The !Kung Bushmen of Botswana," in *Hunters and gatherers today.* Edited by M. G. Bicchieri. New York: Holt, Rinehart and Winston.

Morgan, Lewis Henry. 1954. *League of the Ho-De-No-Sau-Nee or Iroquois.* Vol 1. New Haven: Human Relations Area Files.

———. 1965. *Houses and house-life of the American aborigines.* Chicago: University of Chicago Press.

———. 1974. *Ancient society.* Gloucester, Mass.: Peter Smith.

Richards, Cara B. 1957. "Matriarchy or mistake: The role of Iroquois women through time." *Proceedings of the 1957 Annual Spring Meeting, American Ethnological Society,* pp. 36–45.

Rogers, Edward S. 1972. "The Mistassini Cree," in *Hunters and gatherers today.* Edited by M. G. Bicchieri. New York: Holt, Rinehart and Winston.

Rosaldo, Michelle Zimbalist, and Louise Lamphere. Editors. 1974. *Woman, culture, and society.* Stanford: Stanford University Press.

Sacks, Karen. 1975. "Engels revisited: Women, the organization of production, and private property," in *Toward an anthropology of women.* Edited by Rayna R. Reiter. New York: Monthly Review.

Sahlins, Marshall D. 1961. The segmentary lineage: An organization of predatory expansion. *American Anthropologist* 63:322–45.

Sanday, Peggy R. 1974. "Female status in the public domain," in *Woman, culture, and society.* Edited by Michelle Zimbalist Rosaldo and Louise Lamphere. Stanford: Stanford University Press.

Schlegel, Alice. Editor. 1977. *Sexual stratification: A cross-cultural view.* New York: Columbia University Press.

Service, Elman R. 1966. *The hunters.* Englewood Cliffs: Prentice-Hall.

Speck, Frank G. 1926. Culture problems in northeastern North America. *Proceedings of the American Philosophical Society* 65:273–311.

Spencer, Baldwin, and F. J. Gillen. 1968. *The native tribes of Central Australia.* New York: Dover.

Tindale, Norman B. 1972. "The Pitjandjara," in *Hunters and gatherers today.* Edited by M. G. Bicchieri. New York: Holt, Rinehart and Winston.

Turnbull, Colin M. 1972. *The mountain people.* New York: Simon and Schuster.

Wallerstein, Immanuel. 1974. The rise and future demise of the world capitalist system: Concepts for comparative analysis. *Comparative Studies in Society and History* 16:387–415.

SEVEN

Art, Science, or Politics? The Crisis in Hunter-Gatherer Studies

◆

Richard B. Lee

In the complex history of hunter-gatherer studies, several overlapping and at times antagonistic discourses can be discerned. However, one critique has emerged that would render all hunter-gatherer discourses irrelevant and do away with the concept altogether. The paper explores the poststructuralist roots of this "revisionism" and then argues why the concept of hunter-gatherer continues to be politically relevant and empirically valid. However, if they are to fulfill their promise of illuminating an increasingly fragmented and alienating modernity, hunter-gatherer studies will have to become more attuned to issues of politics, history, context, and reflexivity.

Hunter-gatherer studies have had a rather stormy history. The field has always been marked by controversy, and even the concept of hunter-gatherers itself has waxed and waned in importance. There have been periods in the history of anthropology when the very concept was tabooed, others when it was popular. Within the discipline today, the idea of hunter-gatherer has radically different receptions. Some see it as totally absurd, a derivative of outmoded evolutionary theory, while others see it as an eminently sensible category of humanity with a firm anchor in empirical reality. I noted a strong tendency toward the latter view at the Sixth Conference on Hunter-Gatherers (CHAGS) at Fairbanks, May–June 1990. At least no one advocated canceling the sixth CHAGS for lack of subject matter.

Even if it is agreed that hunters and gatherers exist, almost everything else about them is a matter for contestation. While some fields have crystallized a canon, there is no danger of that in hunter-gatherer studies; the field remains as fractious and controversy-prone as ever. And in recent years a new element has been added to the many voices within the field, a body of opinion that would call into question the entire enterprise and abolish the concept of hunter-gatherers altogether. It would be hard to imagine a more fundamental challenge. Therefore, the purpose of this article is to define the range of anthropological practices that constitute hunter-gatherer studies today and to explore the roots—social, ideological, and epistemological—of the field's crisis in representation.

Some of these difficulties become apparent at the outset when we try to define what we mean by hunter-gatherers.[1] *Economically* we are referring to those people who have historically lived by gathering, hunting, and fishing, with minimal or no agriculture and with no domesticated animals except for the dog. *Politically* gatherer-hunters are usually labeled as "band" or "egalitarian" societies in which social groups are small, mobile, and unstratified, and in which differences of wealth and power are minimally developed.

Obviously there is a degree of fit between "forager" subsistence strategies and "band" social organization, but the fit is far from perfect. Strictly economic definitions of foragers will include a number of peoples with ranking, stratification, and even slavery—the Northwest Coast groups—while the notion of "egalitarian bands" will include a number of small-scale horticultural and pastoral societies—in Amazonia, for example, and some Siberian "small peoples."

Recent attempts to clarify these ambiguities have led to the useful distinction between "generalized" and "complex" hunter-gatherers (Price and Brown 1985; see also Woodburn's immediate/delayed return distinction [1980], and Testart 1988). It is the first category—peoples who hunted and gathered and who were organized into egalitarian bands—that will be the main focus of this discussion, though both simple nonforagers and complex foragers will be referred to from time to time.

The fluctuating fortunes of hunter-gatherer studies are tied as well to ambiguities that lie at the root of the field of anthropology itself; not the least of which revolves around the much debated concept of the primitive. Many would argue along with Stanley Diamond (1974:118) that the "search for the primitive" is the heart of anthropology's unique role in the human sciences. And much of the history of hunter-gatherer studies is linked to our multifaceted understandings of the primitive, either in Diamond's sense, in the quest for origins and fundamentals, or in what Lévi-Strauss terms anthropology's deeper purpose "to bear testimony to future generations of the ingeniousness, diversity, and imagination of our species" (1968:349).

But for other anthropologists the preoccupation with the primitive is an anachronism. For some the primitive is an illusion, an arbitrary construction of the disembodied "other" divorced from history and context (e.g., Clifford 1983; Sperber 1985; Wagner 1981). The result of this ambiguity is that there is a body of opinion in anthropology—not unconnected to views in other disciplines about "the end of history" and particularly among postmodernists—which would find anthropology's preoccupation with the primitive an acute embarrassment; as a consequence, the concept of hunter-gatherers becomes moot (Wilmsen 1989:xi–xviii, 1–6).

A second area of ambiguity is the nature of the anthropological enterprise itself. Anthropology has never declared itself unequivocally on the matter of whether it is a particularizing, historical discipline interested in understanding unit cultures, or whether it is a generalizing, nomothetic science searching for the broadest possible explanatory frameworks. Hunter-gatherer studies broadly defined have vigorous adherents of both these tendencies, going right back to Boas (1935, 1966) and Kroeber (1925) exemplifying the first tendency, and Steward (1936, 1938) and Radcliffe-Brown (1922, 1931) the second.

The history of hunter-gatherer studies, especially since the "Man the Hunter" conference in 1966 (Lee and DeVore 1968), illustrates both anthropology's ambiguities and the problematic role of hunter-gatherer studies within it. Among the persistent issues of the 1970s, 1980s, and 1990s have been debates on the following:

1. Evolutionism. The use and misuse of hunter-gatherer data to understand the fossil record and/or the evolution of human behavior has long been a contentious issue, as has been the concept of evolutionism itself. Hunter-gatherer studies have tended to enjoy respectability among some evolutionists (Isaac 1978; Lancaster 1978; Tanner and Zihlman 1976) and to be viewed with suspicion by others (Wobst 1978; Foley 1988).

2. Optimal Foraging Strategies. Modelers of the behavioral ecology of hunter-gatherers have continued to advocate a nomothetic research strategy and to refine quantitative methodologies at a time when much of the field was moving in the opposite direction. It has been the focus of notable research (Winterhalder and Smith 1981; Hawkes, Hill, and O'Connell 1982; Hill and Hawkes 1983) but also of some pointed critiques (Keene 1983; Martin 1983).

3. Woman the Gatherer. Feminist agendas and priorities have entered hunter-gatherer discourse initially through the ecological issue, raised in "Man the Hunter," of whether women's work in gathering plant foods is not more important to subsistence than men's hunting. This has led to a number of books and articles on gender, women's work, and women's power in foraging society. A significant segment of feminist anthropology has drawn heavily on hunter-gatherer studies (Slocum 1975;

Begler 1978; Dahlberg 1981; Hunn 1981; Leacock 1981; Sacks 1979; Tanner and Zihlman 1976).

4. World View and Symbolic Analysis. Studies of the systems of meaning that give shape and coherence to hunter-gatherer identity and cosmology have been increasingly in evidence as a countercurrent to and implicit critique of the predominant ecological orientation of much of hunter-gatherer studies (Myers 1986b; Ridington 1990; Brody 1981; Endicott 1979).

5. Hunter-Gatherers in Prehistory. Archeologists have always had a strong interest in hunter-gatherer ethnography and its uses for interpreting the past (Binford 1978; Yellen 1977; Keene 1991). Currently, archeological interest in foragers exceeds by a wide margin interest by social and cultural anthropologists. Increasingly, archeologists are working directly with contemporary gatherer-hunters under the rubric of ethnoarcheology, and the questions archeologists ask are often quite different from the problematics within which social anthropologists work (Binford 1980; Paynter 1989; Yellen 1990; Wiessner 1982).

6. Hunter-Gatherers in History. The links of foraging peoples with the wider world, both in the present and in the past, have been a growing focus stimulated in part by world-systems analysis and by the publication of Wolf's *Europe and the People without History* (1982; see also Schrire 1984; Wilmsen 1988, 1989; Headland and Reid 1989). One effect of this move toward historicizing has been to call into question the very idea of hunter-gatherers, and to argue seriously that they are a noncategory, a construction of the observers.

Two Cultures, or Three, or Four?

What analytical framework would be most useful and productive in sorting out the complex currents and countercurrents in the study of hunting and gathering peoples today? It might be helpful to recall C. P. Snow's famous essay, "The Two Cultures" (1959), in which he explored the eternal conflict between two irreconcilable academic subcultures: the *humanistic* and the *scientific*. [2] In the first, scholarship was devoted to the study of meanings and interpretation in great works of art and literature. In the second, scholarship was dedicated to systematic and rigorous investigation of natural laws and general principles governing the natural and human world.

Anthropology is an apt example of a discipline that finds itself straddling the boundaries of C. P. Snow's two cultures. Within the discipline today there is a powerful current moving toward the view of anthropology as essentially a humanistic, even literary discipline, where truth, apart from the poetic variety, is unattainable. An equally strong current moves in the opposite direction, embracing the promise and moral authority of science and strengthening its commitment to improved techniques of data collection and measurement, coupled with more (not less) rigorous application of theory. The first sees itself as modeled after literature and literary criticism, the second draws its inspiration from theoretical biology and evolutionary ecology as well as an updated and recharged structural-functionalism.[3]

Within hunter-gatherer studies, the struggles and contradictions between the humanistic and scientific cultures are played out in a number of ways. While the scientists are gathering data for the construction of mathematical models of forager predator-prey behavior, the humanists, working sometimes among the same people, are collecting life histories of elders and recording and interpreting cosmologies and religious beliefs.

But there is a third culture embedded in current anthropological practice. This school sees neither humanistic nor scientific discourses as adequate to account for the past, present, and future of anthropological subjects. Raising issues of context and history, and placing foragers in regional systems, some scholars focus on the overriding issue of the relations of foragers with the world system. I will call this the "culture" of political economy.

The first anthropological perspective draws its inspiration from the interpretivist, structuralist, and hermeneutic traditions of Clifford Geertz (1973), Claude Lévi-Strauss (1963), Mary Douglas (1966), Victor Turner (1969), and James Clifford (1988; Clifford and Marcus 1986); the second from the positivist and adaptationist current of Julian Steward (1936, 1938), Lew Binford (1978, 1980), and others (e.g., Harris 1979); and the third from the critical Marxist tradition in which Eric Wolf and Sidney Mintz are situated (Wolf 1982; Mintz 1985; Leacock 1981; see also Roseberry 1989; Patterson and Gailey 1987). Each approach has a distinctive methodological stance and each has made important contributions to hunter-gatherer studies. In fact, however much one may profess allegiance to one or another of the three cultures, in practice elements of all three approaches are frequently employed in contemporary research projects (for a classic example of synthesis, see Sahlins 1968).

My first intention in writing this paper was to give a critical appraisal of research contributions to hunter-gatherer studies from each of the anthropological traditions. But a prior question must be addressed, an issue that poses a challenge to the entire collective enterprise so fundamental that to ignore it would be to fiddle while Rome burns.[4] Following the lead of Foucault, Derrida, and the French poststructuralists, several anthropologists have declared hunter-gatherer a noncategory, a construction of observers mired in one or another brand of romantic idealism. The claims of this group are so far-reaching and so ill-contained within the paradigm space of the three cultures that they could be said to constitute a fourth culture rendering irrelevant large parts of the other three.

Revisionism, as it has been called, combining *some* elements of political economy with *some* elements of poststructuralism, presents a fundamental challenge to the way that anthropologists have looked at hunter-gatherers for the past 30 years. It posits that foragers are not what they appear to be; and it proposes a drastic rethinking of our subject. Schrire poses the revisionist challenge in these terms:

> There can be no doubt that, one way or another, all [ethnographies of hunter-gatherers] describe societies coping with the impact of incursions by foreign forces into their territories. . . . The big question that arises is, are the common features of hunter-gatherer groups, be they structural elements such as bilateral kinship systems or behavioral ones such as the tendency to share food, a product of interaction with us? Are the features we single out and study held in common, not so much because humanity shared the hunter-gatherer life-style for 99% of its time on earth, but because the hunter-gatherers of today, in searching for the compromises that would allow them to go on doing mainly that, have reached some subliminal consensus in finding similar solutions to similar problems? (1984:18)

And Wilmsen, writing of the Kalahari San puts it this way:

> The current status of the San-speaking peoples on the rural fringe of African economies can be accounted for only in terms of the social policies and economies of the colonial period and its aftermath. Their appearance as foragers is a function of their relegation to an underclass in the playing out of historical processes that began before the current millennium and culminated in the early decades of this century. *The isolation in which they are said to be found is a creation of our view of them, not of their history as they lived it.* This is as true of their indigenous material systems as it is of their incorporation in wider spheres of political economy of southern Africa. (1989:3, emphasis added)

There are two components to the revisionist critique, and it is essential to recognize the distinction between them. First there is the argument from history (see, e.g., Myers 1988:262–64; Headland and Reid 1989) that accuses past ethnographers of misreading or ignoring history and political economy and hence of treating the society in question as more bounded, more isolated, and more pristine than it really is. Political-economic revisionism argues that foragers have been integrated into larger regional or even international structures of power and exchange for so long that they can reveal nothing about the hunter-gatherer way of life. Evidence of trade and political domination is cited in support of this thesis. Linked to this line of critique is the purported discovery in hunter-gatherers of relations of domination and wealth accumulation previously associated with class societies (Price and Brown 1985; Flanagan 1989; Legros 1985).[5]

These critiques raise important issues, yet in terms of method, the argument remains on familiar terrain: one examines the historical, archeological, or other data and tests the merits of competing hypotheses against these data. Were the hunter-gatherers in question isolated? What does archeology reveal? What is the most parsimonious explanation for the observed facts? This is what Jacqueline Solway and I did in a recent *Current Anthropology* article titled "Foragers, Genuine or Spurious" (1990), meeting the issues raised by revisionists with empirical data that refuted their position.

The poststructuralist criticism, by contrast, takes a much more radically skeptical line. This view, linked to some versions of postmodernism, to deconstruction, and to a variety of other current schools, argues that there is no truth, only regimes of truth and power, and that all anthropology is powerfully shaped by the cultural constructions of the observer. Thus, ethnographic writing (about foragers or anybody else) has more in common with the historical novel and other works of fiction than it has with a scientific treatise. Therefore, the task of ethnography becomes immeasurably more problematic; truth is at best partial, flawed, obscured, and above all *relative*.[6]

This argument has radical implications for methodology. The production of knowledge has left the realm of empirical investigation and analytical methods of the past can no longer be relied upon. One can no longer utilize, for example, the etic/emic distinction because science after all is really only "Western emic" (Marcus and Fischer 1986:180–81). The use of Occam's Razor or the law of parsimony to choose between the merits of two competing explanations is no longer admissible because all are "true" at some level

What impact does this have on the study of foragers? Political economists and poststructuralists have tended to make the same critique of ethnographic practice, but as we shall see, for rather different reasons. Both argue the extraordinary proposition that the natives are "Us," and both put into question the assumption that hunter-gatherers, whatever they may be, represent the "other." The political economists argue that the natives are to all intent like Euro-Americans, because relations of domination and/or merchant capital reached the Arctic or the Ituri Forest or Sarawak long before ethnographers did and, therefore, tributary or mercantilist or capitalist relations of production have transformed foragers into people like ourselves, as parts of larger systems with hierarchies, commodities, exploitation, and other inequities and all their accompanying social consequences (Schrire 1984:18). Poststructuralists take the view that because anthropologists (like everyone else) are prisoners of their own ideology, as a consequence they can see in the "other" only a flawed perception of themselves. Thus, in either scenario, the "other" is declared a noncategory.

If the revisionist/poststructuralist position merits serious consideration— and the sheer volume of journal articles on these topics suggests that it does— then a major tenet of anthropology from Boas forward—that anthropology is the study of difference—becomes untenable. Or if "difference" is to be preserved as an anthropological problematic, then anthropology becomes the study of difference mutually constructed by powerful masters and powerless subalterns within a single world system.

In what follows I will explore the roots of the curious proposition that the natives are only different in surface features and that in truth they are "us." I see it as a peculiar expression of the intellectual culture of Late Capitalism. Anthropological revisionism lies at the intersection of two major tenets of contemporary Western thought: Proposition 1—*Nothing is real;* and Proposition 2—*The "system" is all-powerful.*

Nothing Is Real

We live in an era in which the line between real and nonreal has become dangerously blurred. What is real has become a scarce commodity and the pursuit of the "real" sometimes becomes a desperate search. Under capitalism, as Marshall Berman (quoting Marx) titles his book, "all that is solid melts into air" (1983). We don't have to search far for evidence of this proposition. The Disney corporation produces and distributes in a single fiscal year, perhaps in a single week, more fantasy material to more people than entire archaic civilizations could produce in a century. States of the Left, Right, and Center and their bureaucracies also produce prodigious volumes of fantasy, and through advertising and other media elites deploy enormous manipulative power (Ewen 1976). A recent ad for cigarettes (typical of the thousands that bombard Euro-Americans daily) has a picture of a carefully posed professional model, turned out as a fashion photographer, pretending to photograph another professional model herself posing, surrounded by other posed models in postures of forced gaiety. The caption: "Real People/Real Taste."

To protect the psyche from this type of assault, consumers and citizens in the West (and East) can be forgiven for erecting a shell of cynicism as a survival strategy under conditions of extreme debasement of the currency of reality. In fact it is hard to imagine keeping your sanity by any other means. This position of cool detachment and ironic distanciation has been considered the hallmark of the "postmodern condition" (Lyotard 1984; Sloterdijk 1987; Jameson 1984).

The world of scholarship has not escaped these massive social and psychological forces. In *The Invention of Tradition* (1983) Hobsbawm and Ranger and others show how allegedly hallowed customs handed down from the past are in fact the product of recent history. In his method of deconstruction, Derrida has argued that history is akin to a literary text and, like all texts, is ultimately unknowable (1976, 1978). It seems a short step to extending a critical and debunking discourse to all anthropological subjects.

But along the way there has been a slippage. The tools of deconstruction, developed to debunk and call into question the high and mighty, are now being applied to the powerless. Where the invention-of-tradition perspective was initially deployed to deconstruct the public rituals of the 19th-century British monarchy or pomp and circumstance in colonial India, it was now being generalized to question the claims to authenticity of small peoples. In his influential work, *The Predicament of Culture,* James Clifford shows how the Mashpee Indians construct their identity *de novo* in order to meet the exigencies of a court case (Clifford 1988). Similar arguments (but with less sympathy for the subalterns) have been made for the Maori by Hanson (1989) and for the ancient Hawaiians by Bergendorff, Hasager, and Henriques (1988; see also the reply by Sahlins 1989).[7]

The situation within anthropology is paralleled by the impact of poststructuralism on the broad front of the social sciences. Foucault's famous dictum (1976a, 1976b) that there is no truth, only regimes of truth and power, was originally intended as a critique of arbitrary power, but by showing the fragility of all truth-claims it has had the effect of undermining the legitimacy as well of oppositional movements for justice against these same powers (Taylor 1984; Habermas 1987).

There is a kernel of truth to the idea that all societies in the world are products of interaction with other societies and world society. Modern ethnography is a product of the Enlightenment and is a form of practice in which members of our academic subculture observe the other; as the late Kathleen Gough reminded us, anthropology is a child of imperialism. And then there are cases like the Philippine Tasaday, where a perfectly reasonable Southeast Asian semi-hunter-gatherer group, of which many examples exist, was seized on by the *National Geographic* and other media and popularized as the "Lost Stone Age" find of the century. Their recent exposure, and the media circus surrounding them, certainly fuels the cynicism that is itself the source of postmodernist sensibilities (Lee 1992; see also Dumont 1988; Berreman 1991; Duhaylungsod and Hyndman 1992).

Nevertheless, to succumb to the enticements of the poststructuralists or revisionists would be a disaster. Where I part company with the poststructuralists is in the view that our knowledge of the other—being filtered through perceptions, language, and culture—is so suspect that subjects can only be provisionally and arbitrarily constructed. It is striking how the largely male, White, and Western poststructuralists are proclaiming the death of the subject, precisely at the moment when alternative voices—women, people of color, Third World and aboriginal peoples—are struggling to constitute themselves as subjects of history, as the makers of their own history (Mascia-Lees, Sharpe, and Cohen 1989; see also Spivak 1988).

I do not believe that anthropologists are nearly so powerless before the awesome task of representing the other's reality, or that the ethnography of the 1960s or 1970s was so flawed that it has to be discarded. Adam Kuper, in a recent critique of postmodernism, points out that the methodologies of the 1960s were not so very different from those of the present,[8] and that their results were subjected to the critical scrutiny of peer review and comparative evidence. Kuper argues, and I would agree, that the view that ethnographic writing is more akin to fiction than it is to science does not accord with the history of the discipline. If the ethnographers of that not-so-distant era had passed their fiction off as science their readership and their peers would not have stood for it (Kuper 1990). (For other critiques of "postmodernism" that attempt to reconstruct the "realist" foundations of social science epistemologies see Mascia-Lees, Sharpe, and Cohen 1989; Roth 1989; Sangren 1988; Gellner 1988; Lovibond 1989; Soper 1991; see also Bhaskar 1979, 1986.)

Strictly speaking, the position taken by poststructuralists is not that *nothing* is real, since all take as given the existence of the power elite, of the state and its bureaucracies, and of the world system and its awesome power and reach. Therefore it would be more accurate to represent Proposition 1 as "Nothing is real . . . except power," which brings us directly to the second of our Propositions.

The "System" Is All-Powerful

The core proposition, "nothing is real," is reinforced by and reacts synergistically with the proposition, "the 'system' is all-powerful." We are living through a time in which history is accelerated; as the modern system continues to grow, things are moving faster and faster. Events and processes that unfolded over centuries are compressed into decades or years, and what transpired on a scale of years now unfolds in the space of months or weeks (Piel 1972:17–48; Harvey 1985:6–35). We need to put the revisionist debate in the context of this recent history.

Not everyone within hunter-gatherer studies has paused to reflect on the titanic forces that are transforming the world before our eyes. The era of Late Capitalism is witnessing the accumulation of capital on an unprecedented scale, the rise of the multinational corporation, and the phenomenal growth of the state as an apparatus for shaping and controlling human behavior (Chomsky 1989; Hardison 1989). In addition, one must try to comprehend the accelerating and expanding networks of information transfer on a world scale. Through television, e-mail, modems, cellular phones, fax, and other technologies it is possible to touch any part of the world in seconds, and through these same media we can dispose of all the world's accumulated knowledge and images with the push of a button—what Frederic Jameson has called "a decentered global network of microcircuits and blinking lights."

It is not surprising that this power of instantaneous communication, combined with the vast output of the culture industries mentioned above, and the centralizing power of the state, leads to fantasies of omniscience and omnipotence for the small minority of the world's population that has access to such tools (Berman 1983). Late Capitalism consumes the past with amazing rapidity, spews it out with such dizzying speed that it has the effect of obliterating the past, including the past of even 20 years ago.[9] All these processes tend to endow the force of capitalism with a mystique of enormous reach and totalizing power.[10]

Externally, the spread of worldwide capitalism, sporadic and localized in the 18th century, a flood in the 19th and early 20th century, has become a veritable avalanche in the last third of the 20th century.[11] As John Bodley, Shelton Davis, and others have pointed out, the world's tribal peoples are sitting directly in the path of the world's largest multinational corporations (Bodley 1982, 1988; Davis 1977; see also Jorgensen 1990). The scale of this penetration has increased in many cases by orders of magnitude in 10 or 20 years. To take an example, when I first arrived in Maun, Botswana, in 1963 there was a single tour operator taking tourists into the Okavango Swamps. Today there are over 80 operators; many of them offer to take clients to the last of the River Bushmen, a man who now gets "discovered" 40 or 50 times a year. The Dobe area in 1963–64 was even more isolated than the Okavango Swamps. In that era it received one motor vehicle visit every four to six weeks, for a total of 9 to 13 vehicles per year. In 1987 I counted a vehicle *every four to six hours* for an annual total of 1,400 to 2,100, a one- to two-hundredfold increase. Tom Headland notes that at the turn of the century there were 500 agriculturists in the vicinity of his Agta communities in northeastern Luzon. Today there are 30,000 (personal communication, 1990).

The Penan (or Punan) of Sarawak carried on regular long-distance trade with the coastal Dyak for hundreds of years; the impact of this trade on Penan institutions is the subject of another intense revisionist debate (Hoffman 1986; Brosius 1988).[12] But whatever their links to the coast may have been historically, they are nothing compared to the impact of the Japanese multinationals clear-cutting the rain forest at a rate faster than that in the Amazon. The Penan are now fighting for their lives as the multinationals, in conjunction with the state government (many of whose ministers hold logging concessions), clear-cut the Penans' traditional foraging areas, leaving them destitute and forcing them into government resettlement schemes. The Penan have mounted roadblocks to stop the bulldozers, and hundreds of Penan have been arrested, but the logging goes on (Burger 1990:94–95; Colchester 1989; CBC 1990; see also Hong 1987). Similar examples could be drawn from virtually any part of the First, Second, or Third Worlds. This is the context of accelerating and massive change in which the field of hunter-gatherer studies is situated, and this is the source of the crisis of representation that the field is undergoing.

The point I want to emphasize is that fieldworkers who arrive in the 1980s and 1990s and observe these appalling conditions find it unbelievable that 30, 20, or even 10 years earlier, observers could have found societies with band structure, kinship, and subsistence patterns still functioning. Instead of reflecting on the magnitude of the changes in that 10- or 20-year period, these revisionists immediately assume that the earlier studies were wrong and they go on to blithely project the contemporary patterns of destruction or outside domination back into the past.

Universalizing the present is the obverse of the equally flawed history that postulates pristine hunter-gatherers roaming the forest the year before the anthropologist arrives. While the latter view has correctly come in for a wave of criticism, it could be argued that the revisionists' willingness to project the present onto the past indicates an enchantment with the power of Capital that is, at base, no less romantic and uncritical than the much-criticized enchantment with the pristine or primitive other.

Mythologizing Pre-revisionist Ethnography

It would be foolish to argue that studies of hunters and gatherers prior to, say, 1970 were above reproach and therefore immune to criticism. Just as it would be equally foolish to argue that prior to 1970 all hunter-gatherers lived a pristine existence. Scholars working in that era made mistakes, and that includes myself. My own thinking has undergone continual reassessment, and it might be appropriate at this point to dispel some of the myths that have grown up about exactly what Kalahari ethnographers stand for.

One misconception is that pre-revisionist ethnographers believed the San were pristine hunter-gatherers (Wilmsen 1989:3, 6, 10, 33–43ff; Wilmsen and Denbow 1990:503–7). But as early as 1965 I pointed out that the great majority of the ethnic San—about 80%—were herders or farmers, or were existing as clients or servants on Black cattle posts and on commercial ranches (Lee 1965:20). Also in the 1960s I wrote in detail about the impact on the Dobe !Kung of European hunters and traders going back to the 1870s (Lee 1965:53–68).

A second myth concerns the notion that despite recognizing changes elsewhere, ethnographers have maintained a vision of the Dobe !Kung as unchanging in the face of overwhelming evidence to the contrary (e.g., Wilmsen and Denbow 1990:520; Gordon 1984). At all stages of fieldwork Kalahari ethnographers have grappled with this issue and have tried to give a scrupulous accounting of the non-!Kung elements present in the Dobe area, including the Herero presence, the Tswana presence, and the "European" presence. Any illusions I might have harbored about !Kung pristine conditions were dispelled by the late 1960s when new information came to light. When it became apparent, for example, that the actual economic circumstances of the !Kung had been misread, I was at pains to correct first impressions (note that even in 1976 the word "pristine" appears in quotation marks):

> As our field work continued, a more realistic picture of the "pristine" nature of the Dobe Area began to emerge. Most of the men of the Dobe area had had some experience at some point in their lives of herding the Bantu cattle, and about 20 percent of the young men were working on the cattle at any one time. Some had even owned goats or cattle in the past. Similarly the !Kung were not total strangers to agriculture. Many had learned the techniques by assisting their Bantu neighbors in planting, and in years of good rainfall some had planted small plots themselves and had harvested crops. (1976:18)

Far from holding a rigid and unchanging view of hunter-gatherers, there is evidence that many (but not all) students of the subject have changed their thinking over the years, and these changes have taken the field away from the position of the 1960s: that studies of contemporary hunter-gatherers are primarily a tool for understanding the evolution of human behavior. Two of these changes in particular are worth noting.

Recognizing that foragers have coexisted with farmers sometimes for centuries, *yet have remained foragers,* has moved a number of scholars toward a much more complex understanding of the historical position of foragers. Some of the same evidence that led revisionists to discard the very concept of hunter-gatherers led the editors and authors of *Politics and History in Band Societies* (Leacock and Lee 1982:1–20) in a different direction. The book was structured around the argument that hunter-gatherers can only be understood by seeing how some of them have been involved with farmers for a long time yet have retained their cultural identity.[13]

Understanding hunter-gatherer ecology, however important, is not enough. One has to look at the internal dynamics and the articulation of this internal system with wider histories. This has led to a second change in the thinking of a number of anthropologists, a shift away from an emphasis on hunting and gathering as modes of subsistence, toward the broader concept of "communal mode of production."

From Subsistence Ecology to Mode of Production

As I have discussed elsewhere (Lee 1981, 1988, 1990), communal relations of production are a widespread and well-documented phenomenon. Yet, despite their ubiquity, the subject has been woefully undertheorized. Communal relations of production are observed among the !Kung as well as among a number of hunter-gatherers in a wide variety of historical settings. They are also found among peoples with mixed economies of foraging and horticulture, such as the Iroquois (Trigger 1987, 1990), the Sharanahua (Siskind 1980), and the Batek (Endicott 1979). They are found even among former foragers in peripheral capitalism, such as aboriginal fringe dwellers in Darwin, Australia (Sansom 1980).[14]

Accepting the *existence* of communal relations of production in diverse settings among foragers and (some) nonforagers, the next question is how this is to be explained. I find it extremely difficult to accept that all these diverse instances are to be seen, as revisionists have argued, strictly as societal impoverishment resulting from exploitation by larger and more powerful societies (Schrire 1984:18; Gordon 1984:220; Wilmsen 1983, 1989).

The explanation lies, rather, in one remarkable organizational principle shared by band societies and peoples like them: the ability to reproduce themselves while limiting the accumulation of wealth and power. Such societies operate within the confines of a metaphorical ceiling and floor: a ceiling above which one may not accumulate wealth and power and a floor below which one may not sink. These limits on both aggrandizement and destitution are maintained by powerful social mechanisms known as leveling devices (Lee 1990:242–45). Such societies therefore have social and political resources of their own and are not just sitting ducks waiting to adopt the first hierarchical model that comes along. Clastres (1989) said it best when he said that for these kinds of societies the main problem was resisting becoming a state; by this he meant resisting not only the imposition of a state from outside but also resisting the pressures building up within, pressures leading toward accumulation and concentration of wealth and power.

Clastres did not imply that the nonstate societies lived in a state of perfect equality, nor would I. Hunter-gatherers may exhibit differences in wealth and power and they are certainly *not* nonviolent.[15] I prefer to follow the argument developed by Harriet Rosenberg in her recent research on !Kung aging and caregiving (1990). Rosenberg uses the term "entitlement" to account for the ways in which !Kung elderly were cared for by relatives and nonrelatives alike, such that no one, not even childless people, would be denied access to support in old age. This was part of a general phenomenon in !Kung society in which everyone claimed and was recognized as being "entitled" to the necessities of life, by right of being a member of the society.

> !Kung elders do not see themselves as burdens. They are not apologetic if they are not able to produce enough to feed themselves. They expect others to care for them when they can no longer do so. Entitlement to care is naturalized within the culture. Elders do not have to negotiate care as if it were a favor; rather it is perceived as a right. (Rosenberg 1990:29)

Will the "Real" San Please Stand Up?

The Kalahari revisionists claim to be restoring the San to history, but it is a curious view of history that the only way you can historicize foragers is to make them into pastoralists (or serfs) in the past! This seems to be an instance of life imitating art—of granting all agency to the dominating society whether capitalist or tributary, and making the histories of these diverse societies entirely reactive.[16] Solway and I (1990) have shown that while some San peoples did become peasants and serfs of Black overlords, others did not. The !Kung San of the Dobe area lay outside of the main routes of trade and spheres of tributary power. They defended their lands against incursions from Blacks and Whites, and when they entered into client relations with Black patrons they did so on terms that were more favorable than that prevailing in other parts of the Kalahari. The result is that when systematic ethnographic study began in the 1950s and 1960s, observers found a society with a number of key institutions—language, kinship, ritual practices—intact, while other institutions—land tenure, dispute settlement, political dynamics—were clearly in a state of flux (Marshall 1976; Lee and DeVore 1976; Lee 1979; Shostak 1981; Solway and Lee 1990; Yellen 1977).

Why did these distinctive institutions persist? They should not be seen simply as holdovers or survivals from the past kept in place by the weight of tradition. This trivializes their significance. These institutions are essential elements of cultural survival and they must be reproduced anew in each generation. Their presence is as good an index as any of the cultural viability and vitality of peoples like the !Kung.[17]

What is at issue here is whether foragers broadly represent a diverse but nevertheless identifiable form of human society with characteristic social and economic properties, or whether the foragers' identity dissolves and merges with that of serf, servant, client, slave, or rural proletariat.

What is the !Kung view of their own history? The !Kung see themselves as a people, increasingly circumscribed and threatened, but a people nonetheless with a strong sense of themselves. When told that they were really tributary appendages, long integrated into the economies of their more powerful neighbors, they were surprised and not a little offended.[18]

History and Identity of Hunter-Gatherers: Two Views

This brings us to two views of history and identity. One starts from cultural difference and postulates that there are cultures out there, which exist independent of academic constructions of them; for hunter-gatherers there is a lived reality regardless of whether or not they trade or render tribute to their neighbors. The other view sees historical status as constituted *only* by membership in a regional trading bloc, by subject status in a chiefdom or state, or by the production of a commodity for exchange; in other words, historical visibility can only be achieved through a relationship with *other* systems. The question that arises is whether that part of their history is the only thing or even the main thing that we want to know about hunter-gatherers.

Leacock and I (1982) argued that foraging societies can only be understood as the product of a triple dynamic: first, the internal dynamic of communal foraging relations of production; second, the dynamics of their historical interactions with farmers, herders, and states; and third, the dynamic of articulation and incorporation within the modern world system. The difference between this position and the revisionist one is the latter's privileging the operation of the second and third dynamics at the expense of the first. The revisionist position accords minimal reality to foraging as a distinct mode of life, what Tim Ingold (1990:130) has recently called "a radically alternative mode of relatedness."[19]

These two views of hunter-gatherers inscribe alternate discourses about the current conjuncture. The first says we are living in a time when the world is young, in flux, and still in the process of formation; some of the antecedent societal forms are still there to be observed and experienced. The people we have come to call hunter-gatherers are examples, to varying degrees, of alternative ways of life, examples of difference. The other discourse says no, the world is old, what you are seeing is not difference, it is just another aspect of us, created by the same forces, the same "system" that created us. In my view this second discourse contains a number of unexamined assumptions about the transformative power of commodities, and about the ability of mercantile and tributary systems to project their power and to impose their will on the peoples on their periphery.[20]

How will we ever sort out the conflicting claims of the differing schools of thought in hunter-gatherer studies? Given the enormous load of ideology in hunter-gatherer studies, along with most branches of scholarship, I want to reiterate a plea for the importance of empirical evidence; I am as much opposed to mindless empiricism as anyone, but without empirical evidence debates will disintegrate into ideological name-calling.

What is urgently needed in this era of disillusion is the middle path: a working discipline that sees science, humanism, and critical reflection as three components of a single field; scholars need empiricism tempered by reflexivity and a dialectic between the two. All of this should be framed within a sense of history and political economy, to ensure that a scholar's situated history and the relationship between scholar and subject are not lost. Scholars must interrogate assumptions as the poststructuralists suggest, but after that, I for one would like to get on with it. If sound methods demonstrate that hunter-gatherers are historically serfs or pastoralists or whatever, then so be it. But the current crop of revisionist arguments are dubious, to say the least.[21] The task of situating hunter-gatherers historically has barely begun, and there remains a great deal of scope for archeological, ethnographic, and ethnohistoric investigations to resolve the question of to what degree hunter-gatherers can be said to be culturally autonomous or integrated into larger systems at various points in their histories.[22] I also suggest that these questions will motivate the production of the kinds of knowledge that will be used by future generations, sifted and resifted long after the debates of this decade fade into the past.

To recover a link to the real world, to empirical reality, is precisely what some scholars tried to do in the 1960s with the work diaries, demography, subsistence ecology, and careful ethnography (e.g., Helm 1965; Hiatt 1965; Marshall 1961; Rose 1960). This is a scholarly tradition that many are carrying on today, while constantly improving their methods. But empiricism, however critically informed, is not the whole story. Self-definitions change. In the 1960s, many anthropologists saw themselves as crusading empiricists, replacing speculation with facts, but it is now possible to recognize that, like all scholars in the human sciences, the ethnographers of the 1950s and 1960s were also storytellers, weavers of narratives (after all, the origin of the word "text" is from "textiles"). It was not only a question of *what* they had to say but also *how* they said it. To this extent those who emphasize anthropology's affinities to literature *do* have a point.[23]

As Donna Haraway has noted (1989), one of the master narratives constructed (in part) from hunter-gatherer data has been the story of human nature and life in the "state of nature": who we are as a species, our past, and by implication our future. The poststructuralist project focuses our attention almost exclusively on the "constructedness" of these narratives. But just because they are constructed doesn't mean that they have no claim to empirical validity or that the search for knowledge of the past is an illegitimate enterprise. Ethnographic analogy to the past does involve leaps of extrapolation and therefore must be treated with extreme caution, but the archeological record can and does provide direct knowledge of the distant past.

The problem remains, however, that like ethnography archeological interpretations of the past are no less shaped by the ideological forces of the present. This highlights the critical need for maintaining and enlarging the sphere of knowledge—in both archeology and ethnography—that transcends the ideological battles of each era: the need for a version of anthropology that is both critical and empirical (cf. O'Meara 1989; Carrithers 1990).

Given the difficulties of living up to the demands of doing this kind of work and the many pitfalls, it is surprising how much good work is being done in hunter-gatherer studies. Rejecting the view of foragers as timeless primitives *or* as rural proletarians, there are those who would see hunting and gathering as a way of life that exists in the present yet is different from Western urban modes of life. To varying degrees these students attempt to maintain a sense of balance and proportion between the reality of their scholarly world and the reality of their subjects, and between the methodological demands of the three cultures.[24]

One trend that seems to be present in all three methodological currents is a move by some (but by no means all) away from seeing hunting and gathering peoples as *objects* of anthropological inquiry, to a situation in which they become the *subjects* of their own history and often the directors of their own research. This has paralleled the development of political consciousness among indigenous people. As foragers and former foragers have become more involved in struggles for their rights, hunter-gatherer studies have become much more of a collaborative enterprise: working *with* the people in their struggles to determine their futures.[25]

Perhaps the most significant development of the last decade is indigenous peoples speaking to us in their own voices; for example, the Canadian Innu, Lubicon, Teme-Augama, and others in Richardson (1989). The Gitksan and Wet'suet'en people of British Columbia are good examples of former (and continuing) foragers who have addressed the larger public directly in a variety of voices and settings, including the courts (Sterritt 1989; People of 'Ksan 1980; Gisday Wa and Delgum Uukw 1989). Increasingly, indigenous peoples are making political alliances with environmentalists, feminists, youth groups, and peoples of color.

On this new and expanded political terrain an interesting question concerns how hunters and gatherers themselves regard hunter-gatherer studies. Clearly the cultural renaissance under way in a number of native communities has generated considerable interest in "traditional" ethos and world view, governance, subsistence, arts, crafts, ethnobotany, and healing; for these and other spheres of knowledge, the elders and anthropological texts are the main sources of information.[26]

Conclusion

This article has delineated the crisis of representation in hunter-gatherer studies and has attempted to comprehend the underlying epistemological and ideological roots of the crisis. The field of hunter-gatherer studies has been undergoing a series of transformations and the original raison d'être has required reassessment. Yet, despite the fundamental challenges of the "revisionists," it can be argued that a core of relevance to both scholarly and indigenous peoples' agendas remains in hunter-gatherer studies; that the field is responding to this challenge is indicated by the shift away from simplistic evolutionary arguments toward more nuanced, historically sensitized, and critical understandings. In this respect the altered contours of hunter-gatherer studies represent a successful incursion by humanists and political economists on a terrain that had been largely dominated by natural-science-oriented methods and philosophies.

In the preface to *Man the Hunter*, DeVore and I wrote, "We cannot avoid the suspicion that many of [the contributors] were led to live and work among the hunters because of a feeling that the human condition was likely to be more clearly drawn here than among other kinds of societies" (Lee and DeVore 1968:ix). I now believe this is wrong. The human condition is about poverty, injustice, exploitation, war, suffering. To seek the human condition one must go, as Wolf and Hansen (1975) did, to the barrios, shantytowns, and palatial mansions of Rio, Lima, and Mexico City, where massive inequalities of wealth and power have produced fabulous abundance for some and misery for most. When anthropologists look at hunter-gatherers they are seeking something else: a vision of human life and human possibilities without the pomp and glory, but also without the misery and inequity of state and class society.

Almost all of humanity lives today in highly organized bureaucratized societies of enormous scale and systematic inequalities. Hunter-gatherers, in spite of the inducements (or threats?) to become incorporated, choose for whatever reasons to resist and to live lives very different from that of the majority. The pace is slower, technology simpler, numbers smaller, inequality less, and the relationship to land and resources—the sense of place—is on a radically different basis. Following Clastres, I have argued that what sets hunter-gatherers apart is their ability to reproduce themselves *while severely limiting* the accumulation and concentration of wealth and power. This feature they share with a number of simple horticultural and pastoral societies. Since the accumulation of wealth and power (and resistance to it) is the driving force of much of human history, it follows that societies that don't have this dynamic must have a dynamic of a different sort: what Tim Ingold has called a "different kind of sociality" (1990:130–31).

If indigenous peoples want to adopt a Western (or Soviet) way of life, the door is open; in fact, the pressures to conform are immense. The fact that this has not happened, that some foragers still pursue alternative lifeways not in isolation but in full awareness of alternatives, is a persuasive argument against the two propositions that framed the present essay. *There is something out there beyond the reach of the world system (capitalist or otherwise). The "system" is powerful but not omnipotent.* Pockets of resistance persist and show us that even in this hard-bitten postmodern age other ways of being are possible.

Since so many of the world's intractable problems derive from the gigantic maldistribution of wealth and power, it stands to reason that societies that can reproduce themselves without exploitation have a great deal to teach us. As the world's peoples struggle to redefine alternative visions in the aftermath of the Cold War, I am convinced that hunter-gatherer studies, far from being the fantasy projection of uncritical romantics, have a role to play: in the movement for justice for indigenous peoples, and as part of a larger movement to recapture wholeness from an increasingly fragmented and alienating modernity.

NOTES

This paper was presented at the Sixth International Conference on Hunting and Gathering Societies (CHAGS), Fairbanks, Alaska, May 27–June 1, 1990, and is published here with permission of the CHAGS organizing committee, chaired by Linda Ellanna. The author would like to thank the following colleagues and friends for useful input in the development of this paper: Michael Asch, Victor Barac, John Barker, Alan Barnard, Liz Cashdan, Julie Cruikshank, Richard Daly, Pat Draper, I. Eibl-Eibesfeldt, Bion Griffin, Matthias Guenther, Henry Harpending, Bob Hitchcock, Tim Ingold, Dick Katz, Tom Patterson, Nick Peterson, Phillip Smith, Harriet Rosenberg, Jackie Solway, Eric Smith, Verna St. Dennis, Polly Wiessner, Eric Wood, and John Yellen. These critics are not responsible, of course, for any errors of fact or interpretation. Versions of this paper have been presented at seminars at the Universities of British Columbia, Victoria, Simon Fraser, and Washington. Critical comments by colleagues and students at these institutions were instrumental in further clarifying the issues presented here.

1. Whether hunter-gatherers are more accurately called gatherer-hunters to acknowledge the predominance of gathered foods over game is an issue I have addressed in detail elsewhere (Lee 1979). The term "foragers" is an economical shorthand that does not prejudge the issue either way (e.g., Lee 1981).

2. Snow's position in turn can be traced back to a 19th-century critical Romanticism, which saw science as providing an ideological basis for the spread and destructive effects of capitalism. (I thank Victor Barac for this observation.)

3. The first draft of this paper had been completed before I became aware of Michael Carrithers's (1990) article, which also develops the figure of the "two cultures" as a means of comprehending contemporary anthropology.

4. While work from this prospective still constitutes only a small fraction of hunter-gatherer research, it would be a serious error to ignore, as many within the field have, its profound implications, not only for researchers but, more important, for the anthropological subjects themselves.

5. For a thoughtful and balanced discussion of this issue see Paynter 1989.

6. For a late conversion to relativism see Leach 1989; on the fallacy of "hyperrelativism" see Trigger 1989.

7. Wilmsen uses the Hobsbawm and Ranger thesis to the same effect in a section of his book entitled "The Invention of 'Bushmen'" (1989:24–26).

8. As a case in point, Wilmsen, after stating that his "book is . . . not an ethnography" and proclaiming the end of "the ethnographic era of anthropology" (1989:xii), goes on to devote several hundred pages to the presentation of "ethnographic" data on the San in the form of ethnohistory, genealogies, demography, economic anthropology, and subsistence ecology.

9. David Lowenthal (1985) has offered a provocative discussion of how both selective cultural amnesia and an obsession with the past characterize contradictory contemporary views of history.

10. The feeling of omniscience and instant global communication was nowhere more clearly expressed than in the television coverage of the first days of the war in the Persian Gulf, where major developments were seen as they occurred during North American prime time.

11. Many of these ideas are drawn from the works of Ernest Mandel (1978), Fred Jameson (1984), and the thought of Marshall MacLuhan.

12. Hoffman has argued, like Wilmsen, that the Penan were locked into the coastal trade centuries ago and had long since become subjects of coastal suzerains. Brosius and others have made the case for a greater degree of Penan autonomy.

13. Of this volume Bender and Morris write: "The publication of *Politics and History in Band Societies*... demolish[ed] the notion that contemporary gatherer-hunter societies were in any sense 'pristine'" (1988:6). A similar point is made by John Wright (1989:535) and by Donna Haraway (1989:194–97, 227), who clearly locates Lee as a member of the "revisionists." The revisionists for their part seem to prefer to retain a 1960s image of hunter-gatherer studies as a more convenient straw-person.

14. Some would argue, along with Phillip E. L. Smith, that communal relations and other aspects of foraging lifeways can be discerned in frontier European populations like the transhumant English settlers in Newfoundland from the 18th century on (Smith, personal communication, 1991).

15. For example, the appearance of slavery in complex foraging societies like those of the Northwest Coast (Donald 1983), and of other forms of inequality elsewhere (e.g., Legros 1985; Flanagan 1989), need to be seriously studied. And Clastres's own treatment of several topics—for one, gender—leaves much to be desired.

16. Bender and Morris in their introduction to Volume 1 of *Hunters and Gatherers* (Ingold, Riches, and Woodburn 1988a) perceptively make a similar critique of the revisionist view of history; (1988:7–14):

> Above all the message of *[Politics and History in Band Societies]* must be that gatherer-hunters have their own history. An understanding of the processes of encapsulation has to work in tandem with an understanding that gatherer-hunter variability, past or present, has an internal dynamic. Change in gatherer-hunter societies does not wait upon the arrival of land-hungry farmers, nor upon capitalist penetration. (1988:13–14)

17. Having said this, there is still room to accommodate Alan Barnard's (1988) arguments that ethnicity and identity of San peoples are constructed in part from their mutual accommodations and antagonisms with other peoples.

18. Not only is the assertion of their "subjugation" vehemently denied by the !Kung themselves, but their view of the timing of the entrance of non-!Kung into their lands directly contradicts the "revisionist" position. When !Kung elders were asked to identify which of their African neighbors—the Hereros, Tswanas, or BaYei—first came into their land, they insisted it was none of them: the Europeans came first, followed by other Africans (Solway and Lee 1990:115). Since the Europeans only arrived in the 1870s, this renders moot the revisionist argument that the !Kung of the Dobe area were subjugated in the 1st millennium A.D. !Kung oral histories of the colonial period are presented in Lee (1991).

19. In fact, Ingold has argued that hunter-gatherer sociality is of such a different order that the term "society" is inappropriate with reference to them and should be reserved for describing post-forager peoples (1990:130–31) .

20. In the Kalahari, for example, there are a number of problems in applying 20th-

century patterns of power-holding and projecting them back into the past of the Dobe !Kung. For over 90% of the centuries of San/Black interaction, the putative overlords were not capitalists or even mercantilists, but African kin-ordered and tributary formations. In order for the revisionist model to work in this prehistoric context one has to endow 1st- and 2nd-millennium chiefdoms (if that is what they were) with the same predatory impulses and the same ability to exercise power across great distances that the historic Tswana chiefdoms briefly possessed in the 19th century, under the intense pressure of the Boer military threat and the competition of the British traders and imperialists. Despite the claims of the revisionists (e.g., Wilmsen and Denbow 1990:449–503), there is no convincing evidence that any group in what is now northwestern Botswana had that kind of power before the late 19th century, least of all the Tswana chiefdom, the weakest of the eight major tribes that made up the Tswana nation (Tlou 1985).

21. For a critique of revisionist historiography in the Kalahari see Lee and Guenther (1991).

22. For two excellent examples of how this can be done see Trigger (1990) and Hunn (1990).

23. As I wrote in 1979:

> Modern anthropology no longer believes that the scientist of culture is neutral: today's epistemology includes *the observer along with the "natives" in the field of view.* When acknowledged and used creatively the observer's likes and dislikes, his [sic] prejudices and enthusiasms, become an instrument of discovery, a part of the learning process itself and not external to it. (Lee 1979:8, emphasis in original)

24. While an inventory of recent work in hunter-gatherer studies is far beyond the scope of this paper, a few examples from two of the "paradigms" are appended to illustrate the abundance of work in the 1980s and 1990s (see also Note 23).

"Scientists": Ingold (1986a, 1986b), Woodburn (1980, 1982, 1988), and Wiessner (1982); Winterhalder (1990), Smith (1988); see also Winterhalder and Smith (1981); Smith and Boyd (1990), Vierich (1982), Cashdan (1987, 1990), Griffin (1989), Kent (1989), and the Harvard Pygmy project (Bailey and Peacock 1988; Bailey et al. 1989).

"Humanists": Brody (1981), Myers (1986b), Ridington (1990), Shostak (1981), Cruikshank (1991), Bird-David (1990). For some interesting recent work on Western perceptions and constructions of hunter-gatherers see Dumont (1988), Sponsel (1992), Armitage and Kennedy (1989); see also Myers (1986a). (For various combinations of all three paradigms see Ingold, Riches, and Woodburn [1988a, 1988b].)

25. This renegotiated ethnographic ethic can be seen clearly in the work of some of the "political economists": Asch (1984), Chance (1990), Daly (1988), Duhaylungsod and Hyndman (1992), Feit (1985, 1991), Hitchcock (1977, 1988), Hitchcock and Brandenburgh (1990), Hunn (1990), Kidd (1990), Peterson (1982, 1985), Peterson and Matsuyama (1991), Sansom (1985), and

Tanner (1979). Special mention should be made of the work of Megan Biesele and John Marshall, who have been working with the !Kung San of Namibia through the most dramatic changes in their history (Biesele and Weinberg 1990).

26. On this score I found it instructive that so many members of indigenous Alaskan organizations endorsed the 1990 Fairbanks Conference on Hunting and Gathering Societies, not only contributing papers and workshops but also supporting CHAGS financially. These sponsors included Bering Straits Native Corporation, NANA Regional Corporation Inc., Interior Fish Processors of Alaska, and the Interior Mayors' Association of Alaska.

REFERENCES

Armitage, Peter, and J. C. Kennedy
1989   Redbaiting and Racism in Labrador and Quebec. Canadian Review of
        Sociology and Anthropology 18(4):798–817.

Asch, Michael
1984   Home and Native Land: Aboriginal Rights and the Canadian
        Constitution. Toronto: Methuen.

Bailey, R., and N. Peacock
1988   Efe Pygmies of Northeast Zaire: Subsistence Strategies in the Ituri Forest.
        In Uncertainty in the Food Supply. G. A. Harrison and A. Boyce, eds.
        Pp. 88–117. Cambridge: Cambridge University Press.

Bailey, R. C., G. Head, M. Jenike, B. Owen, R. Rechtman, and E. Zechenter
1989   Hunting and Gathering in Tropical Rain Forest: Is It Possible? American
        Anthropologist 91:59–82.

Barnard, Alan
1988   Cultural Identity, Ethnicity and Marginalization among the Bushmen of
        Southern Africa. *In* New Perspectives on the Study of Khoisan. Rainer
        Vossen, ed. Pp. 9–27. Hamburg: Helmut Buske Verlag.

Begler, E.
1978   Sex, Status, and Authority in Egalitarian Society. American
        Anthropologist 80:571–88.

Bender, Barbara, and Brian Morris
1988   Preface. *In* Hunters and Gatherers, Vol. 1: History, Evolution and Social
        Change. T. Ingold, D. Riches, and J. Woodburn, eds. Pp. 4–14. London:
        Berg.

Bergendorff, Steen, Ulla Hasager, and Peter Henriques
1988   Mythopraxis and History: On the Interpretation of the Makahiki. Journal
        of the Polynesian Society 97:391–408.

Berman, Marshall
1983   All That Is Solid Melts into Air. New York: Simon and Schuster.

Berreman, Gerald
1991   The Incredible "Tasaday": Deconstructing the Myth of a "Stone-Age"
        People. Cultural Survival Quarterly 15(1):3–46.

Bhaskar, Roy
1979   The Possibility of Naturalism: A Philosophical Critique of the Human
        Sciences. Brighton, UK: Harvester Press.
1986   Scientific Realism and Human Emancipation. London: Verso.
Biesele, Megan, and Paul Weinberg
1990   Shaken Roots: The Bushmen of Namibia. Johannesburg: EDA
        Publications.
Binford, Lewis R.
1978   Nuniamiut Ethnoarchaeology. New York: Academic Press.
1980   Willow Smoke and Dogs' Tails: Hunter-Gatherer Settlement Systems and
        Archaeological Site Formation. American Antiquity 45:4–20.
Bird-David, Nurit
1990   The Giving Environment: Another Perspective on the Economic System
        of Gatherer-Hunters. Current Anthropology 31(2):189–96.
Boas, Franz
1935   Kwakiutl Culture as Reflected in Mythology. New York: Memoirs of the
        American Folklore Society, 28.
1966   Kwakiutl Ethnography. Helen Codere, ed. Chicago: University of Chicago
        Press.
Bodley, John
1982   Victims of Progress. Menlo Park, CA: Cummings.
1988   Tribal Peoples and Development Issues: A Global Overview. Mountain
        View, CA: Mayfield.
Brody, Hugh
1981   Maps and Dreams. Harmondsworth: Penguin.
Brosius, Peter
1988   A Separate Reality: Comments on Hoffman's *The Punan: Hunters and
        Gatherers of Borneo*. Borneo Research Bulletin 20(2):81–105.
Burger, Julian
1990   The Gaia Atlas of First Peoples: A Future for the Indigenous World. New
        York: Doubleday.
Carrithers, Michael
1990   Is Anthropology Art or Science? Current Anthropology 31:263–82.
Cashdan, Elizabeth
1987   Trade and Its Origins on the Botetli River. Journal of Anthropological
        Research 43:121–38.
1990 [ed.] Risk and Uncertainty in Tribal and Peasant Economies. Boulder, CO:
        Westview Press.
CBC (Canadian Broadcasting Corporation)
1990   The Fate of the Forest. Toronto: CBC: "Ideas" Programme Transcript.
Chance, Norman A.
1990   The Inupiat and Arctic Alaska: An Ethnography of Development. Fort
        Worth, TX: Holt, Rinehart and Winston.
Chomsky, Noam
1989   Necessary Illusions: Thought Control in Democratic Societies. The
        Massey Lectures. Montreal: CBC Enterprises.

Clastres, Pierre
    1989   Society against the State: Essays in Political Anthropology. New York: Zone Books.
Clifford, James
    1983   On Ethnographic Authority. Reflections 1:118–45.
    1988   The Predicament of Culture: Twentieth Century Ethnography, Literature, and Art. Cambridge, MA: Harvard University Press.
Clifford, James, and George Marcus, eds.
    1986   Writing Culture: The Poetics and Politics of Ethnography. Berkeley: University of California Press.
Colchester, Marcus
    1989   Pirates, Squatters and Poachers: The Political Ecology of Dispossession of the Native Peoples of Sarawak. London and Kuala Lumpur: Survival International and INSAM Malaysia.
Cruikshank, Julie
    1991   Life Lived Like a Story: Lifestories of Three Yukon Native Elders. Lincoln: University of Nebraska Press.
Dahlberg, Frances, ed.
    1981   Woman the Gatherer. New Haven, CT: Yale University Press.
Daly, Richard
    1988   Land Ownership among British Columbia First Nations. Paper presented to First Nations Land Ownership Conference, Vancouver, B.C., Justice Institute, Oct. 1988.
Davis, Shelton
    1977   Victims of the Miracle: Development and the Indians of Brazil. New York: Cambridge University Press.
Derrida, Jacques
    1976   Of Grammatology. Baltimore, MD: Johns Hopkins University Press.
    1978   Writing and Difference. Chicago: University of Chicago Press.
Diamond, Stanley
    1974   In Search of the Primitive: A Critique of Civilization. New Brunswick, NJ: Transaction Books.
Donald, Leland
    1983   Was Nuu-chah-nulth-aht (Nootka) Society Based on Slave Labor? In The Development of Political Organization in Native North America. Elisabeth Tooker, ed. 1979 Proceedings of the American Ethnological Society. Pp. 108–19. Washington, DC: American Ethnological Society.
Douglas, Mary
    1966   Purity and Danger. New York: Praeger.
Duhaylungsod, Levita, and David Hyndman
    1992   Behind and Beyond the Tasaday: The Untold Struggle over Resources of Indigenous Peoples. In The Tasaday Controversy. Tom Headland, ed. Washington, DC: American Anthropological Association Special Publication.

Dumont, Jean-Paul
  1988   The Tasaday, Which and Whose? Towards the Political Economy of an
          Ethnographic Sign. Cultural Anthropology 3:261–75.
Endicott, Kirk
  1979   Batek Negrito Religion. Cambridge: Cambridge University Press.
Ewen, Stuart
  1976   Captains of Consciousness: Advertising and the Social Roots of
          Consumer Culture. New York: McGraw-Hill.
Feit, Harvey
  1985   Legitimation and Autonomy in James Bay Cree Responses to Hydro-
          Electric Development. In Indigenous Peoples and the Nation-State. Noel
          Dyck, ed. Pp. 27–66. St. John's, Newfoundland: Memorial University
          Press.
  1991   Gifts of the Land: Hunting Territories, Guaranteed Incomes and the
          Construction of Social Relations in James Bay Cree Society. In Cash,
          Commoditisation and Changing Foragers. N. Peterson and T.
          Matsuyama, eds. Senri Ethnological Studies No. 30. Pp. 223–68. Osaka:
          National Museum of Ethnology.
Flanagan, James
  1989   Hierarchy in Simple "Egalitarian" Societies. Annual Review of
          Anthropology 18:245–66.
Foley, Robert
  1988   Hominids, Humans and Hunter-Gatherers: An Evolutionary
          Perspective. In Hunters and Gatherers, Vol. 1: History, Evolution
          and Social Change. T. Ingold, D. Riches, and J. Woodburn, eds.
          Pp. 207–21. London: Berg.
Foucault, Michel
  1976a   Truth and Power. In Power/Knowledge. C. Gordon, ed. (Reprinted in The
          Foucault Reader, P. Rabinow, ed., pp. 51–75, Random House, 1984.)
          New York: Pantheon.
  1976b   The Archaeology of Knowledge. New York: Harper and Row.
Geertz, Clifford
  1973   The Interpretation of Cultures: Selected Essays. New York: Basic Books.
Gellner, Ernest
  1988   The Stakes in Anthropology. American Scholar 57:17–32.
Gordon, Robert
  1984   The !Kung in the Kalahari Exchange: An Ethnohistorical Perspective.
          In Past and Present in Hunter-Gatherer Studies. Carmel Schrire.
          Pp. 195–224. Orlando, FL: Academic Press.
Griffin, P. Bion
  1989   Hunting, Farming, and Sedentism in a Rain Forest Foraging Society. In
          Farmers as Hunters: Implications of Sedentism. Susan Kent, ed. Pp.
          60–70. Cambridge: Cambridge University Press.

Habermas, Jürgen
  1987   Modernity: An Incomplete Project. *In* Interpretive Social Science: A
          Second Look. Paul Rabinow and William M. Sullivan, eds. Pp. 141–56.
          Berkeley: University of California Press.
Hanson, Allan
  1989   The Making of the Maori: Culture Invention and Its Logic. American
          Anthropologist 91:890–902.
Haraway, Donna
  1989   Primate Visions: Gender, Race and Nature in the World of Modern
          Science. New York: Routledge, Chapman and Hall.
Hardison, O. B., Jr.
  1989   Disappearing through the Skylight: Culture and Technology in the
          Twentieth Century. Baltimore, MD: Penguin.
Harris, Marvin
  1979   Cultural Materialism: The Struggle for a Science of Culture. New York:
          Vintage.
Harvey, David
  1985   Consciousness and the Urban Experience: Studies in the History and
          Theory of Capitalist Urbanization. Baltimore, MD: Johns Hopkins
          University Press.
Hawkes, Kirsten, Kim Hill, and James O'Connell
  1982   Why Hunters Gather: Optimal Foraging and the Ache of Eastern
          Paraguay. American Ethnologist 9:379–98.
Headland, Tom, and Lawrence Reid
  1989   Hunters-Gatherers and Their Neighbors from Prehistory to the Present.
          Current Anthropology 30:43–66.
Helm, June
  1965   Bilaterality in the Socio-Territorial Organization of the Arctic Drainage
          Dene. Ethnology 4:361–85.
Hiatt, Les
  1965   Kinship and Conflict: A Study of an Aboriginal Community in Northern
          Arnhem Land. Canberra: Australian National University Press.
Hill, Kim, and Kirsten Hawkes
  1983   Neotropical Hunting among the Ache of Eastern Paraguay. *In* Adaptive
          Responses of Native Amazonians. R. Hames and W. Vickers, eds.
          Pp. 139–88. New York: Academic Press.
Hitchcock, Robert
  1977   Kalahari Cattle Posts. Gaborone: Government of Botswana.
  1988   Monitoring Research and Development in the Remote Areas of
          Botswana. Gaborone: Government Printer.
Hitchcock, Robert, and Rodney Brandenburgh
  1990   Tourism, Conservation and Culture in the Kalahari Desert, Botswana.
          Cultural Survival Quarterly 14:20–24.
Hobsbawm, Eric, and T. O. Ranger, eds.
  1983   The Invention of Tradition. Cambridge: Cambridge University Press.

Hoffman, Carl
   1986   The Punan: Hunters and Gatherers of Borneo. Ann Arbor: UMI Research
          Press.
Hong, Evelyne
   1987   Natives of Sarawak: Survival in Borneo's Vanishing Forest. Pulau Pinang,
          Malaysia: Institut Masyarakat.
Hunn, Eugene
   1981   On the Relative Contribution of Men and Women to Subsistence among
          Hunter-Gatherers of the Columbia Plateau: A Comparison with
          Ethnographic Atlas Summaries. Journal of Ethnobiology 1:124–34.
Hunn, Eugene, with James Selam and family
   1990   Nch'i-Wána, "The Big River": Mid-Columbia Indians and Their Land.
          Seattle: University of Washington Press.
Ingold, Tim
   1986a The Appropriation of Nature: Essays on Human Ecology and Social
          Relations. Manchester: Manchester University Press.
   1986b Evolution and Social Life. Cambridge: Cambridge University Press.
   1990   *Comment on* "Foragers, Genuine or Spurious: Situating the Kalahari San
          in History," by J. Solway and R. Lee. Current Anthropology 31:130–31.
Ingold, Tim, David Riches, and James Woodburn, eds.
   1988a Hunters and Gatherers, Vol 1: History, Evolution and Social Change.
          London: Berg.
   1988b Hunters and Gatherers, Vol 2: Property, Power and Ideology. London:
          Berg.
Isaac, Glynn
   1978   The Food-Sharing Behavior of Protohuman Hominids. Scientific
          American 238(4):90–108
Jameson, Frederic
   1984   Postmodernism, or the Cultural Logic of Late Capitalism. New Left
          Review 146:53–92.
Jorgensen, Joseph
   1990   Oil-Age Eskimos. Berkeley: University of California Press.
Keene, Art
   1983   Biology, Behavior, and Borrowing: A Critical Examination of Optimal
          Foraging Models in Archaeology. *In* Archaeological Hammers and
          Theories. A. Keene and J. Moore, eds. New York: Academic Press.
   1991   Archeology and the Heritage of Man the Hunter. Reviews in
          Anthropology 16:133–47.
Kent, Susan, ed.
   1989   Farmers as Hunters: Implications of Sedentism. Cambridge: Cambridge
          University Press.
Kidd Dorothy
   1990   Ikajurti, The Helper: Midwifery in the Arctic (film). Ottawa: Inuit
          Broadcasting Corporation, and Pauktuutit, the Inuit Women's
          Association.

Kroeber, A. L.
    1925   Handbook of the Indians of California. Washington, DC: Bureau of American Ethnology Bulletin No. 78.

Kuper, Adam
    1990   Ethnographic Practice. Unpublished ms., Department of Human Sciences, Brunel University, Uxbridge, Middlesex, England.

Lancaster, Jane
    1978   Carrying and Sharing in Human Evolution. Human Nature (2):82–89.

Leach, Edmund
    1989   *Review of* Works and Lives, by C. Geertz. American Ethnologist 16:137–41.

Leacock, Eleanor
    1981   Myths of Male Dominance. New York: Monthly Review Press.

Leacock, Eleanor, and Richard Lee, eds.
    1982   Politics and History in Band Societies. Cambridge: Cambridge University Press.

Lee, Richard
    1965   Subsistence Ecology of !Kung Bushmen. Doctoral dissertation in Anthropology, University of California, Berkeley. Ann Arbor: University Microfilms.
    1976   Introduction. *In* Kalahari Hunter-Gatherers: Studies of the !Kung San and Their Neighbors. R. Lee and I. DeVore, eds. Pp. 3–24. Cambridge, MA: Harvard University Press.
    1979   The !Kung San: Men, Women and Work in a Foraging Society. New York: Cambridge University Press.
    1981   Is There a Foraging Mode of Production? Canadian Journal of Anthropology 2:13–19.
    1988   Reflections on Primitive Communism. *In* Hunters and Gatherers, Vol. 1: History, Evolution and Social Change. T. Ingold, D. Riches, and J. Woodburn, eds. Pp. 252–68. London: Berg.
    1990   Primitive Communism and the Origins of Social Inequality. *In* The Evolution of Political Systems: Sociopolitics in Small-Scale Sedentary Societies. Steadman Upham, ed. Pp. 225–46. Cambridge: Cambridge University Press.
    1991   Solitude or Servitude: !Kung Images of the Colonial Encounter. Paper presented in the symposium, "Narratives of Resistance: History, Ethnography and Power." Meetings of the Canadian Anthropology Society, London, Ontario, May 1991.
    1992   Making Sense of the Tasaday *In* The Tasaday Controversy. Tom Headland, ed. Washington, DC: American Anthropological Association Special Publication.

Lee, Richard, and Irven DeVore, eds.
    1968   Man the Hunter. Chicago: Aldine.
    1976   Kalahari Hunter-Gatherers: Studies of the !Kung San and Their Neighbors. Cambridge, MA: Harvard University Press.

Lee, Richard, and Mathias Guenther
1991   Oxen or Onions: The Search for Trade (and Truth) in the Kalahari.
        Current Anthropology 32.
Legros, Dominique
1985   Wealth, Poverty, and Slavery among 19th Century Tutchone,
        Athapaskans. Research in Economic Anthropology 7:37–64.
Lévi-Strauss, Claude
1963   Structural Anthropology. New York: Basic Books.
1968   The Concept of Primitiveness. In Man the Hunter. R. Lee and I. DeVore,
        eds. Pp. 349–52. Chicago: Aldine.
Lovibond, Sabrina
1989   Feminism and Postmodernism. New Left Review 178:5–28
Lowenthal, David
1985   The Past Is a Foreign Country. Cambridge: Cambridge University Press.
Lyotard, Jean François
1984   The Postmodern Condition: A Report on Knowledge. Minneapolis:
        University of Minnesota Press.
Mandel, Ernest
1978   Late Capitalism. London: New Left Books.
Marcus, George, and Michael Fischer
1986   Anthropology as Cultural Critique: An Experimental Moment in the
        Human Sciences. Chicago: University of Chicago Press.
Marshall, Lorna
1961   Talking, Sharing and Giving: Relief of Social Tensions among the !Kung
        Bushmen. Africa 31:231–49.
1976   The !Kung of Nyae Nyae. Cambridge, MA: Harvard University Press.
Martin, J.
1983   Optimal Foraging Theory: A Review of Some Models and Their
        Applications. American Anthropologist 85:612–29.
Mascia-Lees, Frances, Patricia Sharpe, and Colleen Ballerino Cohen
1989   The Post-Modernist Turn in Anthropology: Cautions from a Feminist
        Perspective. Signs15(1):7–33.
Mintz, Sidney
1985   Sweetness and Power: The Place of Sugar in Modern History. New York:
        Viking Press.
Myers, Fred
1986a   The Politics of Representation: Anthropological Discourse and Australian
        Aborigines. American Ethnologist 13:430–47.
1986b   Pintupi Country, Pintupi Self: Sentiment, Place and Politics among
        Western Desert Aborigines. Washington, DC: Smithsonian Institution
        Press.
1988   Critical Trends in the Study of Hunter-Gatherers. Annual Review of
        Anthropology 17:261–82.
O'Meara, J. Tim
1989   Anthropology As Empirical Science. American Anthropologist 91:
        354–69.

Patterson, Tom, and Christine Gailey, eds.
  1987   Power Relations and State Formation. Washington, DC: American
          Anthropological Association.
Paynter, Robert
  1989   The Archaeology of Equality and Inequality. Annual Review of
          Anthropology 18:369–99
People of 'Ksan
  1980   Gathering What the Great Nature Provided: Food Traditions of the
          Gitksan. Vancouver: Douglas and McIntyre.
Peterson, Nicholas
  1982   Aboriginal Land Rights in the Northern Territory of Australia. In Politics
          and History in Band Societies. E. Leacock and R. Lee, eds. Pp. 441–62.
          Cambridge: Cambridge University Press.
  1985   Capitalism, Culture and Land Rights. Social Analysis 18:85–101.
Peterson, Nicholas, and Toshio Matsuyama, eds.
  1991   Cash, Commoditisation and Changing Foragers. Senri Ethnological
          Studies No. 30. Osaka: National Museum of Ethnology.
Piel, Gerard
  1972   The Acceleration of History. New York: Knopf.
Price, T., and J. Brown, eds.
  1985   Prehistoric Hunter-Gatherers: The Emergence of Social Complexity.
          Orlando, FL: Academic Press.
Radcliffe-Brown, A. R.
  1922   The Andaman Islanders. Cambridge: Cambridge University Press.
  1931   The Social Organization of Australian Tribes. Sydney: Oceania
          Monographs, 1.
Richardson, Boyce, ed.
  1989   Drumbeat: Anger and Renewal in the Indian Country. Toronto:
          Summerhill Press/Assembly of First Nations.
Ridington, Robin
  1990   Little Bit Know Something: Stories in a Language of Anthropology.
          Vancouver: Douglas and McIntyre.
Rose, Frederick G. G.
  1960   Classification of Kin, Age Structure and Marriage amongst the Groote
          Eylandt Aborigines: A Study in Method and Theory of Australian
          Kinship. Berlin: Akademie Verlag.
Roseberry, William
  1989   Anthropologies and Histories: Essays in Culture, History, and Political
          Economy. New Brunswick, NJ: Rutgers University Press.
Rosenberg, Harriet G.
  1990   Complaint Discourse, Aging, and Caregiving among the !Kung San of
          Botswana. In The Cultural Context of Aging. Jay Sokolovsky, ed. Pp.
          19–41. New York: Bergin and Garvey.
Roth, Paul A.
  1989   Ethnography without Tears. Current Anthropology 30:555–69.

Sacks, Karen
  1979   Sisters and Wives. Urbana: University of Illinois Press.
Sahlins, Marshall
  1968   Notes on the Original Affluent Society. *In* Man the Hunter. R. Lee and I.
          DeVore, eds. Pp. 85–89. Chicago: Aldine.
  1989   Captain Cook at Hawaii. Journal of the Polynesian Society 98:371–423.
Sangren, Steven
  1988   Rhetoric and the Authority of Ethnography: "Postmodernism" and the
          Social Reproduction of Texts. Current Anthropology 29:405–35.
Sansom, Basil
  1980   The Camp at Wallaby Cross: Aboriginal Fringe Dwellers in Darwin.
          Canberra: Australian Institute of Aboriginal Studies.
  1985   Aborigines, Anthropologists and Leviathan. In Indigenous Peoples and
          the Nation-State. Noel Dyck, ed. Pp. 67–94. St. John's, Newfoundland:
          Memorial University Press.
Schrire, Carmel
  1984   Past and Present in Hunter-Gatherer Studies. Orlando, FL: Academic
          Press.
Shostak, Marjorie
  1981   Nisa: The Life and Words of a !Kung Woman. London: Allen Lane.
Siskind, Janet
  1980   To Hunt in the Morning. New York: Oxford University Press.
Slocum, Sally
  1975   Woman the Gatherer. *In* Towards an Anthropology of Women. R. Reiter,
          ed. Pp. 36–50. New York: Monthly Review Press.
Sloterdijk, Peter
  1987   Critique of Cynical Reason. Minneapolis: University of Minnesota Press.
Smith, Eric A.
  1988   Risk and Uncertainty in the "Original Affluent Society": Evolutionary
          Ecology of Resource-Sharing and Land Tenure. *In* Hunters and
          Gatherers, Vol. 1: History, Evolution and Social Change. T. Ingold, D.
          Riches, and J. Woodburn, eds. Pp. 222–51. London: Berg.
Smith, Eric A., and Robert Boyd
  1990   Risk and Reciprocity: Hunter-Gatherer Socioecology and the Problem of
          Collective Action. *In* Risk and Uncertainty in Tribal and Peasant
          Economies. E. Cashdan, ed. Pp. 167–95. Boulder, CO: Westview Press.
Snow, C. P.
  1959   The Two Cultures and the Scientific Revolution. New York: Cambridge
          University Press.
Solway, Jacqueline, and Richard Lee
  1990   Foragers, Genuine or Spurious: Situating the Kalahari San in History.
          Current Anthropology 31:109–46.
Soper, Kate
  1991   Postmodernism, Subjectivity and the Question of Value. New Left Review
          186:120–28.

Sperber, Dan
    1985   On Anthropological Knowledge. New York: Cambridge University Press.
Spivak, Gayatri C.
    1988   Can the Subaltern Speak? *In* Marxism and the Interpretation of Culture.
            Cary Nelson and Lawrence Grossberg, eds. Pp. 271–313. Urbana:
            University of Illinois Press.
Sponsel, Leslie
    1992   Our Fascination with the Tasaday: Anthropological Images and the Image
            of Anthropology. *In* The Tasaday Controversy. Tom Headland, ed.
            Washington, DC: American Anthropological Association Special
            Publication.
Sterritt, Neil J.
    1989   Gitksan and Wet'suwet'en: Unflinching Resistance to an Implacable
            Invader. *In* Drumbeat: Anger and Renewal in the Indian Country. B.
            Richardson, ed. Pp. 265–94. Toronto: Summerhill Press/Assembly of
            First Nations.
Steward, Julian
    1936   The Economic and Social Basis of Primitive Bands. *In* Essays in
            Anthropology in Honor of A. L. Kroeber. R. H. Lowie, ed. Pp. 331–50.
            Berkeley: University of California Press.
    1938   Basin-Plateau Aboriginal Sociopolitical Groups. Bureau of American
            Ethnology Bulletin No. 120. Washington, DC: Smithsonian Institution.
Tanner, Adrian
    1979   Bringing Home Animals: Religious Ideology and Mode of the Production
            of the Misstassini Cree Hunters. London: Hurst.
Tanner, Nancy, and Adrienne Zihlman
    1976   Women in Evolution 1: Innovation and Selection in Human Origins.
            Signs 1:585–608.
Taylor, Charles
    1984   Foucault on Freedom and Truth. Political Theory 12(2):152–83.
Testart, Alain
    1988   Some Major Problems in the Social Anthropology of Hunter-Gatherers.
            Current Anthropology 29:1–31.
Tlou, Thomas
    1985   A History of Ngamiland 1750 to 1906: The Formation of an African
            State. Gaborone: Macmillan.
Trigger, Bruce
    1987   The Children of Aetaentsic. Revised edition. Montreal: McGill-Queens
            University Press.
    1989   Hyperrelativism, Responsibility and the Social Sciences. Canadian Review
            of Sociology and Anthropology 26(5):776–97.
    1990   Maintaining Economic Equality in Opposition to Complexity: An
            Iroquoian Case Study. *In* The Evolution of Political Systems: Sociopolitics
            in Small-Scale Sedentary Societies. Steadman Upham, ed. Pp. 109–46.
            Cambridge: Cambridge University Press.

Turner, Victor
1969   The Ritual Process. Chicago: Aldine.
Vierich, Helga
1982   Adaptive Flexibility in a Multi-Ethnic Setting. *In* Politics and History in Band Societies. E. Leacock and R. Lee, eds. Pp. 213–22. Cambridge: Cambridge University Press.
Wa, Gisday, and Delgam Uukw
1989   The Spirit in the Land: The Opening Statement of the Gitksan and Wet'suwet'en Hereditary Chiefs in the Supreme Court of British Columbia. Gabriola, BC: Reflections Press.
Wagner, Roy
1981   The Invention of Culture. Chicago: University of Chicago Press.
Wiessner, Polly
1982   Risk, Reciprocity and Social Influences on !Kung San Economics. *In* Politics and History in Band Societies. E. Leacock and R. Lee, eds. Pp. 61–84. Cambridge: Cambridge University Press.
Wilmsen, Edwin
1983   The Ecology of Illusion: Anthropological Foraging in the Kalahari. Reviews in Anthropology 10:9–20.
1988   We Are Here: The Politics of Aboriginal Land Tenure. Berkeley: University of California Press.
1989   Land Filled with Flies: A Political Economy of the Kalahari. Chicago: University of Chicago Press.
Wilmsen, Edwin, and James Denbow
1990   Paradigmatic History of San-Speaking Peoples and Current Attempts at Revision. Current Anthropology 31(5):489–524.
Winterhalder, Bruce
1990   Open Field, Common Pot: Harvest Variability and Risk Avoidance in Agricultural and Foraging Societies. *In* Risk and Uncertainty in Tribal and Peasant Economies. E. Cashdan, ed. Pp. 67–87. Boulder, CO: Westview Press.
Winterhalder, Bruce, and Eric A. Smith, eds.
1981   Hunter Gatherer Foraging Strategies: Ethnographic and Archeological Analyses. Chicago: University of Chicago Press.
Wobst, Martin
1978   The Archaeo-Ethnology of Hunters and Gatherers, or, The Tyranny of the Ethnographic Record in Archaeology. American Antiquity 43:303–9.
Wolf, Eric R.
1982   Europe and the People without History. Berkeley: University of California Press.

Wolf, Eric, and Edward Hansen
  1975   The Human Condition in Latin America. New York: Columbia
          University Press.
Woodburn, James
  1980   Hunters and Gatherers Today and Reconstruction of the Past. *In* Soviet
          and Western Anthropology. E. Gellner, ed. London: Duckworth.
  1982   Egalitarian Societies. Man (n.s.) 17:431–51.
  1988   African Hunter-Gatherer Social Organization: Is It Best Seen as a Product
          of Encapsulation. *In* Hunters and Gatherers, Vol. 1: History, Evolution
          and Social Change. T. Ingold, D. Riches, and J. Woodburn eds. Pp.
          31–64. London: Berg.
Wright, John
  1989   *Review of* Politics and History in Band Societies, edited by E. Leacock
          and R. Lee. Journal of Southern African Studies 15:535–36.
Yellen, John
  1977   Archaeological Approaches to the Present. New York: Academic Press.
  1990   The Present and Future of Hunter-Gatherer Studies. *In* Archaeological
          Thought in America. C. C. Lamberg-Karlovsky, ed. New York:
          Cambridge University Press.

EIGHT

The Future of
Hunter-Gatherer Research

◆

Ernest S. Burch, Jr.

Hunter-gatherer research has enjoyed a tremendous expansion in interest and involvement among anthropologists over the past thirty years. However, as we approach the end of the century, the field faces a major crisis. This paper reviews the practical, methodological, and conceptual dimensions of this crisis and discusses the implications of the trends in each. Research on foraging societies is likely to be very different in the next quarter century than it was in the last, and hunter-gatherer studies may cease to exist as a distinct specialty within sociocultural anthropology.[1]

The history of every scientific field is characterized by cycles, each of which has periods of growth, crisis, and renewal (Kuhn 1970). The field of hunter-gatherer studies has experienced extraordinary growth since the conferences that spawned it a quarter of a century ago. Now, however, there is reason to believe that it is approaching a time of crisis. As is true in science generally, this crisis is in many respects a consequence of the enormous increase in knowledge that occurred during its period of growth. In contrast to the usual situation in the more advanced sciences, however, where critical periods typically involve a growing disjunction between theory and evidence, the crisis in hunter-gatherer studies is multidimensional. Richard Lee's (1992) recent discussion of this crisis dealt primarily with its philosophical aspects. In the present paper, I discuss its practical, methodological, and conceptual aspects. Each of these problem areas is distinct and needs to be discussed separately.

Practical Problems

The practical problems in hunter-gatherer research are due to the fact that there are few if any societies of foragers left in the world that have not been profoundly affected by, and to some extent integrated into, much larger-scale

Reprinted with permission of the publisher from *Key Issues in Hunter-Gatherer Research*, Ernest Burch, Jr., and Linda J. Ellanna, eds., Oxford, UK: Berg Publishers. Copyright © 1994 Berg Publishers.

systems (see Peterson 1991a, 1991b). In short, the very subject matter of our investigations is disappearing. This problem has been with us since the beginning, but each year it becomes more acute than it was previously.

One of the most important consequences of the disappearance of viable, autonomous foraging societies is that, in most cases, it is difficult, if not impossible, to replicate earlier research. Lee (1992:38) commented on this problem:

> [F]ieldworkers who arrive in the 1980s and 1990s and observe [the current] appalling conditions [in Botswana] find it unbelievable that 30, 20, or even 10 years earlier, observers could have found societies with [traditional] band structure, kinship, and subsistence patterns still functioning. Instead of reflecting on the magnitude of the changes in the 10- or 20-year period, these revisionists immediately assume that the earlier studies were wrong and they go on to blithely project the contemporary patterns . . . back into the past.

In my judgment this is an enormous problem in contemporary hunter-gatherer research, and it is likely to get worse in the future. I also think it is worth more emphasis than Lee gave it.[2]

The problem of replicability is clearly illustrated by my own experience. During the winter of 1969–1970 I made a major effort to reconstruct the nineteenth-century social history of northern and northwestern Alaska, an area of approximately 170,000 square miles occupied primarily by Iñupiat Eskimos. I was thrilled to find that, of the roughly eleven thousand Iñupiat living in the region at the time, perhaps two hundred could still speak knowledgeably about various aspects of life during their grandparents' and great-grandparents' times. Of those, perhaps thirty commanded reasonably authoritative (and mutually consistent) information on early- and mid-nineteenth-century social boundaries, intersocietal relations, population movements, historical changes, and other phenomena in which I was interested. I had the privilege of working with about half of the larger group, and two-thirds of the experts. Indeed, it was the latter who really taught me how to do historical research (Burch 1991).

By 1990, one generation later, almost everyone in the earlier pool of informants was either dead or else too old to be of help, and all of the experts were gone. Their descendants knew little or nothing about the subjects on which their own parents and grandparents had been so informative, and most of them found my questions to be incomprehensible. In short, by 1990 I could not replicate even my own research of twenty years before. How, then, is a graduate student just beginning work in northern Alaska to know whether or not what I have written has any basis in empirical fact? Where my findings disagree with those of other authors, how is anyone to determine who is correct?

These problems, of course, pervade social scientific research, but they are much more acute for students of small-scale societies than for anyone else.

Fortunately for me, there is enough information in the records of early-nineteenth-century European explorers of northern Alaska to corroborate at least the basic outlines of the picture presented to me by Iñupiat elders in 1970. Most other parts of the world inhabited in recent decades by foraging societies are not so well endowed with useful early historic sources. It seems to me that the only recourse for future investigators in those areas, and to a large extent even in northern Alaska, is anthropologically oriented but otherwise standard historiographic research, in which the original field notes of earlier field investigators serve as primary sources.[3] In order for this to be possible, these notes have to be accessible to future generations of researchers, and also to the descendants of the people with whom they are concerned. In order for them to be accessible they must be donated to an archive where they can be properly curated, on the one hand, and made available to interested parties, on the other.[4]

The disposition of field notes should not be left to the discretion of heirs. There is an unfortunate tendency among heirs to think that anthropological field notes can be sold for vast sums of money. That is virtually never the case. While waiting for this illusory windfall to come about, the notes (including photographs, maps, tapes, etc.) may not be properly stored, and they certainly will not be made accessible to others. Eventually the heirs may give up in disgust and throw them out, or they might donate them to an archive many years later or they might not do anything but have them included in their own estate. The only satisfactory solution is for the author to bequeath them to an appropriate archive, and to do so immediately.[5]

These considerations suggest that hunter-gatherer research may soon become historically oriented rather than field oriented. But before I continue with this topic, there is another one that should be mentioned, namely, "readback."

Readback is a term used by some in Alaska to refer to the phenomenon of native informants giving anthropologists information on their ancestors' way of life that they themselves acquired from reading anthropological reports and publications.[6] In other words, they are "reading back" the results of previous anthropological research, rather than sharing knowledge acquired directly from elders among their own people. Reading may actually be helpful if it stimulates young people to question their elders about customs no longer practiced, and thus become independently informed. More often, however, it results in anthropologists essentially talking to each other (or even to themselves) through the intermediary and filter of a native informant. Newcomers to an area where people are literate must pay particular attention to this possibility.

One may suspect that the problem exists when (literate) teenagers and young adults seem to know more about the old ways than their (nonliterate) elders do.

Returning to the question of the temporal orientation of hunter-gatherer research, I believe it is fair to say that the extremely rapid change that has characterized the few remaining foraging societies over the past twenty-five years does indeed mean that it will become primarily retrospective in nature. I agree with Eric Smith (1991:3) that foraging as an activity is still amenable to fruitful study now, and it probably will be for many years to come. But the hunting involved will be carried out by marginal members of large-scale social systems, rather than by core members of small-scale systems. Other elements of forager life may persist as well, but hunter-gatherer ways of life as coherent systems are no longer amenable to direct observation, except in very few cases.

There are at least two ways for scholars to deal with this problem. One way is to shift the primary research procedure from participant-observation in an ongoing system to the reconstruction of a previously existing one. To some extent, this is possible through ethnographic research (Burch 1988; Henige 1982), but even the best reconstruction cannot yield the kind of observational details and nonmaterial nuances that gave the studies of the Basarwa carried out in the 1960s, for example, their enduring value.[7] As time passes and even more changes occur, archival and archaeological research will steadily replace ethnographic fieldwork as the major means of testing theories about the structure of hunter-gatherer societies.

A sign that the trend is already underway is the growing involvement of prehistorians (e.g., Bettinger 1987, 1991; Davis and Reeves, eds. 1990; Jochim 1976; Price and Brown, eds. 1985; Williams 1974) in systematic research on theoretical questions relating to foraging societies. In addition, many archaeological journals are at least as likely to publish papers dealing with theoretical questions about foraging societies as more ethnographically oriented journals.

Another way for scholars to deal with the dramatic changes occurring among contemporary hunting-gathering peoples is to shift the focus of their attention from the structure of such societies to social change. In studies with this orientation, theoretical interest inevitably shifts away from the ultimate objective of developing generalizations about foraging societies to formulating theories about social change. Often the shift is even greater: from theoretical concerns of any kind to real world problems of applied research. It is in this area, it seems to me, that the future of ethnographic fieldwork among hunter-gatherers lies.

The extent to which research on the structure of foraging societies has been replaced by a concern with the survival problems of contemporary hunter-gatherers has been dramatically demonstrated at the International Conferences on Hunting and Gathering Societies (CHAGS). Many of the papers included in the published collections of papers from CHAGS-4 (Ingold, Riches, and Woodburn, eds. 1988a, 1988b) are oriented to this problem area, and those from CHAGS-1 (Leacock and Lee, eds. 1982), CHAGS-3 (Schrire, ed. 1984; Wilmsen, ed. 1989) and one of the volumes from CHAGS-5 (Altman, ed. 1989) focus on this issue. At CHAGS-6, by my count, some 55 percent of the papers dealt with social change; if the papers based primarily on archaeological data are excluded, the proportion rises to nearly 70 percent. One must conclude from these figures that social change and practical problems already have become the dominant foci in studies of contemporary hunter-gatherers.

The Methodological Problem

The second major problem confronting hunter-gatherer studies is methodological: to what extent can a general model of foraging societies be developed on the basis of research on recent or contemporary foragers? The basic answer to that question is very simple: a model can be developed on the basis of any data, or even through pure intuition. The critical issue is not the basis on which a model is developed, but the extent to which it increases our understanding of the relevant phenomena in an empirically supportable way.

The fundamental principles here are as follows: if a measurably distinct class of societies—e.g., foraging societies—can be delineated, and if an empirically testable model of that class can be developed, then the model should apply to all members of that class, regardless of when they existed in time (cf. Schrire 1980; Woodburn 1980). The same would be true of any other class of societies—industrialized, agrarian, and state. To this effect, Lewis Binford was recently quoted by Bower (1989: 264): "It is obvious that there are no pristine hunter-gatherers [living today], but to say you cannot generalize in any way to the past because modern behavior is unique is, in essence, an attack on science." I agree.

A model that purports to be a truly general representation of the structure of gatherer-hunter societies should be tested against evidence from simple, intermediate, and complex foraging societies, both historic and prehistoric. To my knowledge, no model encompassing this range has ever been produced. Most of the theoretical work has been at the simple end of the continuum, particularly in the immediate-return category. At this level examples abound.[8] Whether or not any of these models holds up against data from the Upper Paleolithic era or some other early time period remains an open question.

The extent to which one may extrapolate from historic foraging societies to ancient ones is one of the main issues in the current revisionist debate (see chapter 1, this volume). On one side, the generalists (Richard Lee in particular [e.g., 1979:432]), hold that a general model of the structure of foraging societies can be developed, at least in principle.[9] To the extent that it is developed, it should apply equally to both ancient and contemporary systems of foragers. On the other side, the historical particularists (Headland and Reid 1989; Schrire 1980; Wilmsen 1983, 1989a, 1989b; Wilmsen and Denbow 1990) argue that contemporary foraging peoples in general, and the Basarwa in particular, have long histories during which all or most of them have been in direct or indirect contact with pastoralists or agriculturalists of various kinds.[10] These contacts have significantly affected the way they operate, they say, and thus cannot be equated in any way with societies that were in existence several millennia ago.

Unfortunately, most of the people engaged in this debate lack the comparative macrosociological perspective (Fallers 1968:564) that is most relevant here. Insofar as the argument concerns entire societies, the basic issues are the following: (1) Is the specific unit under study a separate society or a subsystem of some other society? (2) If it is a separate society, does it meet the defining criteria of the class of foraging societies? If the system in question is a society, and if it meets the defining criteria of the foraging type, then one may legitimately use data on that system in critiquing or building general models of hunter-gatherer societies—regardless of how long the society in question has been in contact with agriculturists, and regardless of whether it had an agrarian subsistence base itself at some earlier point in time.[11] If either criterion is not met, however, then the data cannot be used in that way. But in order to use this approach, one must employ the concept of society in a serious way.

"Society" is one of the most fundamental and widely used concepts in the social sciences, yet it is probably employed with less consistency than any other. Ingold (in Solway and Lee 1990:131) recently maintained that the concept should not be applied to foragers at all because "the very notion of 'society' locks the people into an externally imposed frame that is structured by relations of domination and subordination." After having spent three decades studying more than thirty early historic Eskimo societies (Burch 1980, 1986) that were not dominated by or subordinate to anyone, I find this an untenable assertion.

Of course much depends on how one defines society. Ingold did not indicate the definition that guided his remarks. The definition that has proven useful to me was formulated by Marion J. Levy, Jr. (1952:113), quoted here from a later work (1966:20–21).

> A society is a system of social action: (1) that involves a plurality of interacting individuals whose actions are [carried out] in terms of the system concerned and who are recruited at least in part by their own

sexual reproduction, (2) that constitutes a set of social structures such that action in terms of them is at least in theory capable of self-sufficiency for the maintenance of the plurality of individuals involved, and (3) that is capable of existing long enough for the production of stable adult members of the system of action from the infants of the members.

A society is essentially what most of us think of as a country, in the modern world; with hunter-gatherers and other small-scale societies, the referent is often less apparent, especially to outsiders such as anthropologists.

It is not appropriate here to discuss all of the implications of this definition, but a few are so frequently distorted or misunderstood (e.g., by Mayhew 1968) that some comments are in order. First, since a society is defined as a type of system, like every kind of system, it has a boundary, a singular discontinuity between it and its social and material environments (Sim and Smallen 1972:2). Just how a society's boundary is manifested is not specified or implied by the definition, and hence may vary from one case to another. The definition does not state or even imply that a society is a closed system, which would be nonsense; if there is such a thing as a closed system, it is the universe as a whole. However, it does imply that if a given social system is a society, then its members will have the means of dealing sufficiently effectively with external phenomena (e.g., members of other societies, the nonhuman environment) to persist long enough for infants to become stable adults. The length of the maturation period will vary from one case to another, but presumably it will be at least eighteen years in the case of immediate-return hunter-gatherers, and twice that (or more) in the case of highly modernized societies.

Second, the definition does not state or imply that a society is self-sufficient for any commodity. However, it clearly implies that if a given social system is a society, its members will have available a means of acquiring from elsewhere the commodities they need that they cannot produce in sufficient quantities themselves for the system to persist for the specified time period.

Third, the stipulation about "stable adults" does not indicate a set of psychological superpersons or optimally adapted individuals of some kind. It merely requires a set of individuals who are capable of filling the various roles differentiated in the system successfully enough for the system to persist for the length of time stipulated by the definition.

Finally, it is appropriate to note that, unlike most definitions of society, this one does not contain a provision for a discrete territory. Thus, conceivably, it would be possible to have a society without any territory at all, societies with interlocking territories, or a society whose territory is enclosed within that of a larger system. If Gypsies are or were members of one or more distinct societies, they would be examples of the first possibility. Australian Aborigine societies, with widely scattered sacred sites, might be an example of the second possibility. And most historically documented hunter-gatherer societies definitely were examples of the third possibility. In any event, given this definition, whether or not a society is associated with a discrete territory is a matter of empirical observation, not of definition.

The major weaknesses of Levy's definition derive from measurement problems. How does one definitively determine, for example, whether a given system of action is "at least in theory capable of self-sufficiency for the maintenance" of a set of individuals, or whether a system is "capable of existing long enough" to produce stable adults? These problems are particularly acute at opposite ends of the complexity continuum: with highly modernized societies, which are highly interdependent, and with very small-scale societies (such as most hunter-gatherer societies), where even extended families are highly self-sufficient.

Many of my students and colleagues have told me that the measurement problems are fatal to this definition. My response is to challenge them to demonstrate either that we do not need a concept of "society" (by whatever name) in the social sciences, or to come up with a more fruitful definition themselves. So far they have done neither. If measurement difficulties are considered fatal to a concept in the social sciences, then we must get rid of many others as well: power, responsibility, fear, affection, role, love, belief, centralization, solidarity, cognition, complexity—the list goes on and on. But no one is suggesting that we discard these concepts for the very good reason that they are important for an understanding of human affairs.

As a final comment on this particular issue, I wish to point out that if physicists had discarded theoretically significant concepts simply because their referents were difficult to measure, the most highly advanced of all sciences would still be back in the stone age. When physicists are confronted with a measurement problem relating to a theoretically significant issue, they get to work and try to devise ways to solve the problem. Sometimes it takes decades of strenuous effort by some of the best minds in the business. Social scientists should have the same attitude.

One of the major virtues of Levy's definition is its usefulness in determining the level of generalization on which comparisons and theoretical statements can be made. Given his definition, all social systems are either (1) societies (e.g., the United States, Japan), (2) subsystems of societies (e.g., the U.S. Congress, the John Doe family), or (3) systems interrelating the members of two or more societies (e.g., the United Nations, CHAGS-6) (cf. Etzioni

1970:71). This is an issue that few writers have confronted, yet it is clear that if we are ever to speak about such things as band societies and industrialized societies, then we must have either a definition of society that encompasses both, or some other concept that serves exactly the same purpose. Theoretical work will not make much progress if such a fundamental term is held to mean one thing in one context and something quite different in another.

The society issue fits into the context of the revisionist debate in the following way. If it can be shown that a given population of historic foragers— the Dobe !Kung of the early 1960s, for example—constituted the membership of a distinct society (as opposed to a subsystem of a larger society), then information about it is appropriate for use in formulating or testing theories about the structure of any and all hunter-gatherer societies, past, present, or future.[12] If, however, they already had been incorporated into a larger system, then their appropriateness becomes problematic. I suspect that when Lee, Marshall, Silberbauer, and Tanaka did their work among the Basarwa in the 1950s and 1960s, at least some indigenous societies were still in operation. By the time the revisionists got there, just a few years later, that was no longer the case. It does not take very long for the transition to be made.[13]

I predict that, unless and until this issue is sorted out, both in general and in many specific empirical cases, hunter-gatherer studies will not contribute much in the way of general theory to social science as a whole.

The Conceptual Problem

The third and final major element in the crisis facing hunter-gatherer studies concerns the very concept of "hunter-gatherer society." The issues here occur at two levels. At the more general level, the question is, does a class of empirical referents for the concept hunter-gatherer society exist? Arcand (1981:39, 1988) has answered this question in the negative. At the more specific level, the question is, even if a class of empirical referents for the hunter-gatherer society concept can be shown to exist, is there anything distinctive enough about the societies in it for the class to have any analytic utility or theoretical significance? Arcand (1981, 1988) and Hamilton (1982), among others, have also answered this question in the negative. In their general reviews of the state of hunter-gatherer studies, both Barnard (1983) and Myers (1988) have, not surprisingly, regarded these questions as being of fundamental importance: if hunting-gathering societies do not exist, or if there is nothing distinctive about them even if they do exist, then the whole subfield of hunter-gatherer research is based on a mirage.

It seems to me that the question concerning the existence of hunter-gatherer societies, in contradiction to Arcand, must be answered positively. If they do not exist now as distinct societies, surely they did at one time; I have studied nearly three dozen of them myself. But regarding whether foraging societies constitute a class that is distinctive in significant ways from all other types of society, I have to agree with Arcand and Hamilton: they do not.

A few authors have formulated alternative classifications of small-scale societies (see the discussions in Barnard 1983 and Myers 1988), but no one has dealt with the entire range from the simplest to the most complex within the framework of a single scheme. As Arcand (1981:41) noted, the differences across this range are so great that in *The Hunters*, Elman Service (1979:3) had to exclude most foraging societies from his purview; the book would have been more accurately titled "band societies." The problem is compounded by the apparent fact that many simple agrarian societies have more in common with foraging societies than they do with other agrarian systems, while just the reverse is true of complex foraging societies.[14]

It is easy to understand why most anthropologists have had difficulty confronting this issue. We know that foraging societies occurred first in human history. There is also no doubt that the agrarian revolution came much later and that it led to enormous changes in human affairs. Given these facts, it does not take much of a creative leap to conclude that foraging and agrarian societies must somehow be fundamentally different from one another. This view is supported by the Marxist obsession with modes of production, with an obvious division between foraging and agrarian modes (Ingold 1988; Keenan 1977; Lee 1981a, 1990; Meillassoux 1973).

In my judgment, the most definitive division of small-scale societies identified so far is not between foraging and agrarian, but between immediate-return and delayed-return societies, in Woodburn's (1972, 1979, 1982; Barnard and Woodburn 1988) terms, or nonstoring and storing societies in Testart's terms (1982). As Testart (1982:530) put it,

> Agriculturalists and storing hunter-gatherers together are neatly in opposition to nonstoring hunter-gatherers. The conclusion to be drawn is certainly not the presence of agriculture or its absence which is the relevant factor when dealing with such societies, but rather the presence or absence of an economy with intensive storage as its cornerstone.

Immediate-return or "generalized" hunter-gatherer societies are so unlike all others that, as Birdsell (1973:338) once noted, it is difficult even for anthropologists who have not personally experienced one to conceive how they can exist; it is almost impossible for nonanthropologists to do so.

Having set off immediate-return societies at the simple end of the range of complexity from all other foraging societies, the next question is what to do with the rest—which includes all other societies in world history. I think that Service (1975:70) correctly identified the next dividing line when he distinguished between segmental and (by implication) nonsegmental societies. He defined the former as those "composed of equal and similar component groups (normally kin groups like clans or lineages)." Segmental societies thus lack both an office (chief) and a subsystem (council) having a society-wide span of control (or authority); they consist entirely of networks of segments. Nothing is stated or implied about their economic base, so presumably foraging, pastoral, and agricultural economies are all possible within the storing segmental sphere. However, it is one thing to assert that this division makes sense, and quite another to demonstrate it—which I do not have the space to do here, and which I have not done elsewhere. This distinction thus must be regarded as being of hypothetical significance until its ramifications are worked out and tested.

Just what label should be used to identify the class of small-scale societies that are not segmental was not specified by Service. The next category included in his scheme (1975:71ff.) was chiefdoms, which are societies in which an office associated with a society-wide span of authority is differentiated. This strikes me as a reasonable possibility, although there may be cases in which a council, rather than an office, is the unifying element in the system. Whatever the label, the important point is that even at this level of complexity, both hunter-gatherer and agrarian societies belong to the same class.

One could proceed in this manner right on up the scale of complexity. At some point—certainly once industrialized societies have been reached, but probably well before that—hunter-gatherer societies would eventually drop out of consideration. There is no need for present purposes to pursue the matter further. The basic point has been made already: there is too much variation within the class of hunter-gatherer societies to make it a useful category for theoretical purposes.

Conclusions

This essay began with an assertion that, despite the enormous recent growth of the field, hunter-gatherer research is approaching a time of crisis. This crisis involves three main elements: (1) the likelihood that much of the subject matter of the field is about to disappear; (2) a profound disagreement about the logic used in extrapolating from field studies to general theory; and (3) the likelihood that the field is based on an unfruitful concept in the first place. Any one of these factors could be enough to destroy a field; the three together may prove to be overwhelming.

Colleagues who reviewed a draft of this paper were appalled at these

seemingly negative conclusions. One even expressed the view that they are a re-
pudiation of all of the research that has been done over the past thirty years. In
bringing the paper to a close, it is appropriate to address these concerns.

In the first place, I did not use the term "crisis" by accident. Because of the
problems outlined above, I feel quite safe in saying that hunter-gatherer research in the next quarter century will be a fundamentally different enterprise
than it was in the last. If crisis is too alarming a word, perhaps "threshold" will
do, but it does not convey the tension I see growing in the field.

Second, far from repudiating all the work that has been done in the last
thirty years, the crisis I have outlined is a tribute to it. Although hunter-
gatherer studies have hardly reached the level of theoretical sophistication of
the fields discussed in Kuhn's *Structure of Scientific Revolutions* (1970), our
crisis, like those that have occurred over the centuries in physics, is the result
of our success. We have learned so much in the last three decades that the
framework of inquiry and debate has changed fundamentally. We now must
rethink the whole enterprise.

NOTES

1. I thank Bernard Arcand, Harvey A. Feit, Richard B. Lee, Marion J. Levy, Jr.,
   Carmel Schrire, Eric A. Smith, and Edwin S. Wilmsen for comments on an earlier
   version of this paper. All of the views expressed here are, of course, my own.
2. For similarly brief but telling comments on the rate of change in foraging societies
   and on the implications of this change for research, see C. Berndt (1981:170–71)
   and Silberbauer (1991:97, 98). For a debate on the subject, see Birdsell (1970).
3. It will, of course, be possible for investigators to doctor their field notes.
   Fabricated "original" documents are a common concern in historiography, and
   they sometimes appear in the natural sciences as well. They are unlikely to be any
   worse in anthropology than in any other field. One way to make the authenticity
   of one's own notes more convincing to future scholars is to keep the originals on
   file after they have been transcribed in more elegant fashion.
4. I was pleased to note that the participants in a recent Wenner-Gren symposium
   on preserving anthropological records also came to this conclusion (*Anthropology
   Newsletter* 1992:8; Silverman [1993]). As this volume goes to press (in early
   1994), a number of anthropological associations around the world are considering
   whether or not to pass resolutions embodying the conclusions of this symposium.
5. Copyright to the notes should also be part of the bequest, since the transfer of the
   physical material does not convey ownership of the copyright. Otherwise, researchers will have to track down all of the heirs of the deceased anthropologist
   and get written releases from them prior to any extensive use of unpublished material. The directors of any established archive may be expected to use good judgment regarding the use of the material under their care.
6. I am grateful to Edwin S. Hall, Jr., for introducing me to the concept of readback.

7. Whatever the outcome of the revisionist debate regarding evolutionary questions, the basic ethnographic data published by Richard Lee (e.g., 1979, 1984) and his colleagues (e.g., Lee and DeVore, eds. 1976), George Silberbauer (1981) and Jiro Tanaka (1980), will have a permanent place in the anthropological literature. The same can be said about all of the good field studies that were carried out during the early modern period of hunter-gatherer research.

8. The focus here is on models of the structure of entire societies. Examples include Birdsell (1958, 1968, 1970, 1973), Ingold (1980, 1987, 1988), Jochim (1976), Lee (1968, 1976, 1979, 1981a, 1981b, 1984, 1988, 1990), Sahlins (1968, 1972), Service (1962, 1975, 1979), Testart (1982), Williams (1974), and Woodburn (1968, 1972, 1979, 1982; Barnard and Woodburn 1988). Models of aspects of societies, such as foraging strategy, camp distribution, and local group size, are too numerous to mention here.

9. This is the general issue in the debate. Two more specific ones, which are too detailed to discuss here, are the extent to which the specific model based on the Basarwa actually applies to the Paleolithic era, and the extent to which it has been claimed by its developers to apply to the Paleolithic era.

10. The label "historical particularism" is taken from Lewin (1988:1148).

11. If enough foraging societies could be identified so that there would be samples of those not in contact with agrarian societies and with no history of agrarian production, those in contact with agrarian societies, and those that had an agrarian economy at some previous time—it would be interesting to see if there were systematic differences among them. If there are, then the historical particularist position would gain in credence.

12. Recently Binford (1990:137) maintained that "most of the historically documented [foragers] are irrelevant as analogs for Pleistocene terrestrial hunters." If he is correct about the importance of aquatic resources in the historic period and the lack thereof in the Pleistocene era, he may be right—insofar as direct analogs are concerned. It does not follow that the general structure of forager societies differed between the two periods.

13. See, e.g., Sugawara (1991) and Tanaka (1991). In the case of my own research among the Eskimos of northwestern Alaska and the central Canadian subarctic, most of the societies ceased to exist some 110 and 65 years ago, respectively.

14. Just why some agrarian societies should be less complex than any foraging societies is an interesting question that needs to be investigated.

REFERENCES

Altman, John C., ed. 1989 *Emergent inequalities in Aboriginal Australia.* Sydney: University of Sydney. (Oceania monograph no. 38.)

Arcand, Bernard 1981 The Negritos and the Penan will never be Cuiva. *Folk* 23:37–43.

———, 1988 Il n'y a jamais eu de société de chasseurs-cueilleurs. *Anthropologie et Sociétés* 12(1):39–58.

Barnard, Alan 1983 Contemporary hunter-gathers: Current theoretical issues in ecology and social organization. *Annual Review of Anthropology* 12:193–214.

Barnard, Alan, and James Woodburn 1988 Property, power and ideology in hunter-gathering societies: An introduction. In *Hunters and gatherers 2: property, power and ideology.* Tim Ingold, David Riches, and James Woodburn, eds., pp. 4–31. Oxford: Berg Publishers Limited.

Berndt, Catherine H. 1981 Interpretations and "facts" in aboriginal Australia. In *Woman the gatherer.* Frances Dahlberg, ed., pp. 153–203. New Haven: Yale University Press.

Bettinger, Robert L. 1987 Archaeological approaches to hunter-gatherers. *Annual Review of Anthropology* 16:121–42.

——, 1991 *Hunter-gatherers: Archaeological and evolutionary theory.* New York: Plenum Press.

Binford, Lewis R. 1990 Mobility, housing, and environment: A comparative study. Journal of Anthropological Research 46(2):119–52.

Birdsell, Joseph B. 1958 On population structure in generalized hunting and collecting populations. *Evolution* 12(2):189–205.

——, 1968 Some predictions for the Pleistocene based on equilibrium systems among recent hunter-gatherers. In *Man the hunter.* Richard B. Lee and Irven DeVore, eds., pp. 229–40. Chicago: Aldine Publishing Company.

——, 1970 Local group composition among the Australian Aborigines: A critique of the evidence from fieldwork conducted since 1930. *Current Anthropology* 11(2):115–142.

——, 1973 A basic demographic unit. *Current Anthropology* 14(4):337–56.

Black, Mary B. 1977 Ojibwa power belief system. In *The Anthropology of Power,* R. D. Fogelson and R. N. Adams, eds. New York: Academic Press.

Bower, Bruce 1989 A world that never existed. *Science News* 135(17):264–66.

Burch, Ernest S., Jr. 1980 Traditional Eskimo societies in northwest Alaska. *Senri Ethnological Studies* 4:253–304.

——, 1986 The Caribou Inuit. In *Native peoples: The Canadian experience.* R Bruce Morrison and C. Roderick Wilson, eds., pp. 106–33. Toronto: McClelland and Stewart.

——, 1988 The method of ethnographic reconstruction. Paper presented at the Sixth Inuit Studies Conference. Copenhagen, Denmark. 17–20 October.

——, 1991 From skeptic to believer: The making of an oral historian. *Alaska History* 6(1):1–16.

Davis, Leslie B., and Brian O. K. Reeves, eds. 1990 *Hunters of the recent past.* Boston: Unwin Hyman. (One world archaeology 15.)

Etzioni, Amitai 1970 Toward a macrosociology. In *Theoretical sociology: Perspectives and developments.* John C. McKinney and Edward A. Tiryakian, eds., pp. 69–97. New York: Meredith Corporation.

Fallers, Lloyd A. 1968 Societal analysis. In *International encyclopedia of the social sciences,* vol. 14. David L. Sills, ed., pp. 562–72. New York: Macmillan Free Press.

Hamilton, Annette 1982 The unity of hunting-gathering societies: Reflections on economic forms and resource management. In *Resource managers: Northern American and Australian hunter-gatherers.* Nancy M. Williams and Eugene S. Hunn, eds., pp. 229–47. Boulder: Westview Press, Inc. (AAAS selected symposium 67.)

Headland, Thomas N., and Lawrence A. Reid 1989 Hunter-gatherers and their neighbors from prehistory to the present. *Current Anthropology* 30(1):43–66.

Henige, David 1982 *Oral historiography.* Essex: Longman Group U.K. Ltd.

Ingold, Tim 1980 *Hunters, pastoralists and ranchers: Reindeer economies and their transformations.* Cambridge: Cambridge University Press.

———, 1987 *The appropriation of nature: Essays on human ecology and social relations.* Iowa City: University of Iowa Press.

———, 1988 Notes on the foraging mode of production. In *Hunters and gatherers 1: History, evolution and social change.* Tim Ingold, David Riches, and James Woodburn, eds., pp. 269–85. Oxford: Berg Publishers Ltd.

Ingold, Tim, David Riches, and James Woodburn, eds. 1988a *Hunters and gatherers 1: History, evolution and social change.* Oxford: Berg Publishers Ltd.

———, 1988b *Hunters and gatherers 2: Property, power and ideology.* Oxford: Berg Publishers Limited.

Jochim, Michael A. 1976 *Hunter-gatherer subsistence and settlement: A predictive model.* New York: Academic Press.

Keenan, Jeremy 1977 The concept of the mode of production of hunter-gatherer societies. African Studies 36(1):57–69.

Kuhn, Thomas S. 1970 *The structure of scientific revolutions.* 2d ed. Chicago: University of Chicago Press. (International encyclopedia of unified science, vol. 2, no. 2.)

Leacock, Eleanor, and Richard B. Lee, eds. 1982 *Politics and history in band societies.* New York: Cambridge University Press.

Lee, Richard B. 1968 What hunters do for a living, or, how to make out on scarce resources. In *Man the hunter.* Richard B. Lee and Irven DeVore, eds., pp. 30–48. Chicago: Aldine Publishing Company.

———, 1976 !Kung spatial organization. In *Kalahari hunter-gatherers: Studies of the !Kung San and their neighbors.* Richard B. Lee and Irven DeVore, eds., pp. 73–97. Cambridge: Harvard University Press.

———, 1979 *The !Kung San: Men, women and work in a foraging society.* Cambridge: Cambridge University Press.

———, 1981a Is there a foraging mode of production? Canadian Journal of Anthropology 2(1):13–19.

———, 1981b Politics, sexual and nonsexual, in an egalitarian society: The !Kung San. In *Social inequality: Comparative and developmental approaches.* Gerald D. Berreman, ed., pp. 83–102. New York: Academic Press.

———, 1984 *The Dobe !Kung.* New York: Holt, Rinehart and Winston.

———, 1988 Reflections on primitive communism. In *Hunters and gatherers 1: History, evolution and social change.* Tim Ingold, David Riches, and James Woodburn, eds., pp. 252–68. Oxford: Berg Publishers Limited.

———, 1990 Primitive communism and the origin of social inequality. In *The evolution of political systems: Sociopolitics in small-scale sedentary societies.* Steadman Upham, ed., pp. 225–46. Cambridge: Cambridge University Press.

————, 1992 Art, science or politics? The crisis in hunter-gatherer studies. *American Anthropologist* 94(1):31–54.

Lee, Richard B., and Irven DeVore, eds. 1976 *Kalahari hunter-gatherers: Studies of the !Kung San and their neighbors.* Cambridge: Harvard University Press.

Levy, Marion J., Jr. 1952 *The structure of society.* Princeton: Princeton University Press.

————, 1966 *Modernization and the structure of societies: A setting for international affairs.* Princeton: Princeton University Press.

Lewin, Roger 1988 New views emerge on hunters and gatherers. *Science* 240(4856):1146–48.

Mayhew, Leon W. 1968 Society. In *International Encyclopedia of the Social Sciences.* David L. Sills, ed., pp. 577–86. New York: Macmillan Free Press.

Meillassoux, Claude 1973 On the mode of production of the hunting band. In *French perspectives in African studies.* Pierre Alexandre, ed., pp. 187–203. Oxford: Oxford University Press for the International African Institute.

Myers, Fred R. 1988 Critical trends in the study of hunter-gatherers *Annual Review of Anthropology* 17:261–82.

Peterson, Nicolas 1991a Introduction: Cash, commoditisation and changing foragers. *Senri Ethnological Studies* 30:1–16.

————, 1991b Cash, commoditisation and authenticity: When do Aboriginal people stop being hunter-gatherers? *Senri Ethnological Studies* 30:67–90.

Price, T. Douglas, and James A. Brown, eds. 1985 *Prehistoric hunter-gatherers: The emergence of cultural complexity.* Orlando: Academic Press, Inc.

Sahlins, Marshall 1968 *Tribesmen.* Englewood Cliffs: Prentice-Hall.

————, 1972 Stone age economics. Chicago: Aldine-Atherton, Inc.

Schrire, Carmel 1980 An inquiry into the evolutionary status and apparent identity of San hunter-gatherers. *Human Ecology* 8(1):9–32.

————, 1984 Wild surmises on savage thoughts. In *Past and present in hunter gatherer studies: Selections from the proceedings of the Third International Conferences on Hunter-Gatherers.* Carmen Schrire, ed., pp. 1–25. New York: Academic Press.

Service, Elman R. 1962 *Primitive social organization: An evolutionary perspective.* New York: Random House.

————, 1975 *Origins of the state and civilization: The process of cultural evolution.* New York: W. W. Norton, Inc.

————, 1979 The hunters. 2d ed. Englewood Cliffs, N.J.: Prentice-Hall.

Silberbauer, George B. 1981 *Hunter and habitat in the central Kalahari Desert.* Cambridge: Cambridge University Press.

————, 1991 Morbid reflexivity and overgeneralization in Mosarwa studies. *Current Anthropology* 32(1):96–99.

Silverman, Sydel 1993 Preserving the anthropological record. *Current Anthropology* 34(1):100–102.

Sim, Francis M., and David Smallen 1972 Defining system boundaries. Paper presented at the annual meeting of the Canadian Sociology and Anthropology Association. May 31. Montreal.

Smith, Eric Alden 1991 *Inujjuamiut foraging strategies: Evolutionary ecology of an Arctic hunting community.* New York: Aldine De Gruyter.

Solway, Jacqueline S., and Richard B. Lee 1990 Foragers, genuine or spurious? Situating the Kalahari San in history. *Current Anthropology* 31(2):109–46.

Sugawara, Kazuyoshi 1991 The economics of social life among the central Kalahari San (G//anakhwe and G/wikhwe) in the sedentary community at !Koi!kom. *Senri Ethnological Studies* 30:91–116.

Tanaka, Jiro 1980 *The San, hunter-gatherers of the Kalahari: A study in ecological anthropology.* David W. Hughes, trans. Tokyo: University of Tokyo Press.

———, 1991 Egalitarianism and the cash economy among the central Kalahari San. Senri Ethnological Studies 30:117–34.

Testart, Alain 1982 The significance of food storage among hunter-gatherers: Residence patterns, population densities, and social inequalities. *Current Anthropology* 23(5):523–37.

Williams, B. J. 1974 A model of band society. *American Antiquity* 39(4) part 2. (Memoir #29).

Wilmsen, Edwin N. 1983 The ecology of illusion: Anthropological foraging in the Kalahari. *Reviews in Anthropology* 10(1):9–20.

———, 1989a *Land filled with flies: A political economy of the Kalahari.* Chicago: University of Chicago Press.

———, 1989b Those who have each other: San relations to land. In *We are here: Politics of aboriginal land tenure.* Edwin N. Wilmsen, ed., pp. 43–67. Berkeley: University of California Press.

Wilmsen, Edwin N., and James R. Denbow 1990 Paradigmatic history of San-speaking peoples and current attempts at revision. *Current Anthropology* 31(5):489–524.

Wilmsen, Edwin N., ed. 1989 *We are here: Politics of aboriginal land tenure.* Berkeley: University of California Press.

Woodburn, James C. 1968 An introduction to Hadza ecology. In *Man the hunter.* Richard B. Lee and Irven DeVore, eds., pp. 49–55. Chicago: Aldine Publishing Company.

———, 1972 Ecology, nomadic movement and the composition of the local group among hunters and gatherers: An east African example and its implications. In *Man, settlement and urbanism.* Peter J. Ucko, Ruth Tringham, and G. W. Dimbleby, eds., pp. 194–206. London: Duckworth.

———, 1979 Minimal politics: The political organization of the Hadza of North Tanzania. In *Politics in leadership: A comparative perspective.* William A. Shack and Percy S. Cohen, eds., pp. 244–46. Oxford: Clarendon Press.

———, 1980 Hunters and gatherers today and reconstruction of the past. In *Soviet and Western Anthropology.* Ernest Gellner, ed., pp. 95–117. London: Duckworth.

———, 1982 Egalitarian societies. *Man* 17(3):431–51.

PART III

HUNTER-GATHERERS AND VISIONS OF THE FUTURE

In chapter 9, "The Transformation of the Kalahari !Kung," John E. Yellen describes what happens to hunter-gatherers when they come into contact with a market economy. The answer is disturbing: apparently they become as acquisitive as anyone else. Why do cultures whose traditions of sharing and limited wants have endured for thousands of years suddenly turn acquisitive and develop unlimited wants for the items of Western material culture? An answer to this question may hold the key to a sustainable future.

Chapter 10, Tim Flannery's "So Varied in Detail—So Similar in Outline," from his book *The Future Eaters: An Ecological History of the Australian Lands and People*, offers a geological, ecological, and anthropological perspective on the more than 60,000-year history of the Aboriginal settlement of Australia. Flannery's contribution adds another—and disturbing—perspective to the hunter-gatherer debate. From the geological record, it is clear that humans have always had a profound effect on ecosystems. It is Flannery's thesis that "future eating" is a characteristic of human beings; that is, people always consume the very resources they need for their own future. Environmental factors also have profound effects on human cultures, as illustrated by the interesting case of the El Niño southern oscillation (ENSO), which, Flannery argues, has kept the Aboriginal population low. Flannery gives many examples of cultural and ecological coevolution in which social customs act to conserve scarce natural resources. Nevertheless, his description of the devastating effect of hunter-gatherers on the native species and ecosystems of an entire continent is a disturbing complement to the essays in this volume.

Chapter 11, John Zerzan's "Future Primitive," is an unequivocal argument for the superiority of the hunter-gatherer way of life. The oneness with other humans and other species characteristic of small-scale societies has been well documented by anthropologists and early explorers. Zerzan's chapter draws on these accounts to explore the relationships among foraging, freedom, and power. Rejecting the postmodern notion that power is a defining characteristic of every society, he concludes, "This is a lie unless we accept the death of nature and renounce what once was and what we can find again" (p. 274).

Finally, in chapter 12, "A Post-Historic Primitivism," the late Paul Shepard takes the hunter-gatherer debate to a new level. His spirited defense of the "savage mind" extols not only the ecological and social sustainability of these societies but also the fundamental truth of the preagricultural "nonlinear codification of reality."

Recent discoveries have given credence to Shepard's argument that the lives of our prehistoric hunter-gatherer ancestors were richer and more creative than are the lives of most members of today's industrial society. Recent discoveries of magnificent Upper Paleolithic art and a flute in a cave inhabited by Neanderthals some 80,000 years ago attest to this creativity. Shepard also argues that hunting is an ancient part of human existence, as demonstrated by a recent find in Germany of a 400,000-year-old wooden spear.

The response of most people when confronted with the success of the hunter-gatherer way of life is, "Yes, but you can't go back." Shepard answers this directly (p. 314):

> You can go out or back to a culture even if its peoples have vanished, to retrieve a mosaic component, just as you can transfer a species that has been regionally extirpated, or graft healthy skin to a burned spot from a healthy one. The argument that modern hunting-gathering societies are not identical to paleolithic peoples is beside the point. It may be true that white, ex-Europeans cannot become Hopis or Kalahari Bushmen or Magdalenian bison-hunters, but removable elements in those cultures can be recovered or recreated, which fit the predilection of the human genome everywhere.

NINE

The Transformation
of the Kalahari !Kung

◆

John E. Yellen

We study history to understand the present. Yet sometimes the present can help to clarify the past. So it is with a San-speaking people known as the !Kung—a group of what were once called African Bushmen. (The exclamation point is pronounced as a click.) Dramatic changes now occurring in the !Kung culture are illuminating a major problem in anthropology: Why did most hunting and gathering societies disappear rapidly after coming in contact with societies that kept domesticated animals and plants?

This swift disappearance is puzzling. After all, hunting for animals and gathering wild plants was a robust enough strategy to ensure the survival of anatomically modern human beings from their emergence more than 50,000 years ago until some time after the first animals and plants were domesticated, roughly 10,000 years ago. Conventional wisdom suggests that many traditional societies, recognizing the nutritional advantages of herding and agriculture, simply abandoned their old practices once they learned about newer subsistence strategies. Yet a number of observations indicate that dissatisfaction with foraging is apparently the wrong explanation in many instances.

Archaeologists have shown, for example, that foraging can actually be more beneficial than herding and farming. Detailed analyses of skeletal remains reveal that in parts of North America a shift to agriculture was in fact detrimental to nutrition, health and longevity for certain groups. Similarly, in modern times it has become clear that when droughts strike southern Africa, groups that rely heavily on hunting and gathering tend to be affected less severely than groups that depend primarily on water-hungry herds and crops.

Moreover, foraging probably is not as taxing and unfruitful as it is stereotypically portrayed. Richard B. Lee, when he was a doctoral student at the

This contribution originally appeared in *Scientific American,* April 1990. Reprinted with permission.

University of California at Berkeley in the 1960's, found that the !Kung, who at the time were among the few groups in the world still obtaining most of their food by foraging, did not live on the brink of starvation, even though they inhabited the harsh Kalahari Desert. (The !Kung occupy the northwest corner of Botswana and adjacent areas of Namibia and Angola.) Indeed, they spent only several hours each day seeking food.

What, then, accounts for the decline of foraging societies? No one can say definitely, but glimmers of an answer that may have broad application are emerging from studies focusing on the recent changes in the !Kung way of life. Today young boys no longer learn to hunt, and some of the behavioral codes that gave the society cohesion are eroding. One major catalyst of change appears to have been a sudden easy access to goods. Perhaps a similar phenomenon contributed to the demise of past foraging societies.

It is fortunate that a rather detailed portrait of the !Kung's traditional culture was compiled before the onset of dramatic change. Many investigators deserve credit for what is known, including the independent anthropologist Lorna Marshall, who began studying the group in 1951, and Irven DeVore, Lee and other participants in what was called the Harvard Kalahari Project. One aim of the project, which officially ran from the late 1960's into the 1970's (and in which I participated as a doctoral student), was to understand how traditional hunting and gathering societies functioned.

Any description of the !Kung begins most appropriately with a brief history of the peoples in southern Africa. Before the start of the first millennium A.D., Africa south of the Zambezi River was still populated exclusively by foragers who almost certainly were of short stature, had light-brown skin and spoke what are called Khoisan languages (all of which, like those in the San group, include clicks). In the still more distant past, the various groups had apparently shared a common language and culture and then, as they spread out, adapted to the specific conditions of the regions where they settled. Some had adjusted to the seasonal cold of the Drakensberg Mountains, others to the coastal areas (with their wealth of fish), and still others to the drier conditions of the deserts and other inland areas.

The various groups were what archaeologists call late Stone Age peoples; their knife blades and scraping tools were made of stone and specialized for particular tasks. As yet there were none of the hallmarks of so-called Iron Age peoples: domesticated goats, sheep and cattle; cultivated grains such as millet and sorghum; pottery; and smelted and forged iron and copper.

The first Iron Age influences appeared in southern Africa some time early in the first millennium A.D., when, according to the archaeological record, occasional goods and domesticated animals were introduced, presumably by trade with peoples in more northern territories. The items were soon followed by Iron Age settlers themselves. These newcomers from the north spoke mostly Bantu languages and, compared with the foragers, were taller and darker-skinned. Either directly or indirectly, all of the foraging groups were eventually exposed to the new settlers and technologies and, later, to waves of European intruders: the Dutch and the Portuguese beginning in the 15th and 16th centuries and then the English and Germans as well.

Artifacts as well as journals of European settlers indicate that some of the hunting and gathering groups were exterminated by the intruders. In most other instances, according to clues provided by genetic studies, linguistic analyses and other methods, groups broke up (forcibly or otherwise), often merging with their new neighbors through intermarriage.

In certain cases, foragers were able to maintain a distinct genetic and cultural identity. Some of them, changing many practices, became transformed into new cultures. (For example, the first Dutch settlers, arriving at the southern tip of Africa, met "Hottentots," Khoisan speakers who herded flocks of sheep, goats and cows.) In the Karroo Desert of South Africa and in the northern Kalahari, however, a few hunting and gathering societies—among them, the !Kung—not only stayed intact but also apparently held onto many of their old ways.

Indeed, even as late as 1968, when I first visited the Kalahari as part of the Harvard project, most !Kung men and women in the Dobe region of Botswana still dressed in animal skins and subsisted primarily by hunting and gathering. (Dobe is the site most intensively studied by the project; the people there are, by all indications, quite representative of the !Kung over a broader area.) It is true that iron had long since replaced stone in tools, and plastic and metal containers had supplanted their ceramic counterparts. Yet men still hunted with bows and poisoned arrows, and women set out daily with digging sticks to seek edible plants.

At least it seemed to us that the people we met were behaving much as their ancient ancestors had. Some scholars dissent from that view, contending that the forerunners of 20th-century foragers were probably altered radically by contact with Iron Age peoples. If so, they say, modern foragers, including the !Kung, may reflect but little of the past.

In my view, strong evidence suggests that the !Kung studied in the early years of the Harvard project were very much like their distant forebearers. For example, I have determined that the range of stone tools excavated from what is now !Kung territory remained remarkably constant into the late 19th century (when the grandparents of modern !Kung adults would have been born).

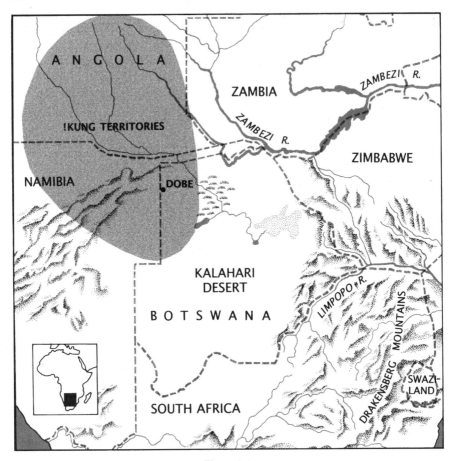

Figure 9.1
Southern Africa is home to many indigenous groups of San speakers (formerly known as Bushmen), including some who lived essentially as hunters and gatherers, or foragers, well into the 20th century. The !Kung, perhaps the best studied of the San, occupy the Kalahari Desert in parts of Botswana, Namibia and Angola. Much of what is known of the group has been gleaned from anthropological and archaeological studies conducted by a number of investigators in the Dobe region of Botswana.

This finding means that the region was probably populated continuously by one cultural group and that its foraging and manufacturing practices remained essentially unaffected by Iron Age influences.

What were the traditional ways of the !Kung? Observations made back in the 1950's and 1960's reveal that the group's strategy for obtaining food—and in fact its entire social organization—was exquisitely adapted for survival in the Kalahari. There, rainfall can vary dramatically from year to year and region to region, giving rise to profound shifts in the availability of food.

When it came to securing food, the !Kung followed what I call a generalist strategy. Rather than specializing in the pursuit of a limited number of species, as could be done in more predictable environments, they cast their foraging "net" broadly and so could usually find something to eat even if favored foods were in short supply. Remarkably, Lee found that males hunted more than 60 animal species, ranging in size from hare to buffalo. Females recognized more than 100 edible plant species, collecting perhaps a dozen varieties in a single day.

Certain accepted foraging guidelines minimized competition for the desert's limited resources. For example, groups of people were loosely organized into bands, and each band had the right to seek food in specified areas. During the dry season the members of a single band would congregate, setting up camps near a water hole (a year-round source of drinking water) understood to belong to that band. From the camps, individuals or small clusters of people would fan out each day to forage. During the rest of the year, when rainfall was more frequent and rain collected in shallow depressions in the ground known as pans, bands would disperse; small groups foraged in less trafficked areas, staying for as short as a day (and rarely as long as two months) before moving on.

The band system actually made it easy for people to migrate to more desirable places when the territory allotted to a given band was unproductive or becoming depleted. Band membership was rather fluid, and so a family could readily join a different band having more luck.

Consider the options open to a husband and wife, who would have had few possessions to hamper their travels. They could claim the right to join the bands available to both sets of parents, which means that at least four territories were open to them. Moreover, they could join any band in which their brothers or sisters had rights. If the couple also had married children, they might, alternatively, forage anywhere the children's spouses could; indeed, parents frequently arranged their children's marriages with an eye to the accompanying territorial privileges. Individuals could also claim band memberships on the basis of certain less direct kinship ties and on friendship.

The social values of the !Kung complemented this flexible band system, helping to ensure that food was equitably distributed. Most notably, an ethic of sharing formed the core of the self-described !Kung system of values. Families were expected to welcome relatives who showed up at their camps. Moreover, etiquette dictated that meat from large kills be shared outside the immediate family, which was obviously a sound survival strategy: a hunter who killed a large antelope or the like would be hard pressed, even with the help of his wife and children to eat all its meat. By distributing his bounty, the hunter ensured that the recipients of his largess would be obliged to return the favor some time in the future.

Table 9.1
Average Number of Species

Time Period	Large Mammals Greater Kudu/Cattle	Medium Mammals Steenbok/Goat	Small Mammals Springhare/Porcupine	Reptiles and Amphibians Puff Adder/Bullfrog	Birds Guinea Fowl/Chicken
1944–1962	1.40	2.40	1.80	0.80	1.20
1963–1968	2.86	2.86	2.14	1.71	1.86
1970–1971	2.33	3.33	2.33	1.67	1.33
1972–1975	2.00	2.75	2.00	1.25	2.25

!Kung diet remained varied between 1944 and 1975, according to an analysis of animal bones excavated from dry-season camps at Dobe. The author identified and counted the number of bones at each camp during four periods. (Selected examples are shown.) The balance across categories changed little, indicating that variety was maintained, as was the !Kung's generalist food-securing strategy. The persistance of a diverse diet even after domesticated animals were acquired in the 1970's indicates that the group had not become dependent on their herds, which apparently were viewed as foraging resouces like any others. Hence, the popular notion that dissatisfaction with foraging caused hunting and gathering societies of the past to abandon their old way of life does not seem to hold true for the Dobe !Kung.

Similarly, individuals also established formal relationships with nonrelatives in which two people gave each other gifts such as knives or iron spears at irregular intervals. Reciprocity was delayed, so that one partner would always be in debt to the other. Pauline Weissner, when she was a graduate student at the University of Michigan at Ann Arbor, analyzed those reciprocity relationships and concluded that individuals purposely selected gift-giving partners from distant territories. Presumably it was hoped that a partner would have something to offer when goods were difficult to obtain locally. Hence, in the traditional !Kung view of the world, security was obtained by giving rather than hoarding, that is, by accumulating obligations that could be claimed in times of need.

Clearly, mobility was a critical prerequisite for maintaining reciprocity relationships over long distances and for making it possible to move elsewhere when foraging conditions were unfavorable. The !Kung system of justice had the same requirement of ready movement. Like many other traditional foraging groups, the !Kung society was acephalous, or headless: no one was in charge of adjudicating disputes. When disagreements became serious, individuals or groups of disputants simply put distance between themselves, claiming membership in widely separated bands. As long as everyone could carry their few possessions on their backs, and so could relocate with ease, the approach worked well.

The traditional !Kung, then, were well suited to the Kalahari. They were generalists who lived by the ethic of sharing, ensuring that those who were less successful at finding food could usually be fed nonetheless. Because families owned no more than they could carry, they were able to travel at will whenever resources became scarce or disputes too heated.

By 1975, however, the !Kung were undergoing a cultural transition—at least so it seemed by all appearances at Dobe. I left there in 1970 and returned in the middle of the decade. I found that, in the interim, many families had taken on the ways of the neighboring Bantu. A number had planted fields and acquired herds of goats along with an occasional cow. Fewer of the boys were learning to hunt; traditional bows and arrows were still produced but mostly for eventual sale on a worldwide curio market. The people wore mass-produced clothing instead of animal skins, and traditional grass huts were for the most part replaced by more substantial mud-walled structures, which were now inhabited for longer periods than in the past.

An influx of money and supplies had clearly played a part in many of these changes. Botswana became an independent nation in 1966, after having been the British protectorate Bechuanaland. The new government began to encourage the keeping of livestock and the development of agriculture, such as by giving donkeys to the !Kung for pulling simple plows. And it arranged for the routine purchase of traditional handicrafts (for example, bead necklaces), thereby injecting extraordinary sums of money into the community. Later, when the !Kung in Namibia (then a colony of South Africa) were brought into the South African Army, the !Kung in Botswana received more infusions of cash and goods, mainly via interactions with kin.

Yet the exact meaning of such surface changes remained unclear. To what extent did the livestock and fields, the new clothes and the sturdier huts reflect a weakness in the glue that held !Kung society together? Why had the men and women, who had long been successful as foragers and who were not coerced into changing, decided to take on the burdens of herds and crops and to otherwise allow their mobility to be compromised? Archaeological work I undertook at Dobe between 1975 and 1982 (first as a research associate at the Smithsonian Institution and then as an employee of the National Science Foundation), together with observations made by other workers during the same period, provides some hints.

To be frank, when I returned in 1975, a methodological question preoccupied me. I hoped to learn about what happened to the bones of hunted animals after the carcasses were discarded and became buried naturally in the ground; such information was important for developing archaeological techniques to determine how people in the past killed, butchered and cooked animals. I thought that by locating the remains of old cooking hearths at Dobe, around which families ate, I might gather a good collection of bones—the remains of meals—on which to test a few ideas. Later I realized the data I had collected in the course of this endeavor might also say something about the transformation of the !Kung.

As part of my studies I identified and mapped the locations of huts and their associated hearths dating back to 1944. I then dug up bones that had been dropped in and around the hearths and identified the species to which they belonged. In visits made after 1975, I no longer collected bones, but I continued to map contemporary camps; in the end, I accumulated almost 40 years of settlement data.

The camps were usually occupied by the same extended family and close relatives, such as in-laws, although the specific mix of individuals changed somewhat from year to year. At the older sites, where all visible traces of occupation had disappeared, the huts and the hearths (which were normally placed outside a hut's entryway) were identified with the help of family members who actually remembered the placements.

My data supported the conclusion that by the mid-1970's long-standing !Kung values, such as the emphasis on intimacy and interdependence, were no longer guiding behavior as effectively as they once did. The data also indicated that, despite appearances to the contrary, the !Kung had retained their foraging "mentality." These generalists had taken up herding as if their goats and few cows were no different from any other readily accessible foraging resource. This surprising discovery meant that factors other than a failure of the food-securing system were at the root of the !Kung transformation.

My sense that traditional values were losing their influence over behavior came mainly from my analyses of the maps I had drawn (combined with other observations). Traditional !Kung camps, as depicted in the first 25 or so maps, were typically arranged in a circle, and most entrances faced inward. The huts were also set close together, so that from the entrance of one of them it was possible to see into most of the others.

The camp arrangement remained close and intimate until the early 1970's. Then suddenly the distance between huts increased significantly. At the same time, the circular pattern yielded to linear and other arrangements that gave families more privacy; also, in the last two camps I mapped (dating to 1981 and 1982), many of the hearths, which had been central to much social interaction, were located inside the huts instead of in front of them. The changes occurred so abruptly that the pattern of camp design can be said to have been unambiguously transformed from "close" to "distant" within a few years. By implication, such changes in camp design indicate that major changes in social norms for openness and sharing occurred as well in the early to middle 1970's.

This conclusion is consistent with other evidence. In 1976 Diane E. Gelburd, then a graduate student at George Washington University, inventoried the material possessions of individuals at Dobe and compared her data with a survey Lee had conducted in 1963. Whereas Lee found that most people could carry all their worldly belongings with ease, Gelburd found a dramatically different situation.

She showed that many !Kung owned large items, such as plows and cast iron pots, which are difficult to transport. With their newfound cash they had also purchased such goods as glass beads, clothing and extra blankets, which they hoarded in metal trunks (often locked) in their huts. Many times the items far exceeded the needs of an individual family and could best be viewed as a form of savings or investment. In other words, the !Kung were behaving in ways that were clearly antithetical to the traditional sharing system.

Yet the people still spoke of the need to share and were embarrassed to open their trunks for Gelburd. Clearly, their stated values no longer directed their activity. Although spoken beliefs and observed behavior do not coincide perfectly in any society, at Dobe in 1976 the disjunction had become extreme.

In what way did my other data set—the animal bones—clarify the causes of the social changes apparent by the 1970's? The presence of domesticated animals and cultivated fields at Dobe caused me to wonder if the changes I saw in the !Kung could be traced through some sequence of events to discontent with foraging. If the bones revealed that by the mid-1970's the !Kung derived meat almost exclusively from domesticated animals, the conclusion could then be entertained that a shift in subsistence strategy had preceded other dramatic social changes and, hence, might have somehow given rise to them.

My data confirmed earlier impressions that through the 1950's the !Kung were almost exclusively hunters and gatherers: in sites dating from that period, the bones of domesticated animals are rare. Then, in the 1960's, the consumption of goat and cattle increased markedly; in fact, by 1974 and 1975 these animals were consumed more than any others. The frequency with which chicken was consumed also increased during that period, although the Dobe !Kung never did eat very much of this Western staple. At the same time—from 1944 to 1975—the once great popularity of certain wild animals waned, including the greater kudu (a large antelope regularly hunted in the dry season) and two smaller antelopes (the steenbok and duiker).

A cursory look at these data might have suggested that the !Kung were indeed abandoning hunting. Yet a closer examination revealed that cattle essentially substituted for kudu, both of which are large animals, and that goats, which approximate steenbok and duiker in size, directly replaced those animals in the diet. It also turns out that the number of species represented at each camp remained essentially the same, as did the mix of small, medium and large species. That is, if the meat diet of the !Kung in the 1940's normally consisted of 10 species, of which 50 percent were small, 30 percent medium and 20 percent large, roughly the same numbers would be found in a 1975 camp, although the species in each category might differ.

These findings show that the !Kung did not reduce the variety in their diet, as would be expected if they had abandoned the traditional, generalist strategy and had committed themselves to becoming herders, who typically are dependent on just a few animal species. Hence, I realized that although anthropologists might view "wild" and "domestic" animals as fundamentally different, the !Kung as late as 1975 did not make such a distinction. From the !Kung perspective, goats were essentially the same as any other medium-size animal (in that they provided a reasonable yield of meat and were relatively easy to carry), and cows were the same as other large creatures. If an animal was easy to obtain, the !Kung ate it, but they apparently did not come to depend on their herd animals to the exclusion of all others.

Anecdotal information supports the assessment that the !Kung of 1975 did not view themselves as herders. For instance, whereas Bantu groups, who depend on their herds for food and prestige, would quickly kill a hyena that preyed on their animals, many !Kung men would not bother to do so. I believe the !Kung would have been less indifferent if they had considered their herds

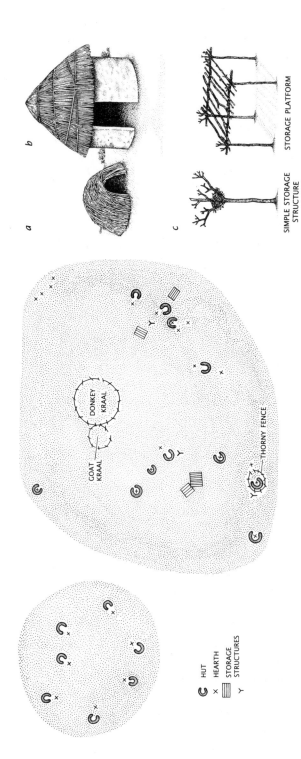

HUT   **C**
HEARTH   ×
STORAGE STRUCTURES   ▥
    Y

DONKEY KRAAL

GOAT KRAAL

THORNY FENCE

a

b

c

SIMPLE STORAGE STRUCTURE   STORAGE PLATFORM

Figure 9.2

Arrangements of camps changed markedly between 1944 and 1982. The changes, revealed by a series of maps much like these of dry-season camps, seem to reflect a decline in the cohesion of !Kung society. Until the early 1970's the traditional !Kung camp (*left*) was intimate: closely spaced huts roughly described a circle, and the entryways faced inwards so that from a single vantage one could see into many huts. The arrangements changed abruptly (*center*): the average distance between huts increased, and the cir-cular arrangement yielded to linear and other private arrays. The dwellings—which in the past were made of branches and grass (*a*) and now resembled the semipermanent mud-walled huts of the Bantu (*b*)—were sometimes isolated and fenced. Hearths, formerly the focal point of social exchange, were moved inside many huts. Kraals (pens for animals) gained a central place in camp, and private food-storage structures (*c*) joined the landscape.

to be all-important sources of meat. Similarly, they seemed to conceive of agriculture and wage labor undertaken for the Bantu and anthropologists—activities they pursued on a part-time, short-term basis—much as they perceived herding: as foraging resources just like any other.

Thus, well into the 1970's, the !Kung retained their generalist strategy, limiting their reliance on any one type of resource. Obviously that approach was adaptable enough to permit the transition from a foraging to a more mixed economy without disrupting social functioning.

If neither empty bellies nor coercion initiated the !Kung's transformation, what did? The impetus may well have come largely from internal stresses generated by the desire to have the material goods that had become readily accessible. The following scenario—based in part on my map data, Gelburd's work and my interactions with the !Kung over the years—is one plausible sequence of events that may have occurred. The scenario does not attempt to be a comprehensive description of how and why the !Kung culture has changed, but it does describe some of the major processes that seem to be driving the society's transformation.

Once the !Kung had ready access to wealth, they chose to acquire objects that had never before been available to them. Soon they started hoarding instead of depending on others to give them gifts, and they retreated from their past interdependence. At the same time, perhaps in part because they were ashamed of not sharing, they sought privacy. Where once social norms called for intimacy, now there was a disjunction between word and action. Huts faced away from one another and were separated, and some hearths were moved inside, making the whole range of social activities that had occurred around them more private. As the old rules began to lose their relevance, boys became less interested in living as their fathers had. They no longer wished to hunt and so no longer tried to learn the traditional skills; instead they preferred the easier task of herding.

Meanwhile the acquisition of goods limited mobility, a change that came to be reflected in the erection of semi-permanent mud-walled huts. The lack of mobility fueled still more change, in part because the people could no longer resolve serious arguments in the traditional manner, by joining relatives elsewhere in !Kung territories.

With the traditional means of settling disputes now gone, the !Kung turned to local Bantu chiefs for arbitration. In the process they sacrificed autonomy and, like other San groups, increased their reliance on, and incorporation into, Bantu society. In fact, many !Kung families currently have close relationships with individual Bantu and look on them as protectors.

For their part, the Bantu have accepted the role, often speaking of "my Bushmen." Marriage of !Kung women to Bantu men is now fairly common, an ominous sign for the cohesion of !Kung society. The children of these unions obtain full rights within the Bantu system, including the right to inherit livestock, and are more likely to think of themselves as Bantu than as !Kung.

Genetic studies of many Bantu-speaking peoples in southern Africa show that Khoisan speakers have been melding into Bantu societies for centuries. Very possibly some of those Khoisan groups and similar ones elsewhere in the world followed a course something like the modern !Kung at Dobe are following now; that is, the acquisition of goods led to a lack of mobility and to societal stresses fatal to the group's cohesion.

Today the issue of whether the !Kung experience is applicable to foraging societies of the past can best be resolved by comparing the forces acting on the !Kung with those acting on the remnants of other foraging societies in Africa, Asia and South America. These groups merit intense and immediate scrutiny. If they are ignored, an important opportunity to understand more about the ways of past foraging groups and about the forces leading to their demise will soon pass forever.

FURTHER READING

Kalahari Hunter-Gatherers: Studies of the !Kung San and Their Neighbours. Edited by Richard B. Lee and Irven DeVore. Harvard University Press, 1976.

The !Kung of Nyae Nyae. Lorna Marshall. Harvard University Press, 1976.

The !Kung San: Men, Women and Work in a Foraging Society. Richard B. Lee. Cambridge University Press, 1979.

Optimization and Risk in Human Foraging Strategies. John E. Yellen in *Journal of Human Evolution*. Vol. 15, pages 733–50; 1986.

TEN

So Varied in Detail—
So Similar in Outline

◆

Tim Flannery

I have taken the title for this chapter from the epigraph of a seminal work on Aboriginal lifestyles and environments called *Aboriginal Man and Environment in Australia.* It is a quote from the explorer Edward John Eyre, writing in 1845, who said that Aboriginal culture was:

> so varied in detail, though so similar in general outline and character, that it will require the lapse of years, and the labours of many individuals, to detect and exhibit the links which form the chain of connection in the habits and history of tribes so remotely separated; and it will be long before any one can attempt to give to the world a complete and well-drawn outline of the whole.

Time has proven Eyre correct, for despite many partially successful attempts, there is still no complete overview of Aboriginal lifestyles and cultures. These cultures are the result of over 40 000 years of coadaptation with Australian ecosystems. The experience and knowledge encompassed therein is perhaps the single greatest resource that Australians living today possess, for without it we have no precedence; no guide as to how humans can survive long-term in our strange land.

The relatively few technological changes in the archaeological record of the Aborigines may suggest a kind of cultural stasis. Several researchers have argued for change in the form of an 'intensification' of Aboriginal activity over the past 5000 years, resulting in an increase in population, but this is yet to be conclusively demonstrated. Overall, it appears that Aboriginal cultures have changed slowly over the last 12 000 years when compared with those of people living on other continents. Part of the perception of slow change, at least, is

This chapter originally appeared in *The Future Eaters: An Ecological History of the Australian Lands and People* by Tim Flannery. Reprinted with permission. Copyright © 1995 by Reed Books Australia.

due to the very incomplete nature of the archaeological record and the fact that many of the cultural adaptations of the Aborigines do not leave evidence in the archaeological record. Where the record is more complete, or where details of lifestyles are known, there is much greater evidence of cultural change and adaptation, at least at the local level.

There are other ways of viewing this apparent stasis. While it is true that the cultural change experienced by the Aborigines over the last 12 000 years was relatively slow, this period represents perhaps only the last one-sixth of their tenure in Australia. It is entirely possible that cultural change had been extremely rapid in the millennia following initial colonisation and that things changed so little in the last 12 000 years because so much cultural adaptation happened over the previous 50 000. Changes seen over the last 12 000 years may, in this context, be seen merely as exceedingly fine tuning of the relationship between the Aborigines and their environment.

Today, the lifestyles of all Aborigines are grossly altered by the European economy. In many regions of Australia very little is known of how people lived in the past, and what little is known is difficult to interpret. For those who recorded Aboriginal lifestyles did not see through the eyes of an historical ecologist. For these reasons, the archaeological record assumes great importance in interpreting the vital matters of lifestyle and human impact. It is, however, an extremely limited record, providing glimpses of now-vanished tribes even more elusive than the thin, wailing songs captured on wax cylinders in Central Australia by the great Professor Baldwin Spencer a century ago. More ghostly indeed than the fading sepia images of proud, naked men and women, that inform us of how life once was in Australia.

A first and most crucial deficit in the Australian archaeological record is the virtual complete absence of a beginning. Living Australians know, from their own life experiences, how good life can be for the first generations of future eaters,* to whom fall the lion's share of resources. The archaeological record and early history of New Zealand speaks eloquently of how dire the situation becomes when that first, full harvest is exhausted. Yet on both of these matters, the archaeological record of the Aborigines is silent. This is presumably because these initial phases of human adaptation are brief—a few hundred years at most in the infinity of time. Unless those few hundred years lie in the very recent past, time will destroy all traces of them. In the extraordinarily long history of the Aborigines, those phases may have passed over 40 000 years ago. Thus there is only a slim chance indeed that we will ever know much about this part of Aboriginal history.

This lack of a beginning is a great pity, for adaptation proceeds fastest when

*Editor's note: Flannery uses the term future eaters to describe people whose behavior destroys the basis for future human existence.

ecological pressure is greatest; and pressure is greatest during the resource crash that occurs in the first millennium following settlement. Many of the most important practices and beliefs that were to be crucial in determining the course of Aboriginal cultural evolution were probably shaped during that missing millennium.

Despite its shortcomings, the great strength of the Australian archaeological record is the enormously long, stable and slowly evolving relationship it documents between a people and their land. In some rare instances, such as that of the rock art galleries of Arnhem Land, it is a detailed record. Much, however, is quite literally skeletal, consisting of stone tools and bones. It tells us very little about the cultural and social life that the people of the time must have enjoyed and little of the forces that brought about social and cultural change. Indeed, often the record is barely sufficient to detect the small, incremental changes in diet and technology that reveal ecological coadaptation. Despite its many deficiencies, it is important to examine the archaeological record before making observations about the fundamental underpinnings of the lifestyle of the modern Aborigines.

There is little evidence for marked, continent-wide technological change in the archaeological record of the Aborigines before 6000 years ago. Perhaps the most striking change occurring before then is the loss of the great, waisted axes that have been found in archaeological deposits as far afield as Kangaroo Island and New Guinea's Huon Peninsula. People may have ceased manufacturing these axes as long as 40 000 years ago. As their function is not clear, it is difficult to interpret their economic importance, or whether they were replaced by superior tools.

At least three major changes can be detected among the stone tools that have been made in Australia over the past 6000 years. None, however, present unequivocal evidence for a major shift in the economy of a people. Instead, some may mark shifts in their spiritual and social life. The most striking of these changes concerns the development of the edge-ground axe, a clearly recognisable stone artefact with which many Australian farmers are familiar, having ploughed them from the soil of their fields.

About 5000 years ago, the manufacture of these splendid stone axes with their fine, ground edge, became popular throughout Australia.[14] Although at first sight they appear to mark a revolution in the relationship between humans and trees, this has proved not to be the case. For such axes are not particularly suitable for cutting down trees. Although commonly referred to as axes, these tools are in fact hatchets as they are wielded with one hand. A New Guinean friend who used an edge-ground axe in his youth to clear gardens, described their action (in Melanesian Pidgin) as *'chew 'im down diwai* [tree]'and laughed at the enormous effort put into felling trees before steel axes were introduced by Australian kiaps. The much tougher hardwoods of Australia would have been even less amenable to felling with such implements. Thus it seems likely that these fine axes were used primarily for shaping wooden tools and enlarging pre-existing tree hollows to reach possums or honey, rather than felling trees. Indeed, these are precisely the uses that were recorded for these axes by early observers of Aboriginal culture.

While the technological significance of the edge-ground axe may have been limited, its potential social significance was enormous. This is because superior stone suitable for the manufacture of edge-ground axes can be obtained at only a few quarries around Australia. As items of trade, edge-ground stone axes were enormously valued, for they are beautiful and much time goes into their manufacture. The quest to obtain axes often saw people undertaking journeys of hundreds of kilometres. Such journeys resulted in social ties that may otherwise never have been consolidated. As will be explained below, it is precisely such changes that may have been the most important ones in helping the Aborigines to flourish in Australia's environment.

A second technological development in stone-working technology which can be traced in the archaeological record is the adoption, in northern Australia about 6000 years ago, of bifacial stone points.[14] Their use rapidly spread into southern Australia, but by 3000 years ago they were being abandoned in the south. It was only in the north, where they originated, that their use persisted into historic times. Although it is difficult to know precisely why this kind of stone point began to be used, one possibility is that it enhanced the aerodynamic properties of spears, particularly those launched from woomeras. This theory has never been tested, and if correct, the reason as to why bifacial points should have been abandoned in the south has never been satisfactorily explained.

A variety of other tools, such as backed blades and tiny, geometric stone tools known as microliths, spread rapidly across Australia some 4500 years ago.[14] Their function is still unclear, but many researchers postulate that microliths were used as sharpened barbs on spears. Debate still rages concerning the origins of the tiny and unusual microliths. Similar tools were in use in south Asia at about the same time. Indeed, similar tools were in use in other parts of the world for 20 000 years before this. Thus it seems possible, but not certain, that the technology was passed from Asia to Australia.

If we shift from the examination of stone to bone in the archaeological record, we find evidence for several other widespread changes. The dingo was the first domesticated animal to reach Australia. It was adopted enthusiastically by the Aborigines and rapidly spread throughout the continent. Only

Tasmania, being cut off by Bass Strait, was inaccessible to it. It is difficult to assess the impact of the dingo on the economy of the Aborigines. There is some evidence that it may have had a large initial impact, for when Tasmanian Aborigines acquired dogs from European settlers, they quickly turned them to use in hunting marsupials. The Tasmanian marsupials had evolved no strategy for dealing with dog predation and thus dogs may have found it particularly easy to catch them. In this situation, dogs may have been a very valuable asset. Marsupials may have acted similarly on the mainland before they became used to dingos.

But by the time of European contact with the Aborigines of mainland Australia, the situation was very different. Early observers noted that Aborigines living in more open habitats rarely used dogs for hunting. Their presence is often a positive disadvantage, as they disturb prey before the hunter is able to stalk close enough to launch his spear. The advantage of acquiring dingos may also have been lessened once feral populations had become established. Dingos are efficient hunters of the larger marsupials and feral populations may have actually reduced the numbers of these important prey species that were available to Aborigines.

Again, although the economic value of the acquisition of the dingo remains equivocal, its social role was clear. Eric Rolls, in his book *From Forest to Sea*, puts the relationship as well as anyone ever has:

> Aborigines naturally adopted dingos as hunting aids, as companions, as warmth on freezing desert nights. There soon began the long, strange, inadvertent association of Aborigines and dogs. They treasured them, they treasure them, but they showed no rational concern for their welfare . . . Old men and old women welcomed them as sleeping companions—the more dingos they had the warmer they slept—so they broke their forelegs to keep them in camp. When they moved around, they might carry one or two and leave the others to die.[10]

The other great social value of dingos was to alert people to the arrival of strangers at a camp and particularly to scare away nocturnally active dangerous spirits.

Prior to the introduction of the dingo some 3500 years ago, Australia had experienced a period of relative ecological stability. It had suffered no extinctions since the great wave that carried off the megafauna over 30 000 years earlier. Three species fell victim to the dingo on the Australian mainland, but all survived in Tasmania, where the dingo was never present. The Tasmanian tiger *(Thylacinus cynocephalus)* and Tasmanian devil *(Sarcophilus harrisii)* were probably affected through direct competition for resources and became extinct on the mainland soon after the arrival of the dingo. Their extinction may indicate that dingos had greatly reduced the prey available to both carnivorous marsupials and humans.

The only prey species that appears to have been exterminated by the dingo is the flightless Tasmanian native hen *(Gallinula mortierii)*. This chicken-sized bird grazes on short grass sward, which is often maintained by grazing marsupials. Four thousand years ago it inhabited the alpine areas of south-eastern Australia. It was probably relict in these areas, for during the last ice age it was more widespread on the mainland, occurring as far north as Queensland. It may be that dingos were able to destroy it because it favoured short grasslands which are precisely the same kind of habitat that dogs perform best in. While its extinction may have been a loss to the Aborigines of the high country, it clearly had only a local impact.

A final, fascinating study which has arisen from the examination of bones is the remarkable work of Dr Steven Webb of the University of New England.[13] In the early 1980s, before so many human remains had been lost from Australian museums, Webb examined virtually every human bone in museum collections for signs of stress caused by disease and starvation. He found that there was a substantial increase in the incidence of such stresses with time. Just why this occurred remains unclear. It may be that it reflects a strengthening of ENSO [el Niño Southern Oscillation], or indeed the opposite, for if ENSO weakened, human populations may increase, leading to increased competition for food and a greater chance of disease transmission.

Curiously, Webb also found that the incidence of stress varied around the continent, with the greatest levels in the central Murray River area and coastal New South Wales. Both of these areas—but along the Murray in particular—supported higher human population densities than were normal for Australia. Webb speculates that the high incidence of evidence of diseases among bones from the central Murray may have been caused by a unique lifestyle that led to osteoarthritis. Victorian groups suffered seasonal and acute stress, perhaps due to the harshness of winter there.

Clearly, Webb's study is of enormous potential importance in understanding the past. Rapidly developing technologies for examining bones, such as CAT scans, would almost certainly have seen even more extraordinary advances in this area. Unfortunately, now this will never happen, for increasingly, museums are yielding to pressure from lobby groups and are giving over Aboriginal osteological material for reburial. Those bones once belonged to people for whom it was not possible to write to their descendants about how life was for them. But through studying the ancient bones, living Aborigines can read in each the very personal story of a life led so very long ago. As bleak as it is to be a future eater, it is as nothing compared with the tragedy of obliterating one's past.

One area of Australia preserves a far more detailed and informative record of cultural change than any other. This is Arnhem Land, which shelters one of the greatest, if not *the* greatest, concentration of ancient art on Earth. There, people have been painting the walls of rockshelters for 18 000 years. Researchers are now beginning to understand the significance of various painting styles and are coming up with a chronology for the works. Some individual paintings are even able to be dated.[12]

Analysis of the Arnhem Land art galleries has revealed some extraordinary things. Some paintings dating to over 3000 years ago, for example, show people holding boomerangs. The Aborigines who inhabit Arnhem Land today do not possess boomerangs and have no traditions regarding them. This seemed like a mysterious loss until researchers noted that spear throwers were not depicted in the older art. Then it was discovered that at about 3000 years ago the vegetation of Arnhem Land became denser. Boomerangs can only be used effectively in open country and in forest the spear, especially if propelled by the ingenious woomera or spear thrower, is a far superior weapon.

There are still many mysteries regarding the Arnhem Land paintings. Some dating to about 3000 years ago show people using a short, trident-like spear. Its points are barbed and spread widely (Taçon, personal communication). No-one living today can determine its use.

Other changes recorded in the art are those concerning food resources and even the fighting of pitched battles. The study of Australia's rock art is still young, but it promises to be a treasure-trove of information when further research is completed.

It is now time to look at Aboriginal cultures as they were in 1788, to see what was recorded before they were disrupted and to determine what these early observations can add to our understanding of the ecology of the Aborigines.

The traditional European view of Aboriginal cultures has been that, by and large, life has 'stood still' for the Aborigines since they had arrived in Australia. This view was based upon the observations by anthropologists and others that Aborigines had arrived in Australia in the stone age and were still in it by the time Cook arrived. This is a very superficial and naive view. The truth, as always in such matters, is far more complex. Indeed, I suspect that many of the features of Aboriginal lifestyles that we continue to view as primitive are highly specialised responses to Australian conditions.

A fascinating study of Aboriginal settlement patterns was undertaken by the anthropologist Joseph Birdsell in the 1950s.[2] He tested the simple premise that Aboriginal population density was directly related to rainfall. He found that throughout much of the continent the basic relationship held good. But he also concluded, from reading early ethnographies, that the average size of an Aboriginal 'tribe' was 500 individuals. Remarkably, this is the same population size that geneticists postulate is needed for long-term survival of mammalian populations. Birdsell found that it was only in very unusual circumstances that larger tribes existed and that very few areas of Australia he examined had dramatically denser populations than the average. Indeed the only exceptions in terms of population density were the tribes inhabiting the Murray River drainage system, where the population density could have been as great as 40 times the average for Australia overall. This exceptional density was permitted by the nutrients and water carried to the lower reaches of the Murray River from a very large catchment. This concentration of resources created a uniquely rich environment that allowed an exceptional buildup of population.

One of the things that Birdsell's study tells us, I think, is that the Aborigines of most of Australia were living a delicately balanced existence, for their population was kept very close to the limit of viability dictated by genetics. In order to maintain this number, during bad times they had to use every resource available, as well as to develop some ingenious social arrangements. An analysis of just what constraints they laboured under and what solutions they developed to overcome them, forms the bulk of the discussion below.

The most striking features of Aboriginal lifestyles to nineteenth-century Europeans were doubtless the absence of agriculture, widespread nomadism, its associated simple dwellings and limited material possessions. We now know that it is rather deceptive to view these features in isolation, for they were part of an adaptational response that included religious beliefs and social customs which, as a whole, maintained a balance between Aborigines and their environment. In order to understand that adaptational response it is necessary to examine all of these factors. There is no better place to start than the lack of agriculture.

A lack of agriculture has long been cited as evidence of the 'backwardness' or 'laziness' of Aborigines. It was indeed the basis of the British legal concept of *terra nullius*. *Terra nullius* gave the British a moral right to occupy 'unused' lands and to the English, Australia appeared to be one vast, unused land. To them, the very essence of ownership constituted tilling of the soil.

I have long been uneasy with the idea that the lack of agriculture by Aborigines is a primitive trait retained from remote ancestors. This is because it seems probable that humans have been practicing rudimentary forms of agriculture for many tens of thousands of years. As I will discuss below in relation to New Guinea, the boundary between agriculture and wild harvesting seems to disappear when food-gathering practices are examined in detail. In some areas of Australia there is indeed evidence for 'plant curation'. The most important was broad-acre management using fire, but because of the multiplicity of uses that Aborigines put fire to, it is difficult to evaluate from the perspective of plant curation alone.

More exclusively agricultural in nature are the practices of small-scale curation, such as the removal of competing plant species, the diversion of small streams to provide water to certain food plants and the transplantation of useful plant species. Some of these small-scale practices are perhaps hundreds of thousands of years old. Some were, I think, part of the behavioural repertoire of the first Aborigines. What is remarkable is that in Australia, these practices, with the exception of fire, seem to have survived only in exceptional circumstances. Over most of the continent, even the relatively small investment of time and energy in agriculture that such practices entail may have been uneconomical.

There are a number of reasons why agriculture may have been down-played in the economic activities of the Aborigines. One way of understanding this is to seek examples from elsewhere in the world where people have abandoned agriculture. An extraordinary example has been recorded among people living in coastal areas of Europe some 5000–4000 years ago. There, people abruptly abandoned agriculture and began to harvest increased numbers of maritime resources, particularly seals. In this case, an increase in the biological productivity of the North Sea, with a corresponding rise in seal numbers, might have been responsible.[3] This example is interesting, for it shows that agriculture does not always pay, even where conditions are favourable. Clearly, a similar scenario could not apply in Australia, where marine resources are so limited. So other reasons must be sought.

The lack of agriculture among Aborigines was certainly not brought about by a lack of plant species suitable for cultivation; for among the indigenous flora of Australia there are yams, taro, nardoo and various grasses, relatives of most of which have been cultivated elsewhere. There are also various members of the family Solanaceae (including tomato, potato, tobacco, capsicum and other species which have been widely cultivated). In addition, various tree species such as *Macadamia, Terminalia* and *Araucaria,* produce nut crops which are important cultivars in the Pacific and elsewhere.

It is true that Australia's poor soils mitigate against the development of agriculture, yet New Guinea also has only small areas of fertile soils, but agriculture there is a venerable and profitable tradition. So an argument based upon poor soils alone is not entirely convincing.

The real reasons, I suspect, lie in the effect of ENSO on productivity in Australia. ENSO brings more variability and unpredictability in weather patterns to the eastern two-thirds of Australia than are experienced almost anywhere. Even with all of the benefits of irrigation, a modern transportation system, a worldwide economic system and extraordinary storage technology, Australian agriculture is at the mercy of ENSO. Australian agricultural industries often find it hard to fill orders placed the previous year because of drought, fire or flood, all spawned by ENSO. Thus, with its two- to eight-year-long cycle, ENSO makes life a gamble even for the most prepared of farmers.

It is easy to imagine the difficulties that Aboriginal people may have encountered had they attempted to intensify plant management into agriculture. Were they living in an area with tolerably good soils and if ENSO was kind, they may have done very well for a couple of years, increasing their numbers and investing effort in the development of a permanent camp. Then, one year, no useful rain would fall. Even if they had storable food on the scale that European farmers use to get through the winter, it would have been insufficient to save them, for the critical difference between ENSO and a European winter is predictability. European farmers know, with a margin of error of a couple of weeks, how long winter will last and they plan accordingly. We owe the great mid-winter feast—so beloved by our pagan ancestors that upon being missionised they changed its name to Christmas and continued to celebrate it—to such knowledge and planning. The fact that the Europeans could, in the face of dismal mid-winter, consume vast amounts of foodstuffs with alacrity, is remarkable testimony to the predictability of the coming spring.

In contrast, an ENSO drought might last for months—or years. It may be followed by useful rain or devastating floods. Without a tight social and economic network that spans a continent and the technology necessary to store and transport vast amounts of food, such obstacles are probably insurmountable difficulties for agriculturalists. It makes an enormous amount of sense to me to see the lack of agriculture by Australian Aborigines as a fine-tuned adaptation to a unique set of environmental problems, rather than as a sign of 'primitiveness'.

I think that the same can be said for patterns of Aboriginal settlement and resource use. Nomadism was clearly an adaptation to tracking the erratic availability of resources as they are dictated by ENSO. Nomadism has a great cost, for possessions must be kept to a minimum. The Aboriginal tool kit was thus rather limited, consisting of a number of usually light, mostly multipurpose implements. Investment in shelter construction is likewise constrained by such a lifestyle, for there is no point in building large and complex structures when ENSO may dictate that the area be deserted for an unknown period at any time.

Before moving on, it is worth mentioning that none of the characteristics of Aboriginal culture discussed above have a genetic basis. In the past, people have argued that Aborigines were, by virtue of their supposedly primitive condition, incapable of 'advancing' by adoption of agriculture and a settled life.

That this is demonstrably untrue is shown by the very early development of agriculture by their New Guinean relatives, who are genetically and technologically extremely similar to the Australian Aborigines. Indeed, at the time agriculture was developing in New Guinea, people could have walked over dry land from Tasmania to Irian Jaya.

To return to the issue of human adaptation to Australian conditions, how do we make sense of other aspects of Aboriginal lifestyles in light of ENSO? In this regard, I think that it is singularly shortsighted to try to understand the ecology of the Aborigines solely through their technology and economy. This is because the nature of the conditions that they were adapting to made the social contract of extraordinary importance and down played the significance of technology. Just why technological advances were relatively unimportant I will explain below. But now we must look at the nature of the social contract in Aboriginal society.

An important facet of the cultural life of the Aborigines is that extraordinary social obligations must sometimes be honoured. This is because in the most difficult of droughts, people abandon their land temporarily and seek refuge with neighbours. It takes remarkably strong social bonds for people to share their limited resources with guests at such times. Doubtless, warfare and bad relations between neighbours existed in Aboriginal Australia, but they appear to have been common only in those few areas where population density was high or the impact of ENSO lessened. One example comes from densely populated Arnhem Land, where approximately 25 per cent of males of reproductive age were killed in inter-tribal skirmishes. Intriguingly, the Aborigines living in the south-west of Western Australia had a well-developed system of 'payback', remarkably like that existing in New Guinea today.[5] This region is almost unique in Australia in that neither ENSO nor monsoon variability has a marked effect. It is possible that this relative climatic predictability accounts for some anomalously high population densities recorded there, as well as for the development of the payback system.

Despite these exceptions, when looked at overall, Aboriginal society clearly lacked the degree of xenophobia and constant warfare exhibited by the people inhabiting New Guinea and New Zealand. This was due, I suspect, to the development of harmonious and extensive social networks, the existence of which was imperative if people were to survive ENSO.

Other factors selected for widespread social networks. ENSO and the inherent poverty of Australian ecosystems have kept Aboriginal populations close to the lower limit for long-term genetic survival. This has made neighbours with whom one can intermarry one of the most valued resources.

Just how the social life of Aborigines was organised in light of these conditions is revealed through an examination of Aboriginal religion. Religion is one of the most omnipresent features of Aboriginal culture. Today, even in the face of rapid cultural change, the effects of traditional Aboriginal religion remain strong. They are manifested in land claims, social obligations, rules of marriage and other practices. Through sacred sites and land claims, they are having an important impact on all Australians.

In pre-contact times, religious beliefs manifested themselves in every aspect of an Aboriginal person's life. Religion was the main controller of peoples' lives and movements in a way matched only, in European culture, among the inmates of the stricter Catholic monasteries. Even now, in remote areas religious beliefs dictate whom a person will marry, when certain tracts of land are burned and when they are left idle, when a person will visit another group and even what a person will eat and when. All of these things have an economic impact, and economic and long-term religious interests coincide closely.

The reason why long-term economic concerns and religious belief coincide so perfectly in Aboriginal society, is, I suspect, because Aboriginal religious beliefs have been evolving for tens of thousands of years. In effect, they embody hundreds of generations of accumulated wisdom regarding the environment and how best to utilise it without destroying it.

As noted above, Aboriginal religion regulates the social life of a people by determining when, given the right environmental conditions, ceremonies will occur and who will take part in them and what obligations will be carried by whom as a result of them. It also determines, very exactly, who will marry whom. This is often known long before a person is born. Thus, religion tightly controls a people's social relationships and it determines where the genes of an individual will be spread. Perhaps, over 40 000 or more years of experience with Australian environments, Aborigines found that the best way to 'codify' their relationships in order to achieve maximum genetic fitness where potential partners were few, was through strict adherence to invariable religious observance.

Nomadism and low population densities mean that opportunities for contact among people of different groups is very limited. For this reason, the great tribal meetings, known by Europeans as corroborees, were critically important events for Aborigines. Corroborees often involved hundreds of participants drawn from several tribal groups. There, contacts were made, social obligations renewed and opportunities for individuals to move from one tribe to another, either through marriage, or for reasons of initiation, were created.

Despite their importance, corroborees could only take place in exceptional circumstances, for enough food had to be present in one place to feed hundreds of people for weeks. In the drier parts of Australia this was a particularly severe problem, for it was only following exceptionally good rains that favoured areas contained the requisite resources. Elsewhere, people were less constrained by their environment. A few groups were fortunate enough to have a reliable resource such as the bunya pine *(Araucaria bidwilli)* of south-east Queensland, which produced nutritious nuts in abundance every three years and to which people flocked from miles around.

An interesting variation on the corroboree is the *Rom* ritual of Arnhem Land, which involves visits by the performers of the *Rom* ceremony to distant parts and results in the cementing of numerous social obligations. It is interesting to hear the words of an Arnhem Land elder concerning the impact that transport by car and plane has on the ancient visiting ceremonies such as *Rom:*

> we're getting friends; we want to make friends. For a long time now we had no friends, too far away. But now with planes and cars it's all right. We are one fullblood Aborigines.[6]

Similar visiting or corroboree-like ceremonies occurred throughout Australia. They were highly successful in linking the scattered bands and in providing information about distant groups. An extreme example is provided by Daisy Bates, who records that people living at Ooldea in South Australia had detailed knowledge about the tribal relationships of individuals who lived up to 1600 kilometres away.[1] It is all too easy to see ENSO as an unmitigated disaster for Aborigines. But in truth there were also some great benefits. The size of hunter-gatherer populations is determined by the resources available at the worst of times. This is because humans reproduce slowly and live a very long time. This reproductive strategy means that a bad season can reduce a population so greatly that it takes a long time for it to recover. During the long period that the population is recovering, the people will be living at a level well below the carrying capacity of the land. This means that many resources will be easily available. Researchers have calculated that, in normal times, hunter-gatherers utilise only 20–30 per cent of the resources available. This probably results from the occasional hard season which periodically devastates the population.

In Australia, ENSO produces such wild swings in climate that the hard times are extraordinarily hard, even though they may be experienced as rarely as once every few decades. Despite their infrequency, these events may keep populations at a lower level than they would otherwise reach, giving people a relatively easy living, with a choice of resource options, in the good times.

Because resources are normally more than sufficient for people in such situations, they have much leisure time. During their stay with the Anbarra people at Anadjerraminyia outstation, Drs Betty Meehan and Rhys Jones calculated that the Anbarra obtained about 50 magpie geese daily, which is at least one goose per adult in the camp. This food was obtained during some 10 minutes' work each morning and evening by three or four men, who admittedly were using shotguns. Nonetheless, the amount of time invested in these 'wild goose chases' was a mere one or two man-hours per day.[9]

Much of the leisure time of the Anbarra was utilised in the pursuit of religious and social goals, with ritual business totalling at least 40 man-hours per day. This division of time, with much devoted to social activities, seems rather typical of Aborigines living throughout Australia.

Richard Gould, who has lived with the Aborigines of the Western Desert, notes that resources in this inhospitable corner of Australia are sufficient so that even prepared plant food is occasionally in surplus and is discarded, people saying that they are not hungry for any more of it. Yet the Western Desert Aborigines have fewer plant staples (10) than has been recorded for any other group of Aborigines, or indeed any desert-dwelling hunter-gatherers living anywhere on earth.[4] Incredibly, in times of mild drought, the number of plant species supplying staples drops to three, yet the volume of food usually remains sufficient to feed the people. In very bad times, however, things are different. The lack of food and water forces people to abandon their territories and seek refuge among neighbours.[4]

The easy life that was created most of the time by ENSO made it possible for Aborigines to invest heavily in ritual and religion. Religion, in turn, codified ecological wisdom. Advances in technology which made the gathering of food easier were, in these circumstances, secondary considerations. Because of their role in trade, stone axes may have been more important socially than economically. It seems that, as with fire, ENSO reinforces a self-perpetuating loop that drives society inexorably in one direction.

Before moving on, it is worth noting the adaptations that have occurred on a regional level among Aborigines who find themselves in a particular environment and fine-tune their ecology to local conditions. There is considerable diversity in the resources utilised around Australia, perhaps because of the ENSO-influenced low populations and resource excess that exist most of the time. Thus, in some areas, people concentrated on shellfish, in others on fish and in yet others on small mammals. The vegetable foods also varied. Yet in all, these were essentially small-scale variations, which is remarkable considering that Australia is an enormous continent, spanning environments as diverse as rainforest and desert. Before European contact it was home to some 300 000–600 000 people who spoke 250 distinct languages and who were members of hundreds of different 'tribes'. Europe, by comparison, appears to be linguistically homogeneous. Yet the diversity of lifestyles lived by the Europeans, including as it does, farmer, herder and fisherman, is far greater than that seen in Australia.

This overarching similarity of Aboriginal culture throughout the continent is most striking. It may have its roots in the broad social networks of the Aborigines, which allowed for wide diffusion of ideas and technologies. It is clear that both trade and ceremonies linked Aborigines across the continent and that songs and dances were passed from group to group, often over enormous distances. Roth, the great recorder of the ways of the Queensland Aborigines, noted that in the late nineteenth century a ceremony, the *Molonga,* which originated in the Selwyn Ranges of north-western Queensland, was passed on to groups living as far away as Adelaide and Alice Springs.[11] Likewise, stone axes quarried near Mount Isa made their way to areas as distant as the Gulf of Carpentaria and the Great Australian Bight, while pearl shell from the Kimberley was traded deep into southern Australia. There can be little doubt that people and ideas travelled with these songs and goods. People certainly knew of each other—and the general lay of the land—in areas far distant from their own territories.

These great social networks, so important in linking widely scattered people in a people-poor land, were probably the great achievement of the Aborigines. Of land and food they normally had plenty. It was people that they needed, yet neighbours often lived far away. To build 'ropes' with distant groups, some perhaps meeting on only three or four occasions over a lifetime, was the great challenge.

Finally, we must consider the relationship between Aboriginal people and their food species. Despite the early exploitation that probably led to the demise of the megafauna, by 1788 Aboriginal societies had developed a large number of rather sophisticated practices for conserving animal resources. Unfortunately, the environmental implications of many Aboriginal practices have been lost, for they vanished before the study of ecology was understood by researchers. But some striking examples have recently been recognised in regard to hunting. One of the most interesting concerns the tradition of 'story places' in the rainforests of north Queensland.

Even today, the Aboriginal people of the Cooktown area regard certain mountain summits as 'story places'. The Aborigines believe that these places are inhabited by spirits and should on no account be entered. The most important story places in the lands of the Gugu-Yalandji people of the Cooktown area are the summits of Mount Finnigan and Mount Misery. Until hunting ceased in relatively recent times, these were the only areas where Bennett's tree-kangaroo *(Dendrolagus bennettianus)* was regularly seen.[8]

Bennett's tree-kangaroo was among the most important of game animals to the Gugu-Yalandji people in traditional times. Until the 1960s they hunted it avidly with dogs. In some ways it was an easy target, for once a dog had located the tree that a tree-kangaroo was resting in, it rarely escaped the humans who climbed after it. This hunting pressure had greatly reduced the population and early zoologists often recorded just how rare tree-kangaroos were in north

Queensland. Carl Lumholtz, a biologist who visited the Atherton Tablelands area in 1882–83, was determined to obtain a specimen of a tree-kangaroo. The specimens he sent back to Europe were eventually named Lumholtz tree-kangaroo *(Dendrolagus lumholtzi)* in his honour.

Lumholtz searched for months in prime habitat with a party of Aboriginal hunters, yet had this to report:

> We searched the scrubs in the vicinity thoroughly and found many traces of boongary [tree-kangaroo] in the trees but they were all old. It could be hunted more easily here, for the reason that the lawyer palm is rare, and consequently the woods are less dense. The natives told me that their 'old men' in former times had killed many boongary in these woods.[7]

It was only when Lumholtz entered a wild and precipitous region, where 'progress was difficult and it was almost impossible to find a suitable place to camp', that he finally saw his first tree-kangaroo.

If this were the state of affairs throughout the entire distribution of tree-kangaroos, they would long ago have become extinct due to overhunting. They survived because there were a few special places, including some prime tree-kangaroo habitat, where they remained unhunted. These were the story places of the Cooktown and Atherton Aborigines.

The development of story places was probably the very best solution available to Aborigines faced with the problem of maintaining a sustainable resource of tree-kangaroos. The usual European solution to such a problem would be to limit the number of tree-kangaroos taken, either by restricting access to them to a privileged class, or licensing and setting an annual quota. These were not really options for Aboriginal people, for they lived in scattered groups which were only irregularly in contact with one another and they lacked a centralised authority structure. In any case, the European solutions may have been inherently inferior, for in the variable Australian environment, the sustainable yield of tree-kangaroos may have varied wildly from year to year and thus have been exceedingly difficult to determine.

The story places were clearly defined and extensive areas of prime tree-kangaroo habitat which humans never entered. They acted as reservoirs for sustainable populations of tree-kangaroos, from which animals could disperse into hunted areas. This happened in a number of ways. Tired old males were kicked out of their territories in the story places by younger rivals, while the young of the year dispersed from there to find new homes. All of these individuals took up residence in the suitable yet heavily hunted habitats outside the story places and it was these animals that had, for tens of thousands of years, provided protein to the Gugu-Yalandji and other groups without driving tree-kangaroos to extinction.

Interestingly, the New Guineans with whom I have worked also had story places to protect tree-kangaroos. In 1985 I discovered a hitherto unknown species of tree-kangaroo in the remote Torricelli Mountains of Papua New Guinea. It is one of the very largest of the tree-kangaroos—a magnificent black creature with a short face and long, dense fur. Known to the Olo people as *Tenkile,* it had clearly become very rare by the 1980s, as one after the other, its story places lost their sacredness in the eyes of the local people and were hunted out. I witnessed the demise of the last story place in 1990.

It was a mountain summit called Sweipini—an eerie place of gnarled, stunted trees covered in long wisps of moss. It seems to be eternally shrouded in mist; a place where the strange calls of birds of paradise can be heard, but the birds themselves are only rarely glimpsed as they feed upon the red fruit of a palm that grows only on the mossy summits. At the centre of Sweipini, near the mountain summit itself, is a small circular lake that was once the most sacred place in the entire Olo region. The Olo believe that the lake was inhabited by gigantic eels which, if ever woken, would cause terrible weather that would destroy everyone's gardens, resulting in widespread starvation. A variety of frogs acted as the eels' sentinels. Only one old man, the most senior traditional landowner, was allowed to enter the area, for the frogs knew his face. If the frogs saw the face of a stranger, they would all begin to croak, thus waking the great eels.

Sweipini was the last refuge of the *Tenkile* in the area and was widely acknowledged as such by the local people. But in 1990 some village men decided that the huge 'devil eels' should be exorcised by the local Catholic priest, a delightful Irishman who has devoted his life to improving things for the people of the region. To comply with his parishioners' wishes and in the great tradition of the Catholic Church, he undertook the arduous walk to the remote lake. In a long ceremony he exorcised the devil eels. Everyone went home pleased, but over the next month 11 adult *Tenkile* were captured at Sweipini, including females with young. When I finally entered Sweipini in late 1990, tree-kangaroos were no longer in evidence.

Sadly, the senior landowner and guardian of the place was dismayed at this turn of events, being upset that the eels had been exorcised and the tree-kangaroos destroyed. Yet he was helpless against village pressure to resist the 'Christianising' event. With his help, I tried to convince the local people that there was real wisdom in their ancestors' decision to leave places like Sweipini to the spirits and tree-kangaroos. Once broken however, taboos are not easily repaired and it seems likely that the respect with which people once regarded Sweipini will never be fully restored.

Tragically, unless story places can be protected, or, as has happened in Australia, local people stop hunting, species like tree-kangaroos are doomed. Already, after just 50 years of hunting, the *Tenkile* has vanished from many previous strongholds. The next few decades will probably see it vanish from its last.

REFERENCES

1. Bates, D. (1985). *The native tribes of Western Australia.* National Library of Australia, Canberra.
2. Birdsell, J. B. (1953). Some environmental and cultural factors influencing the structure of Australian Aboriginal populations. *American Naturalist* 87:171–207
3. Burenhalt, G. (general editor) (1993). *The Illustrated Encycloapedia of Humankind.* Vols.1 + 2. Harper, San Francisco.
4. Gould, R. A. (1991). Arid-land foraging as seen from Australia: adaptive models and behavioural realities. *Oceania* 62:12–33.
5. Green, N. (1984). *Broken Spears: Aboriginals and Europeans in the southwest of Australia.* Focus Education Services. Cottesloe.
6. Hiatt, L. (1986). *Rom* in Arnhem Land. Pp 5–14 *In* S.A. Wild (ed.). Rom, *an Aboriginal Ritual of Diplomacy.* Institute of Aboriginal Studies, Canberra.
7. Lumholtz, C. (1889). *Among Cannibals.* J. Murray, London.
8. Martin, R. (1992). Of Koalas, tree-kangaroos and man. *Australian Natural History* 24:22–31.
9. Meehan, B. and Jones, R. (1986). Pp 15–32. *In* S.A. Wild (ed.). Rom, *an Aboriginal Ritual of Diplomacy.* Institute of Aboriginal Studies, Canberra.
10. Rolls, E. (1993). *From Forest to Sea.* University of Queensland Press.
11. Roth, H. L. (1897). *Ethnographical Studies Among the North-West-Central Queensland Aborigines.* Brisbane.
12. Taçon, P. (1993). Art of the Land. Pp 158–59. *In* G. Burenhalt (ed.). *The Illustrated History of Humankind.* Vol. 1. Harper, San Francisco.
13. Webb, S. (1984). *Prehistoric Stress in Australian Aborigines.* Ph.D. thesis, Prehistory, Research School of Pacific Studies. Australian National University.
14. White, J. P. (1993). Australia: the different continent. Pp 207–27. *In* G. Burenhalt (ed.). *The Illustrated Encyclopaedia of Humankind.* Vol. 2. Harper, San Francisco.

ELEVEN

Future Primitive

◆

John Zerzan

Division of labor, which has had so much to do with bringing us to the present global crisis, works daily to prevent our understanding the origins of this horrendous present. Mary Lecron Foster (1990) surely errs on the side of understatement in allowing that anthropology is today "in danger of serious and damaging fragmentation." Shanks and Tilley (1987b) voice a rare, related challenge: "The point of archaeology is not merely to interpret the past but to change the manner in which the past is interpreted in the service of social reconstruction in the present." Of course, the social sciences themselves work against the breadth and depth of vision necessary to such a reconstruction. In terms of human origins and development, the array of splintered fields and sub-fields—anthropology, archaeology, paleontology, ethnology, paleobotany, ethnoanthropology, etc., etc.—mirrors the narrowing, crippling effect that civilization has embodied from its very beginning.

Nonetheless, the literature can provide highly useful assistance, if approached with an appropriate method and awareness and the desire to proceed past its limitations. In fact, the weakness of more or less orthodox modes of thinking can and does yield to the demands of an increasingly dissatisfied society. Unhappiness with contemporary life becomes distrust with the official lies that are told to legitimate that life, and a truer picture of human development emerges. Renunciation and subjugation in modern life have long been explained as necessary concomitants of "human nature." After all, our pre-civilized existence of deprivation, brutality, and ignorance made authority a benevolent gift that rescued us from savagery. 'Cave man' and 'Neanderthal' are still invoked to remind us where we would be without religion, government, and toil.

This ideological view of our past has been radically overturned in recent decades, through the work of academics like Richard Lee and Marshall Sahlins. A nearly complete reversal in anthropological orthodoxy has come

This chapter originally appeared in *Future Primitive and Other Essays* (1994) by John Zerzan. Reprinted with permission.

about, with important implications. Now we can see that life before domesti-cation/agriculture was in fact largely one of leisure, intimacy with nature, sen-sual wisdom, sexual equality, and health. This was our human nature, for a couple of million years, prior to enslavement by priests, kings, and bosses.

And lately another stunning revelation has appeared, a related one that deepens the first and may be telling us something equally important about who we were and what we might again become. The main line of attack against new descriptions of gatherer-hunter life has been, though often indi-rect or not explicitly stated, to characterize that life, condescendingly, as the most an evolving species could achieve at an early stage. Thus, the argument allows that there was a long period of apparent grace and pacific existence, but says that humans simply didn't have the mental capacity to leave simple ways behind in favor of complex social and technological achievement.

In another fundamental blow to civilization, we now learn that not only was human life once, and for so long, a state that did not know alienation or domination, but as the investigations since the '80s by archaeologists John Fowlett, Thomas Wynn and others have shown, those humans possessed an in-telligence at least equal to our own. At a stroke, as it were, the 'ignorance' thesis is disposed of, and we contemplate where we came from in a new light.

To put the issue of mental capacity in context, it is useful to review the var-ious (and again, ideologically loaded) interpretations of human origins and de-velopment. Robert Ardrey (1961, 1976) served up a bloodthirsty, macho ver-sion of prehistory, as have to slightly lesser degrees, Desmond Morris and Lionel Tiger. Similarly, Freud and Konrad Lorenz wrote of the innate depravity of the species, thereby providing their contributions to hierarchy and power in the present.

Fortunately, a far more plausible outlook has emerged, one that corre-sponds to the overall version of Paleolithic life in general. Food sharing has for some time been considered an integral part of earliest human society. Jane Goodall (1971) and Richard and Mary Leakey (1978), among others, have concluded that it was the key element in establishing our uniquely Homo de-velopment at least as early as two million years ago. This emphasis, carried for-ward since the early '70s by Linton, Zihlman, Tanner, and Isaac, has become ascendant. One of the telling arguments in favor of the cooperation thesis, as against that of generalized violence and male domination involves a dimin-ishing, during early evolution, of the difference in size and strength between males and females. Sexual dimorphism, as it is called, was originally very pro-nounced including such features as prominent canines or 'fighting teeth' in males and much smaller canines for the female. The disappearance of large male canines strongly suggests that the female of the species exercised a selec-tion for sociable, sharing males. Most apes today have significantly longer and larger canines, male to female, in the absence of this female choice capacity (Zihlman 1981, Tanner 1981).

Division of labor between the sexes is another key area in human beginnings, a condition once simply taken for granted and expressed by the term hunter-gatherer. Now it is widely accepted that gathering of plant foods, once thought to be the exclusive domain of women and of secondary importance to hunting by males, constituted the main food source (Johansen and Shreeve 1990). Since females were not significantly dependent on males for food, it seems likely that rather than division of labor, flexibility and joint activity would have been central (Bender 1989). As Zihlman (1981) points out, an overall behavioral flexibility may have been the primary ingredient in early human existence. Joan Gero (1991) has demonstrated that stone tools were as likely to have been made by women as by men, and indeed Poirier (1987) reminds us that there is "no archaeological evidence supporting the contention that early humans exhibited a sexual division of labor." It is unlikely that food collecting involved much, if any, division of labor and probably that sexual specialization came quite late in human evolution (Zihlman 1981).

So if the adaptation that began our species centered on gathering, when did hunting come in? Binford (1984) has argued that there is no indication of use of animal products (*i.e.* evidence of butchery practices) until the appearance, relatively quite recent, of anatomically modern humans. Electron microscope studies of fossil teeth found in East Africa (Walker 1984) suggest a diet composed primarily of fruit, while a similar examination of stone tools from a 1.5-million-year-old site at Koobi Fora in Kenya (Keeley and Toth 1981) shows that they were used on plant materials. The small amount of meat in the early Paleolithic diet was probably scavenged, rather than hunted (Ehrenberg 1986).

The 'natural' condition of the species was evidently a diet made up largely of vegetables rich in fiber, as opposed to the modern high fat and animal protein diet with its attendant chronic disorders. Though our early forbears employed their "detailed knowledge of the environment and cognitive mapping" (Zihlman 1981) in the service of a plant-gathering subsistence, the archaeological evidence for hunting appears to slowly increase with time (Hodder 1991).

Much evidence, however, has overturned assumptions as to widespread prehistoric hunting. Collections of bones seen earlier as evidence of large kills of mammals, for example, have turned out to be, upon closer examination, the results of movement by flowing water or caches by animals. Lewis Binford's "Were There Elephant Hunters at Tooralba?" (1989) is a good instance of such a closer look, in which he doubts there was significant hunting until 200,000 years ago or sooner. Adrienne Zihlman (1981) has concluded that "hunting arose relatively late in evolution," and "may not extend beyond the last one hundred thousand years." And there are many (*e.g.* Straus 1986; Trinkhaus

1986) who do not see evidence for serious hunting of large mammals until even later, *viz.* the later Upper Paleolithic, just before the emergence of agriculture.

The oldest known surviving artifacts are stone tools from Hadar in eastern Africa. With more refined dating methods, they may prove to be 3.1 million years old (Klein 1989). Perhaps the main reason these may be classified as representing human effort is that they involve the crafting of one tool by using another, a uniquely human attribute so far as we know. Homo habilis, or 'handy man,' designates what has been thought of as the first known human species, its name reflecting association with the earliest stone tools. Basic wooden and bone implements, though more perishable and thus scantily represented in the archaeological record, were also used by Homo habilis as part of a "remarkably simple and effective" adaptation in Africa and Asia (Fagan 1990). Our ancestors at this stage had smaller brains and bodies than we do, but Poirier (1987) notes that "their postcranial anatomy was rather like modern humans," and Holloway (1972, 1974) allows that his studies of cranial endocasts from this period indicate a basically modern brain organization. Similarly, tools older than two million years have been found to exhibit a consistent right-handed orientation in the ways stone has been flaked off in their formation. Right-handedness as a tendency is correlated in moderns with such distinctly human features as pronounced lateralization of the brain and marked functional separation of the cerebral hemispheres. Klein (1989) concludes that "basic human cognitive and communicational abilities are almost certainly implied."

Homo erectus is the other main predecessor to Homo sapiens, according to longstanding usage, appearing about 1.75 million years ago as humans moved out of forests into drier, more open African grasslands. Although brain size alone does not necessarily correlate with mental capacity, the cranial capacity of Homo erectus overlaps with that of moderns such that this species "must have been capable of many of the same behaviors" (Ciochon, Olsen and Tames 1990). As Johanson and Edey (1981) put it, "If the largest-brained erectus were to be rated against the smallest-brained sapiens—all their other characteristics ignored—their species names would have to be reversed." Homo Neanderthalus, which immediately preceded us, possessed brains somewhat larger than our own (Delson 1985, Holloway 1985). Though of course the much-maligned Neanderthal has been pictured as a primitive, brutish creature—in keeping with the prevailing Hobbesian ideology—despite manifest intelligence as well as enormous physical strength.

Recently, however, the whole species framework has become a doubtful proposition (Rightmire 1990). Attention has been drawn to the fact that fossil specimens from various Homo species "all show intermediate morphological traits," Leading to suspicion of an arbitrary division of humanity into separate taxa (Gingerich 1979; Tobias 1982). Fagan (1989), for example, tells us that "it is very hard to draw a clear taxonomic boundary between Homo erectus and archaic Homo sapiens on the one hand, and between archaic and anatomically modern Homo sapiens on the other." Likewise, Foley (1989): "The anatomical distinctions between Homo erectus and Homo sapiens are not great." Jelinek (1978) flatly declares that "there is no good reason, anatomical or cultural" for separating erectus and sapiens into two species, and has concluded (1980) that people from at least the Middle Paleolithic onward "may be viewed as Homo sapiens." The tremendous upward revision of early intelligence, discussed below, must be seen as connected to the present confusion over species, as the once-prevailing overall evolutionary model gives way.

But the controversy over species categorization is only interesting in the context of how our earliest forbears lived. Despite the minimal nature of what could be expected to survive so many millennia, we can glimpse some of the texture of that life, with its often elegant, pre-division of labor approaches. The 'tool kit' from the Olduvai Gorge area made famous by the Leakeys contains "at least six clearly recognizable tool types" dating from about 1.7 million years ago (Leakey and Leakey 1978). There soon appeared the Acheulian handaxe, with its symmetrical beauty, in use for about a million years. Teardrop-shaped, and possessed of a remarkable balance, it exudes grace and utility from an era much prior to symbolization. Isaac (1986) noted that "the basic needs for sharp edges that humans have can be met from the varied range of forms generated from 'Oldowan' patterns of stone flaking," wondering how it came to be thought that "more complex equals better adapted." In this distant early time, according to cut-marks found on surviving bones, humans were using scavenged animal sinews and skins for such things as cord, bags, and rugs (Gowlett 1984). Further evidence suggests furs for cave wall coverings and seats, and seaweed beds for sleeping (Butzer 1970).

The use of fire goes back almost two million years and might have appeared even earlier but for the tropical conditions of humanity's original African homeland, as Poirier (1987) implies. Perfected fire-making included the firing of caves to eliminate insects and heated pebble floors, amenities that show up very early in the Paleolithic.

As John Gowlett (1984) notes, there are still some archaeologists who consider anything earlier than Homo sapiens—a mere 30,000 years ago—as greatly more primitive than we "fully human" types. But along with the documentation, referred to above, of fundamentally 'modern' brain anatomy even in early humans, this minority must now contend with recent work depicting complete human intelligence as present virtually with the birth of the Homo species. Thomas Wynn (1985) judged manufacture of the Acheulian handaxe to have required "a stage of intelligence that is typical of fully modern adults." Gowlett, like Wynn, examines the required "operational thinking involved in the right hammer, the right force and the right striking angle, in an ordered sequence and with flexibility needed for modifying the procedure. He contends that manipulation, concentration, visualization of form in three dimensions, and planning were needed, and that these requirements "were the common property of early human beings as much as two million years ago, and this," he adds, "is hard knowledge, not speculation."

During the vast time-span of the Paleolithic, there were remarkably few changes in technology (Rolland 1990). Innovation, "over 2½ million years measured in stone tool development was practically nil," according to Gerhard Kraus (1990). Seen in the light of what we now know of prehistoric intelligence, such 'stagnation' is especially vexing to many social scientists. "It is difficult to comprehend such slow development," in the judgment of Wymer (1989). It strikes me as very plausible that intelligence, informed by the success and satisfaction of a gatherer-hunter existence, is the very reason for the pronounced absence of 'progress'. Division of labor, domestication, symbolic culture—these were evidently refused until very recently.

Contemporary thought, in its postmodern incarnation, would like to rule out the reality of a divide between nature and culture; given the abilities present among people before civilization, however, it may be more accurate to say that, basically, they long chose nature over culture. It is also popular to see almost every human act or object as symbolic, a position which is, generally speaking, part of the denial of a nature versus culture distinction. But it is culture as the manipulation of basic symbolic forms that is involved here. It also seems clear that reified time, language (written, certainly, and probably spoken language for all or most of this period), number, and art had no place, despite an intelligence fully capable of them.

I would like to interject, in passing, my agreement with Goldschmidt (1990) that "the hidden dimension in the construction of the symbolic world is time." And as Norman O. Brown (1959) put it, "life not repressed is not in historical time," which I take as a reminder that time as a materiality is not inherent in reality, but a cultural imposition, perhaps the first cultural imposition, on it. As this elemental dimension of symbolic culture progresses, so does, by equal steps, alienation from the natural.

Cohen (1974) has discussed symbols as "essential for the development and maintenance of social order." Which implies—as does, more forcefully, a great deal of positive evidence—that before the emergence of symbols there was no condition of dis-order requiring them. In a similar vein, Lévi-Strauss (1953) pointed out that "mythical thought always progresses from the awareness of oppositions toward their resolution." So whence the absence of order, the conflicts or 'oppositions'? The literature on the Paleolithic contains almost nothing that deals with this essential question, among thousands of monographs on specific features. A reasonable hypothesis, in my opinion, is that division of labor, unnoticed because of its glacially slow pace, and not sufficiently understood because of its newness, began to cause small fissures in the human community and unhealthy practices vis-à-vis nature. In the later Upper Paleolithic, "15,000 years ago, we begin to observe specialized collection of plants in the Middle East, and specialized hunting," observed Gowlett (1984). The sudden appearance of symbolic activities (*e.g.* ritual and art) in the Upper Paleolithic has definitely seemed to archaeologists one of prehistory's "big surprises" (Binford 1972), given the absence of such behaviors in the Middle Paleolithic (Foster 1990). But signs of division of labor and specialization were making their presence felt as a breakdown of wholeness and natural order, a lack that needed redressing. What is surprising is that this transition to civilization can still be seen as benign. Foster (1990) seems to celebrate it by concluding that the "symbolic mode . . . has proved extraordinarily adaptive, else why has Homo sapiens become material master of the world?" He is certainly correct, as he is to recognize "the manipulation of symbols [to be] the very stuff of culture," but he appears oblivious to the fact that this successful adaptation has brought alienation and destruction of nature along to their present horrifying prominence.

It is reasonable to assume that the symbolic world originated in the formulation of language, which somehow appeared from a "matrix of extensive non-verbal communication" (Tanner and Zihlman 1976) and face-to-face contact. There is no agreement as to when language began, but no evidence exists of speech before the cultural 'explosion' of the later Upper Paleolithic It seems to have acted as an "inhibiting agent," a way of bringing life under "greater control" (Mumford 1972), stemming the flood of images and sensations to which the pre-modern individual was open. In this sense it would have likely marked an early turning away from a life of openness and communion with nature, toward one more oriented to the overlordship and domestication that followed symbolic culture's inauguration. It is probably a mistake, by the way, to assume that thought is advanced (if there were such a thing as 'neutral' thought, whose advance could be universally appreciated) because we actually think in language; there is no conclusive evidence that we must do so (Allport 1983). There are many cases, involving stroke and like impairments, of patients who have lost speech, including the ability to talk silently to themselves, who were fully capable of coherent thought of all kinds. These data strongly suggest that "human intellectual skill is uniquely powerful, even in the absence of language" (Donald 1991).

In terms of symbolization in action, Goldschmidt (1990) seems correct in judging that "the Upper Paleolithic invention of ritual may well have been the keystone in the structure of culture that gave it its great impetus for expansion."' Ritual has played a number of pivotal roles in what Hodder (1990) termed "the relentless unfolding of symbolic andsocial structures" accompanying the arrival of cultural mediation. It was as a means of achieving and consolidating social cohesion that ritual was essential; totemic rituals, for example, reinforce clan unity.

The start of an appreciation of domestication, or taming of nature, is seen in a cultural ordering of the wild, through ritual. Evidently, the female as a cultural category, *viz.* seen as wild or dangerous, dates from this period. The ritual 'Venus' figurines appear as of 25,000 years ago, and seem to be an example of earliest symbolic likeness of women for the purpose of representation and control. Even more concretely, subjugation of the wild occurs at this time in the first systematic hunting of large mammals; ritual was an integral part of this activity (Frison 1986).

Ritual, as shamanic practice, may also be considered as a regression from that state in which all shared a consciousness we would now classify as extrasensory (Leonard 1972). When specialists alone claim access to such perceptual heights as may have once been communal, further backward moves in division of labor are facilitated or enhanced. The way back to bliss through ritual is a virtually universal mythic theme, promising the dissolution of measurable time, among other joys. This theme of ritual points to an absence that it falsely claims to fill, as does symbolic culture in general.

Ritual as a means of organizing emotions, a method of cultural direction and restraint, introduces art, a facet of ritual expressiveness. "There can be little doubt," to Gans (1985), "that the various forms of secular art derive originally from ritual." We can detect the beginning of an unease, a feeling that an earlier, direct authenticity is departing. La Barre (1972), I believe, is correct in judging that "art and religion alike arise from unsatisfied desire." At first, more abstractly as language, then more purposively as ritual and art, culture steps in to deal artificially with spiritual and social anxiety.

Ritual and magic must have dominated early (Upper Paleolithic) art and were probably essential, along with an increasing division of labor, for the coordination and direction of community (Wymer 1981). Similarly, Pfeiffer (1982) has depicted the famous Upper Paleolithic European cave paintings as the original form of initiating youth into now complex social systems; as necessary for order and discipline (Jochim 1983). And art may have contributed to the control of nature, as part of development of the earliest territorialism, for example (Straus 1990).

The emergence of symbolic culture, with its inherent will to manipulate and control, soon opened the door to domestication of nature. After two million years of human life within the bounds of nature, in balance with other wild species, agriculture changed our lifestyle, our way of adapting, in an unprecedented way. Never before has such a radical change occurred in a species so utterly and so swiftly (Pfeiffer 1977). Self-domestication through language, ritual, and art inspired the taming of plants and animals that followed. Appearing only 10,000 years ago, farming quickly triumphed; for control, by its very nature, invites intensification. Once the will to production broke through, it became more productive the more efficiently it was exercised, and hence more ascendant and adaptive.

Agriculture enables greatly increased division of labor, establishes the material foundations of social hierarchy, and initiates environmental destruction. Priests, kings, drudgery, sexual inequality, warfare are a few of its fairly immediate specific consequences (Ehrenberg 1986; Wymer 1981; Festinger 1983). Whereas Paleolithic peoples enjoyed a highly varied diet, using several thousand species of plants for food, with farming these sources were vastly reduced (White 1959).

Given the intelligence and the very great practical knowledge of Stone Age humanity, the question has often been asked, "Why didn't agriculture begin at, say, 1,000,000 B.C. rather than about 8,000 B.C.?" I have provided a brief answer in terms of slowly accelerating alienation in the form of division of labor and symbolization, but given how negative the results were, it is still a bewildering phenomenon. Thus, as Binford (1968) put it, "The question to be asked is not why agriculture . . . was not developed everywhere, but why it was developed at all." The end of gatherer-hunter life brought a decline in size, stature, and skeletal robusticity (Cohen and Armelagos 1984, Harris and Ross 1981), and introduced tooth decay, nutritional deficiencies, and most infectious diseases (Larsen 1982; Buikstra 1976; Cohen 1981). "Taken as a whole . . . an overall decline in the quality—and probably the length—of human life," concluded Cohen and Armelagos (1984).

Another outcome was the invention of number, unnecessary before the ownership of crops, animals, and land that is one of agriculture's hallmarks. The development of number further impelled the urge to treat nature as something to be dominated. Writing was also required by domestication, for the earliest business transactions and political administration. Lévi-Strauss (1955) has argued persuasively that the primary function of written communication was to facilitate exploitation and subjugation; cities and empires, for example, would be impossible without it. Here we see clearly the joining of the logic of symbolization and the growth of capital.

Conformity, repetition, and regularity were the keys to civilization upon its triumph, replacing the spontaneity, enchantment, and discovery of the pre-agricultural human state that survived so very long. Clark (1979) cites a gatherer-hunter "amplitude of leisure," deciding "it was this and the pleasurable way of life that went with it, rather than penury and a day-long grind, that explains why social life remained so static."One of the most enduring and widespread myths is that there was once a Golden Age, characterized by peace and innocence, and that something happened to destroy this idyll and consign us to misery and suffering. Eden, or whatever name it goes by, was the home of our primeval forager ancestors, and expresses the yearning of disillusioned tillers of the soil for a lost life of freedom and relative ease.

The once-rich environs people inhabited prior to domestication and agriculture are now virtually nonexistent. For the few remaining foragers there exist only the most marginal lands, those isolated places as yet unwanted by agriculture. And surviving gatherer-hunters, who have somehow managed to evade civilization's tremendous pressures to turn them into slaves (*i.e.* farmers, political subjects, wage laborers), have all been influenced by contact with outside peoples (Lee 1976; Mithen 1990).

Duffy (1984) points out that the present day gatherer-hunters he studied, the Mbuti Pygmies of central Africa, have been acculturated by surrounding villager-agriculturalists for hundreds of years, and to some extent, by generations of contact with government authorities and missionaries. And yet it seems that an impulse toward authentic life can survive down through the ages. "Try to imagine," he counsels, "a way of life where land, shelter, and food are free, and where there are no leaders, bosses, politics, organized crime, taxes, or laws. Add to this the benefits of being part of a society where everything is shared, where there are no rich people and no poor people, and where happiness does not mean the accumulation of material possessions." The Mbuti have never domesticated animals or planted crops.

Among the members of non-agriculturalist bands resides a highly sane combination of little work and material abundance. Bodley (1976) discovered that the San (a.k.a. Bushmen), of the harsh Kalahari Desert of southern Africa, work fewer hours, and fewer of their number work, than do the neighboring cultivators. In times of drought, moreover, it has been the San to whom the farmers have turned for their survival (Lee 1968). They spend "strikingly little time laboring and much time at rest and leisure," according to Tanaka (1980), while others (e.g. Marshall 1976) have commented on San vitality and freedom compared with sedentary farmers, their relatively secure and easygoing life.

Flood (1983) noted that to Australian Aborigines "the labour involved in tilling and planting outweighed the possible advantages." Speaking more generally, Tanaka (1976) has pointed to the abundant and stable plant foods in the society of early humanity, just as "they exist in every modern gatherer society." Likewise, Festinger (1983) referred to Paleolithic access to "considerable food without a great deal of effort," adding that "contemporary groups that still live on hunting and gathering do very well, even though they have been pushed into very marginal habitats."

As Hole and Flannery (1963) summarized: "No group on earth has more leisure time than hunters and gatherers, who spend it primarily on games, conversation and relaxing." They have much more free time, adds Binford (1968), "than do modern industrial or farm workers, or even professors of archaeology."

The non-domesticated know that only the present can be total. This by itself means that they live life with incomparably greater immediacy, density and passion than we do. It has been said that some revolutionary days are worth centuries; until then "We look before and after," as Shelley wrote, "And sigh for what is not . . . ."

The Mbuti believe (Turnbull 1976) that "by a correct fulfillment of the present, the past and the future will take care of themselves." Primitive peoples do not live through memories, and generally have no interest in birthdays or measuring their ages (Cipriani 1966). As for the future, they have little desire to control what does not yet exist, just as they have little desire to control nature. Their moment-by-moment joining with the flux and flow of the natural world does not preclude an awareness of the seasons, but this does not constitute an alienated time consciousness that robs them of the present.

Though contemporary gatherer-hunters eat more meat than their prehistoric forbears, vegetable foods still constitute the mainstay of their diet in tropical and subtropical regions (Lee 1968; Yellen and Lee 1976). Both the Kalahari San and the Hadza of East Africa, where game is more abundant than in the Kalahari, rely on gathering for eighty percent of their sustenance (Tanaka 1980). The !Kung branch of the San search for more than a hundred different kinds of plants (Thomas 1968) and exhibit no nutritional deficiency. This is similar to the healthful, varied diet of Australian foragers (Flood 1983). The overall diet of gatherers is better than that of cultivators, starvation is very rare, and their health status generally superior, with much less chronic disease (Lee and DeVore 1968).

Laurens van der Post (1958) expressed wonder at the exuberant San laugh, which rises "sheer from the stomach, a laugh you never hear among civilized people." He found this emblematic of a great vigor and clarity of senses that yet manages to withstand and elude the onslaught of civilization. Truswell and Hansen (1976) may have encountered it in the person of a San who had survived an unarmed fight with a leopard; although injured, he had killed the animal with his bare hands.

The Andaman Islanders, west of Thailand, have no leaders, no idea of symbolic representation, and no domesticated animals. There is also an absence of aggression, violence, and disease; wounds heal surprisingly quickly, and their sight and hearing are particularly acute. They are said to have declined since European intrusion in the mid-19th century, but exhibit other such remarkable physical traits as a natural immunity to malaria, skin with sufficient elasticity to rule out post-childbirth stretch marks and the wrinkling we associate with ageing, and an 'unbelievable' strength of teeth: Cipriani (1966) reported seeing children of 10 to 15 years crush nails with them. He also testified to the Andamese practice of collecting honey with no protective clothing at all; "yet they are never stung, and watching them one felt in the presence of some age-old mystery, lost by the civilized world."

DeVries (1952) has cited a wide range of contrasts by which the superior health of gatherer-hunters can be established, including an absence of degenerative diseases and mental disabilities, and childbirth without difficulty or pain. He also points out that this begins to erode from the moment of contact with civilization.

Relatedly, there is a great deal of evidence not only for physical and emotional vigor among primitives but also concerning their heightened sensory abilities. Darwin described people at the southernmost tip of South America who went about almost naked in frigid conditions, while Peasley (1983) observed Aborigines who were renowned for their ability to live through bitterly cold desert nights "without any form of clothing." Lévi-Strauss (1979) was astounded to learn of a particular [South American] tribe which was able to "see the planet Venus in full daylight," a feat comparable to that of the North African Dogon who consider Sirius B the most important star; somehow aware, without instruments, of a star that can only be found with the most powerful of telescopes (Temple 1976). In this vein, Boyden (1970) recounted the Bushman ability to see four of the moons of Jupiter with the naked eye.

In *The Harmless People* (1959), Elizabeth Marshall Thomas told how one Bushman walked unerringly to a spot in a vast plain, "with no bush or tree to mark place," and pointed out a blade of grass with an almost invisible filament of vine around it. He had encountered it months before in the rainy season when it was green. Now, in parched weather, he dug there to expose a succulent root and quenched his thirst. Also in the Kalanari Desert, van der Post (1958) meditated upon San/Bushman communion with nature, a level of experience that "could almost be called mystical. For instance, they seemed to know what it actually felt like to be an elephant, a lion, an antelope, a steenbuck, a lizard, a striped mouse, mantis, baobab tree, yellow-crested cobra or starry-eyed amaryllis, to mention only a few of the brilliant multitudes through which they moved." It seems almost pedestrian to add that gatherer-hunters have often been remarked to possess tracking skills that virtually defy rational explanation (*e.g.* Lee 1979).

Rohrlich-Leavitt (1976) noted, "The data show that gatherer-hunters are generally nonterritorial and bilocal; reject group aggression and competition; share their resources freely; value egalitarianism and personal autonomy in the context of group cooperation; and are indulgent and loving with children."

Dozens of studies stress communal sharing and egalitarianism as perhaps the defining traits of such groups (Marshall 1976; Sahlins 1968; Pilbeam 1972; Damas 1972; Lafitau 1974; Tanaka 1976, 1980; Riches 1982; Mithen 1990). Lee (1982) referred to the "universality among foragers" of sharing, while Marshall's classic 1961 work spoke of the "ethic of generosity and humility" informing a "strongly egalitarian" gatherer-hunter orientation. Tanaka provides a typical example: "The most admired character trait is generosity, and the most despised and disliked are stinginess and selfishness."

Baer (1986) listed "egalitarianism, democracy, personalism, individuation, nurturance"' as key virtues of the non-civilized, and Lee (1988) cited "an absolute aversion to rank distinctions" among "simple foraging peoples around the world." Leacock and Lee (1982) specified that "any assumption of authority" within the group "leads to ridicule or anger among the !Kung, as has been recorded for the Mbuti (Turnbull 1962), the Hadza (Woodburn 1980) and the Montagnais-Naskapi (Thwaites 1906), among others."

"Not even the father of an extended family can tell his sons and daughters what to do. Most people appear to operate on their own internal schedules," reported Lee (1972) of the !Kung of Botswana. Ingold (1987) judged that "in most hunting and gathering societies, a supreme value is placed upon the principle of individual autonomy," similar to Wilson's finding (1988) of "an ethic of independence" that is "common to the focused open societies." The esteemed field anthropologist Radin (1953) went so far as to say: "Free scope is allowed for every conceivable kind of personality outlet or expression in primitive society. No moral judgment is passed on any aspect of human personality as such."

Turnbull (1976) looked on the structure of Mbuti social life as "an apparent vacuum, a lack of internal system that is almost anarchical." According to Duffy (1984), "the Mbuti are naturally acephalous—they do not have leaders or rulers, and decisions concerning the band are made by consensus." There is an enormous qualitative difference between foragers and farmers in this regard, as in so many others. For instance, agricultural Bantu tribes (*e.g.* the Saga) surround the San, and are organized by kingship, hierarchy, and work; the San exhibit egalitarianism, autonomy, and sharing. Domestication is the principle which accounts for this drastic distinction.

Domination within a society is not unrelated to domination of nature. In gatherer-hunter societies, on the other hand, no strict hierarchy exists between the human and the non-human species (Noske 1989), and relations among foragers are likewise non-hierarchical. The non-domesticated typically view the animals they hunt as equals; this essentially egalitarian relationship is ended by the advent of domestication.

When progressive estrangement from nature became outright social control (agriculture), more than just social attitudes changed. Descriptions by sailors and explorers who arrived in "newly discovered" regions tell how wild mammals and birds originally showed no fear at all of the human invaders. A few contemporary gatherers practiced no hunting before outside contact, but while the majority certainly do hunt, it is not normally an aggressive act. Turnbull (1965) observed Mbuti hunting as quite without any aggressive spirit, even carried out with a sort of regret. Hewitt (1986) reported a sympathy bond between hunter and hunted among the San Bushmen he encountered in the 19th century.

As regards violence among gatherer-hunters, Lee (1988) found that "the !Kung hate fighting, and think anybody who fought would be stupid." The Mbuti, by Duffy's account (1984), "look on any form of violence between one person and another with great abhorrence and distaste, and never represent it in their dancing or playacting." Homicide and suicide, concluded Bodley (1976), are both "decidedly uncommon" among undisturbed gatherer-hunters. The 'warlike' nature of Native American peoples was often fabricated to add legitimacy to European aims of conquest (Kroeber 1961); the foraging Comanche maintained their non-violent ways for centuries before the European invasion, becoming violent only upon contact with marauding civilization (Fried 1973).

The development of symbolic culture, which rapidly led to agriculture, is linked through ritual to alienated social life among extant foraging groups. Bloch (1977) found a correlation between levels of ritual and hierarchy. Put negatively, Woodburn (1968) could see the connection between an absence of ritual and the absence of specialized roles and hierarchy among the Hadza of Tanzania. Turner's study of the west African Ndembu (1957) revealed a profusion of ritual structures and ceremonies intended to redress the conflicts arising from the breakdown of an earlier, more seamless society. These ceremonies and structures function in a politically integrative way. Ritual is a repetitive activity for which outcomes and responses are essentially assured by social contact; it conveys the message that symbolic practice, via group membership and social rules, provides control (Cohen 1985). Ritual fosters the concept of control or domination, and has been seen to tend toward leadership roles and centralized political structures. A monopoly of ceremonial institutions clearly extends the concept of authority, and may itself be the original formal authority.

Among agricultural tribes of New Guinea, leadership and the inequality it implies are based upon participation in hierarchies of ritual initiation or upon shamanistic spirit-mediumship. In the role of shamans we see a concrete practice of ritual as it contributes to domination in human society.

Radin (1937) discussed "the same marked tendency" among Asian and North American tribal peoples for shamans or medicine men "to organize and develop the theory that they alone are in communication with the supernatural." This exclusive access seems to empower them at the expense of the rest: Lommel (1967) saw "an increase in the shaman's psychic potency . . . counterbalanced by a weakening of potency in other members of the group." This practice has fairly obvious implications for power relationships in other areas of life, and contrasts with earlier periods devoid of religious leadership.

The Batuque of Brazil are host to shamans who each claim control over certain spirits and attempt to sell supernatural services to clients, rather like priests of competing sects (S. Leacock 1988). Specialists of this type in "magically controlling nature . . . would naturally come to control men, too," in the opinion of Muller (1961). In fact, the shaman is often the most powerful individual in pre-agricultural societies; he is in a position to institute change. Johannessen (1987) offers the thesis that resistance to the innovation of planting was overcome by the influence of shamans, among the Indians of the American Southwest, for instance. Similarly, Marquardt (1985) has suggested that ritual authority structures have played an important role in the initiation and organization of production in North America. Another student of American groups (Ingold 1987) saw an important connection between shamans' role in mastering wildness in nature and an emerging subordination of women.

Berndt (1974) has discussed the importance among Aborigines of ritual sexual division of labor in the development of negative sex roles, while Randolph (1988) comes straight to the point: "Ritual activity is needed to create 'proper' men and women." There is "no reason in nature" for gender divisions, argues Bender (1989). "They have to be created by proscription and taboo, they have to be 'naturalized' through ideology and ritual."

But gatherer-hunter societies, by their very nature, deny ritual its potential to domesticate women. The structure (non-structure?) of egalitarian bands, even those most oriented toward hunting, includes a guarantee of autonomy to both sexes. This guarantee is the fact that the materials of subsistence are equally available to women and men and that, further, the success of the band is dependent on cooperation based on that autonomy (Leacock 1978; Friedl 1975). The spheres of the sexes are often somewhat separate, but inasmuch as the contribution of women is generally at least equal to that of men, social equality of the sexes is a key feature of forager societies (Ehrenberg 1989). Many anthropologists, in fact, have found the status of women in forager groups to be higher than in any other type of society (Leacock 1978).

In all major decisions, observed Turnbull (1970) of the Mbuti, "men and women have equal say, hunting and gathering being equally important." He made it clear (1981) that there is sexual differentiation—probably a good deal more than was the case with their distant forbears—"but without any sense of superordination or subordination." Men actually work more hours than women among the !Kung, according to Post and Taylor (1984).

It should be added, in terms of the division of labor common among contemporary gatherer-hunters, that this differentiation of roles is by no means universal. Nor was when the Roman historian Tacitus wrote, of the Fenni of the Baltic region, that "the women support themselves by hunting, exactly like the men . . . count their lot happier than that of others who groan over field labor." Or when Procopius found, in the 6th century A.D., that the Serithifinni of what is now Finland "neither till the land themselves, nor do their women work it for them, but the women regularly join the men in hunting."

The Tiwi women of Melville Island regularly hunt (Martin and Voorhies 1975) as do the Agta women in the Philippines (Estioko-Griffen and Griffen 1981). In Mbuti society, "there is little specialization according to sex. Even the hunt is a joint effort," reports Turnbull (1962), and Cotlow (1971) testifies that "among the traditional Eskimos it is (or was) a cooperative enterprise for the whole family group."

Darwin (1871) found another aspect of sexual equality: " . . . in utterly barbarous tribes the women have more power in choosing, rejecting, and tempting their lovers, or of afterwards changing their husbands, than might have been expected." The !Kung Bushmen and Mbuti exemplify this female autonomy, as reported by Thomas (1959; 1965). "Women apparently leave a man whenever they are unhappy with their marriage," concluded Begler (1978). Marshall (1970) also found that rape was extremely rare or absent among the !Kung.

An intriguing phenomenon concerning gatherer-hunter women is their ability to prevent pregnancy in the absence of any contraception (Silberbauer 1981). Many hypotheses have been put forth and debunked, e.g. conception somehow related to levels of body fat. What seems a very plausible explanation is based on the fact that undomesticated people are very much more in tune with their physical selves. Foraging women's senses and processes are not alienated from themselves or dulled; control over childbearing is probably less than mysterious to those whose bodies are not foreign objects to be acted upon.

The Pygmies of Zaire celebrate the first menstrual period of every girl with a great festival of gratitude and rejoicing (Turnbull 1962). The young woman feels pride and pleasure, and the entire band expresses its happiness. Among agricultural villagers, however, a menstruating woman is regarded as unclean and dangerous, to be quarantined by taboo (Duffy 1984). The relaxed, egalitarian relationship between San men and women, with its flexibility of roles and mutual respect, impressed Draper (1975); a relationship, she made clear, that endures as long as they remain gatherer-hunters and no longer.

Duffy (1984) found that each child in an Mbuti camp calls every man father and every woman mother. Forager children receive far more care, time, and attention than do those in civilization's isolated nuclear families. Post and Taylor (1984) described the "almost permanent contact" with their mothers and other adults that Bushman children enjoy. !Kung infants studied by Ainsworth (1967) showed marked precocity of early cognitive and motor skills development. This was attributed both to the exercise and stimulation produced by unrestricted freedom of movement, and to the high degree of physical warmth and closeness between !Kung parents and children (see also Konner 1976).

Draper (1976) could see that "competitiveness in games is almost entirely lacking among the !Kung," as Shostack (1976) observed "!Kung boys and girls playing together and sharing most games." She also found that children are not prevented from experimental sex play, consonant with the freedom of older Mbuti youth to "indulge in premarital sex with enthusiasm and delight" (Turnbull 1981). The Zuni "have no sense of sin," Ruth Benedict (1946) wrote in a related vein. "Chastity as a way of life is regarded with great disfavor . . . Pleasant relations between the sexes are merely one aspect of pleasant relations with human beings . . . Sex is an incident in a happy life."

Coontz and Henderson (1986) point to a growing body of evidence in support of the proposition that relations between the sexes are most egalitarian in the simplest foraging societies. Women play an essential role in traditional agriculture, but receive no corresponding status for their contribution, unlike the case of gatherer-hunter society (Whyte 1978). As with plants and animals, so are women subject to domestication with the coming of agriculture. Culture, securing its foundations with the new order, requires the firm subjugation of instinct, freedom, and sexuality. All dis-order must be banished, the elemental and spontaneous taken firmly in hand. Women's creativity and their very being as sexual persons are pressured to give way to the role, expressed in all peasant religions, of Great Mother, that is, fecund breeder of men and food.

The men of the South American Munduruc, a farming tribe, refer to plants and sex in the same phrase about subduing women: "We tame them with the banana" (Murphy and Murphy 1985). Simone de Beauvoir (1949) recognized in the equation of the plow and the phallus a symbol of male authority over women. Among the Amazonian Jivaro, another agricultural group, women are beasts of burden and the personal property of men (Harner 1972); the "abduction of adult women is a prominent part of much warfare" by these lowland South American tribes (Ferguson 1988). Brutalization and isolation of women seem to be functions of agricultural societies (Gregor 1988), and the female continues to perform most or even all of the work in such groups (Morgan 1985).

Head-hunting is practiced by the above-mentioned groups, as part of endemic warfare over coveted agricultural land (Lathrap 1970); head-hunting and near-constant warring are also witnessed among the farming tribes of Highlands New Guinea. Lenski and Lenski's 1974 researches concluded that warfare is rare among foragers but becomes extremely common with agrarian societies. As Wilson (1988) put it succinctly, "Revenge, feuds, rioting, warfare and battle seem to emerge among, and to be typical of, domesticated peoples."

Tribal conflicts, Godelier (1977) argues, are "explainable primarily by reference to colonial domination" and should not be seen as having an origin "in the functioning of precolonial structures." Certainly contact with civilization can have an unsettling, degenerative effect, but Godelier's Marxism (*viz.* unwillingness to question domestication/production), is, one suspects, relevant to such a judgment. Thus it could be said that the Copper Eskimos, who have a significant incidence of homicide within their group (Damas 1972), owe this violence to the impact of outside influences, but their reliance on domesticated dogs should also be noted.

Arens (1979) has asserted, paralleling Godelier to some extent, that cannibalism as a cultural phenomenon is a fiction, invented and promoted by agencies of outside conquest. But there is documentation of this practice (Tuzin 1976) among, once again, peoples involved in domestication. The studies by Hogg (1966), for example, reveal its presence among certain African tribes, steeped in ritual and grounded in agriculture. Cannibalism is generally a form of cultural control of chaos, in which the victim represents animality, or all that should be tamed (Sanday 1986). Significantly, one of the important myths of Fiji Islanders, "How the Fijians first became cannibals," is literally a tale of planting (Sahlins 1983). Similarly, the highly domesticated and time-conscious Aztecs practiced human sacrifice as a gesture to tame unruly forces and uphold the social equilibrium of a very alienated society. As Norbeck (1961) pointed out, non-domesticated, "culturally impoverished" societies are devoid of cannibalism and human sacrifice.

As for one of the basic underpinnings of violence in more complex societies, Barnes (1970) found that "reports in the ethnographic literature of territorial struggles" between gatherer-hunters are "extremely rare." !Kung boundaries are vague and undefended (Lee 1979); Pandaram territories overlap, and individuals go where they please; Hadza move freely from region to region (Woodburn 1968); boundaries and trespass have little or no meaning to the Mbuti (Turnbull 1966); and Australian Aborigines reject territorial or social demarcations. An ethic of generosity and hospitality takes the place of exclusivity (Hiatt 1968).

Gatherer-hunter peoples have developed "no conception of private property," in the estimation of Kitwood (1984). As noted above in reference to sharing, and with Sansom's (1980) characterization of Aborigines as "people without property," foragers do not share civilization's obsession with externals.

"Mine and thine, the seeds of all mischief, have no place with them," wrote Pietro (1511) of the native North Americans encountered on the second voyage of Columbus. The Bushmen have "no sense of possession," according to Post

(1958), and Lee (1972) saw them making "no sharp dichotomy between the resources of the natural environment and the social wealth." There is a line between nature and culture, again, and the non-civilized choose the former.

There are many gatherer-hunters who could carry all that they make use of in one hand, who die with pretty much what they had as they came into the world. Once humans shared everything; with agriculture, ownership becomes paramount and a species presumes to own the world. A deformation the imagination could scarcely equal.

Sahlins (1972) spoke of this eloquently: "The world's most primitive people have few possessions, but they are not poor. Poverty is not a certain small amount of goods, nor is it just a relation between means and ends; above all, it is a relation between people. Poverty is a social status. As such it is the invention of civilization."

The "common tendency" of gatherer-hunters "to reject farming until it was absolutely thrust upon them" (Bodley 1976) bespeaks a nature/culture divide also present in the Mbuti recognition that if one of them becomes a villager he is no longer an Mbuti (Turnbull 1976). They know that forager band and agriculturalist village are opposed societies with opposed values.

At times, however, the crucial factor of domestication can be lost sight of. "The historic foraging populations of the Western Coast of North America have long been considered anomalous among foragers," declared Cohen (1981); as Kelly (1991) also put it, "tribes of the Northwest Coast break all the stereotypes of hunter-gatherers." These foragers, whose main sustenance is fishing, have exhibited such alienated features as chiefs, hierarchy, warfare, and slavery. But almost always overlooked are their domesticated tobacco and domesticated dogs. Even this celebrated 'anomaly' contains features of domestication. Its practice, from ritual to production, with various accompanying forms of domination, seems to anchor and promote the facets of decline from an earlier state of grace.

Thomas (1981) provides another North American example, that of the Great Basin Shoshones and three of their component societies, the Kawich Mountain Shoshones, Reese River Shoshones, and Owens Valley Paiutes. The three groups showed distinctly different levels of agriculture, with increasing territoriality or ownership and hierarchy closely corresponding to higher degrees of domestication.

To 'define' a disalienated world would be impossible and even undesirable, but I think we can and should try to reveal the unworld of today and how it got this way. We have taken a monstrously wrong turn with symbolic culture and division of labor, from a place of enchantment, understanding, and wholeness to the absence we find at the heart of the doctrine of progress. Empty and emptying, the logic of domestication, with its demand to control everything, now shows us the ruin of the civilization that ruins the rest. Assuming the inferiority of nature enables the domination of cultural systems that soon will make the very earth uninhabitable.

Postmodernism says to us that a society without power relations can only be an abstraction (Foucault 1982). This is a lie unless we accept the death of nature and renounce what once was and what we can find again. Turnbull spoke of the intimacy between Mbuti people and the forest, dancing almost as if making love to the forest. In the bosom of a life of equals that is no abstraction, that struggles to endure, they were "dancing with the forest, dancing with the moon."

REFERENCES

The editor and the author have reconstructed for this publication the reference list to this chapter. However, because a number of sources are no longer available, the following reference list is unavoidably incomplete. Citations have nonetheless been retained for works originally referenced.

Ainsworth, Mary. 1967. *Infancy in Uganda Infant Care and the Growth of Love,* Baltimore: Johns Hopkins Press.

Allport, Gordon. 1983. "Language and Cognition" in *Approaches to Language,* ed., R. Harris, New York: Elsevier.

Ardrey, Robert. 1961. *African Genesis,* New York: Macmillan.

Ardrey, Robert. 1976. *The Hunting Hypothesis,* New York: Macmillan.

Arens, W. (1979). *Man Eating Myth: Anthropology and Anthropophagy,* New York: Oxford.

Baer. 1986. [Full reference not available]

Bailey, G.N. and P. Callow. Editors. 1986. *Stone Age Prehistory,* Cambridge: Cambridge University Press.

Barnes. 1970. [Full reference not available]

Beauvoir, Simone De. 1949. *Le Deuxieme Sexe.* Paris: Gallimard.

Begler, Elsie. 1978. "Sex, Status and Authority in Egalitarian Society," *American Anthropologist,* Vol. 80.

Benedict, Ruth. 1946. *Patterns of Culture,* New York: Houghton Mifflin.

Berndt, Ronald. 1974. *Australian Aboriginal Religions,* Leiden: Brill.

Binford, Lewis. 1968. *New Perspectives in Archaeology,* Chicago: Aldine.

Binford, Lewis. 1972. *An Archaeological Perspective,* New York: Seminar Press.

Binford, Lewis. 1984. *Faunal Remains from Klaises River Mouth,* New York: Academic Press.

Binford, Lewis. 1989. "Were There Elephant Hunters at Tooralba?" In Nittecki and Nittecki (Editors) *The Evolution of Hunting,* New York: Academic Press.

Bloch, M. 1977. "The Past and the Present" in *The Present Man,* Vol. 12.

Bodley, John. 1976. *Anthropology and Contemporary Human Problems,* Menlo Park, CA.

Boyden, S. V. Editor. 1970. *The Impact of Civilization on the Biology of Man,* Toronto: Toronto University Press.

Brown, Norman O. 1959. *Life Against Death*, New York: Wesleyan University Press.

Buikstra, Jane. 1976. *Hopewell in the Lower Illinois Valley*, Chicago: Center for American University Press.

Butzer, Karl. 1970. *Environment and Archaeology: An Ecological Approach to Prehistory*, New York: De Gruyter.

Canetti, E. 1978. *The Human Province*, New York: Seabury Press, translated by Joachim Neugroschel.

Ciochon, Olsen, Tames. 1990. [Full reference not available]

Cipriani, Lido. 1966. *The Andaman Islanders*, New York.

Clark, Grahame. 1979. [Full reference not available]

Clark, Grahame and Stuart Piggott. 1965. *Prehistoric Societies*, New York: Penguin Books.

Clark, Grahame. 1977. *World Prehistory in New Perspective*, Cambridge: Cambridge University Press.

Cohen, Mark. 1974. [Full reference not available]

Cohen, Mark. 1981. "Pacific Coast Foragers: Affluent or Overcrowded?" *Senri Ethnological Studies* 9: 275–295.

Cohen, Mark. 1985. "Prehistoric Hunter-Gatherers: The Meaning of Social Complexity," In *Prehistoric Hunter-Gatherers: The Emergence of Cultural Complexity*, T. Douglas Price and James A. Brown, editors. Orlando: Academic Press.

Cohen, Mark and G. Armelagos. Editors. 1984. *Paleopathology and the Origins of Agriculture*, New York: Academic Press.

Coontz, S. and Henderson, P. Editors. 1986. *Woman's Work, Men's Property: The Origins of Class and Gender*, London: Vesco Books.

Cotlow, Lewis. 1971. *Twilight of the Primitive*, New York: Macmillan.

Crader and Isaac. 1981. [Full reference not available]

Dahlberg, Frances. Editor. 1981. *Woman the Gatherer*, New Haven: Yale University Press.

Damas, David. 1972. "Central Eskimo System of Food Sharing" in *Ethnology II*, pp. 220–36.

Darwin, Charles. 1871. *The Descent of Man*, London.

Davies, Nigel. 1981. *Human Sacrifice in History and Today*, New York: Morrow and Company.

DeVries. 1952. *Primitive Man and His Food*, Chicago.

Delson, Eric. 1985. Editor. *Ancestors: The Hard Evidence*, New York: Wiley-Liss.

Diamond, Stanley. 1964. *Primitive Views of the World*, New York: Columbia University Press.

Donald, L. 1991. [Full reference not available]

Draper, P. 1975. "!Kung Women: Contrasts in Sexual Egalitarianism in Foraging and Sedentary Contexts," in *Toward and Anthropology of Women*, edited by R. Reiter, 7–109. New York: Monthly Review Press.

Draper, P. 1976. "Social and Economic Constraints on Child Life among the !Kung," in *Kalahari Hunter-Gatherers*, edited by Richard Lee and Irven Devore, 200–217. Cambridge, MA: Harvard U. Press.

Duffy, Kevin. 1984. [1996] *Children of the Forest: Africa's Mbuti Pygmies*, New York: Waveland Press.

Durant, John, ed. 1989. *Human Origins,* New York: Oxford.

Ehrenberg, Margaret. 1989. *Women in Prehistory,* Norman: University of Oklahoma Press.

Esioko-Griffen, Agnes and Griffen, P. Bion. 1981. "Women the Hunter," in *Woman the Gatherer,* ed. F. Dalhberg. New Haven.

Fagan, Brian. 1989. "The Science of Archaeology Comes of Age," *Archaeology,* Vol. 42.

Fagan, Brian. 1990. *The Journey from Eden,* London.

Farb, Peter and George Armelagos. 1980. Consuming Passions: *The Anthropology of Eating,* Boston: Houghton-Mifflin.

Ferguson, B. 1988. [Full reference not available]

Festinger, Leon. 1983. *The Human Legacy,* New York: Columbia University Press.

Flood, Josephine. 1983. *Archaeology of the Dreamtime: The Study of Prehistoric Australia and Its People,* New York: Angus Robertson.

Foley, Robert. 1989. [Full reference not available]

Foster, Mary LeCren. 1990. "Symbolic Origins and transitions in the Paleolithic," in *The Emergence of Modern Humans,* edited by Paul Mellars. Ithaca, NY.

Foucault, Michael. 1972. *The Archaeology of Knowledge,* Pantheon Books.

Fried, Morton. Editor. 1973. *Explorations in Anthropology,* New York: Thomas Y. Crowell.

Friedl, Ernestine. 1975. *Women and Men: An Anthropological View,* New York: Holt, Rinehart and Winston.

Frison. 1986. "Communal Hunting Strategies," in *The Evolution of Human Hunting,* eds., Nittecki and Nittecki. New York.

Gans, Eric. 1985. *The End of Culture: Toward a Generative Anthropology,* Berkeley: University of California Press.

Gebser, J. 1985. *The Ever Present Origin,* Athens, OH: Ohio University Press, translated by Noel Barsted with Algis Michunas.

Gero, Joan. 1991. "Genderlithics: Women's Role in Stone Tool Production," in *Engendering Archaeology: Women and Prehistory,* eds., Gero and Conkly. Oxford.

Gingerich. 1979. [Full reference not available]

Godelier, Maurice. 1977. *Perspectives in Marxist Anthropology,* New York: Cambridge University Press.

Goldschmidt, Walter. 1990. *The Human Career,* Cambridge: Blackwell.

Goodall. 1971. [Full reference not available]

Gowlett, John. 1984. *Ascent to Civilization: The Archaeology of Early Man,* New York: McGraw-Hill.

Gregor. 1988. [Full reference not available]

Hadingham, Evan. 1979. *Secrets of the Ice Age,* New York: Marboro.

Hadingham, Evan. 1982. *Secrets of the Ice Age: A Reappraisal of Prehistoric Man,* Walker and Company.

Hansen. 1976. [Full reference not available]

Harner, Michael. 1972. *The Jivaro, People of the Sacred Waterfalls,* Berkeley: University of California Press.

Harris, Marvin. 1989. *Our Kind,* New York: HarperCollins.

Harris, Marvin and Eric Ross. 1981. *Food and Evolution,* Philadelphia: Temple University Press.

Hewitt. 1986. [Full reference not available]

Hiatt, L.R. 1968. [Full reference not available]

Hogg, Gary. 1966. *Cannibalism and Human Sacrifice*, New York.

Hole and Flannery. 1963. [Full reference not available]

Holloway, Ralph. 1972. "Australopithicene" Endocasts . . ." in *Primitive Functional Morphology and Evolution*, ed., by R. W. Tuttle. The Hague.

Holloway, Ralph. 1974. *Primate Aggression Territoriality and Xenophobia: A Comparative Perspective*, New York: Academic Press.

Holloway, Ralph. 1985. "The Poor Brian of Homo Sapiens Neanderthalensis . . ." in *The Emergence of Modern Humans*, ed., Paul Mellons. Ithaca, NY.

Horkheimer, M. and T. Adorno. 1972. *Dialectic of Enlightenment*, translated by John Cumming. New York: Continuum.

Ingold, Tim, David Riches and James Woodburn. Editors. 1988. *Hunters and Gathers: History, Evolution and Social change*. Oxford.

Ingold, Tim. 1987. *The Appropriation of Nature: Essays on Human Ecology and Social Relations*, Iowa City: University of Iowa Press.

Isaac, Glynn. 1989. *The Archeology of Human Origins*, Cambridge: Cambridge University Press.

Isaac. 1986. [Full reference not available]

Jelinek, Arthur. 1980. "European Homo Erectus and the Origin of Homo Sapiens," in *Current Argument on Early Man*, edited by L. K. Konigsson. Oxford.

Jelinek. 1978. [Full reference not available]

Jochim, Michael. 1983. "Paleolithic Cave Art in Ecological Perspective," in, edited by Geoff Bailey *Hunter-Gatherer Economy in Prehistory: A European Perspective*, New York: Cambridge University Press.

Johannessen, Sissel. 1987. [Full reference not available]

Johanson, Donald and M.A. Edey. 1981. *Lucy, the Beginnings of Humankind*, New York: Simon and Schuster.

Johanson, Donald and James Shreeve. 1990. *Lucy's Child: The Discovery of a Human Ancestor*, Avon Books.

Keely, L.H. and Toth. 1981. [Full reference not available]

Kelly, Robert. 1991. "Sedentism, Sociopolitical Inequality, and Resource Fluctuations" in *Between Bands and States*, edited by S. Gregg. Carbondale, IL.

Kitwood, Tom. 1984. *Technology, Development and Domination*, Manchester, NJ.

Klein. 1989. [Full reference not available]

Konner. 1976. [Full reference not available]

Kraus, Gerhard. 1990. *Human Origins and Development from and African Ancestry*, London.

Kroeber, Therodora. 1961. *Ishi in Two Worlds: A Biography of the Last Wild Indian in North America*, Berkeley, CA: University of California Press.

LaBarre, Weston. 1972. *Ghost Dance Origins of Religion*, London: Allen and Unwin.

Lafitau, Joseph. 1974. *Customs of the American Indian Compared with the Customs of Primitive Times*, Toronto: Champlain Society.

Larsen, Stephen. 1982. *The Shaman's Doorway: Opening Imaginations to Power and Myth*, Barrytown, NY: Station Hill Press.

Lathrap, Donald Ward. 1970. *The Upper Amazon*, London: Thames and Hudson.

Leacock, Eleanor. 1978. "Women's Status in Egalitarian Society," *Current Anthropology*, Vol. 19.

Leacock, Eleanor and Richard B. Lee. Editors. 1982. *Politics and History in Band Societies*, Cambridge.

Leacock, S. 1988. [Full reference not available]

Leakey, Richard and M. G. Leakey. 1978. *The Fossil Huminids and an Introduction to Their Context 1968–74*, New York: Clarendon.

Lee, Richard. 1968. "What do Hunters do for a Living; or, How to Make out on Scarce Resources," in *Man the Hunter*, R. Lee and I. DeVore (editors) 30–48. Chicago: Aldine.

Lee, Richard. 1972. "Work Effort, Group Structure, and Land Use in Contemporary Hunter-Gatherers," in *Man, Settlement and Urbanism*, P. Ucko, R. Tringham and G. Dimbleby (editors) 177–85. London: Duckworth.

Lee, Richard B. (1976). *Kalahari Hunter-Gathers: Studies of the !Kung San*, Cambridge: Harvard University Press.

Lee, Richard. 1979. *The !Kung San: Men, Women and Work in a Foraging Society*, Cambridge: Cambridge University Press.

Lee, Richard. 1982. "Politics, Sexual and Non-Sexual, in an Egalitarian Society," in *Politics and History in Band Societies*, Eleanor Leacock and Richard Lee (editors) 37–59. Cambridge: Cambridge University Press.

Lee, Richard. 1985. [Full reference not available]

Lee, Richard and Irven DeVore. 1968. *Man the Hunter*, Chicago: Aldine.

Lenski, Jean and Garhard Lenski. 1974. *Human Societies: An Introduction to Macrosociology*, New York: McGraw-Hill.

Leonard, George. 1972. *The Transformation*, New York.

Lévi-Strauss, Claude. 1955. *Tristes Tropiques*, Paris: Plon.

Lévi-Strauss, Claude. 1969. *The Raw and the Cooked*, New York: Harper and Row, translated by J. and D. Weightman.

Lévi-Strauss, Claude. 1979. *Myth and Meaning*, New York: Schocken Books.

Lommel, Andreas. 1967. *The World of the Hearly Hunters*, London: Evelyn, Adams and Mackay.

Marquardt. 1985. [Full reference not available]

Marshall, Lorna. 1961. [Full reference not available]

Marshall, Lorna. 1970. [Full reference not available]

Marshall, Lorna. 1976. *The !Kung of Nyae Nyae*, Cambridge, MA.

Martin, M. Kay and Barbara Voorhies. 1975. *Female of the Species*, New York.

Mithen, Stephen J. 1990. *Thoughtful Foragers: A Study of Prehistoric Decision Making*, New York: Cambridge University Press.

Morgan, Elaine. 1985. *The Descent of Woman*, London.

Muller. 1961. [Full reference not available]

Mumford, Lewis. 1972. *The Ecological Basis of Planning*, New York.

Murphy, Yolanda and Robert Murphy. 1985. *Women of the Forest* (2nd ed.), New York: Columbia University Press.

Norbeck, Edward. 1961. *Religion in Primitive Society*, New York: Harper.

Noske, Barbara. 1989. *Humans and Other Cannibals*, London: Pluto Press.

Peasley. 1983. [Full reference not available]

Pietro. 1511. [Full reference not available]

Pfeiffer, John. 1969. *The Emergence of Man,* New York: McGraw-Hill.

Pfeiffer, John. 1977. *The Emergence of Society: A Pre-History of the Establishment,* New York: McGraw-Hill.

Pfeiffer, John. 1982. *The Creative Explosion,* New York: Harper and Row.

Pilbeam, David. 1972. *The Ascent of Man: An Introduction to Human Evolution,* New York: Macmillan.

Poirier, Frank. 1987. *Understanding Human Evolution,* Englewood Cliffs, NJ: Prentice-Hall.

Post, Laurens van der. 1958. *The Lost World of the Kalahari,* New York: Harcourt-Brace.

Post, Laurens van der and Jane Taylor. 1984. *Testament to Bushmen,* New York.

Radin, Paul. 1937. *Primitive Religion,* New York: Dover Publications.

Radin, Paul. 1953. *The World of Primitive Man,* New York: H. Schuman.

Randolph. 1988. [Full reference not available]

Riches, David. 1982. *Northern Nomadic Hunters-Gatherer: A Humanistic Approach,* New York: Academic Press.

Rightmire, Philip. 1990. *The Evolution of Homo Erectus,* New York: Cambridge University Press.

Rolland, Nicholas. 1990. "Middle Paleolithic Socio-Economic Formations," in *The Emergence of Modern Humans,* ed. by Paul Mellars. Ithaca, NY.

Sagan, Eli. 1985. *At the Dawn of Tryanny,* New York.

Sahlins, Marshall. 1968. "Notes on the Original Affluent Society," in *Man the Hunter,* Richard Lee and Irven DeVore (editors). Chicago: Aldine.

Sahlins, Marshall. 1972. *Stone Age Economics,* Chicago: Aldine.

Sahlins, Marshall. 1983. "Raw Women, Cooked Men, and Other 'Great Things' of the Fugi Islands," in *The Ethnography of Cannibalism,* eds., Brown and Tuzin. Washington.

Sanday, Peggy Reeves. 1986. *Divine Hunger: Cannibalism as a Cultural System,* New York: Cambridge University Press.

Sansom, Basil. 1980. *The Camp at Wallaby Cross,* Canberra: Australian Institute of Aboriginal Studies.

Shanks and Tilley. 1987. [Full reference not available]

Shostack. 1976. [Full reference not available]

Silberbauer, George. 1981. *Hunter and Habitat in the Central Kalahari Desert,* New York: Cambridge University Press.

Spengler, O. 1932. *The Decline of the West,* New York: Knopf.

Straus, Lawrence Guy. 1986. "Hunting in the Upper Paleolithic," in *The Evolution of Human Hunting,* eds., Nittecki. New York.

Straus, Lawrence. 1990. "The Early Paleolithic in Southwest Europe," in *The Emergence of Modern Humans,* Paul Mellons (editor). Ithaca New York: Cornell.

Tanaka, Yasua. 1976. *The San: Hunter-Gatherers of the Kalahari,* Tokyo: Tokyo University Press.

Tanaka, Yasua. 1980. *Somehow Crystal.*

Tanner, Nancy. 1981. *On Becoming Human,* Cambridge.

Tanner and Zihlman. 1976. "Women in Evolution," *Signs,* Vol. 1.

Temple 1976. [Full reference not available]

Thomas, Elizabeth Marshall. 1950. *The Harmless People.*

Thomas. 1965. [Full reference not available]

Thomas. 1968. [Full reference not available]

Thomas. 1981. [Full reference not available]

Thwaites. 1906. [Full reference not available]

Tobias. 1982. [Full reference not available]

Trinkhaus, Erik. 1986. "The Neanderthal and Modern Human Origins," in *The Emergency of Modern Humans,* ed., Paul Mellans. Ithaca, NY.

Turnbull, Colin. 1962. *The Lonely African,* New York: Simon and Schuster.

Turnbull, Colin. 1965. *The Mbuti Pygmies,* New York.

Turnbull, Colin. 1970. *Tradition and Change in African Tribal Life,* Cleveland.

Turnbull, Colin. 1976. *Man in Africa,* New York: Doubleday.

Turnbull, Colin. 1981. "Mbuti Womenhood," in *Women the Gatherer,* Francis Dahlberg (editor). New Haven: Yale University Press.

Turner. 1957. [Full reference not available]

Tuzin, Donald F. 1976. *The Llahita Arapesh: Dimensions of Unity,* Berkeley: University of California Press.

Walker. 1984. [Full reference not available]

Wenke, Robert. 1984. *Patterns in Prehistory,* New York.

White, Leslie. 1959. *The Evolution of Culture,* New York: McGraw-Hill Book Co.

Whyte, Martin King. 1978. *The Status of Women in Preindustrial Societies,* Princeton.

Wilson, Peter J. 1988. *The Domestication of the Human Species,* New Haven.

Woodburn, James. 1968. "An Introduction to Hadza Ecology," in Lee and DeVore's *Man the Hunter,* pp. 49–55. Chicago.

Woodburn, James. 1980. "Hunter Gatherers Today and Reconstruction of the Past," in *Soviet and Western Anthropology,* edited by A. Gellner, 95–117. London: Duckworth.

Wymer, John. 1981. *The Paleolithic Age,* New York: St. Martin's Press.

Wymer. 1989. [Full reference not available]

Wynn, Thomas. 1989. *The Evolution of Spatial Competence,* University of Illinois Press.

Yellen, J. and Lee. 1976. "The Dobe-Duda Environment" in *Kalahari Hunger-Gatherers,* eds., Lee and DeVore. Cambridge, MA.

Zerzan, John. 1988. *Elements of Refusal,* Seattle: Left Bank Books.

Zihlman, Adrienne. 1981. "Women As Shapers of the Human Adaptation," in *Women the Gatherer,* ed., F. Dahlberg. New Haven, CT.

A Post-Historic Primitivism

◆

Paul Shepard

1. The Problem of the Relevance of the Past

History as a Different Consciousness

H. J. Muller's classic *The Uses of the Past: Profiles of Former Societies* presented us with a paradox: "Our age is notorious for its want of piety or sense of the past. . . . Our age is nevertheless more historically minded than any previous age."[1]

Two decades later, with the publication of Herbert Schneidau's *Sacred Discontent*, the paradox vanished in a radical new insight.[2] For Schneidau History was not simply a chronicle, nor even an "interpretation," but a new way of perceiving reality, one that set out to oppose and destroy the vision which preceded it. It does not refer to readers' understanding but to a cognitive style.

History, he said, is the view of the world from the outside. It was "invented" by early Hebrews who took their own alienation as the touchstone of humankind. Especially did they conceive themselves as outside the earth-centered belief systems of the great valley civilizations of their time. Central to those beliefs was cyclic return and its paradigmatic and exemplary stories linking past, present, and future with eternal structure. Schneidau calls this the "mythic" way of life. Alternatively, the view created by the Hebrews and later polished by the Greeks and Christians was that time may produce analogies but not a true embeddedness. All important events resulted from the thoughts and actions of a living, distant, unknowable God. There could never be a return. The only thing of which we could be sure is that God would punish those deluded enough to believe in the powers of the mythic earth or who fell away from the worship of himself.

A perspective on Schneidau's concept of pre-history can be gained from recent studies of a style of consciousness among living, non-historical peoples. Dorothy Lee, describing the Trobriand Islanders, refers to the "non-linear codification of reality"; space which is not defined by lines connecting points: a world without tenses or causality in language, where change is not a becoming but a new are-ness; a journey, not a passage through but a revised at-ness. Walter Ong calls it "an event world, signified by sound," a world composed of interiors rather than surfaces, where events are embedded instead of reading like the lines of a book. Of Eskimos, Bogert O'Brien says, "The Inuit does not depend on objects for orientation. One's position in space is fundamentally relational and based upon activity. The clues are not objects of analysis. . . . The relational manner of orienting is a profoundly different way of interpreting space. First, all of the environment is perceived subjectively as dynamic, experiencing processes. . . . Secondly, the hunter moves as a participant amidst other participants oriented by the action."[3]

For the Hebrews who invented History, the record of the linear sequence of ever-new events would be the Old Testament. By the time we get to Herbert Muller that record has the density of civilized millennia, and could be projected back upon the whole 5,000 years of written words and such records as archaeology offers.

Muller's paradox, of our obsession with and obliviousness toward history, vanishes because we can begin to understand that the passion is an anxiety with our circumstances and our identity, which only grow thicker, like layers of limestone, as we burrow into that vast accumulation. The hidden truth of history is that the more we know the stranger it all becomes. It is human to want to know ourselves from the past, but History's perspective narrows that identity to portraits, ideology, and abstractions to which nation states committed human purpose. True ancestors are absent. Our search simply sharpens desire.

The meaning for our lives, of nature, of purposeful animals, of simple societies, of everything in this "past," is in doubt. We do not feel our ancestors looking over our shoulders or their lives pressing on our own. The past is the temporal form of a distant place. Our view is that you cannot be in two places or two times at once. I speak of this as a "view" in the sense of Ong's observation that the modern West is hypervisual, and my own conviction that what it considers a "view" is a perceptual habit. From this viewpoint we can see mere "oral tradition" as a nadir from which it was impossible to know that water in time's river runs its course but once and that you can no more recover the primordial sense of earth-linked at-homeness than a waterfall can run backward. And further, once we have shaken off that mythic immersion, and put on the garment of dry History, we are unable to shed the detachment and skepticism that define the Western personality, embodied in the written "dialogues" which Robert Hutchins defined as the central feature of the Western civilization.[4]

History not only envisioned, it created sense of the moment. Its content is sometimes delectable, sometimes horrible, but always irretrievable except as beads on the string from which we now dangle. It deals with an arc of time and of measured location; its creative principle being external rather than intrinsic to the world; deity as distant, unknowable and arbitrary. Central to History is a subjectivity which also distances us from our ancestors.

The legacy of History with respect to primitive peoples is threefold: (1) primitive life is devoid of admirable qualities, (2) our circumstances render them inappropriate even if admirable, and (3) the matter is moot, as "You cannot go back."

"You can't go back" shelters a number of corollaries. Most of these are physical rationalizations—too many people in the world, too much commitment to technology or its social and economic systems, ethical and moral ideas that make up civilized sensibilities, and the unwillingness of people to surrender to a less interesting, cruder, or more toilsome life, from which time and progress delivered us. This progress is the work of technology. When technology's "side effects" are bad, progress becomes simply "change," which is, by the same rote, "inevitable." Progress is a visible extension of the precognitive habit of History that influences concept and explanation by modulating understanding. It was not only the mathematicians, astronomers, and philosophers of the modern era who gave us the theoretical basis of progress.

All of these objections—and they seem insurmountable—seem to me to imply a deeper mind-set which does not have to do with the content of history. It is more a reflex than a concept. We care little for its theories or inventions since the time of Francis Bacon or for the moods in Christendom which reversed the older view that things only get worse.

Its true genesis lies in the work of Hebrew and Greek demythologizers. They created a reality focused outside the self, one that could be manipulated the way god-the-potter fingered the world. In rooting out the inner-directed, cyclic cosmos of gentiles and naive barbarians, they destroyed the spiraled form of myth with its rituals of eternal return, its mimetic means of transmitting values and ideas, its role in providing exemplary models, its central metaphor of nature and culture, and most of all as a way of comprehending the past. It began the deconstruction of the empirical wisdom of earlier peoples, and culminated in the monumental Western view of reality whose central theme was the outwardness of nature.

Along with pictorial space and Euclidean time goes the phonetic alphabet as inadvertent "causes" of estrangement.[5] But these are not simply inventions of the post-medieval West. They are markers in the way the world is experienced. Their antecedents occur in the Bronze Age Mediterranean where much of what we call "Western" has its roots.

Elsewhere I have tried to describe this history as a crazy idea, fostered not as a concept so much as the socially sanctioned mutilation of childhood, the training ground of perception, by the blocking of what Erik Erikson called "epigenesis."[6] But, whatever its dynamic, History alters not our interest in the past (witness Muller's observation that we moderns seem more interested than ever), but the work of attention itself, the deep current of precomprehension that runs silently beneath our spoken thoughts.

History and Ambiguity

If we attempt to recover the difficult and "distant" art of tool-flaking we may do so over the objections of modern rationality that denies that the pterodactyl can fly since no one has seen it do so. That is, you cannot know the ancient technique. Not only does History define it as beyond access, but incomprehensible. History thinks its own process is an evolution separating us by our very nature from our past—medieval, Neanderthal or primate.

Central to History is the notion of a fixed essence, an inner state that persists in spite of the contradictions of appearance, that our visible form not only fails to inform but can be made to deceive. Shifting appearance is dangerous, larval forms signify evil. The question of our primate or Neanderthal past cannot be addressed except as alternatives to our present identity. We are predisposed by the immense cultural momentum of History to dismiss such ambiguous assertions as one of a larger class of moot points in which categorical contradiction, the simultaneous reality of two opposing truths about ourselves, is denied.

Equally paradoxical is the matter of being in two times at once, even though our senses tell us that we are not today what we were yesterday. This movement from one state or one thing to another is not so much a problem for human consciousness as for meaning. The liminal or boundary area of categories heightens cognitive intensity. In the historical world, such transformations have been handled by accepting reality as made up of fixed identities, oppositions, and beyond them, transcendent meaning, declaring one of the appearances to be illusory, or by seeing them as good and evil. In all cases except the last the surface or apparent contradiction is cast into doubt in favor of some deeper, hidden, more real reality. Mostly this problem has been met in the West by denying appearance—especially when it shifts or is a larval state—as the true identity and instead postulating essences and spirits within or seeking principles and abstractions as the enduring, unchanging reality, despite outward shape.

In non-Western, non-industrial, and largely non-literate (hence non-historical) societies, external form is dealt with quite differently. Edmund Carpenter cites our difficulty with the visual duck/rabbit pun as our loss of the "multiplicity of thought," a collapse of metaphor in a mind-set related to phonetic writing.[7] A. David Napier has traced the matter in elegant detail in connection with the ritual use of masks as the perceptual means of assenting to a universal principle of shape-shifting. Coupled with dance, this is humankind's central means of reconciliation with a world of changes.[8] The many shapes in such masked dances testify also to a world in which abstractions are given lively form. Ahistorical peoples usually live in worlds where power is plural, as in egalitarian small societies in which leadership is not monopolized but changing and dispersed. The concrete or given model for this discontinuity of emphatic and exemplary qualities is the range of natural species. To varying degrees the animals and plants are regarded as centers, metaphors, and mentors of the different traits, skills, and roles of people. In polytheistic worlds there is no omniscience and no single hierarchy, although there may be said to loom a single creative principle behind it all. Insofar as they model diversity and the polytheistic cosmos, the animals provide metaphors of forms and movements that can be brought ceremonially into human presence, as interlocutors of change. Their heads as masks, the animals in such rites become combinational figures created to give palpable expression to transitional states. The animal mask on the body of a person joins in thought that which is otherwise separate, not only representing human change but conceptualizing shared qualities, so that unity in difference and difference in unity can be conceived as an intrinsic truth. And some animals, by their form or habit, are boundary creatures who signify the passages of human life. Finally, in dance these bodies move to deep rhythms that bind the world and bring the humans into mimetic participation with other beings.

The sophisticated Greeks after the time of Pericles ridiculed these predications, and the Jews and Christians rejected them. The thinness of music and dance in temples, churches, and mosques indicates the minimalizing of what was and is basic to hundreds of different, indigenous religions marked by "mythic" imagination.

The nature of the primitive world is at the center of our dilemma about essence, appearance, and change. Since we are not now what we once were—we are not bacteria or quadruped mammals, or apish hominids, or primitive people living without domesticated plants and animals—the dichotomy is clear enough. We each know as adults that we are no longer a child, yet we are not so sure that our being doesn't still embrace that other self who we were. We are attached to that primitive way of understanding, of double being, in spite of our modern perspective. Depth psychology has led us to understand that this going back is going into ourselves, into what, from the civilized historical view, is a "heart of darkness." Clearly a threat of the loss of self-identity is implied, swallowed by a second nature which is hidden and unpredictable.

As born anti-historians, our secret desire is to explicate the inexplicable, to recover that which is said to be denied. It is a yearning, a nostalgia in the bone, an intuition of the self as other selves, perhaps other animals, a shadow of something significant that haunts us, a need for exemplary events as they occur in myth rather than History. If not a necessity, it is a hunger that can be suppressed and distanced. The experience of that past is in terms of something still lived with, like fire, that still draws us. We cannot explain it, but it is there, made fragile in our psyche and hearts, drowned perhaps in our logic, but unquenchable.

It has been said that those who do not learn from history are doomed to repeat it, and yet by definition it cannot be repeated. Presumably such repetition means analogy. One does not really "go back," but merely discovers similar patterns. To ask the question in the perspective of pre-history: what are we to learn from history? The answer: history rejects the ambiguities of overlapping identity, space and time, and creates its own dilemmas of discontent and alienation from Others, from non-human life, primitive ancestors, and tribal peoples. Failing to enact pre-history, we can live only in history, caught between captivity and escape, afflicted with Henry Thoreau's "life of quiet desperation," now called neurosis. Since history began, most people most of the time have lived under tyrants and demagogues (Mr. Progress, Mr. Collectivity, Mr. Centralized Power, Mr. Growthmania, and Mr. Technophilia). No empire lasts, and when states collapse their subjects are enslaved by other states.

The crucial question of the modern world is, "How are we to become native to this land?" It is a question that history cannot answer, for history is the de-nativizing process. In history "going native" is a madman's costume ball, a child's romp in the attic, a misanthrope's escape.

Unlike History, pre-history does not participate in the dichotomy that divides experience into inherited and acquired. Nor does it imply that our behavior is instinctive rather than learned. It refers us to mythos, the exemplifications of the past-in-the-present. Ancestors are the dreamtime ones, and their world is the ground of our being. They are with us still.

The real lesson of history is that it is no guide. By its own definition, History is a declaration of independence from the deep past and its peoples, living and dead, the natural state of being which is outside its own domain. Indeed, History corrupts the imperatives of pre-history. What are the imperatives? What are we to learn from pre-history? Perhaps as Edith Cobb said of childhood, "The purpose is to discover a world the way the world was made."[9]

2. Savagery—Once More

After 2,500 years of yearning for lost garden paradises in Western mythology perhaps one of the most outrageous ideas of the 20th century was the advocacy of a hunting/gathering model of human life. Much of the world is still caught up in making a transition from an agrarian civilization. A writer for *Horizon* proclaims that "An epoch that started ten thousand years ago is ending. We are involved in a revolution of society that is as complete and as profound as the one that changed man from hunter and food gatherer to settled farmer."[10] He alerts us to the colossal struggle to go forward from the tottering institutions of agricultural life, and I am suggesting that we do move ahead to—of all things—hunting/gathering!

Among the problems that plague the "uses of the past," as H. J. Muller called it, the search for a lost paradise seems to resist the "facts" of history. One wonders whether it is even possible to write about the deep past without nostalgia, or without creating a world that never existed. Its images are a mix of dreams and visions, infantile mnemonics, ethnographic misinformation, and attempts to locate mythological events in geographical space and recorded history. History, indeed, is not exactly anti-myth, dealing as it does with "origins" and recitations of the significant events of the past. But its "past" is radically different from the one shaping human evolution.

It was great fun working on a book on hunter-gatherer people in the early 1970s because almost everything that the layman generally thought to be true of them was wrong. In writing *The Tender Carnivore*[11] I tried to avoid the snare of idealism by disarming my critics in advance. I avoided the beatifying language of Noble Savagery and I engaged Fons von Woerkom to draw chapter headings, as his art was anything but romantic. Even so, the incredulity with which it was greeted was puzzling. Looking back, I now see that the objection was not only that primitive life was inferior and irrelevant, but in the lens of historical memory, inaccessible.

For two centuries the ideology of inevitable change had set its values in contrast to fictional images of the lost innocence of deprived and depraved savage. Forty years ago George Boas traced the history of that idea of the primitive over the last 2,000 years, from early attempts to associate tribal peoples with Biblical paradise, various views of perfection, and the saga of evolving mankind.[12] For the Greeks anyone who lacked civil life in a polis and spoke incoherently (babbled) was a barbarian. Hostility to the idea that we have anything to learn from savages has as long a tradition as the dream itself. Skepticism about the full humanity of the Hyperboreans and Scythians among some Classical authors was opposed by the idealizing of the Celts, the Getae, and the Druids by Herodotus and Strabo.

The Christians got their ideas on prehistory from Plato's Laws via the Romans, which portrayed the pagans as childlike. Spanish endeavors to associate American Indians with European *sylvestres homines*, the wild man, and the legacy of the Greek *barbori* have been reviewed by Anthony Pagdon. He makes some distinctions between Franciscan and Jesuit perception of the Indians, the Franciscans determined to destroy Indian culture in order to Christianize and the Jesuits ignoring the "secular" side of the culture as irrelevant—an ironic twist on holism.[13] Oddly enough, it was the "unnaturalness" of the native peoples rather than their "naturalness" that justified decimation. Natural men, for example, did not eat each other.

In neo-Classical times Dr. Johnson observed that the hope of knowing anything about the people of the past was "idle conjecture." Horace Walpole derided antiquarians' fantasies. Locke and Hume gave us images of slavering brutes as an alternative to Rousseau's fictions of innocence and integrity. Admiral Cook's Polynesia would not look benign after the untamed sons of Adam did him in on the beach at Oahu. The images were part of the heritage of the Roman idea of barbarians, the Christian notion of pagans, and 18th century political philosophy of the benighted savage. Von Herder, Hegel, Compte, and Adelung all strove to disassociate mankind from the "laws of nature," to identify culture with History, to see conscious intellect identified with urban life, property, law, government, and "great art," as the final flowers in the human odyssey. The tradition continues. As M. Navarro said as late as 1924 of the South American Campa, "Degraded and ignorant beings, they lead a life exotic, purely animal, savage, in which are eclipsed the faint glimmerings of their reason, in which are drowned the weak pangs of their conscience, and all the instincts and lusts of animal existence alone float and are reflected. . . ."[14] Or, closer to home, is the testimony of Will Durant, the historian: "Through 97 per cent of history, man lived by hunting and nomadic pasturage. During those 975,000 years his basic character was formed—to greedy acquisitiveness, violent pugnacity and lawless sexuality."[15] Quite apart from anthropology this conglomerate idea of the primitive remains the central dogma of civilization held by modern humanists.

By the end of the 19th century there emerged in the United States a substantial body of admiration for Indian ways. I remember as a boy in the 1930s meeting Ernest Thompson Seton in Santa Fe. He ran a summer camp in which boys came to his ranch to be tutored by local Navajos, bunked in tepees, and lived out the handcraft and nature study ventures of *Two Little Savages*.[16] The image of the American Indians in this dialectic has been reviewed by Calvin Martin, who observes that by the late 1960s the image of the "ecological Indian" was being articulated by Indians themselves, notably Scott Momaday and Vine Deloria. Arrayed against them in postures of "iconoclastic scorn" are experts who pursued an old line in anthropological guise—debunkers of the image of the Noble Savage, which they said merely masked a knave who was not nature's friend but who typically over-killed the game at every opportunity.[17]

Oddly enough, science did not rapidly resolve what seemed to be a question of facts. Geology after Lyell, evolution after Darwin, and archaeological time after Libby's atomic dating complicated but did not settle much. With a slight twist evolution could be the handmaiden of Progress. "It began to look," says Glyn Daniel, "as if prehistoric archaeology was confirming the philosophical and sociological speculations of the mid-nineteenth century scholars."[18] Anthropology idealized value-free science and cultural relativism, thwarting European chauvinism but throwing out the baby with the bath water.

I was, of course, not the first to try to formulate the meaning of hunting-gathering for our own time. But not all efforts to clarify the description of hunters were applied to ourselves. Knowledgeable writers tiptoed among the ferocious critics, pretending that hunting signified only a remote past, as in Robert Ardrey's *Hunting Hypothesis*[19] or John Pfeiffer's *The Emergence of Man*.[20] Nigel Calder's *Eden Was No Garden*[21] and Gordon Rattray Taylor's *Rethink*[22] stirred the pot, but could hardly be said to have influenced, say, the civilized dogma of the modern university. Scholarly silence greeted the English translation of Ortega y Gasset's *Meditations on Hunting*[23] as though an imposter had inserted an aberration in his works.

The message is clear: Advocacy of a way of life that is both repulsive and no longer within reach seems futile. Time is an unreturning arrow. The hunting idea is a barbaric atavism, unwelcome at a time when aggression and violence seem epidemic. The idea is obviously economically impractical for billions of people and incongruent with the growing concern for the rights of animals. Animal protectionists and many feminists seem generally to feel that hunting is simply a final grab at symbolic virility by insensitive, city-bred male chauvinists, or one more convulsion of a tattered and misplaced nostalgia. Less and less, however, is hunting condemned as the brutal expression of tribal subhumans, for that would conflict with modern ethnic liberation.

The idea of inherent "nobility" of the individual savage was laughed out of school a century ago, properly so. Hunter-gatherers are not always pacific (though they do not keep standing armies or make organized war), nor innocent of ordinary human vices and violence. There is small-scale cruelty, infanticide, inability or unwillingness to end intratribal scuffling or intertribal vengeance. From the time of Vasco da Gama Westerners have been fascinated by indigenous punishment for crimes and by cannibalism (although cannibalism is primarily a trait of agri-cultures). Hunter-gatherers may not always live in perfect harmony with nature or each other, being subject to human shortcomings. Nor are they always happy, content, well-fed, free of disease, or profoundly philosophical. Like people everywhere they are, in some sense, incompetent. In "Little Big Man" the Indian actor Dan George did an unforgettable satire on the wise old chief who, delivering his rhetoric of joining the Great Spirit, lies down on the mountain to die and gets only rain in the face for his trouble. Given a century of this kind of scientific dis-illusioning, what is left?

It has been uphill and downhill for the anthropologists all along. The 19th century "humanist anthropologists" like Edward Tylor and Malinowski dismissed native religious rites as logical error, although they allowed that ritual may work symbolically. As to the veracity of their religion, an "embarrassed silence" has marked anthropology ever since, say Bourdillon and Fortes.[24]

Against these relativists there has also been an eccentric group of anthropologists who were not neutral about the tribal cultures. A. O. Hallowell, W. E. H. Stanner, Carleton Coon, and Julian Steward walked a narrow line between science and advocacy. Claude Lévi-Strauss rescued the savage mind. Coon's courage was exemplary. He scorned the "academic debunkers and soft peddlers," including those who spoke of "the brotherhood of man" as contradicting the reality of race.[25] Stanner was perhaps the most eloquent, describing Aboriginal thought as a "metaphysical gift," its idea of the world as an object of contemplation, its lack of omniscient, omnipotent, adjudicating gods—a world without inverted pride, quarrel with life, moral dualism, rewards of heaven and hell, prophets, saints, grace, or redemption. All this among Blackfellows whose "great achievement in social structure" he said was equal in complexity to parliamentary government, a wonderful metaphysic of assent and abidingness, "hopelessly out of place in a world in which the Renaissance has triumphed only to be perverted and in which the products of secular humanism, rationalism and science challenge their own hopes."[26] If any modern intellectuals read him they must have thought he had "gone native" and left his critical intelligence in the outback.

After twenty centuries of ideological controversy it may be impossible to enter the dialogue without trailing some of its biases and illusions. But there is perspective from different quarters—from the study of higher primates, hominid paleontology, paleolithic archaeology, ethology, ecology, field studies of living hunter-gatherers, and direct testimony from living hunter-gatherers.

A turning point was a Wenner-Gren symposium in Chicago and its publication as *Man the Hunter* in 1968.[27] The essays therein reported scientific evidence that the cave man as well as the noble savage was so much urban moonshine. It was a meeting of field workers who had studied living tribal peoples in many parts of the world, coming together and finding common threads that linked diverse hunter-gatherer cultures to one another and to paleolithic archaeology. This shift toward species-specific thinking benefitted from "the new systematics," an evolutionary perspective based on genetics and natural selection articulated by G. G. Simpson, Ernst Mayr, Julian Huxley, and others. *The Social Life of Early Man*[28] was indicative of the new level of continuity among primitive societies, afterwards given cross-cultural generalizations in George Murdock's ethnographic atlas.[29]

Although a few bold voices had been heard among them, such as Marshall Sahlins' *Stone Age Economics,*[30] their own evidence did not make anthropologists into advocates of a new primitivism. Their restraint was no doubt the result of a hard-won professional posture, the 20th century effort to overcome two centuries of ethnocentrism. But it was also the outwash of three generations of cultural relativism by mainstream social science, pioneered by Boas and Kroeber,[31] recently voiced with imperious assurance by Clifford Geertz that "there are no generalizations that can be made about man as man, save that he is a most various animal."[32] Catch them saying that any culture is better than another!

In any case, such a judgment would be irrelevant, since even present-day hunter-gatherers are, by its historical logic, part of an irrecoverable past. Melvin Konner, a Harvard-bred anthropologist, spent years studying the !Kung San of the Kalahari desert of Africa, wrote a fascinating account of his study showing the marvelous superiority of their lives to their counterparts in Cleveland or Los Angeles, and then pulled the covers over his head by saying, "But here is the bad news. You can't go back."[33] One can only be grateful for Loren Eiseley[34] and Laurens van der Post[35] in their admiration of the same Kalahari Bushmen. Perhaps they anticipated what Roger Keesing calls the "new ethnography," which seeks "universal cultural design" based on psychological approaches. "If a cognitive anthropology is to be productive, we will need to seek underlying processes and rules," he says, observing that the old ethnoscience has been undermined by transformational linguistics and its sense of "universal grammatical design." He concludes that "the assumption of radical diversity in cultures can no longer be sustained by linguistics."[36]

So to return to the question—just what is it that is so much better in hunter-gatherer life? How does one encapsulate what can be sifted from an enormous body of scientific literature? It is not only, or even mainly, a matter of how nature is perceived, but of the whole of personal existence, from birth through death, among what history arrogantly calls "pre-agricultural" peoples. In the bosom of family and society, the life cycle is punctuated by formal, social recognition with its metaphors in the terrain and the plant and animal life. Group size is ideal for human relationships, including vernacular roles for men and women without sexual exploitation.[37] The esteem gained in sharing and giving outweighs the advantages of hoarding. Health is good in terms of diet as well as social relationships.[38] Interpenetration with the non-human world is an extraordinary achievement of tools, intellectual sophistication, philosophy, and tradition. There is a quality of mind, a sort of venatic phenomenology. "In a world where diversity exceeds our mental capacity nothing is impossible in our capacity to become human."[39] Custom firmly and in mutual council modulates human frailty and crime. Organized war and the hounding of nature do not exist. Ecological affinities are stable and non-polluting. Humankind is in the humble position of being small in number, sensitive to the seasons, comfortable as one species in many, with an admirable humility toward the universe. No hunter on record has bragged that he was captain of his soul. Hunting, both in an evolutionary sense and individually, is "the source of those saving instincts that tell us that we have a responsibility towards the living world."[40]

To make such statements is to set out the game board for the dialectics of our intellectual life. Graduate students, religious fundamentalists, economists, corporate executives, and numerous others, including a gleeful band of book reviewers, will leap to prove differently. I have a wonderful set of newspaper book reviews of *The Tender Carnivore* with headings like "Professor Says Back to the Cave" and "Aw, Shoot!" And there is always an anthropologist somewhere to point to a tribe which is an exception to one or another of the "typical" characteristics of hunter-gatherers, hence there can be no "universals," and so on.

The most erudite essay on hunting, ancient or modern, is José Ortega y Gasset's *Meditations on Hunting*. He conceives the hunt in terms of "authenticity," especially in its direct dealing with the inescapable and formidable necessity of killing, a reality faced in the "generic" way of being human. He also refers to the hunter's ability to "be inside" the countryside, by which he means the natural system—"wind, light, temperature, round-relief, minerals, vegetation, all play a part; they are not simply there, as they are for the tourist or the botanist, but rather they function, they act." Ultimately, this function is the reciprocity of life and death. The enigma of death and that of the animal are the same, and therefore "we must seek his company" in the "subtle rite of the hunt." In all other kinds of landscape, he says—the field, grove, city, battleground—we see "man travelling within himself," outside the larger reality.

The humanized and domesticated places may have their own domestic reality, but Ortega refers to generic being. Ortega's is a larger understanding; he attends to human "species-specific" traits, and escapes the cultural relativism and social reduction that have dominated anthropology. A biologist turned philosopher/historian, Ortega links "primitive" hunter-gatherers to ourselves.

This is because there are characteristics of humankind, as Eibes-Eibesfeldt tells us,[41] as well as shared characteristics of hunter-gatherers, present and past.

What has been learned about the nature of our own problems in the past twenty years?

Item: Health disorders are increasingly traced to polluting poisons and to a diet of domesticated (i.e., chemically altered or chemically treated) plants and animals. More people every year eat the meat of wild animals, seek "organic" vegetables, and seek alternatives to chemicalized nature.

Item: Evidence indicates that the small, face-to-face, social group works better in the quality of social experience and decision-making for its members and in its efficacy as a functional institution.[42]

Item: Percussive music and great intervals of silence are evidently conducive to our well-being. A meditative stillness, suggests Gary Snyder, was invented by waiting hunters.[43] Perhaps this reflected the poised and ruminating hush of mothers of sleeping infants. High levels of sound have been directly linked to degenerative disease in urban life.

Item: Regular exercise, especially jogging, rare in 1965, was common by 1980. The sorts of exercise for men and women (aerobics, jogging, stretching) correlate with certain routines of life in cynegetic societies. The benefits are not only physical but mental.[44]

Item: One of the hardest stereotypes about the savage to die is gluttony. In arguing that Pleistocene peoples were responsible for the extinctions of large mammals, Paul Martin projected urban greed on the ancient hunters.[45] This preposterous theory ignores fundamental ecology, comparative ethnography, and the anthropological distinctions between people who maximize their take and those who optimize it.[46] Given the whole range of Pleistocene extinctions it is a poor fit in the paleontological and archaeological record.

Item: Childhood among hunter-gatherers better fits the human genome[47] in terms of the experience and satisfaction of both parents and children. I refer to the "epigenetic" calendar, which is based on the complex biological specialization of neoteny, to which human culture is in part mediator and mitigator.

Item: That advanced intelligence not only arrived with hunting and being hunted, but continues to be the central characteristic of the hunt, is still hard to accept for those who think of predation as something like a dogfight. Knowledge is of overwhelming importance in accommodating the whole of society to a "watchful world" and structuring the mentality of the hunter. There are three evolutionary correlates of large cerebral hemispheres: large size, predator-prey interaction, and intense sociality.[48]

Item: The cosmography of tribal peoples is as intricate as any, and marked by a humility which is lacking in civilized society. For example, two of the "principles of Koyukon world view" are "each animal knows way more than you do," and "the physical environment is spiritual, conscious, and subject to rules of respectful behavior."[49] The essays in Gary Urton's *Animal Myths and Metaphors in South America*[50] describe myths of the sort depicted in Huichol yarn paintings of Mexico—visual evocations of stories that integrate the human and non-human in dazzling, sophisticated metaphor.

The Paradox of the Civilized Hunter

There is no room here to review current ideas about hunting by modern, urban people, except to observe that the argument for hunting links primitive and civilized people, past and present. One can split this distinction and say with Barry Lopez that hunting is OK for ethnic groups but not for modern people. I think that view is based mistakenly on the notion that there are vicarious alternatives and reflects a kind of despair over the practical question of how the sheer numbers of people now living could gain the benefits of hunting-gathering.

Anti-hunters are outraged by "sport killing" as opposed to ethnic tradition, pointing for example to the diminished presence of wildlife and to old photographs of white African hunters with numerous dead animals. Who would consider defending such "slaughter"? What is sometimes regarded as vanity needs to be understood in the context of the traditional laying out of the dead animals. One of the most thoughtful modern hunters, C. H. D. Clarke, writes, "The Mexican Indian shamanic deer hunt is as much pure sport as mine, and the parallels between its rituals, where the dead game is laid out in state, and those of European hunts, where the horns sound the 'Sorbiati,' or 'tears of the stag,' over the dead quarry, are beyond coincidence."[51]

Fanatic opposition to hunting suggests that some other fear is at work. Neither the animal protectionists, the animal rights philosophers, nor the feminists hostile to vernacular gender have ecosystems (including the wildness of humans) at heart. When anti-hunters heard that "a Royal Commission on blood sports in Britain reported that deer had to be controlled and that hunting was just as humane as any alternative, these people wanted deer exterminated once and for all, as the only way to deliver the land from the infamy of hunting." In America we have similar ecological blindness regarding the killing of goats on the coastal islands of California and wild horses in national parks. I once heard a nationally known radio commentator, Paul Harvey, complain that the trouble with the idea of national parks protecting both predators and prey animals was that "mercy" was missing. Clarke concludes that the "rejection of hunting is just one in a long list of rejections of things natural," and that hunting will linger as one of the human connections to the natural environment "until the human race has completed its flight from nature, and set the scene for its own destruction."[52]

3. Romancing the Potato

Seventeen years after the publication of *The Tender Carnivore* there is still only speculation among scholars about the "cause" of the first agriculture. It is clear now as it was then, however, that recent hunting-gathering peoples did not joyfully leap into farming. The hunter-gatherers' progressive collapse by invasion from the outside is typified in Woodburn's description of the Haida.[53] For ten millennia there has been organized aggression against hunters, who themselves had no tradition of war or organized armies. The psychology of such assault probably grew out of the territoriality inherent in agriculture and farmers' exclusionary attitude toward outsiders, land hunger growing from the decline of field fertility and the increase in human density, and, with the rise of "archaic high civilizations," social pathologies related to group stresses and insecurity in an economy of monocultures (i.e., grains, goats), and the loss of autonomy in the pyramiding of power. Hunting-gathering peoples have been the victims of these pressures that beset farmers and ranchers, bureaucratically amplified upward in the levels of government.

The old idea that farming favored more security, longer life, and greater productivity is not always correct. For example, Marek Zvelebil, in the *Scientific American* in 1986, says, "Hunting-and-gathering is often thought of as little more than the prelude to agriculture. A reevaluation suggests it was a parallel development that was as productive as early farming in some areas."[54] As for modern agriculture, C. Dean Freudenberger says, "Agriculture, closely related to global deforestation by making room for expanding cropping systems, is the most environmentally abusive activity perpetuated by the human species."[55]

At least six millennia of mixed tending and foraging followed the first domesticated wheat and preceded the first wheel, writing, sewers, and armies. In varying degrees local, regenerative, subsistence economies blended the cultivated and gathered, the kept animal and the hunted. Before cities, the world remained rich, fresh, and partly wild beyond the little gardens and goat pens. Extended family, small-scale life with profound incorporation into the rhythms of the world made this "hamlet society" the best life humans ever lived in the eyes of many. It is this village society of horticulture, relatively free of monetary commerce and outside control, that most idealizers of the farm look to as a model.

Perhaps that image motivated Liberty Hyde Bailey in his turn-of-the-century book, *The Holy Earth*. Yet, his feeling for the land seems betrayed by a drive to dominate. Bailey says, "Man now begins to measure himself against nature also, and he begins to see that herein shall lie his greatest conquests beyond himself; in fact, by this means shall he conquer himself,—by great feats of engineering, by complete utilization of the possibilities of the planet, by vast discoveries in the unknown, and by the final enlargement of the soul; and in these fields shall he be the heroes. The most virile and upstanding qualities can find expression in the conquest of the earth. In the contest with the planet every man may feel himself grow."[56] Tethering the neolithic reciprocity with a nourishing earth, he suddenly jerks us into the heroic Iron Age. In the same book, however, he says, "I hope that some reaches of the sea may never be sailed, that some swamps may never be drained, that some mountain peaks may never be scaled, that some forests may never be harvested."[57] Inconsistent? No, it is an expression of the enclave mentality, the same one that gave us national parks and Indian reservations, the same that gives us wilderness areas.

The ideal of hamlet-centered life is represented by *Mother Earth News*, a search for equilibrium between autonomy and compromise. It is difficult not to be sympathetic. So too do Wes Jackson and the "permaculture" people seem to seek the hamlet life.[58] Their objective of replacing the annual plants with perennials seems laudable enough. Yet they are busily domesticating through selective breeding more wild perennials as fast as possible. They are making what geneticist Helen Spurway called genetic "goofies," the tragic deprivation of wildness from wild things.[59]

Who among us is not touched by the idyll of the family farm, the Jeffersonian yeoman, the placeness and playground of a rural existence? Above all, this way of life seems to have what hunting-gathering does not—retrievability. The yearning for it is not from academic studies of exotic tribal peoples, but is only a generation or two away—indeed, only a few miles away in bits of the countryside in Europe and America. After all, it incorporates part-time hunting and gathering, as though creating the best of all possible worlds. Like many others, I admire Jefferson as the complete man and share the search for peace of mind and good life of its modern spokesmen like Wendell Berry.

Of course, most agriculture of the past five millennia has not been like that. The theocratic agricultural states, from the early centralized forms in ancient Sumer onward, have been enslaving rather than liberating. Even where the small scale seems to prevail, such conviviality is not typical in medieval or modern peasant life with its drudgery, meanness, and suffering at the hands of exploitive classes above it.[60]

The primary feature of the farmer's concept of reality is the notion of "limited good." There is seldom enough of anything. By contrast, the hunter's world is more often rich in signs that guide toward a gifting destiny in a realm of alternatives and generous subsistence. Since they know nature well enough to appreciate how little they know of its enormous complexity, hunter-gatherers are engaged in a vast play of adventitious risk, hypostatized in gambling, a major leisure-time activity. Their myths are rich in the strangeness of life, its unexpected boons and encounters, its unanticipated penalties and mysterious rewards, not as arbitrary features but as enduring, infinitely complex structure. Gathering and hunting are a great, complex cosmology in which a numinous reality is mediated by wild animals. It is a zero-sum game, a matter of leaning toward harmony in a system which they disturb so little that its inter-species parities seem more influenced by intuition and rites than physical actions. Autonomous, subsistence farming or gardening shares much of this natural reverence for the biotic community and the satisfactions of light work schedules, hands-on routines, and sensitivity to seasonal cycles.

But agriculture, ancient and modern, is increasingly faced with a matter of winners and losers, dependence on single crops. Harmony with the world is sustained by enlarging the scope of human physical control or by rites of negotiation with sacred powers, such as sacrifice. The domesticated world reduces the immediate life forms of interest to a few score species which are dependent on human cultivation and care—just as the farmers see themselves, dependent on a master with human-like, often perverse actions. Theirs is a cosmos controlled by powers more or less like themselves, from local bureaucrats up through greedy princes to jealous gods. No wonder they prefer games of strategy and folktales in which the "animals," burlesques of their various persecutors, are outwitted by clever foxes like themselves. The world does not so much have parts as it has sides substructured as class. From simple to complex agriculture these increase in importance as kin connections diminish.

The transition from a relatively free, diverse, gentle subsistence to suppressed peasantry yoked to the metropole is a matter of record. The subsistence people clearly long for genuine contact with the non-human world, independence from the market and the basic satisfaction of a livelihood gained by their own hands. But this distinction among agricultures has its limits and was not apparently in mind when Chief Washakie of the Shoshones said, "God damn a potato." Sooner or later you get just what the Irish got after they thought they had rediscovered Eden in a spud skin.

We may ask whether there are not hidden imperatives in the books of Wendell Berry obscured by the portrayal of the moral quality, stewardship syndrome, and natural satisfactions of farm life. He seems to make the garden and barnyard equivalent to morality and esthetics and to relate it to monotheism and sexual monogamy, as though conjugal loyalty, husbandry, and a metaphysical principle were all one. And he is right. This identity of the woman with the land is the agricultural monument, where the environment is genderized and she becomes the means of productivity, reciprocity, and access to otherness, compressed in the central symbol of the goddess. When the subsistence base erodes this morality changes. Fanaticism about virginity, women as pawns in games of power, and their control by men as the touchstone of honor and vengeance has been clearly shown to be the destiny of sub-equatorial and Mediterranean agriculture.[61] Aldous Huxley's scorn of Momism is not popular today, but there are reasons to wonder whether the metaphors that mirror agriculture are not infantile.[62] (For hunter-gatherers the living metaphor is other species, for farmers it is mother, for pastoralists the father, for urban peoples it has become the machine.)[63]

In time, events and people seem to come back in new guise. I keep thinking that Wendell Berry is the second half-century's Louis Bromfield. Bromfield was a celebrated author and gentleman farmer, known for his conservation practices and the good life on his Ohio farm. He could prove the economic benefit of modern farming by his detailed ledgers. But it was his novels that made him wealthy, and the dirt farmers who were invited along with the celebrities to see his showplace could well ask, "Does Bromfield keep books or do the books keep Bromfield?"

Berry writes with great feeling about fresh air and water, good soil, the sky, the rhythms of the earth, and human sense in these things. But those were not invented by farmers. They are the heritage of the non-domesticated world. Much that is "good" in his descriptions does not derive from its husbandry but from the residual "wild" nature. He accepts Biblical admonishments about being God's steward, responsible for the care of the earth. None of the six definitions of "steward" in my dictionary mentions responsibility toward that which is managed. It refers to one who administers another's property, especially one in charge of the provisions; another way of saying that the world biomes need to be ruled, that nature's order must be imposed from the outside.

Alternatively, one could pick any number of Christian blue-noses, from popes to puritans and apostles to saints, who wanted nothing to do with nature and who were disgusted to think they were part of it. The best that can be said about Christianity from an ecological viewpoint is that the Roman church, in its evangelical lust for souls, is a leaky ship. Locally it can allow reconciliation of its own dogma with "pagan" cults, as when the Yucatan Indians were Christianized by permitting the continued worship of limestone sinks, or *cenotes*, making the Church truly catholic.[64] Similar blending may be seen in eccentrics like St. Francis or Wendell Berry, who voice a "tradition" that never existed.

The worst is difficult to choose, although its shadow may be discerned behind the figure of Berry himself in *The Unsettling of America*, humming his bucolic paeans to the land and clouds and birds as he sits astride a horse, his

feet off the ground, on that domestic animal which more than any other symbolized and energized the worldwide pastoral debacle of the skinning of the
earth, and the pastoralists' ideology of human dissociation from the earth-
bound realm. No wonder the horse is the end-of-the-world mount of Vishnu
and Christ. As famine, death, and pestilence, it was the apocalyptic beast who
carried Middle East sky-worship and the sword to thousands of hapless tribal
peoples and farmers from India to Mexico.

Dealing with Death

Joseph Campbell, who clearly understood the hunter-gatherer life, tried to
have it both ways. The hunters' rituals, he said (capitulating to the 19th century anthropological opinion that primitive religion is simply bad logic), tried
to deny death by the pretense that a soul lived on. "But in the planting societies a new insight or solution was opened by the lesson of the plant world itself, which is linked somehow to the moon, which also dies and is resurrected
and moreover influences, in some mysterious way still unknown, the lunar
cycle of the womb."[65] The planters did indeed lock themselves to the fecundity
and fate of annual grains (and their women to an annual pregnancy). But according to Alexander Marshack the moon's periodicity had long since been observed by hunters. In any case it was not seen by the early planters of the Near
East as a plant but as a bull eaten by the lion sun.

Campbell regards sacrifice as the central rite of agriculture's big idea that the
grain crop is the soul's metaphor. Sacrifice—the offering of fruit or grain, or
the ritual slaughter of an animal or person—is a means of participating in the
great round. But in agriculture participation turns into manipulation. The
game changes from one of chance to one of strategy, from reading one's state
of grace in terms of the hunt to bartering for it, from finding to making, from
a sacrament received to a negotiator with anthropomorphic deities. This transition can be seen in a series of North Asian forms of the ceremony of the slain
bear, from an egalitarian, *ad hoc* though traditional celebration of the wild kill
as a symbolic acceptance of the given to the shaman-centered spectacle of the
sacrifice of a captive bear in order to deflect evil from the village.[66]

The transition from bear hunt to bull slaughter has been traced by Tim
Ingold.[67] Sacrifice does not seem to me to accommodate the "problem of
death" but to domesticate it. It reverses the gift flow idea from receiving according to one's state of grace to bartering, from the animal example of "giving
away" to the animal's blood as currency.

The changes that take place as people are forced from hunting-gathering
to agriculture are not conjectural, but observed in recent times among the
!Kung.[68] Their small-group egalitarian life vanishes beneath chiefdoms, children become excessively attached and more aggressive, there are more

contagious diseases, poorer nourishment, more high blood pressure, earlier menarche, three times as many childbirths per woman, and a loss of freedom in every aspect of their lives.[69] The farmer remains lean if he is hungry, but otherwise his body loses its suppleness. One might well wonder who benefits from all this, and of course the answer is the landholders, middlemen, bureaucrats, white-collar workers, and corporations. It is their spokesmen who echo C. H. Brown's blithe view that "a major benefit of agriculture is that it supports population densities many times greater than those that can be maintained by a foraging way of life." He adds, "Of course, this benefit becomes a liability if broad crop failure occurs."[70] He does not say who benefits from the bigger population density, and he is wrong about the "if" of crop failure—it is only a matter of "when."

Today most of us live in cities but the left-over ideology of farming is the basis, ever since the Greek pastoral poets, Roman bucolics, and later the European rustic artists, of the nature fantasies of urban dwellers. Its images of a happy yeomanry and happy countryside are therapeutic to the abrasions of city life. This potato romance is not only one of celebrating humanity surrounded by genetic slaves and freaks, but of perceiving the vegetable world as a better metaphor. The heritable deformity of cows and dogs is inescapable while carrots and cereal grains seem fresh from the pristine hand of nature. This post-Neolithic dream lends itself, for example, to the recovery of the paradisiacal ecological relations of a no-meat diet.

The Vegetarians

The ethical-nutritional vegetarians, the zucchini-killers and drinkers of the dark blood of innocent soy beans, argue for quantity instead of quality. The Animal Aid Society's "Campaign to Promote the Vegetarian Diet" calculates that ten acres will feed two people keeping cattle, ten eating maize, twenty-four munching wheat, and sixty-one gulping soya.[71] The same space would probably support one or fewer hunter-gatherers. There is nothing wrong with their humane effort "toward fighting hunger in the Third World" of course, but what is life to be like for the sixty-one people and what do we do when there are 122 or 488? And what becomes of the Fourth World of tribal peoples or the Fifth World of non-human life?

The quantitative-mindedness links them philosophically with the nationalistic maximizers who assume that military advantage belongs to the most populous countries, with the politics of growth-economists and with the local greed for sales. Nutritionally, energy increase is no substitute for protein quality, nor adipose fats for the structural fats necessary for growth and repair, nor calories over immune system needs, or over the proportions of vitamins and essential minerals found in animal tissues.

Apart from their demographic and ecological short-sightedness, the vegetarians rightfully reject the fat-assed arrogance of piggish beefsteak-eaters, but
they become slaves to protein hunger, by striving to get eight of the twenty
amino acids that their own bodies cannot make and that meat contains in optimum amounts. The search leads to cereals and legumes, the first are low in
lysine, the second in methionine. Humans with little or no meat must get
combinations of legumes and grain (lentils and rice, rice and beans, corn and
beans), and they must locate a substitute source for vitamin B-12, which
comes from meat.

Just this side of the vegetarians are various degrees of meat eating, and the
same chains of reasoning carry us from red to white meats and from meat to
eggs and milk. Neither domestic cereals nor milk from hoofed animals are
"natural" foods in an evolutionary sense; witness the high levels of immune re-
action, cholesterol susceptibility, and the dietary complications from too much
or too little milling of grains.

Except for a tiny minority, people everywhere, including farmers, prefer to
eat meat, even when its quality has been reduced by domestication. Marvin
Harris has summed up the evidence from ethnology and physiology: "Despite
recent findings which link the over consumption of animal fats and cholesterol
to degenerative diseases in affluent societies, animal foods are more critical for
sound nutrition than plant foods."[72]

Nutritionally, little detailed comparison has been made between domestic
and wild meats. Long-chain fatty-acids, found only in meat, are necessary for
brain development. These come from structural rather than adipose fat. You
can get them in meat from the butcher, but domestic cattle often lack access to
an adequate variety of seeds and leaves to make an optimum proportion of
structural fats.[73] The latter are richest in wild meats.

Theories that attempt to center human evolution around something like
the role of female chimpanzees or to link gathering with a gender-facilitated
evolution by reference to the "vegetarian" diets of primates, neglect the pro-
tein-hunger of primates and their uptake of meat in insect and other animal
materials. The argument that humans are physiologically "closer" to herbivory
than to carnivory, somehow placing women closer to the center of human
being, is a red herring based on a mistaken dichotomy. It simply ignores
human omnivory, signified not only in food preferences but physiologically in
the passage time of food in the gut (longer in herbivores because of the slow di-
gestion of cellulose-rich and fibrous foods, shorter in carnivores). In humans it
is half-length between gorillas and lions.

Among most tribal peoples most of the time meat comprises less than fifty
percent of the total diet, the bulk being made up of a wide variety of fruits and
vegetables. But meat is always the "relish" that makes the meal worthwhile,

and close attention is always paid to the way meat is butchered and shared. Vegetarianism, like creationism, simply re-invents human biology to suit an ideology. There is no phylogenetic felicity in it.

As for the alternatives in turning from the cholesterol of domestic meats, not everything comes up yogurt. Many European restaurants now offer a separate menu of game animals (reared but not domesticated). S. Boyd Eaton and Marjorie Shostak, an M.D. and an anthropologist, comment, "The difference between our diet and that of our hunter-gatherer forebears may hold keys to many of our current health problems. . . . If there is a diet natural to our human makeup, one to which our genes are still best suited, this is it."[74]

4. Cultural Evolution

The casual misuse of "evolution" in describing social change produced enough confusion to mislead generations of students. Every society was said to be evolving somewhere in a great chain of progress. Beginning in a Heart of Darkness in the individual and at the center of remote forests humankind advanced to ethics, democracy, morality, art, and the other benefits of civilization. This ladder probably still represents the concept of the past for most modern, educated people. It is a direct heritage of the Enlightenment and its industrial science, its spectatorship (as in the art museum or at the play), elitism, and the cult of the *polis*.

Recently there have appeared new versions of lifeways that refute a universal yearning toward civilization, from savagery through nomadic pastoralism and various agricultures to a pinnacle of urban existence.[75] The revised version also denies a hierarchy of inherent physical or mental differences among the peoples of different economies.

One modified view presents us with shifts in which societies are compelled to change not so much as an advance as a result of circumstances beyond their control—increased population density and the struggle for power and space. It offers a "circumscription theory." Societies at the denser demographic end show a hierarchical, imperial domain and the loss of local autonomy in which symbols of participation in the larger system replace real participation for the individual. Such societies subjugate or are conquered by others.

In a recent book Allen Johnson and Timothy Earle cite specific examples from first to last.[76] They begin with a description of hunting-gathering at the family-level of economy, characterizing them as low in population density, making personal tools, engaged in annual rhythms of social aggregation and dispersion, informally organized with *ad hoc* leadership, collectively hunting large game, lightly assuming tasks of gathering, without territoriality or war, and with numerous alternatives in "managing risk."

Such easy-going societies continue with minor introduction of domestic plants and animals, at the same time consciously resisting life in denser structures. In villages, however, men begin to fight over "the means of reproduction" and depart from the "modesty and conviviality" found in family-level societies. As "geographical circumscription" closes around them, leaving nowhere to go, there is more bullying, impulsive aggression, revenge, and territoriality. "Scarcity of key resources" and war become "a threat to the daily lives" of these horticulturalists and pig-raisers. As the economy "evolves" the "domestication of people into interdependent social groups and the growth of political economy are thus closely tied to competition, warfare and the necessity of group defense."

As villages get bigger, Johnson and Earle continue, "Big Man" power appears, ceremonial life shifts from cosmos-focused family activity to public affirmation of political rank. Dams and weirs and slaves and food surplus and shortage management occupy the leaders. But "the primary cause of organization elaboration appears to be defensive needs." Among typical yam-growers of the South Pacific "half a mile beyond a person's home lies an alien world fraught with sudden death."

Meanwhile, the pastoralists also "evolve." Their lives are increasingly centralized under patriarchal systems based on "friends" who "help spread the risk" of resource depletion and defense needs. As cattle become currency, raiding and banditry increase in a "highly unpredictable environment." Chiefdoms are subordinated by greater chiefs, who allocate pasture and travel lanes, manage "disagreement resolution" locally, and negotiate alliances and conflict externally. Life is lived in camp, i.e., "a small nucleus of human warmth surrounded by evil." Their equivalents in sedentary towns are concerned with crop monocultures and massive tasks of "governing redistribution," regulating the bureaucracy and management of field use and irrigation works.

When we get to the first true or archaic states, vassalage, standing armies, and taxes make their appearance. "Social circumscription" is added to geographical circumscription. Religion and staple food storage are centralized. As the state matures the peasants emerge with "no end of disagreement and even disparagement" among themselves. They often "live so close to the margin of survival that they visibly lose weight in the months before harvest." As we approach the modern state the authors say, "peasant economics provide a less satisfactory subsistence than the others we have examined," with poor diet, undernourishment, extreme competition, and a meager security experienced as vulnerability to markets controlled from the outside or the arbitrary will of patrons.

Johnson and Earle conclude, at the end of this long road to a "regional polity," that the record is one of endless rounds of population increase and "intensification," producing societies symbolized by their dependence on "starchy staples." All hail the potato.

The authors are careful to remain mere observers. If a book can have a straight face while taking off civilization's pants, here is a wonderful irony, although probably a competent synthesis of the record. Yet euphemisms and semi-technical phrases abound. For "diminished resources" one should read "collapse of life support" or "failed ecosystems." For "local slave management" read "tyranny," for "risk management" simply "debacle." The increasing need for "defense" is frequently mentioned, but who is doing all the offense? How casually and with value-free candor we move from many options in "risk management" to few, from personal tools to work schedules, from ad-hoc leadership to hierarchies of chiefs. Little is said about children, women, the source of slaves, the loss of forests and soil, the scale of tensions between farmers and pastoralists. One has to interpolate the relevant changes in the role and status of women, the lives of children, or the condition of the non-human fellow-beings. The book seems to achieve its objective of combining "economic anthropology and cultural ecology," making disaster humdrum and so inevitable. The recitation of the "evolution of culture" in such expressionless fashion is in fact enormously effective, for the authors seem oblivious to the horrors they describe. I am reminded of academics who reply to descriptions of the biotic costs of civilization with murmurings about how difficult life would be for them without Beethoven, cathedrals, and jurisprudence. But then, it was a tiny elite who benefitted from this "evolution" all along, and I suppose that they can easily imagine that others, in their benighted state, cannot possibly appreciate the gains.

For twenty years my students and colleagues have responded to this scenario by asking why people changed if the old way was better, and then refuse to believe that the majority were compelled by centralized force in which power and privilege motivated the few. Zvelebil says, "The stubborn persistence of foraging long after it 'should' have disappeared is one of the qualities that is contributing to a fundamental reassessment of post-glacial hunting and gathering."

The idea of cultural change as a paradoxical "development" can also be seen in a comparison of American Indian tribes. John Berry and Robert Annis studied differences in six northern Indian tribes using George Murdock's classifications of culture types, "a broad ecological dimension running from agricultural and pastoral interactions with the environment through to hunting and gathering interactions." They describe a corresponding psychological differentiation, defined along this axis.

Agriculture tends to be associated with high food accumulation, population density, social stratification, and compliance. At the other end of the series are the low food accumulators—hunter-gatherers—with a high sense of personal identity, social independence, emphasis on assertion and self-reliance, high self-control, and low social stratification. Berry and Annis see these differences in terms of "cognitive style," "affective style," and "perceptual style."[77] These studies are consistent with the work of Robert Edgerton, who found distinct personality differences between farmers and pastoralists.[78]

What we come to is an uneasy sense of economic determinism. There is a profound similarity of hunter-gatherers everywhere. This convergence demonstrates the niche-like effect of a way of life. The possibilities for human cultural mixtures can be seen in the variety of peoples in the modern world. There seems to be no end to the anthropological exploration of their differences. Still, the surprising thing is not their dissimilarity but the extent of common style. Something enormously powerful binds living hunter-gatherers to those of the past and to modern sportsmen.

They are all engaged in a game of chance amid heterogeneous, exemplary powers rather than in collective strategies of accumulation and control. Their metaphysics conceives a living, sentient, and dispersed comity whose main features are given in narrations that are outside History. Their mood is assent. Their lives are committed to the understanding of a vast semiosis, presented to them on every hand, in which they are not only readers but participants. The hunt becomes a kind of search gestalt. The lifelong test and theme is "learning to give away" what was a gift received in the first place.

There are also convergent likenesses among subsistence farmers, pastoralists, and urban peoples. The economic constraints seem to transcend religions and ethnic differences, to surpass the unique effects of history, to overstep ideology and technology. The philosophies as well as the material cultures of otherwise distant peoples who have similar ecologies seem to converge.

5. Wilderness and Wildness

Wilderness

How are we to translate the question of the hunt into the present? One road leads to the idea of wilderness, the sanctuaries or sacrosanct processes of nature preserved.

The idea of wilderness—both as a realm of purification outside civilization and as a place of beneficial qualities—has strong antecedents in the Western world. In spite of the recent national policies of designating wilderness areas, the idea of solace, naturalness, nearness to fundamental metaphysical forces, escape from cities, access to ruminative solitude, and locus of test, trial, and special visions—all these extend Biblical traditions. As for wildness, I suppose that most people today would say that wilderness is where wildness is, or that wildness is an aspect of the wilderness.

Wilderness is a place you go for a while, an escape to or from. It is a departure into a kind of therapeutic land management, a release from our crowded and overbuilt environment, an esthetic balm, healing to those who sense the presence of the disease but who may have confused its cause with the absence of the therapy. More importantly, we describe it to ourselves in a language invented by art critics, and we take souvenirs of our experience home as photographs. Typically, the lovers of wilderness surround themselves with pictures of mountains or forests or swamps which need not be named or even known, for they are types of scenery. But it is emphatically not scenery which is involved in either the ceremonies of Aborigines or the experience of the hermit saints. Something has intervened between them and the *zeitgeist* of the calendar picture. That something is the invention of landscape.

Wilderness remains for me a problematic theme, intimately associated in the modern mind with landscape. It is a scene through which spectators pass as they would the galleries of a museum. Art historians attribute the origins of landscape (in the Occident) to 16th century perspective painters, but I find a strange analogy to the descriptions of Mesolithic art, where "we are evidently approaching a historical sense. . . . The tiny size of these paintings is something of a shock after the Paleolithic. The immediate impression is of something happening at a great distance, watched from a vantage-point which may be a little above the scene of the action. This weakens the viewer's sense of participating in what is going forward. There is something of a paradox here, for in the graphic art of the paleolithic, though man was seldom shown, he was the invisible participant in everything portrayed, while now that he has moved into the canvas and become a principal, there is a quite new detachment and objectivity about his portrayal."[79] In other words, the first appearance of genre and perspective in pictorial art is Neolithic, and probably expresses a new sense of being outside nature. Something like modern landscape reappears later in Roman mosaics, prior to its rediscovery by Renaissance art, and I take this as evidence of renewed "distancing" and an expression of the Classical rationality that made possible the straight roads across Europe, based on survey rather than old trails.

I owe to David Lowenthall and Marshall McLuhan a debt for diverting me from writing and thinking about wilderness. Graduate work on the history of landscape, published as *Man in the Landscape,* left me susceptible to McLuhan's devastating analysis of 17th century science and art. Linear/mathematical thinking and the representation of places as esthetic objects distanced the observer from rather than connected him to his surroundings.[80] The place was framed. This was the esthetic origin of pictorial vision, of which wilderness is a subject matter.

Lowenthall did not describe so much as embody the humanist position, in which the "love of nature" is understood as an esthetic experience, and any esthetic is a "congeries of feelings," a cultural ripple that can come and go in the dynamics of taste and fashion.[81] Lowenthall is wrong. He misunderstands the truly radical aspect of romanticism, misconstruing it as esthetic or iconographic rather than an effort to reintegrate cognition and feeling in an organic paradigm. But he may be right about landscape. It was the means of perceiving nature according to criteria established by art criticism, the avenue of "landscape" by which people "entered" nature as they did a picture gallery. As long as pictures were regarded as representations, the enthusiasm for landscape could still penetrate all areas of culture, in spite of the estrangement described by McLuhan. By the end of the 19th century the art world moved on to non-objectivity, leaving wilderness with the obsolescence and superficiality with which Lowenthall confused it.

The landscape cannot escape its origins as an objectifying perception, although it may be misused as a synonym for place, terrain, ecosystem, or environment. Photos of it are surrealistic in the sense that they empty the subject of intimate context. As pictures age they add layers of a cold impulse like growing crystals, making the subject increasingly abstract, subjecting real events to a drifting, decadent attention. When 19th century painters discovered photography they were freed, as Cezanne said, from literature and subject matter. Susan Sontag has it right about surrealism: disengagement and estrangement. It is, she says, a separation that enables us to examine dispassionately old photographs of suffering people.[82] It is a form of schizophrenia, a final effect of splitting art from its origins in religion. It becomes seeing for its own sake, what Bertram Lewin has called "neurotic scopophilia."[83] To this I add the photography of nature, which anti-hunters want to substitute for killing and eating. Pictures of nature exactly embody what is meant by wilderness as opposed to that wildness which I kill and eat because I, too, am wild.

Wildness

Thank God Thoreau did not say, "In wilderness is the preservation of the world." Wildness, ever since Starker Leopold's research on heritable wildness in wild turkeys in the mid-1940s and Helen Spurway's "The Causes of Domestication,"[84] has for me an objective reality, or at least a degree of independence from arbitrary definitions.

Wildness occurs in many places. It includes not only eagles and moose and their environments but house sparrows, cockroaches, and probably human beings—any species whose sexual assortment and genealogy are not controlled by human design. Spurway, Konrad Lorenz's observation on the bodily and behavioral forms of domesticated animals, and the genetics of zoo animals provide substance to the concept. The loss of wildness that results in the heritable, blunted, monstrous surrogates for species, so misleading because the plants and animals which seem to be there have gone, are like sanity's mask in the benign visage of a demented friend.

What then is the wild human? Who is it? Savages? Why . . . it is us! says Claude Lévi-Strauss. The savage mind is our mind.[85] Along with our admirable companions and fellow omnivores, the brown rat, raccoon, and crow, not yet deprived of the elegance of native biology by breeding management, it is us! Some among us may be deformed by our circumstances, like obese raccoons or crowded rats, but as a species we have in us the call of the wild.

It is a call corrupted not only by domestication but by the conventions of nature esthetics. The corporate world would destroy wildness in a trade for wilderness. Its intent is to restrict the play of free and selfish genes, to establish a dichotomy of places, to banish wild forms to enclaves where they may be encountered by audiences while the business of domesticating the planet proceeds. The savage DNA will be isolated and protected as esthetic relicts, as are the vestiges of tribal peoples. This includes the religious insights of wild cultures, whose social organization represents exotic or vestigial stages in "our" history or "evolution," their ecological relations translated into museum specimens of primeval economics. My wildness according to this agenda is to be experienced on a reservation called a wilderness, where I can externalize it and look at it.

Instead my wildness should be experienced in the growing of a self that incorporates my identity in places. See Fred Myer, Roy Rappaport, D. H. Stanner, or Gary Snyder on the way the self exists in resonance with specific events in particular places among Australian peoples.[86] The Australian outback is not a great two dimensional space, not a landscape, but a pattern of connections, lived out by walking, ritually linking the individual in critical passages to sacred places and occasions, so that they become part of an old story. To be so engaged is like a hunger for meat, irreducible to starches, the wild aspect of ourselves.

Wild Versus Domestic Metaphysics

The bones I sometimes think I have to pick with Gary Snyder are surely those remaining from a shared hunt and meal, pieces to be mulled over—to mull, from a root word meaning "to grind" or "to pulverize" which I take to mean that we are sitting at a fire together, breaking femurs to get at the marrow or the pith.

He has said that the intent of American Indian spiritual practice is not cosmopolitan. "Its content perhaps is universal, but you must be a Hopi to follow
the Hopi way." A dictum that all of us in the rag-tag tribe of the "Wanta-bes"
should remember. And he has said, "Otherworldly philosophies end up doing
more damage to the planet (and human psyches) than the existential conditions they seek to transcend."[87] But he also refers to Jainism and Buddhism as
models, putting his hand into the cosmopolitan fire, for surely those are two of
those great, placeless, portable, world religions whose ultimate concerns are
not just universal but otherworldly. Yet, without quite understanding why,
from what I have seen of his personal life, there is no contradiction. I suspect
that Snyder in the Sierra Nevada, like Berry in Kentucky and Wes Jackson in
the Kansas prairie, is not so much following tradition but doing what Joseph
Campbell called "creative mythology."

When I am sometimes discouraged by the thought that Gary Snyder has already said everything that needs to be said, as in, for instance, "Good, Wild,
Sacred,"[88] I reawaken my independence of spirit by thinking of his faith in
agriculture and Buddhism, even though in reality he carefully qualifies both.
No matter how benign small-scale garden-horticulture may be, at its center is
the degenerating process of domestication, the first form of genetic engineering. Domestication is the regulated alteration of the genomes of organ-
isms, making them into slaves that cannot be liberated, like comatose patients
hooked without reprieve to the economic machine.

As for coma, the excessive use of slave animals in experimental laboratories,
their fecundating overspill as pets into city streets, and their debasement in factory farms has generated the "humane" movement, the dream of animal rights
groups that by kindness or legislation you can liberate enslaved species. The
clearest analogy is the self-satisfied, affectionate care of slaves by many pre-
Civil War gentry. In our time, a huge, terrible yearning has come into the
human heart for the Others, the animals who nurture us now as from our beginnings. Our gratitude to them is deep—so deep that it is subject to the
pathologies of our crowded lives. In our wild hunger for the recovery of animal
presence we have made and given names to pets, moulded their being after our
cultural emphasis on individuals. Our hunting past tells us that the species is
the "individual," each animal the occasion of the species' soul. Our humane
movement personalizes them instead, losing sight of the species and its
ecology. Worse, that self-proclaimed "kindness" marks the collapse of a
metaphor central to human consciousness, replacing it with the metonymy of
touch-comfort, hence the new jargon of "animal companion" for pet in the
new wave of "animal facilitated therapy." It is a massive, industrial effort
among an amalgam of health workers, veterinarians, pet food manufacturers,
and institutions. The effects of the therapy are undoubtedly genuine, but its

"cognitive style" connects at one end with the hair-splitting philosophical rationality of the animal ethicists and at the other with the maudlin neuropath keeping thirty cats in a three-room city house—an abyssal chaos of purposes and priorities.

The lack of ecological concern in almost all animal ethics is strangely similar to that "embarrassed silence" in anthropology—the posture of detached respect by which all ethnic rites are interpreted as serving social and symbolic functions for an erroneous religion. Animal ethics comes from the same Greek source as all our philosophy, passionately reasoning but grounded in detachment and skepticism. There seems to be no real feeling there for the living world. They simply do not ask whether the Holy Hunt might indeed be so.

As for killing animals to eat, in *The Tender Carnivore* I suggested, taste buds and tongue in cheek, that in an overpopulated world we could free the animals, including ourselves, make hunting possible, and terminate the domestication of multicellular life by eating oil-sucking microbes (which is entirely feasible). To my surprise I find that this is our direction, in our yogurt and cheese rush to avoid killing "higher" animals by substituting down a chain of being, killing asparagus instead of cows or yeasts instead of asparagus. But there is no escape from the reality that life feeds by death-dealing (and its lesson in death-receiving). The way "out" of the dilemma is into it, a way pioneered for us in the play of sacred trophism, the gamble of sacramental gastronomy, central myths of gifts, and chance, the religious context of eating in which the rules are knowing the wild forms who are the game. You cannot sit out the game, but must personally play or hide from it.

This brings us back to Buddhism. I remain a skeptical outsider, unnerved by the works of Gary Snyder and Alan Watts, whose combined efforts I consider to be a possible library on how to live. Still, the Hindus disdained Buddhism when they discovered how abstract and imageless it was, how shorn of group ceremony, the guiding insights of gifted visionaries, and the demonstrable respect for life forms represented in their multitudinous pantheon. The Hindus at least saw personal existence as a good many slices of *dharma* in a variety of species before the individual finally escaped into the absolute, while the Buddhists argued that all you needed was the right discipline and you could exit pronto.

The Buddhists' contemporaries and fellow travelers, the Jains, famous for *ahimsa* (harmlessness), are familiarly portrayed moving insects from the footpath. But this is not because they love life or nature. The Jains are revolted by participation in the living stream and want as little as possible to do with the organic bodies, which are like tar pits, trapping and suffocating the soul. Historically, it would appear that both Buddhists and Jains got something from the Aryans who brought their high-flying earth-escaping gods from

Middle East pastoralism. In the face of these invasions, the Hindus and their unzipped polytheism survived best in the far south of India where the Western monotheists penetrated least.

At a more practical level, everywhere the "world" religions have gone the sacred forests, springs, and other "places" and their wild inhabitants have vanished. The disappearance of respect for local earth-shrines is virtually a measure of the impact of the other-worldly beliefs.

Can there be a world religion of bioregions, a universal philosophy of place, an inhabitation of planet Earth with plural, local autonomy?

Perception as the Dance of Congruity

Rene Dubos once observed that humans can adapt (via culture) to "starless skies, treeless avenues, shapeless buildings, tasteless bread, joyless celebrations, spiritualess pleasures—to a life without reverence for the past, love for the present, or poetical anticipations of the future. Yet it is questionable that man can retain his physical and mental health if he loses contact with the natural forces that have shaped his biological and mental nature."[89] But, unless these "forces" are the characteristics he mentions, what are they? His list is made up entirely of acts within a social and cultural milieu, by customary definition not "natural." Something "natural" looms behind all this, mediated by culture.

Dubos' statement is preceded by the observation that the human genetic makeup was stabilized 100,000 years ago. He quotes Lewis Mumford, "If man had originally inhabited a world as blankly uniform as a 'high rise' housing development, as featureless as a parking lot, as destitute of life as an automated factory, it is doubtful that he would have had a sufficiently varied experience to retain images, mold language or acquire ideas."[90]

What is this something natural necessary to become cultural? What is between culture and nature, betwixt the phenomenal or palpable world and the conceptual and ceremonial expressions of it? Connecting the cognition and the outer world is the event/structure, linking entity and environment. It is perception, the pre-cognitive act, mostly unconscious, which directs attention, favors preferences, governs sensory emphasis, gives infrastructure. Lee and Ong's distinctions between an "acoustical event world" and the "hypervisual culture" is just such a prior mode, giving primordial design to experience, limiting but not formulating the concepts and enactments by which events are represented.[91] Phonetic alphabet, pictorial space, and Euclidean theory are not only ideas and formulas, but frames supporting a kind of liminal foreknowledge of assumptions and inclinations.

Emphasis on perception does not mean that we shape our own worlds irrespective of a reality, or that one person's perceptual process is as reliable as another's. Perception is not another word for taste. In this, says Morris Berman, it transcends "the glaring blind spot of Buddhist philosophy."[92] Its truest expression "by test" (my criteria: quality of life; ecological integrity) in the world is the empirical effect of its contiguity. It is the process of the first steps of directed attention and vigilance. Perceptual habit is style in the sense that Margaret Mead once used the term, to mean a pattern of movement and sensitivity, the lively net of predisposition emerging from our early grounding, finally affecting every aspect of one's expressive life. In our wild aspect such unconscious presentations are centered in dance and narration, surrounded by innumerable and wonderfully varied moral and esthetic presences. It presents us with an intuition of rich diversity whose "forces" are purposeful and sentient. From Dubos' treeless avenues to Mumford's parking lot, it is not a view that is absent, or things or wilderness. It is a way of expecting and experiencing, encountering inhabitance by a vast congregation of others unlike us, yet, like our deepest selves, wild.

6. The Mosaic

We must now close the circle to that sweeping, four-word dictum which is intended to close the door on access to the primitive: "You can't go back."

The Structural Dimension

The hereditary material is organized as a linked sequence of separable genes and chromosomes. This genome is a mosaic of harmonious but distinct entities. This structure makes possible the mutation of specific traits and the independent segregation of traits, the accumulation of multiple factors, and both the hiding and expression of genes.

The structure of the natural community, the ecosystem, is likewise an integrated whole composed of distinct species populations and their niches. The fundamental concept of modern biology is its primary characteristic as a composite of linked and harmonious but separable parts. The whole is neither the sum of its parts nor independent of any of them. As with genes, substitutions occur. A given species can be totally removed by extirpation or introduced into new communities. Witness for example the constitution of the prairie without the buffalo and the continuity of ecosystems after the successful introduction of the starling into North America.

Human culture, being genetically framed and ecologically adapted, is also an integrated conglomerate. Stories, dances, tools, and goods are sometimes completely lost from a society. At others they move from culture to culture, sometimes trailing bits of the context from which they come, sometimes arriving rough-edged and isolate, but being assimilated, modified or not, as a part of the new whole.

There is a common characteristic of each of the above examples from the genome of the individual, the material or expressive culture of a people, and the tapestry of the natural environment. The specific entity involves both a distinct portability and a working embeddedness. The reality is more complex but the principle is true: the capacity for a part to be transferred. It is then part of a new whole. The rest of the totality adjusts, the organism accommodates, the niche system stretches or contracts, the culture is modified.

Societies and cultures are mosaics. They are componential. Their various elements, like genes and persons, can be disengaged from the whole. Contemporary life is in fact just such an accumulation representing elements of different ages and origins, some of which will disappear, as they entered, at different times than others. The phrase "You cannot go back" can only mean that you cannot recreate an identical totality but it does not follow that you cannot incorporate components.

"You can't go back" is therefore a disguise for several assumptions, which in turn may hide ways of perceiving or preconstructing experience. One is the paradigm of uni-direction, the idea that time and circumstances are linear. Yet we "go back" with each cycle of the sun, each turning of the globe. Each new generation goes back to already existing genes, from which each individual comes forward in ontogeny, repeating the life cycle. While it is true that you may not run the ontogeny backwards, you cannot avoid its replays of an ancient genome, just as human embryology follows a pattern derived from an ancestral fish. Most of the "new" events in each individual life are only new within a certain genetic octave and only in their combinations. New genes do occur, but the tempo of their emergence is in the order of scores of thousands of years. The difference between the genomes of chimpanzees and humans is about one percent. Of the 146 amino acids of the Beta chain of blood hemoglobin the gorilla differs from humans at one site, the pig at ten, the horse at twenty-six.[93]

A paradox is evident: newness yet sameness; repetition and novelty, past and present. Recall that the historical consciousness of the West rejects this as illusory ambiguity. The rejection is a characteristic perceptual habit. In tribal life, such matters of identity ambiguity are addressed ritually in the use of animal masks and mimetic dances, on the grounds that we are both animal and human, a matter "understood" by certain animal guides. Genes are not only "how-to" information but are mnemonic, that is, memories. Ceremonies recall. The reconciliation of our own polytheistic zoological selfhood is inherent in our ritualized, sensuous assent of multiple truth. It denies the contradiction, abolishes the either-or dichotomy in the simultaneous multitude that we are. Our primitive legacy is the resolution of contradiction by affirmation of multiplicity, plurality, and change.

In advocating the "primitive" we seem to be asking someone to give up everything, or to sacrifice something: sophistication, technology, the lessons and gains of History, personal freedom, and so on. But some of these are not "gains" so much as universal possessions, reified by a culture which denies its deeper heritage. "Going back" seems to require that a society reconstruct itself totally, especially that it strip its modern economy and reengage in village agriculture or foraging, hence is judged to be functionally impossible. But that assumption misconstrues the true mosaic of both society and nature, which are composed of elements that are eminently dissectible, portable through time and space, and available.

You can go out or back to a culture even if its peoples have vanished, to retrieve a mosaic component, just as you can transfer a species that has been regionally extirpated, or graft healthy skin to a burned spot from a healthy one. The argument that modern hunting-gathering societies are not identical to paleolithic peoples is beside the point. It may be true that white, ex-Europeans cannot become Hopis or Kalahari Bushmen or Magdalenian bison-hunters, but removable elements in those cultures can be recovered or recreated, which fit the predilection of the human genome everywhere.

Three Important, Recoverable Components: The Affirmation of Death, Vernacular Gender, and Fulfilled Ontogeny

Our modern culture or "mosaic" is an otherworldly monotheism littered with the road kills of species. Road kills—such trivial death contrasts sharply to that other death in which circumspect humans kill animals in order to eat them as a way of worship.

This ancient, sacramental trophism is as fundamental to ourselves as to our ancestors and distant cousins. The great metaphysical discovery by the cynegetic world was cyclicity. It emerged in the context of the rites of death, both human and animal, as part of this flow. It is as old as the Neanderthal observation of hibernating bears as models of life given and recovered, and as new as Aldo Leopold's story "Odyssey" in *A Sand County Almanac* telling of an atom from a dead buffalo moving through the chain of photosynthesis, predation, decay, and mineralization. These concepts are about the nutritional value of meat in human metabolism as a reflection of a larger "metabolism," and about the gift of human consciousness in a sentient world in which food-giving symbolizes connectedness. Animals on the medicine wheel of the Plains Indians were said to be those that know how to "give away." "'Each dot I have made with my finger in the dirt is an animal,' said White Rabbit. 'There is no one of any of the animals in this world that can do without the next. Each whole tribe of animals is a Medicine Wheel, in that it is the One Mind. Each dot on the Great Wheel is a tribe of animals. And parts of these tribes must Give-Away in order that they all might grow. The animal tribes all know of this. It is only the tribes of People who are the ones who must learn it."[94]

William Arrowsmith, observing that in our time "we cannot abide the encounter with the 'other,'. . . . We do not teach children Hamlet or Lear because we want to spare them the brush with death. . . . A classicist would call this disease *hybris*. . . . The opposite of *hybris* is *sophrosyne*. This means 'the skill of mortality.'"[95] It is the obverse side of the "giving away" coin, the way of momentarily being White Rabbit, reminding the human hunter that he too once was a prey and, in terms of the cosmic circling-back, still is.

The difficult question of interspecies ethics centers on death-dealing. Death is the great bugaboo. How we resent its connection to food—and to life—and repress the figure of the dying animal. Gary Snyder's reply: "All of nature is a gift-exchange, a potluck banquet, and there is no death that is not somebody's food, no life that is not somebody's death. Is this a flaw in the universe? A sign of the sullied condition of being? 'Nature red in tooth and claw'? Some people read it this way, leading to a disgust with self, with humanity, and with life itself. They are on the wrong fork of the path."

Joseph Campbell has argued rightly that death was a great metaphysical problem for hunters, and concluded wrongly that it was solved by planters with their sacrifices to forces governing the annual sprouting of grain. But it was control, not acquiescence to this great round, that the agriculturalists sought. In the Neolithic, says Wilhelm Dupre, "The individual no longer stands as a whole vis-à-vis the life-community in the sense that the latter finds its realization through a total integration of the individual—as is the case by and large under the conditions of a gathering and hunting economy."[96]

"Hunters" is an appropriate term for a society in which meat, the best of foods, signifies the gift of life, the obtaining and preparation of which ritualizes the encounter of life and death, in which the human kinship with animals is faced in its ambiguity, and the quest of all elusive things is experienced as the hunt's most emphatic metaphor.

Vernacular Gender

And so we bring to and from the mosaic of lifeways the hunt itself. Some feminists object that too much is made of it. But they misunderstand this killing of animals as an exercise of vanity, which they see as characteristic of patriarchy. They note that only a third of the diet is meat, the rest from plants, mostly gathered by women, as though there were a contest to see who really supports the society. In this they merely reverse the sexist view. Like so much of extremist feminism it is just a new "me first." They point out that in most hunting-gathering societies the women gather most of the food that is eaten. This view has the same myopia as that of the vegetarians—the tendency to quantify food value in calories. In any case they are wrong, as meat is so much higher in energy that the net energy gained from hunting is as great as that from gathering.[97]

While it is true that the large, dangerous mammals are usually hunted by men in hunting-gathering societies, it has never been claimed that women only pluck and men only kill. The centrality of meat, the sentient and spiritual beings from whom it comes, and the diverse activities in relationship to the movement of meat and the animal's numinous presence through the society, entail a wide range of roles, many of which are genderized. Insofar as the animal eaten is available because it has learned "to give away," there is no more virtue in the actual chase or killing than the transformation of its skin into a garment, the burying of its bones, the drumming that sustains the dancers of the mythical hunt, or the dandling of infants in such a society as the story of the hunt is told.

Meat, says Konner, is only thirty percent of the !Kung diet, but it equals the nutritional value of the plant foods and produces eighty percent of the excitement, not only during the hunt but in group life. The metaphysics of meat. The hunt itself is a continuum, from its first plan to its storied retelling, from the metaphors on food chains to prayers of apology, this carnivory takes nothing from woman, though it clarifies the very different meaning that different kinds of foods have in expressive culture. Broadly understood, the hunt refers to the larger quest for the way, the pursuit of meaning and contact with a sentient part of the environment, and the intuition that nature is a language. Hunting is a special case of gathering.

A critical dimension of the hunt is the confrontation with death and the incorporation of substance in new life, in all forms of sharing and giving away. Women are traditionally regarded as keepers of the mystery of death-as-the-genesis-of-life, hence the hunt is clearly connected with feminine secrets and powers, and we are not surprised to see Artemis and her other avatars, the archaic "Lady of the Beasts," and the Paleolithic female figurines in sanctuaries where the walls are painted with hunted game. More value is placed on men than women only as the hunt is perverted by sexism and war. Indeed, it is possible that sexism comes into being with the doting on fertility and fecundity in agriculture and the androgenous "reply" of nomadic, male dominated societies of pastoralism.

Hunting has never excluded women, whose lives are as absorbed in the encounter with animals, alive and dead, as those of men. If in some societies the practices of vernacular gender tend more often to relegate to the men the pursuit of large, dangerous game, it relegates to the women the role of singing the spirit of the animal a welcome, and to them the discourse at the hearth where she is the host. Roles and duties are divided, but not to make inequality. Among the Sharanahua of South America, the women, being sometimes meat-hungry, send off the men to hunt and sing the hunters to their task. They are commonly believed to transform men into hunters. Janet Siskind says, "The social pressure of the special hunt, the line of women painted and waiting, makes young men try hard to succeed." Women also hunt. Gathering, like hunting, is a light-hearted affair done by both men and women. The stable sexual politics of the Sharanahua, "based on mutual social and economic dependence, allows for the open expression of hostility," a combination of solidarity and antagonism that "prevents the households from becoming tightly closed units."[98]

Martin Whyte, comparing "cultural features in terms of their evolutionary sequence," concluded that as civilization evolves, "women tend to have less domestic authority, less independent solidarity with other women, more unequal sexual restrictions and perhaps receive more ritualized fear from men and have fewer property rights than is the case in the simpler cultures."[99]

All in all a far cry from the more strident views, whether of feminists, the obsolete social evolution of the neo-Marxists, or the flight from life of the humane animal protectionists. On the whole, plant foods are not shared as ceremoniously as meat. They do not signify the flow of obligations in the same degree. But this is not a statement about women as opposed to men.

The Temporal Mosaic: The Episodic Character of Individual Life

Being individuals slow to reach maturity, we are among the most neotonic of species. This resiliency makes humans prime examples of "K" type species evolution (education, few offspring, slow development). "Culture" constitutes the social contrivances that mitigate neotony. The transformation of the self through aging is inevitable, but whether we move through successive levels of maturity and the fullest realization of our genome's potential depends on the quality of the active embrace of society in all of the nurturance stages. Incomplete, ontogeny runs to the dead end of immaturity and a miasma of pathological limbos.[100]

The important nurturant occasions are like triggers in epigenesis. Neoteny, the many years of individual immaturity, depends on the hands of society to escape itself. This mitigation of our valuable retardation is in part episodic and social, a matching of the calendars of postnatal embryology by the inventions of caregivers. Occasions make the human adult. If culture in the form of society does not act in the ceremonial, tutoring, and testing response to the personal, epigenetic agenda, we slide into adult infantility—madness. This fantastic arrangement is foreshadowed in the nucleus of every cell. It is an expectancy of the genome, fostered by society, enacted in ecosystems.

Two of the transformative stages of human ontogeny have been studied in detail among living hunter-gatherers—infant/caregiver relationships and adolescent initiation. The archaeological record leaves little doubt that we see in them ancient patterns which may be incompletely addressed in ourselves. Foremost is the bonding/separation dynamic of the first two years. The interaction of infant and mother and infant and other caregivers emerges as a compelling necessity, perhaps the most powerful shaping force in the whole of individual experience. The "social skills" of the newborn and the mother's equally indigenous reciprocity create not only the primary social tie but the paradigm for existential attitudes. The lifelong perception of the world as a "counterplayer"—caring, nourishing, instructing, and protecting, or vindictive, mechanical, and distant—arises here.

The process arises in our earliest experience and is coupled to patterns of response. Hara Marano says, "Newborns come highly equipped for their first intense meetings with their parents, and in particular their mothers. . . . Biologically speaking, today's mothers and babies are two to three million years old. . . . When we put the body of a mother close to her baby, something is turned on that is part of her genetic makeup.[101] Details of the socially embedded rhythms of parenthood vary from culture to culture, but they can hardly improve on the basic style or primary forms found in hunter-gatherer groups. Studies of babies and parents in these societies reveal that the intense early attachment leads not to prolonged dependency but to a better functioning nervous system and greater success in the separation process.[102]

Something of the same can be said for the whole of ontogeny, especially those passage-markers by which the caregivers celebrate and energize movement across thresholds by the ripe and ready. Notable among these is adolescent initiation, a subject to which a vast body of science and scholarship has been devoted. Yet again it has fundamental forms for which individual psychology is endowed. Much of modern angst has its roots in the modern collapse of this crucial episode in personal development.

Early experience has this formative and episodic quality, with varying degrees of formality in its context. The hunt is one, bringing into play in the individual the most intense emotions and sense of the mysteries of our existence, to be given a catharsis and mediating transformation. The hunt is a pulse of social and personal preparation, address to presences unseen, skills and strategies, festive events and religious participation. We cannot become hunter-gatherers as a whole economy, but we can recover the ontogenetic moment. Can five billion people go hunting in a world where these dimensions of human existence were played out in a total population of perhaps one million? They can, because the value of the hunt is not in repeated trips but a single leap forward into the heart-structure of the world, the "game" played to rules that reveal ourselves. What is important is to have hunted. It is like having babies; a little of it goes a long way.

Endemic Resources and the Design of a Lifeway—a Post-Historic Primitivism

In her book, *Prehistoric Art in Europe,* N. K. Sandars identifies four strands of the primordial human experience: (1) "The sense of diffused sacredness which may erupt into everyday life," (2) "an order of relationships the categories of which take no account of genetic barriers and which will lead to ideas of metamorphosis inside and outside this life," (3) "unhistorical time" and (4) "the character or position of the medicine man or shaman."[103]

These are not, of course, removable entities as such, but they constitute aspects of the Paleolithic genius, emergent gestalts from the separate and portable elements of a culture. As ideals not one of these is a regression to obsolescence but a forward step to Heidegger's *dasein,* Merleau-Ponty's and Whitehead's event world, Eliade's centrality of the rites of passage, Odum's redaction of ecological entities as process and relationship. It is not a matter of what ought to be done or how life could be, or even of greater meaning and understanding, but of the nature of experience. I would summarize these "experiences" as follows:

1. Therio-metaphysics. Animals as the language of nature, a great Semiosis. Reading the world as the hunter-gatherer reads tracks. The heuristic principle and hermeneutic act of nature and society as the basic metaphor. Eco-predicated logos.

2. The Voice of life. Sound, drum, song, voice, instrument, wind, the essential clue to the livingness of the world. It is internal and external at once, the game told as narrative, the play of chance. In story, Snyder has called it "the primacy of together-hearing."

3. The Fledging and Moulting principle. Epigenesis as the appropriate and sequential coupling of gene and environment, self and other. The ecology of ontogenesis as a resonance between bonding and separation that produces identity. Transitions marked by formal acts of public recognition.

4. Sacramental Trophism. The basic act of communion, transformation, and relatedness, incorporating death as life. It is centered on the act of bringing death and of giving to death as the central celebration of life.

5. The Fire Circle. All forms of social connection in relation to scale. Vernacular gender. Examples: Homeostatic demographic units. The dialectical tribe in Australia: family, band, and tribe affiliation. Sizes 25/500. "In terms of conscious dedication to human relationships that are both affective and effective, the primitive is ahead of us all the way," comments Colin Turnbull.[104]

6. Vocational Instruments. Dealing directly with the means of subsistence by hands-on approach. Tools are a gestural response to life, subordinate to thought, art, and religious forms. Marshack speaks of "the demands of fire culture" as one of lore and skills in which the tale is a "metaphysical gift" making the world "an object of contemplation."

7. Place instead of Space, Moments replace Time, Chance instead of Strategy. Place is at once an external and internal state in a journey home. The place is a process, not coordinates, yet a specific geology, climate, and habitat.

8. Occasions of the Numinous in the relocation of the signs of sacred presence, the mystery of being, and the participatory role of human life, not as ruler or viceroy but as one species of many, in a mood not of guilt or conflict but of affirmation.

9. The escape from domestication, a liberation of nature into itself, including human nature, from the tyranny of the created blobs and the fuzzy goo of emotional—and epoxic glue of ethical—humanism.

Primitivism does not mean a simplified or more thoughtless way of life but a reciprocity with origins, a recovery misconstrued as inaccessible by the ideology of History. In the latter view one puts on costumes and enacts another culture as the French aristocracy imitated shepherds during the Renaissance or as middle class "dropouts" in the 1960s put on gingham gowns and bib overalls.

From the ahistoric perspective you cannot "go back" to recover "lost" realities, nor can you completely lose them. So long as there is a green earth and other species our wild genome can make and find its place. Like many difficult things the transformation cannot be made solely by acts of will. One can simulate the external features of a primitive life—for example, the limitation of possessions and the non-ownership of the land—but something precedes the outward form and its supporting ideology. That something is the way in which the sensuous apprehension is linked to the conceptual world, the establishment early in life of a mode by which experience and ideas interact, in perception.

It is, of course, a cyclic matter in which childhood experience leads to appropriate thought and custom, which in turn mentors individual genesis. Breaking into the circle is hard, as we urban moderns can only start with an idea of it. Rare are those who can make that leap from the idea to the mode without early shaping. As a result most of us get only glimpses of what we might be were we truer to our wildness, among them some of the anthropologists who study tribal peoples. Or, we get intimations from the archetypes arising in our dreams or given in visionary moments.

In sum it is an archetypal ecology, a paraprimitive solution, a Paleolithic counter-revolution, a new cynegetics, a venatory mentation. Whatever it may be called, our best guides, when we learn to acknowledge them, will be the living tribal peoples themselves.

NOTES

Acknowledgment: My thanks to Flo Krall for her careful reading, criticism, and suggestions in the preparation of this paper.

1. Herbert J. Muller, *The Uses of the Past,* Oxford University Press, New York, 1952, p. 38.
2. Herbert Schneidau, *Sacred Discontent,* University of California, Los Angeles, 1976.
3. Bogert O'Brien, "Inuit Ways and the Transformation of Canadian Theology," mss., 1979.
4. Robert Hutchins, Preface to Mortimer J. Adler's Hundred Great Books Series, *The Great Ideas,* Encyclopedia Britannica, Chicago, 1952.
5. Ivan Illich and Barry Sanders, *The Alphabetization of the Popular Mind,* North Point, San Francisco, 1988.
6. Paul Shepard, *Nature and Madness,* Sierra Club Books, San Francisco, 1982.
7. Edmund S. Carpenter, "If Wittgenstein Had Been an Eskimo," *Natural History* 89 (4), Feb., 1980.
8. A. David Napier, *Masks, Transformation, and Paradox,* University of California, Los Angeles, 1986. And see Steven Lonsdale, *Animals and the Origin of Dance,* Thames and Hudson, New York, 1982.
9. Edith Cobb, *The Ecology of Imagination in Childhood,* Columbia University Press, New York, 1978.
10. J. H. Plumb, *Horizon* 41 (3), 1972.
11. Scribners, New York, 1973.
12. George Boas, *Essays on Primitivism and Related Ideas in the Middle Ages,* Johns Hopkins, Baltimore, 1948.
13. Anthony Pagdon, *The Fall of Natural Man,* Cambridge, New York, 1982, p. 78.
14. M. Navarro, *La Tribu Campa,* Lima, 1924, quoted in Gerald Weiss, "Campa Cosmology," *American Museum of Natural History Anthropological Papers,* 52, Part 5, New York, 1975.
15. Dr. Will Durant, "A Last Testament to Youth," *The Columbia Dispatch Magazine,* Feb. 8, 1970.
16. Ernest Thompson Seton, *Two Little Savages,* Doubleday, New York, 1903.
17. Calvin Martan, *Keepers of the Game,* University of California, Los Angeles, 1978.
18. Glyn Daniel, *The Idea of Prehistory,* Penguin, Baltimore, 1962, p. 57.
19. Robert Ardrey, *The Hunting Hypothesis,* Athenaeum, New York, 1976.
20. John Pfeiffer, *The Emergence of Man,* Harper and Row, New York, 1972.

21. Nigel Calder, *Eden Was No Garden,* Holt, New York, 1967.
22. Gordon Rattray Taylor, *Rethink, a Paraprimitive Solution,* Dutton, New York, 1973.
23. José Ortega y Gasset, *Meditations on Hunting,* Scribners, New York, 1972.
24. M. F. C. Bourdillon and Meyer Fortes, eds., *Sacrifice,* Academic Press, New York, 1980.
25. Carleton Coon, *The Story of Man,* Knopf, New York, 1962, p. 187.
26. W. E. H. Stanner, *White Man Got No Dreaming,* Australian National University Press, Canberra, 1979.
27. Richard B. Lee and Irven DeVore, eds., *Man the Hunter,* Aldine, Chicago, 1968.
28. Sherwood L. Washburn, ed., *The Social Life of Early Man,* Aldine, Chicago, 1961.
29. G. P. Murdock, *Ethnographic Atlas for New World Societies,* University of Pittsburgh Press, 1967.
30. Marshall Sahlins, *Stone Age Economics,* Aldine, Chicago, 1972.
31. Derek Freeman, letter, *Current Anthropology,* Oct., 1973, p. 379.
32. Clifford Geertz, "The Impact of the Concept of Culture on the Concept of Man," in Stanley Diamond, *In Search of the Primitive: A Critique of Civilization,* Transaction Books, New Brunswick, 1974, p. 102.
33. Melvin Konner, *The Tangled Wing: Biological Constraints on the Human Spirit,* Harper and Row, New York, 1983.
34. Loren Eiseley, "Man of the Future," *The Immense Journey,* Random House, New York, 1957.
35. Laurens van der Post, *Heart of the Hunter,* Harcourt Brace Jovanovich, New York, 1980.
36. Roger M. Keesing, "Paradigms Lost: The New Ethnography and New Linguistics," *South West Journal of Anthropology* 28: 299–332, 1972.
37. Ivan Illich, *Gender,* Pantheon, New York, 1982.
38. Gina Bari Kolata, "!Kung Hunter-Gatherers: Feminism, Diet, and Birth Control," *Science* 185: 932–34, 1974.
39. Claude Lévi-Strauss, *The Savage Mind,* University of Chicago Press, Chicago, 1966.
40. C. H. D. Clarke, "Venator—the Hunter," mss., n.d.
41. Irenaus Eibes-Eibesfeldt, *Love and Hate,* Holt, Rinehart and Winston, New York, 1971.
42. Jane Howard, "All Happy Clans Are Alike," *The Atlantic,* May, 1978.
43. Gary Snyder, quoted in Peter B. Chowka, "The Original Mind of Gary Snyder," *East-West,* June, 1977.
44. A. H. Ismail and L. B. Trachtman, "Jogging the Imagination," *Psychology Today,* March, 1973.
45. P. S. Martin and H. E. Wright, Jr., eds., *Pleistocene Extinctions: The Search for a Cause,* Yale University Press, New Haven, 1967.
46. Donald K. Grayson, "Pleistocene Avifaunas and the Overkill Hypothesis," *Science* 195: 691–93, 1977. Karl W. Butzer, *Environment and Archaeology,* Aldine, Chicago, 1971, pp. 503ff. Michael A. Joachim, *Hunter-Gatherer Subsistence and*

Settlement: A Predictive Model, Academic Press, New York, 1976. Marvin Harris, "Potlatch Politics and Kings' Castles," *Natural History,* May, 1974.

47. Melvin J. Konner, "Maternal Care, Infant Behavior and Development Among the !Kung," in R. B. Lee and I. DeVore, *Kalahari Hunter Gatherers,* Harvard University Press, Cambridge, 1976.

48. Joachim, op. cit., p. 22. Harry Jerison, *Evolution of the Brain and Intelligence,* Academic, New York, 1973.

49. Richard Nelson, *Make Prayers to the Raven,* University of Chicago Press, Chicago, 1983, p. 225.

50. Gary Urton, ed., *Animal Myths and Metaphors in South America,* University of Utah Press, Salt Lake City, 1985.

51. Clarke, op. cit.

52. Clarke, ibid.

53. James Woodburn, "An Introduction to Hadza Ecology, in Lee and DeVore, *Man the Hunter.*

54. Marek Zvelebil, "Postglacial Foraging in the Forests of Europe," *Scientific American,* May, 1986.

55. C. Dean Freudenberger, "Agriculture in a Post-Modern World," mss. for conference, "Toward a Post-Modern World," Santa Barbara, California, January, 1987.

56. Liberty Hyde Bailey, *The Holy Earth,* Scribners, New York, 1915, p. 83.

57. Ibid., p. 151.

58. Wes Jackson, *New Roots for Agriculture,* Friends of the Earth, San Francisco, 1980.

59. Helen Spurway, "The Causes of Domestication," *Journal of Genetics* 53:325, 1955.

60. Jack M. Potter, *Peasant Society,* Little, Brown, Boston, 1967.

61. Jane Schneider, "Of Vigilance and Virgins: Honor, Shame, and Access to Resources in Mediterranean Societies," *Ethnology* 10:1–24, 1971.

62. Aldous Huxley, "Mother," *Tomorrow and Tomorrow and Tomorrow,* Harper and Row, New York, 1952.

63. Shepard, *Nature and Madness.*

64. Robert Redfield, *The Folk Cultures of Yucatan,* University of Chicago, Chicago, 1941.

65. Joseph Campbell, *The Masks of God,* Viking Press, New York, 1959, vol. 1, p. 180.

66. Paul Shepard and Barry Sanders, *The Sacred Paw: The Bear in Nature, Myth and Literature,* Viking Press, New York, 1985.

67. Tim Ingold, "Hunting, Sacrifice, and the Domestication of Animals," in *The Appropriation of Nature,* University of Iowa Press, Iowa City, 1987.

68. Kolata, op. cit.

69. Patricia Draper, "Social and Economic Constraints on Child Life among the !Kung," in Lee and DeVore, *Kalahari Hunter Gatherers.*

70. C. H. Brown, "Mode of Subsistence and Folk Biological Taxonomy," *Current Anthropology* 26 (1): 43–53, 1985.

71. "Campaign to Promote the Vegetarian Diet," (leaflet), Animal Aid Society, Tonbridge, England, n.d.

72. Marvin Harris, *Sacred Cow, Abominable Pig*, Simon and Schuster, New York, 1985, p. 22.
73. Robert Allen, "Food for Thought," *The Ecologist*, January, 1975.
74. Stanley Boyd Eaton and Marjorie Shostak, "Fat Tooth Blues," *Natural History* 95 (6), July, 1986.
75. Daniel, op. cit.
76. Allen W. Johnson and Timothy Earle, *The Evolution of Human Societies: From Foraging Group to Agrarian State*, Stanford University Press, Stanford, 1987.
77. John W. Berry and Robert C. Annis, "Ecology, Culture and Psychological; Differentiation," *International Journal of Psychology* 9: 173–93, 1974.
78. Robert Edgerton, *The Individual in Cultural Adaptation*, University of California, Los Angeles, 1971.
79. N. K. Sandars, *Prehistoric Art in Europe*, Penguin, Baltimore, pp. 95–96.
80. Marshall McLuhan, *Through the Vanishing Point*, Harper and Row, New York, 1968.
81. David Lowenthall, "Is Wilderness Paradise Now?" *Columbia University Forum* 7 (2), 1964.
82. Susan Sontag, *On Photography*, Dell, New York, 1973.
83. Bertram Lewin, *The Image and the Past*, I.U.P., New York, 1968.
84. Spurway, op. cit., 1968.
85. Lévi-Strauss, op. cit., 1968.
86. Fred Myer, *Pintupi Country, Pintupi Self*, Smithsonian Institution, Washington, D.C., 1986. Myer is following a path laid out by A. Irving Hallowell. For example see Hallowell, "Self, Society, and Culture in Phylogenetic Perspective," in Sol Tax, ed., *The Evolution of Man*, Aldine, Chicago, 1961.
87. Gary Snyder, "On 'Song of the Taste,'" The Recovery of the Commons Project, Bundle #1, North San Juan, Califonia, n.d.
88. Gary Snyder, "Good, Wild, Sacred," *The Co-Evolution Quarterly*, Fall, 1983.
89. Rene Dubos, "Environmental Determinants of Human Life," in David C. Glass, ed., *Environmental Influences*, Rockland University Press, 1968.
90. Ibid., quoted from Lewis Mumford, *The Myth of the Machine*, Harcourt Brace, New York, 1966. Mumford probably got it from Loren Eiseley's "Man of the Future" in *The Immense Journey*.
91. Walter J . Ong, "World as View and World as Event," *American Anthropologist* 71:634–47. Dorothy Lee, "Codifications of Reality: Lineal and Non-Lineal," *Psychosomatic Medicine* 12 (2), 1969.
92. Morris Berman, "The Roots of Reality" (a review of Humberto Maturana and Francisco Varelas, *The Tree of Knowledge*), *Journal of Humanistic Psychology* 29:277–84, 1989.
93. Emile Zuckenkandle, *Scientific American* 212: 63, 1960.
94. Hyemeyohsts Storm, *Storm Arrows*, Harper and Row, New York, 1972.
95. William Ayres Arrowsmith, "Hybris and Sophrosyne," *Dartmouth Alumni Magazine*, July, 1970.
96. William Dupre, *Religion in Primitive Cultures*, Mouton, The Hague, 1975, p. 327.

97. Kevin T. Jones, "Hunting and Scavenging by Early Hominids: A Study in Archaeological Method and Theory," Ph.D. Thesis, University of Utah, 1984.

98. Janet Siskind, *To Hunt in the Morning*, Oxford University Press, New York, 1976, p. 109.

99. Martin King Whyte, *The Status of Women in Preindustrial Societies*, Princeton University Press, Princeton, 1978.

100. Arnold Modell, *Object Love and Reality*, I.U.P., New York, 1968. Chap. 5, "The Sense of Identity: The Acceptance of Separateness."

101. Hara Estroff Marano, "Biology Is One Key to the Bonding of Mothers and Babies," *Smithsonian*, February, 1981.

102. Melvin J. Konner, "Maternal Care, Infant Behavior and Development Among the !Kung," and Patricia Draper, "Social and Economic Constraints on Child Life Among the !Kung," in Lee and DeVore, *Kalahari Hunter Gatherers*.

103. Sandars, op. cit. p. 26.

104. Colin M. Turnbull, *The Human Cycle*, Simon and Schuster, New York, 1983.

About the Contributors

Nurit Bird-David is a lecturer in social anthropology at Tel Aviv University, Tel Aviv, Israel. Her research focuses on hunter-gatherer studies and economic anthropology. She has been a research fellow of New-Hall at Cambridge University and a Smutz Visiting Fellow at Cambridge University.

Ernest Burch, Jr. is a research associate in anthropology with the Smithsonian Institution, Washington, D.C. His main area of research is the native peoples of northern Alaska and the central subarctic Canada. He is co-editor, with Linda Ellanna, of *Key Issues in Hunter-Gatherer Research* (1994).

Tim Flannery is senior research scientist in mammalogy at the Australian Museum in Sydney. He is the author of several books about Australian mammals. He is the author of *The Future Eaters: An Ecological History of the Australian Lands and People* (1995).

Eleanor Leacock was professor of anthropology of the City College of New York and the Graduate Faculty of the City University of New York. She did pioneering work on the cross-cultural study of women, anthropology and education, and anthropological theory. Her books include *The Montagnais "Hunting Territory" and the Fur Trade* (1954), *Teaching and Learning in City Schools: A Comparative Study* (1969), *Politics and History in Band Societies* (1982), and *Myths of Male Dominance* (1982).

Richard B. Lee is professor of anthropology at the University of Toronto. He has studied the hunter-gatherers of southern Africa for three decades. He is coeditor, with Irven DeVore, of *Man the Hunter* (1968) and *Kalahari Hunter-Gatherers* (1976), and the author of *The !Kung San* (1979) and *The Dobe Ju/Hoans* (1993).

Lorna Marshall is an associate of the Peabody Museum, Harvard University and a leading authority on the !Kung of southern Africa. She is the author of *The !Kung of Nyae Nyae* (1976) and many important articles.

Marshall Sahlins is Charles F. Grey Distinguished Service Professor of Anthropology at the University of Chicago. His research interests are the history and ethnography of the Pacific. His books include *Stone Age Economics* (1972), *Islands of History* (1985), and *How Natives Think* (1995)

Paul Shepard was a leading environmental philosopher whose books include *Man in the Landscape* (1967), *The Tender Carnivore and the Sacred Game* (1973), *Nature and Madness* (1982), and *Traces of an Omnivore* (1996). He taught human ecology and natural philosophy at Pitzer College and the Claremont Graduate School.

James Woodburn is senior lecturer in the department of anthropology at the London School of Economics and Political Science. His main research interests are the comparative analysis of hunter-gatherer societies, especially those of sub-Saharan Africa, and economic anthropology.

John Yellen is program director for archaeology at the National Science Foundation.

John Zerzan is a freelance writer and social critic living in Eugene, Oregon. He is the author of *Future Primitive and Other Essays* (1994).

Index